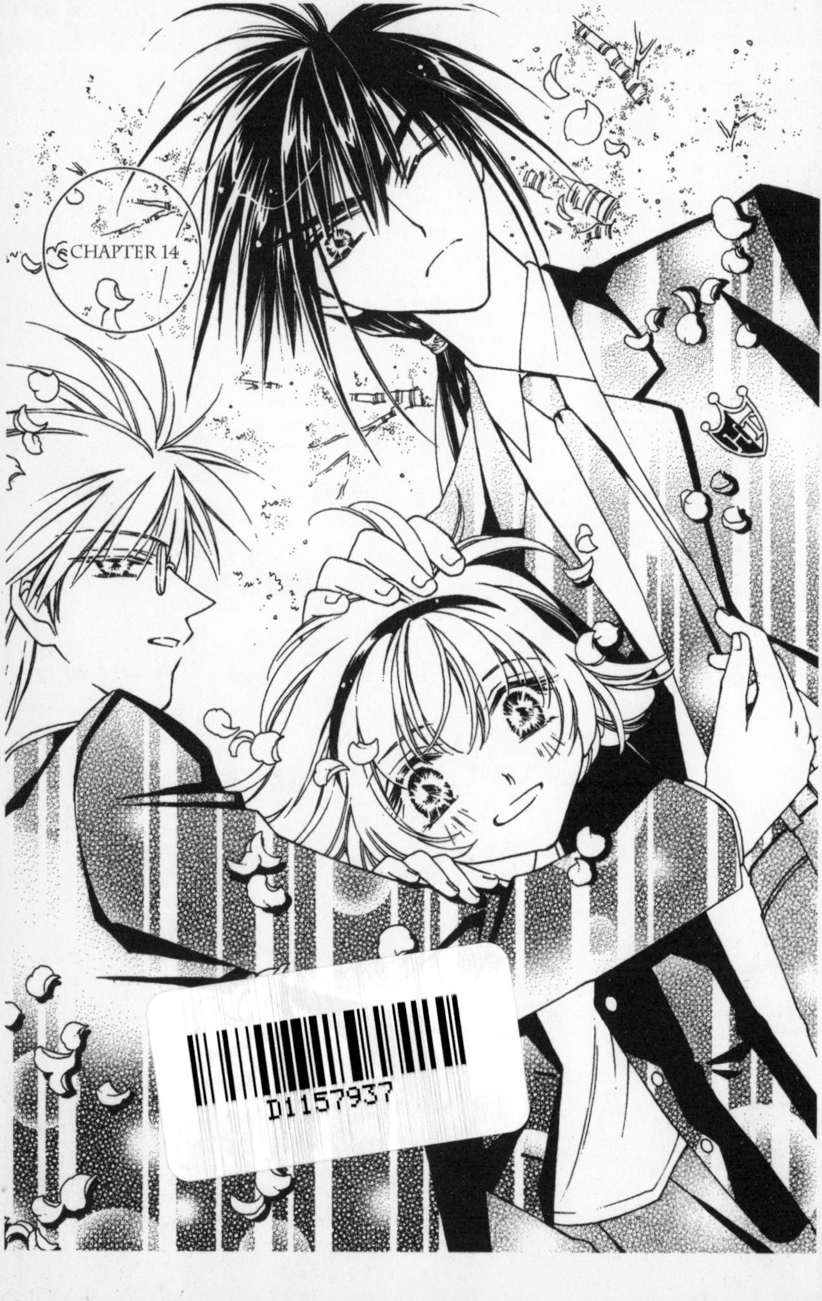
CHAPTER 14

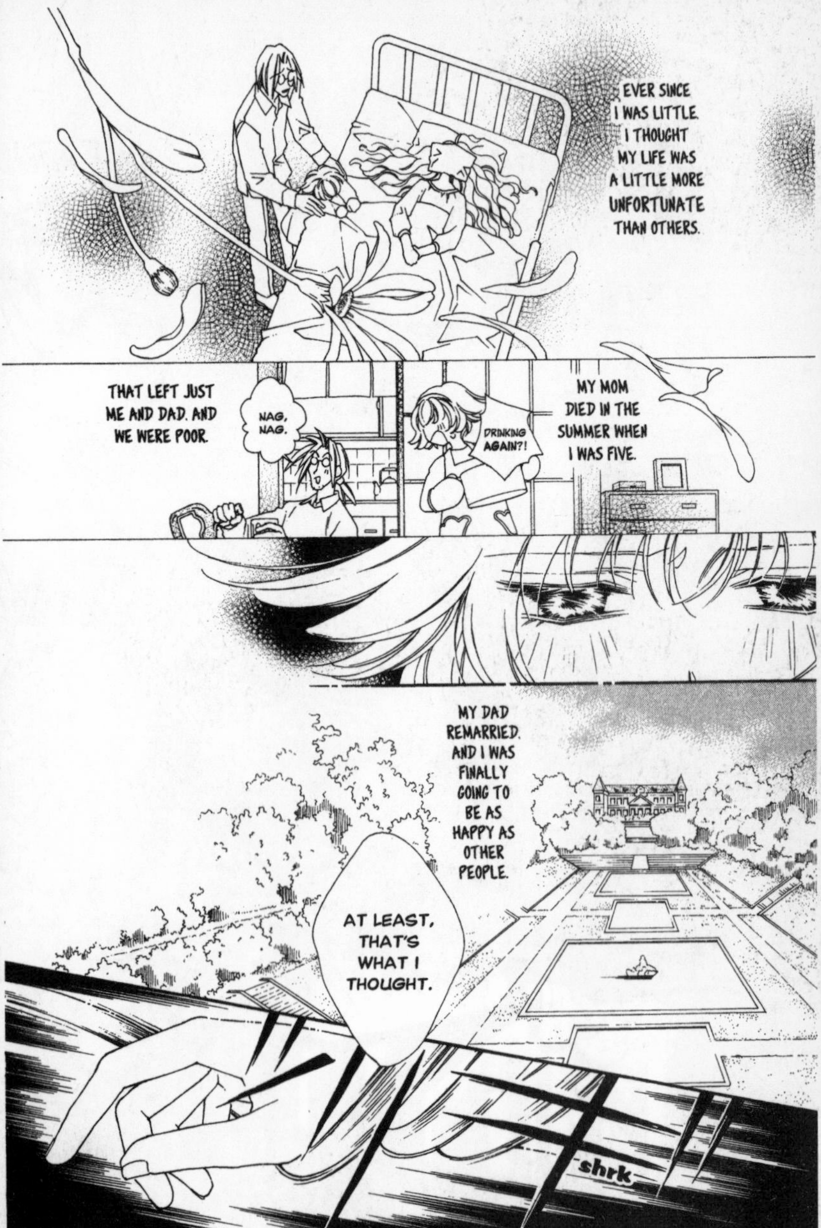
EVER SINCE I WAS LITTLE, I THOUGHT MY LIFE WAS A LITTLE MORE UNFORTUNATE THAN OTHERS.
MY MOM DIED IN THE SUMMER WHEN I WAS FIVE.
DRINKING AGAIN?!
THAT LEFT JUST ME AND DAD, AND WE WERE POOR.
NAG, NAG.
MY DAD REMARRIED, AND I WAS FINALLY GOING TO BE AS HAPPY AS OTHER PEOPLE.
AT LEAST, THAT'S WHAT I THOUGHT.
shrk

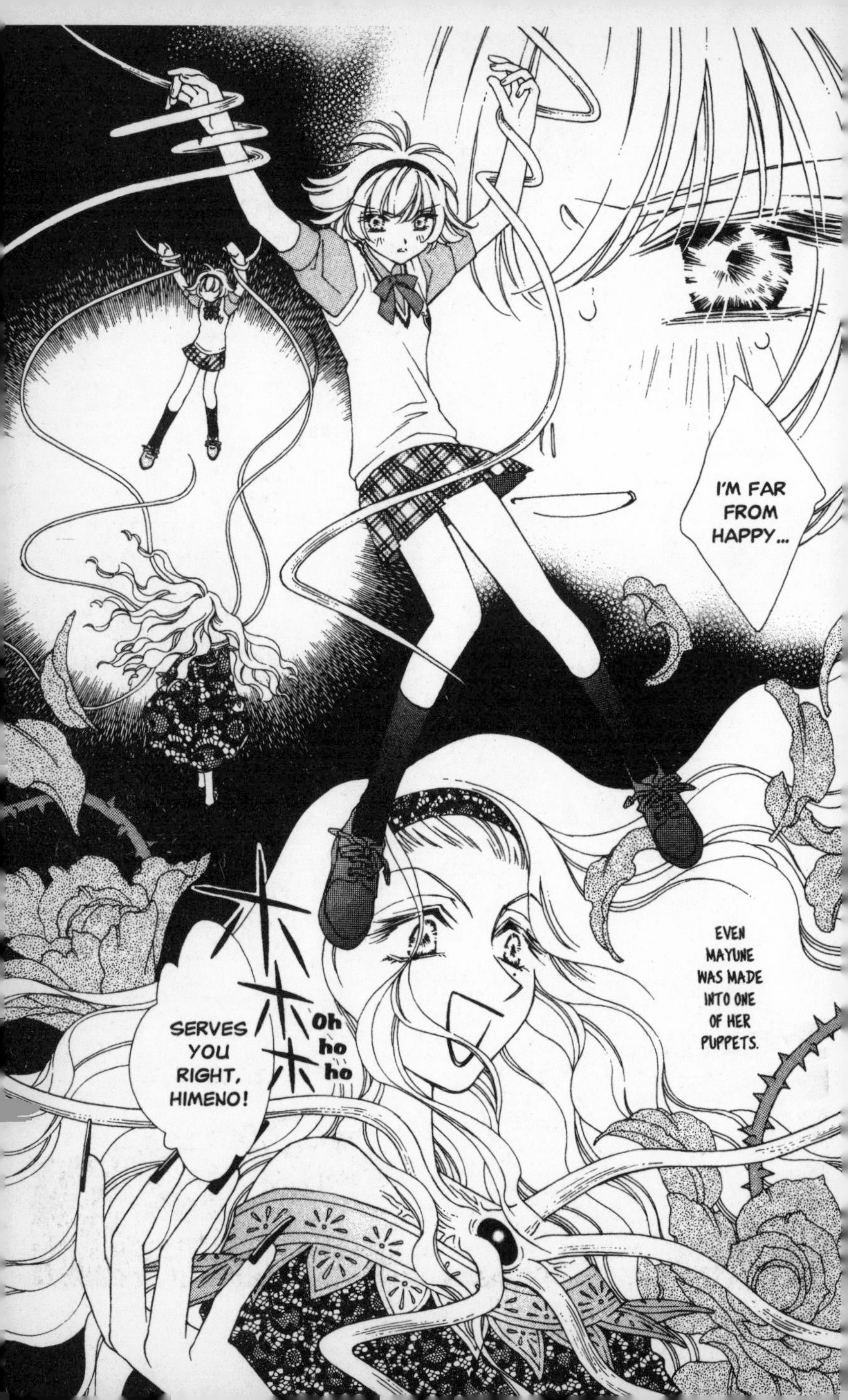
I'M FAR FROM HAPPY...
EVEN MAYUNE WAS MADE INTO ONE OF HER PUPPETS.
Oh ho ho
SERVES YOU RIGHT, HIMENO!

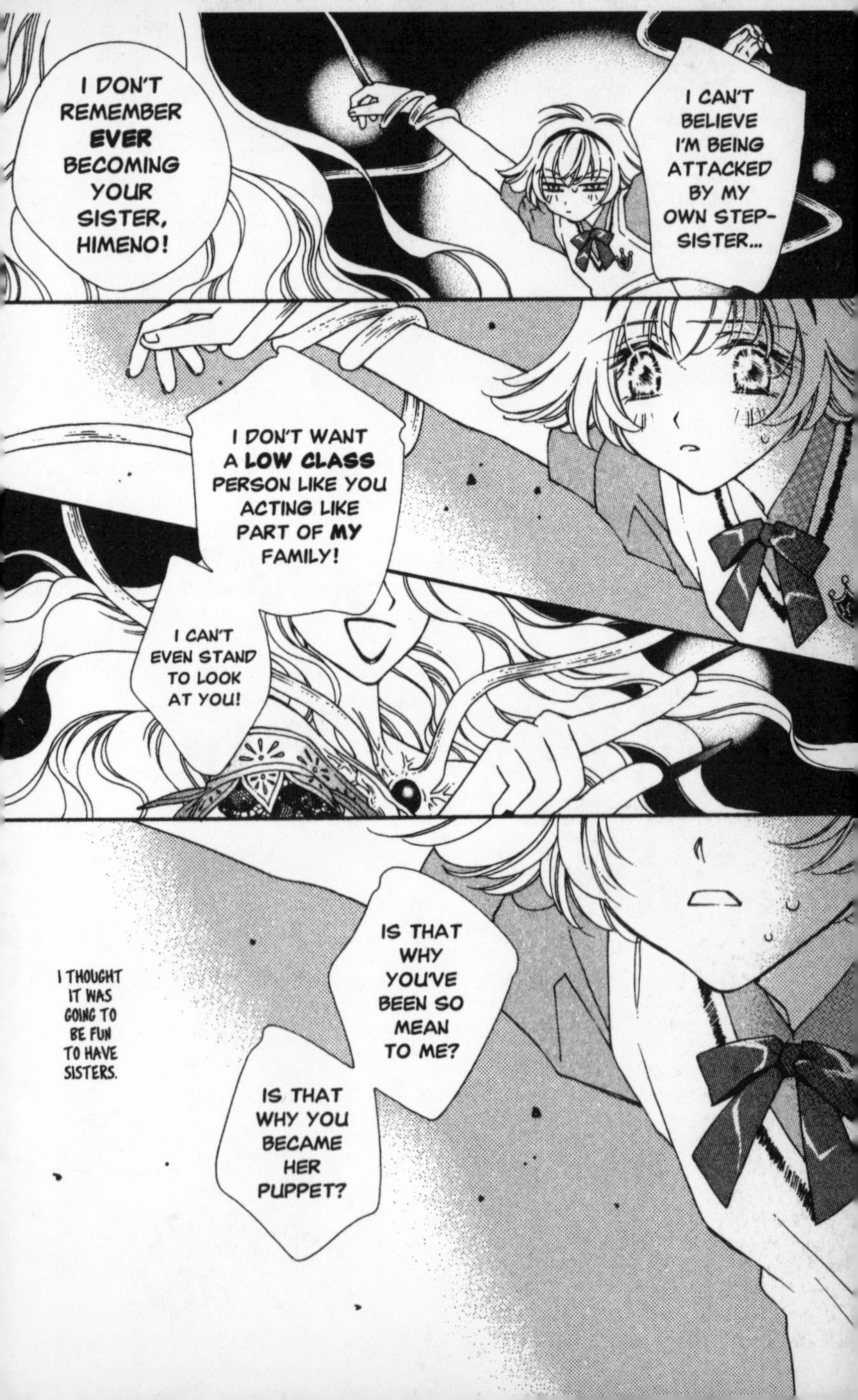
I CAN'T BELIEVE I'M BEING ATTACKED BY MY OWN STEP-SISTER...
I DON'T REMEMBER EVER BECOMING YOUR SISTER, HIMENO!
I DON'T WANT A LOW CLASS PERSON LIKE YOU ACTING LIKE PART OF MY FAMILY!
I CAN'T EVEN STAND TO LOOK AT YOU!
IS THAT WHY YOU'VE BEEN SO MEAN TO ME?
IS THAT WHY YOU BECAME HER PUPPET?
I THOUGHT IT WAS GOING TO BE FUN TO HAVE SISTERS.

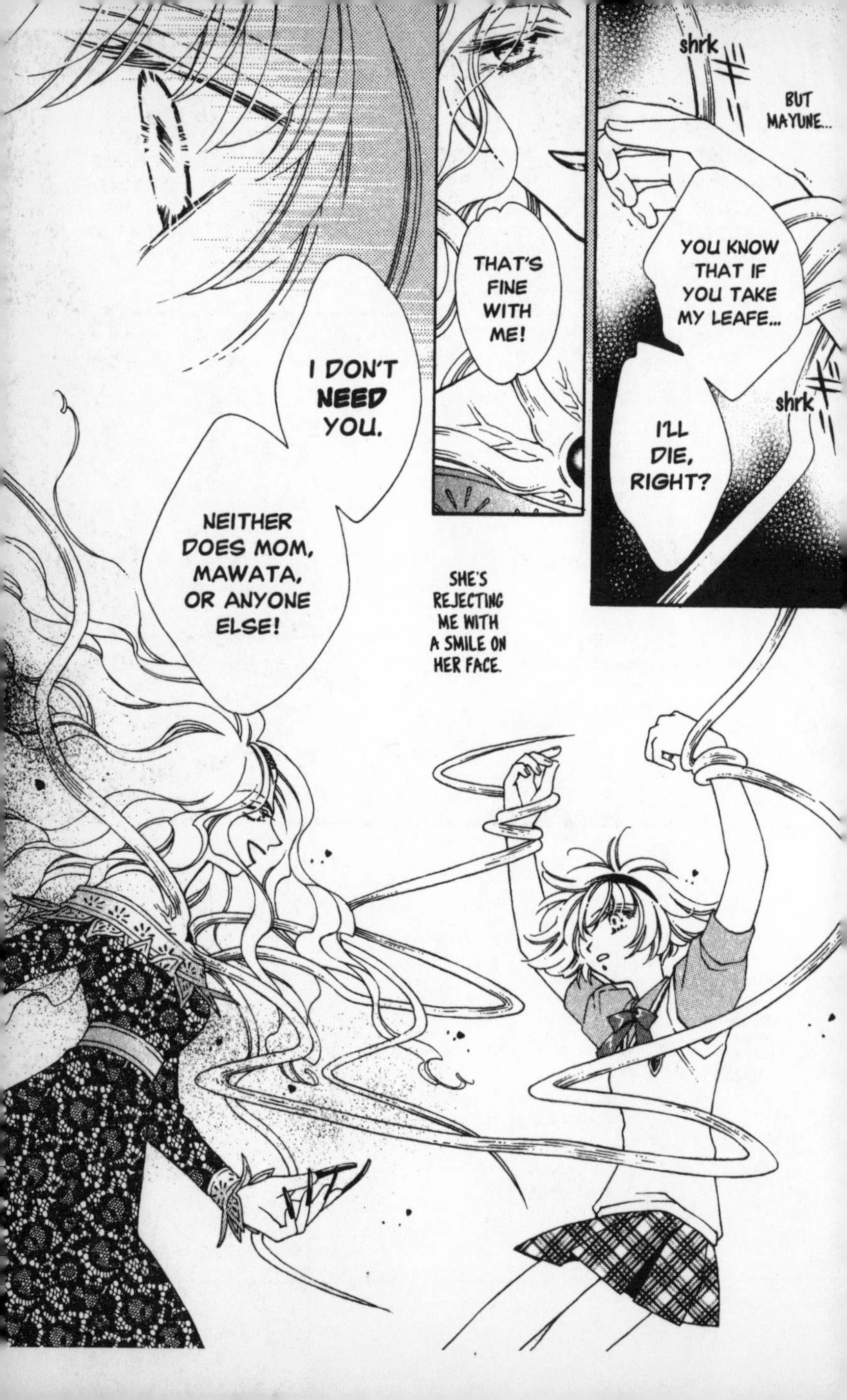
shrk
BUT MAYUNE...
YOU KNOW THAT IF YOU TAKE MY LEAFE...
shrk
I'LL DIE, RIGHT?
THAT'S FINE WITH ME!
I DON'T **NEED** YOU.
NEITHER DOES MOM, MAWATA, OR ANYONE ELSE!
SHE'S REJECTING ME WITH A SMILE ON HER FACE.

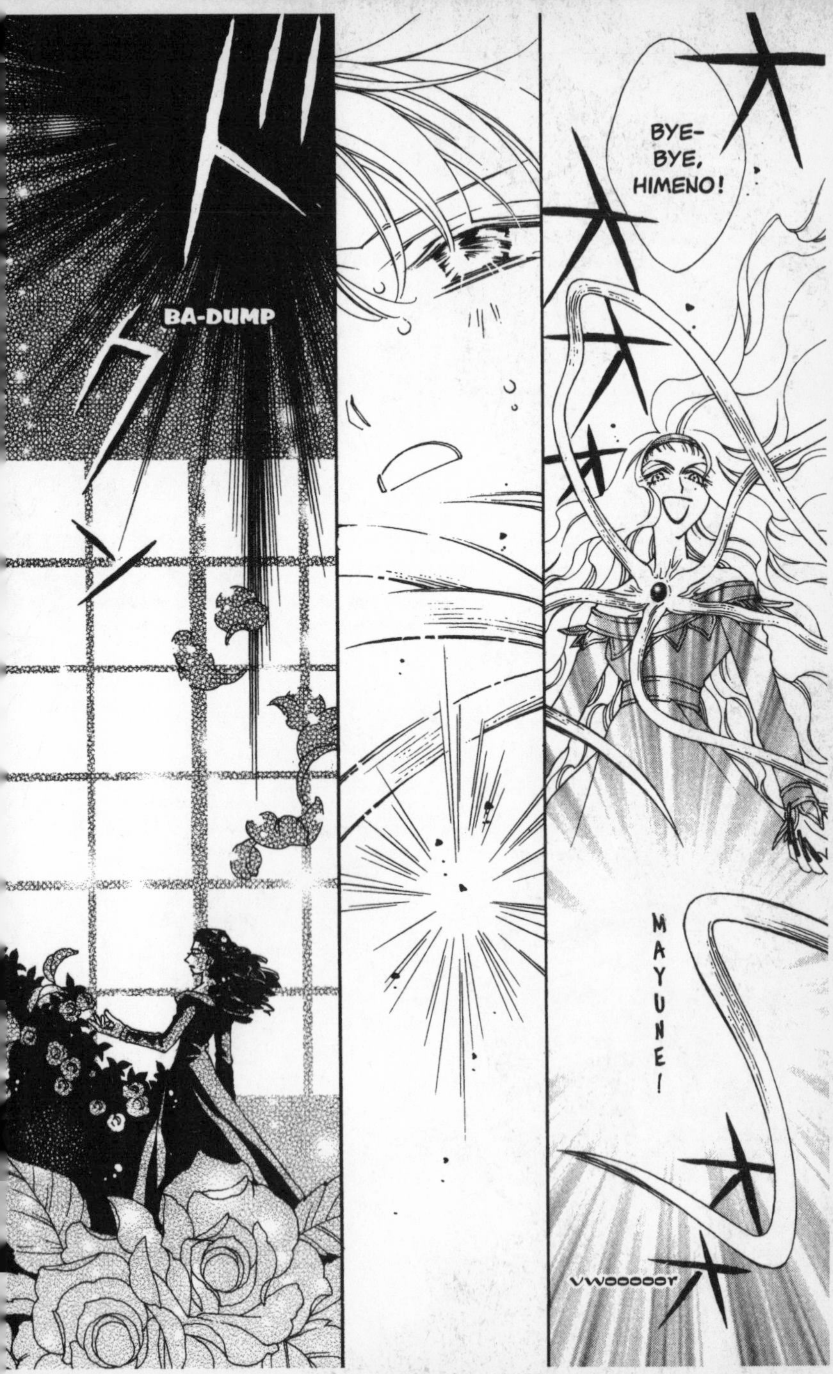
BYE-BYE, HIMENO!
MAYUNE!
VWOOOOOr
BA-DUMP

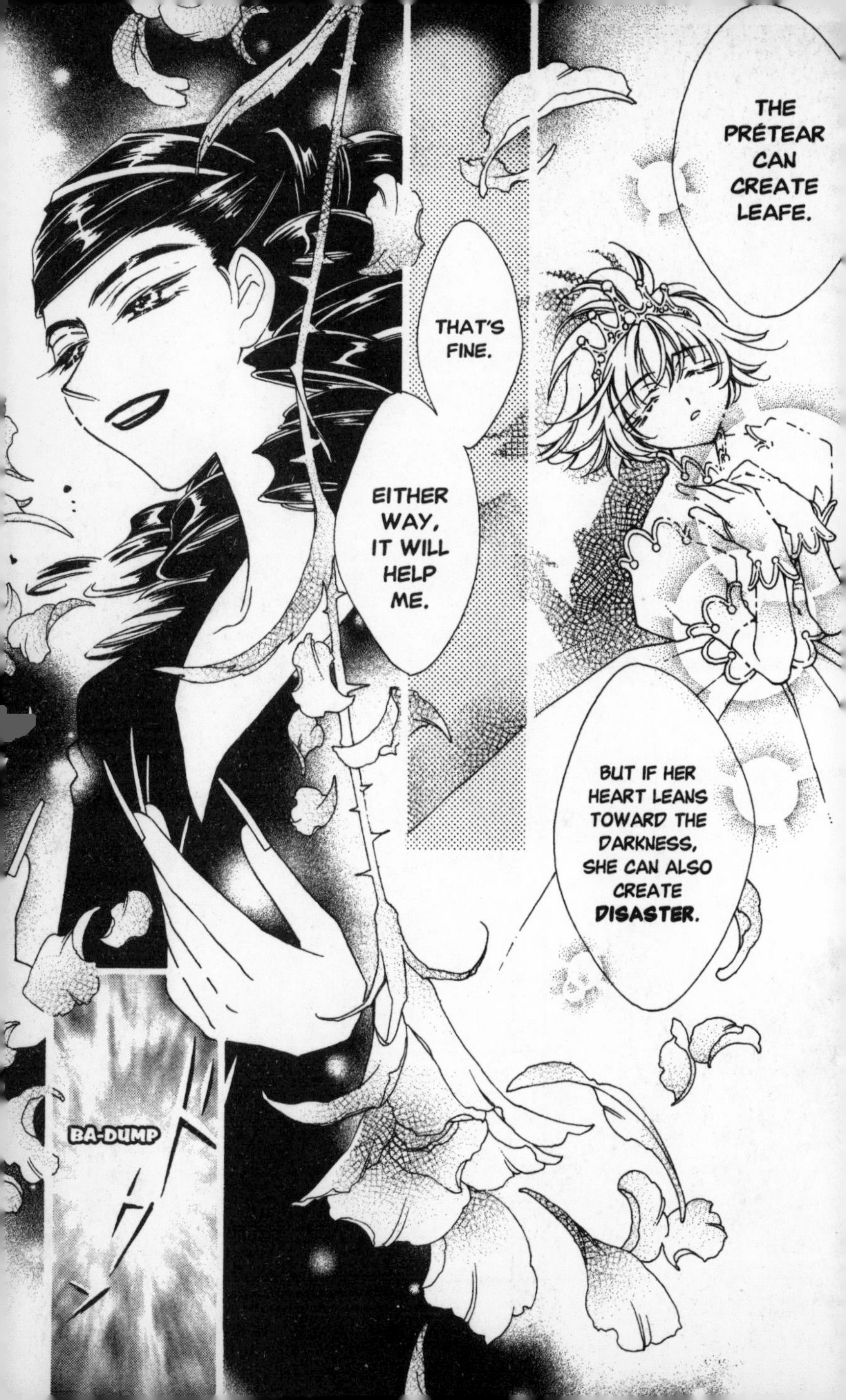
THE PRÉTEAR CAN CREATE LEAFE.
BUT IF HER HEART LEANS TOWARD THE DARKNESS, SHE CAN ALSO CREATE **DISASTER**.
THAT'S FINE.
EITHER WAY, IT WILL HELP ME.
BA-DUMP

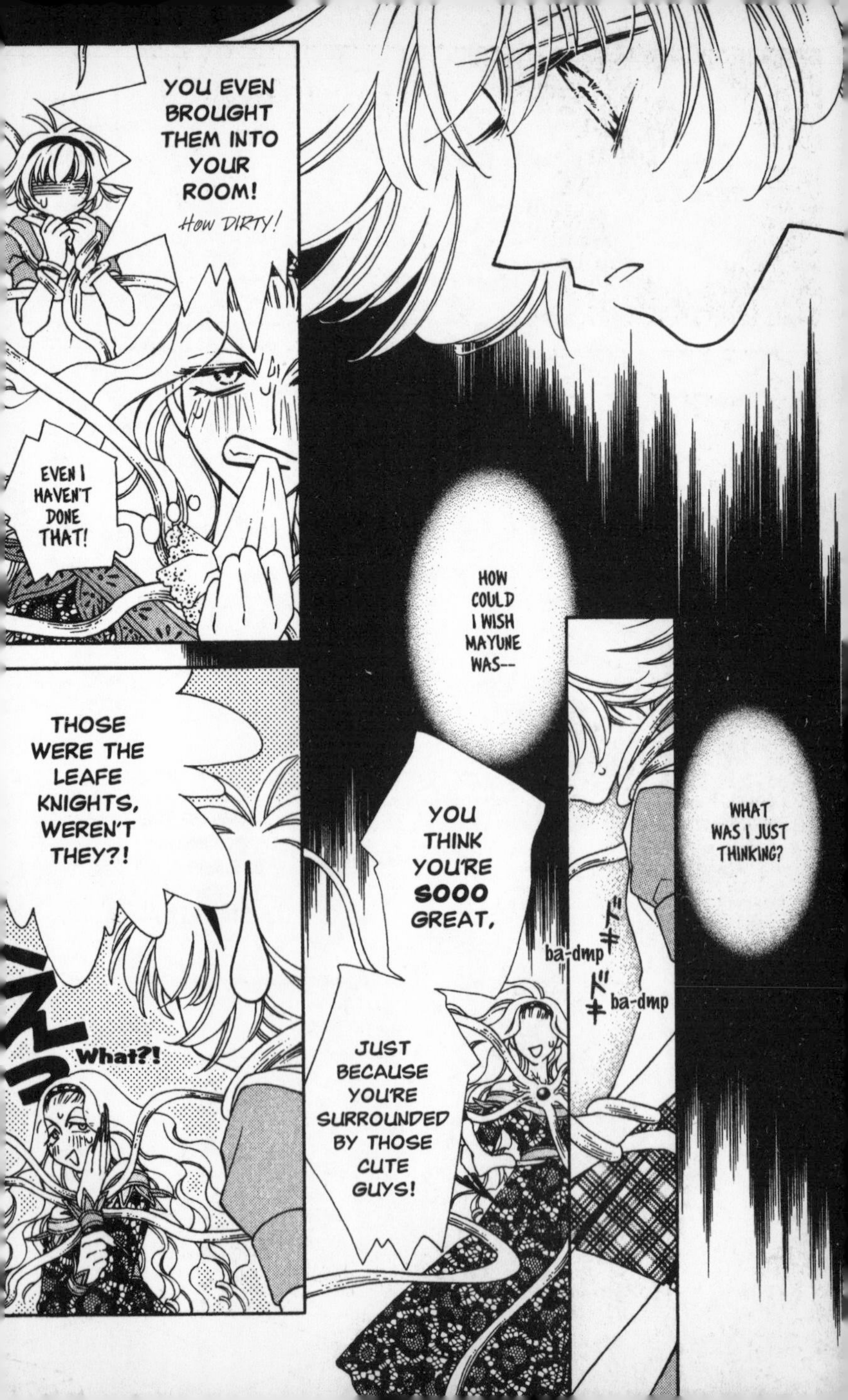
HOW COULD I WISH MAYUNE WAS--
WHAT WAS I JUST THINKING?
ba-dmp
ba-dmp
YOU THINK YOU'RE **SOOO** GREAT,
JUST BECAUSE YOU'RE SURROUNDED BY THOSE CUTE GUYS!
YOU EVEN BROUGHT THEM INTO YOUR ROOM!
How DIRTY!
EVEN I HAVEN'T DONE THAT!
THOSE WERE THE LEAFE KNIGHTS, WEREN'T THEY?!
What?!

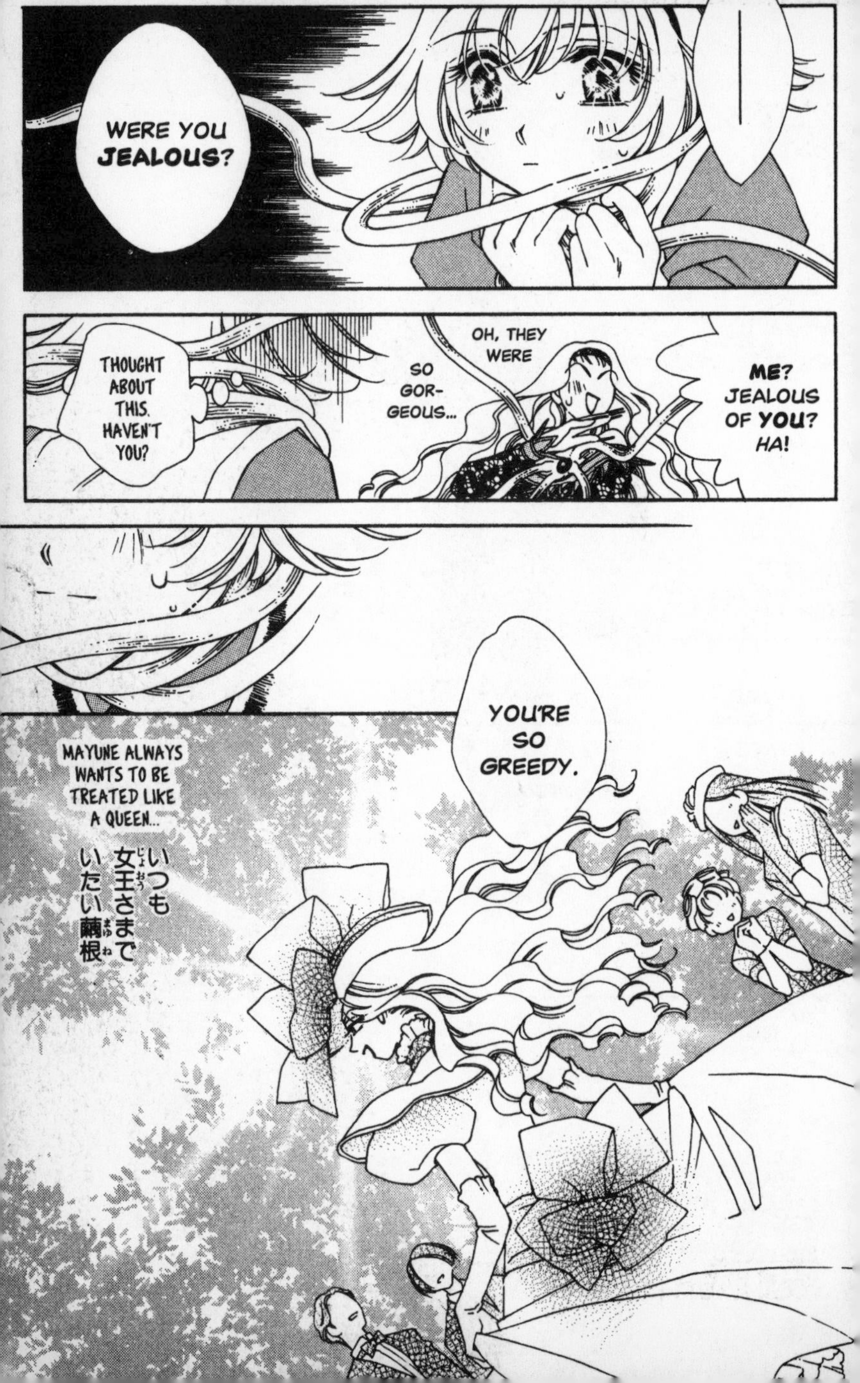
WERE YOU JEALOUS?
ME? JEALOUS OF YOU? HA!
OH, THEY WERE SO GORGEOUS...
THOUGHT ABOUT THIS, HAVEN'T YOU?
YOU'RE SO GREEDY.
MAYUNE ALWAYS WANTS TO BE TREATED LIKE A QUEEN...
いつも女王さまでいたい繭根

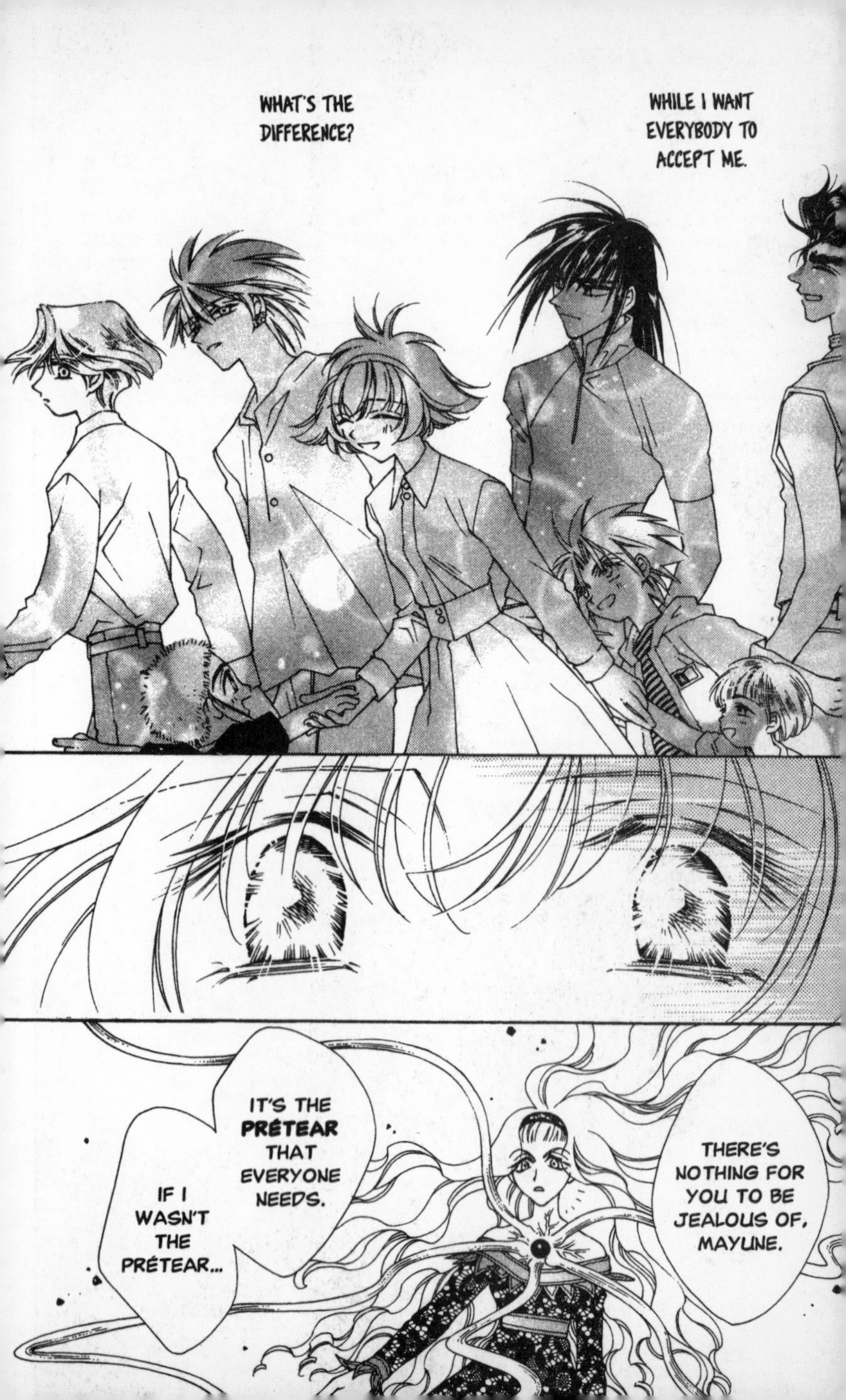
WHILE I WANT EVERYBODY TO ACCEPT ME.
WHAT'S THE DIFFERENCE?
THERE'S NOTHING FOR YOU TO BE JEALOUS OF, MAYUNE.
IT'S THE PRÉTEAR THAT EVERYONE NEEDS.
IF I WASN'T THE PRÉTEAR...

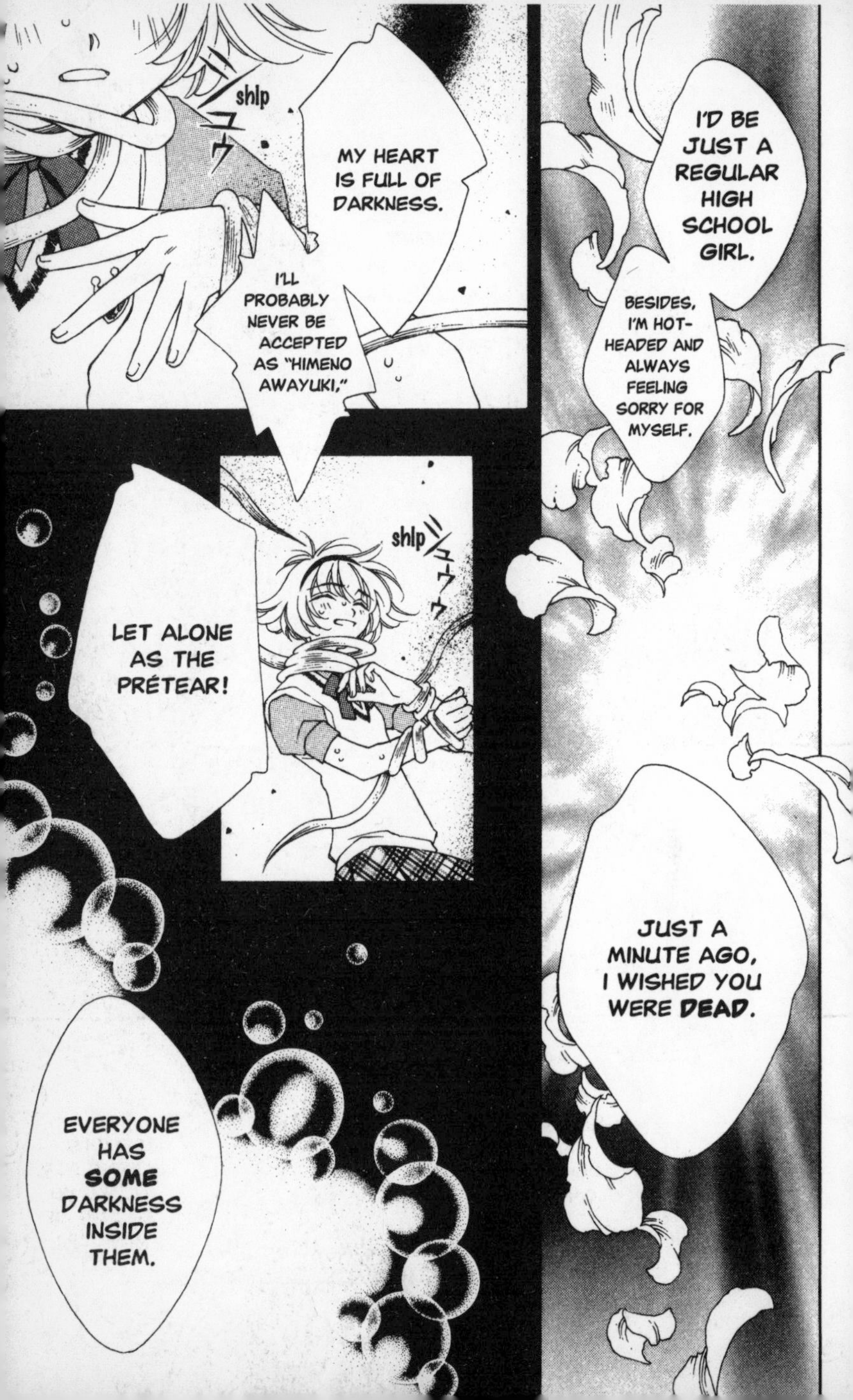
I'D BE JUST A REGULAR HIGH SCHOOL GIRL.
BESIDES, I'M HOT-HEADED AND ALWAYS FEELING SORRY FOR MYSELF.
JUST A MINUTE AGO, I WISHED YOU WERE **DEAD**.
shlp
MY HEART IS FULL OF DARKNESS.
I'LL PROBABLY NEVER BE ACCEPTED AS "HIMENO AWAYUKI,"
shlp
LET ALONE AS THE PRÉTEAR!
EVERYONE HAS **SOME** DARKNESS INSIDE THEM.

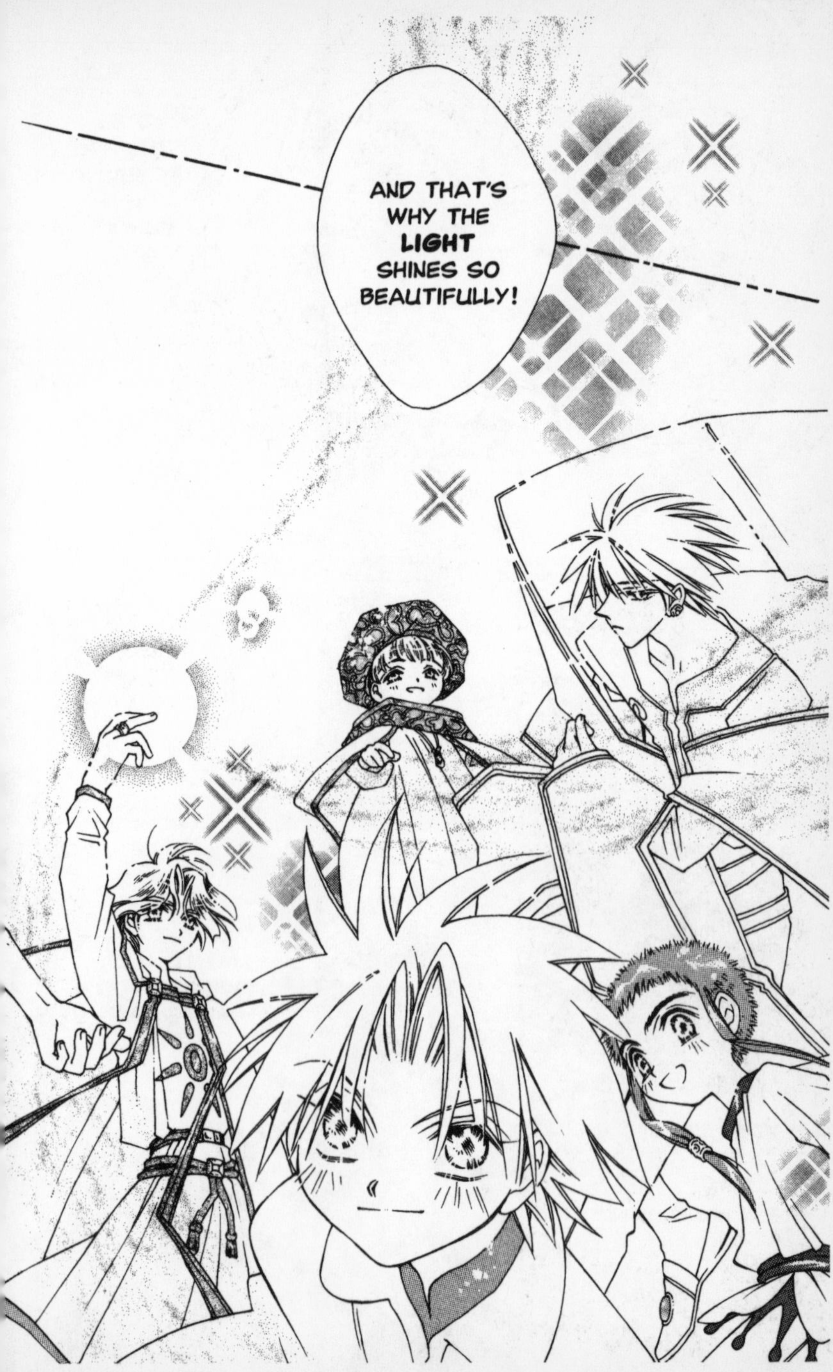
AND THAT'S WHY THE LIGHT SHINES SO BEAUTIFULLY!

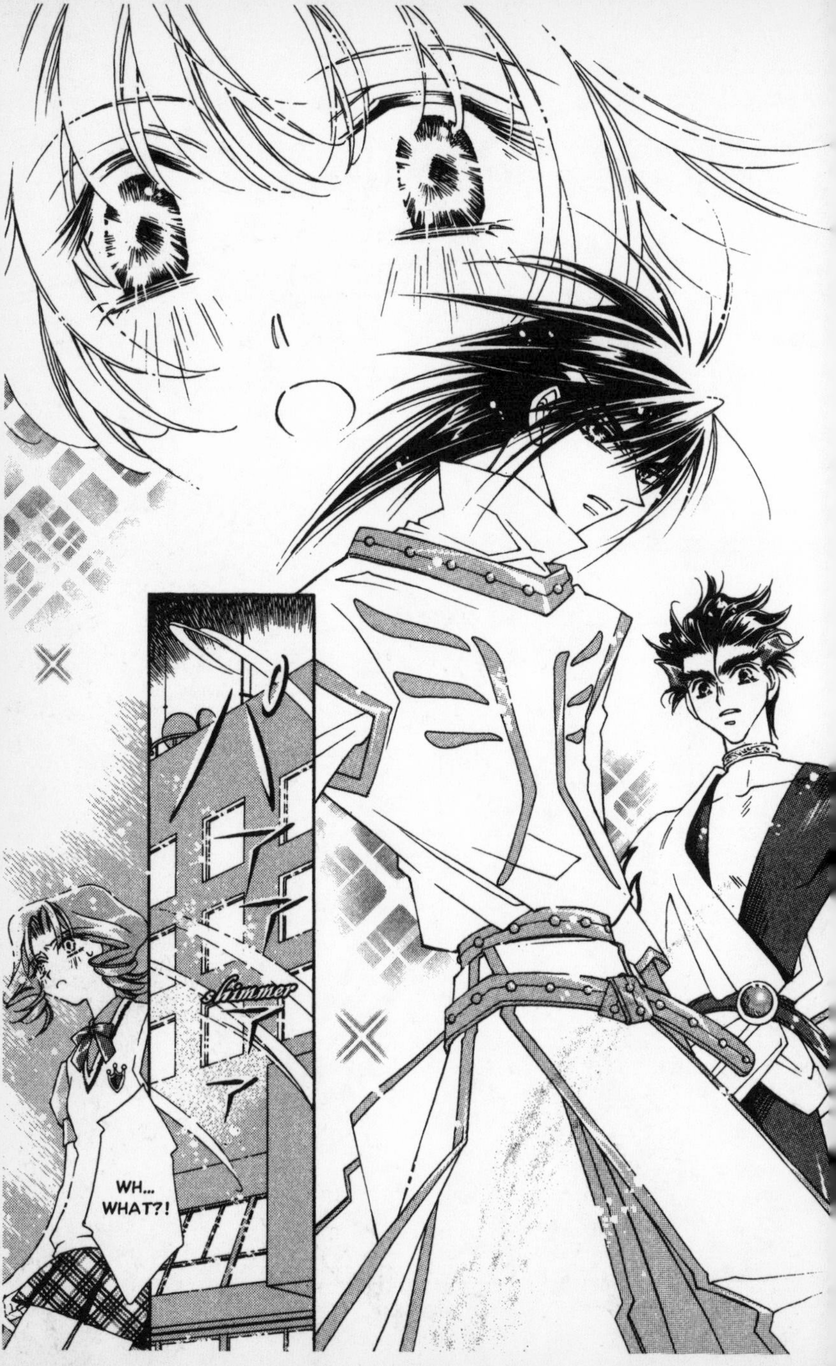
shimmer
WH...
WHAT?!

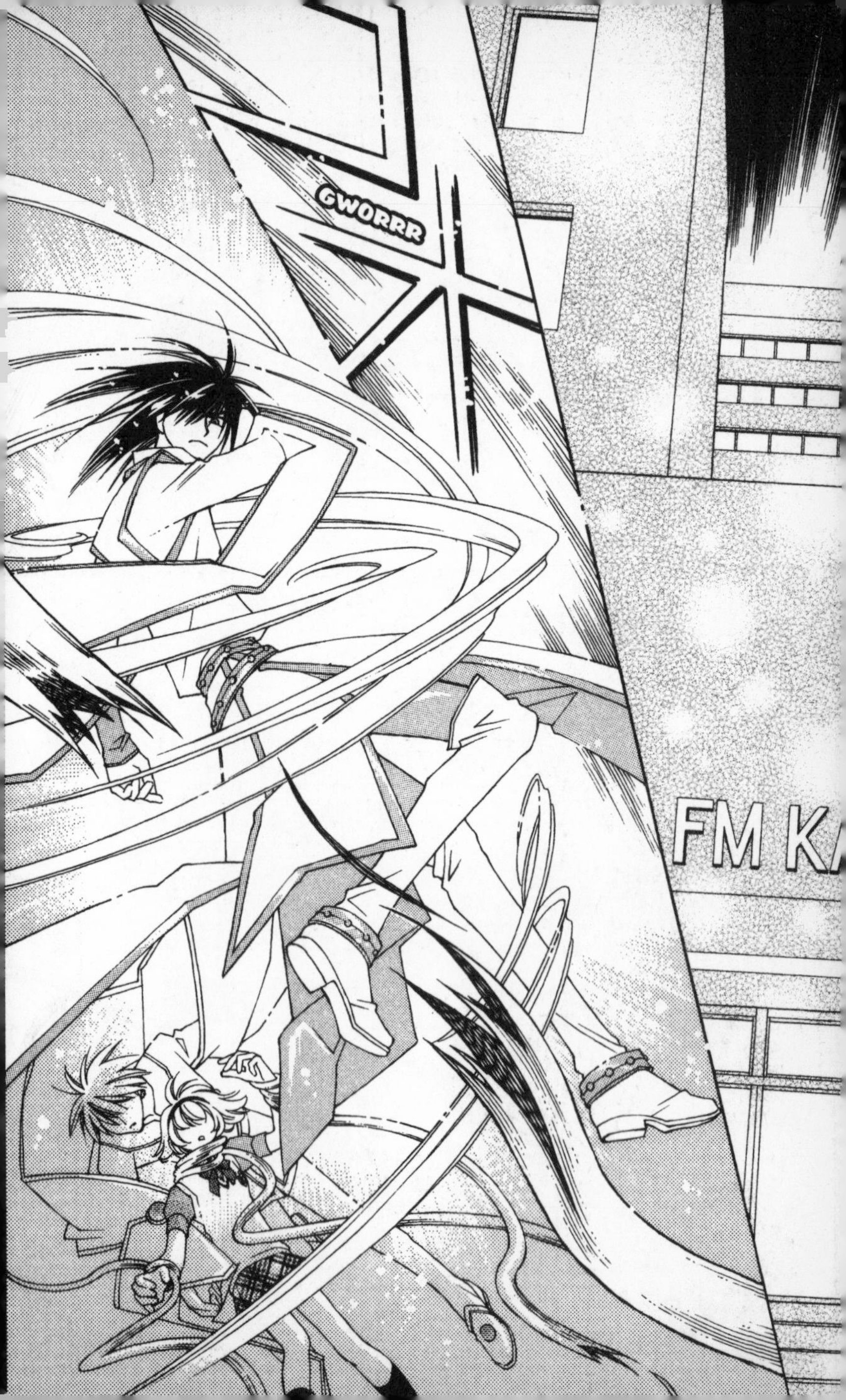
GWORRR
FM KA

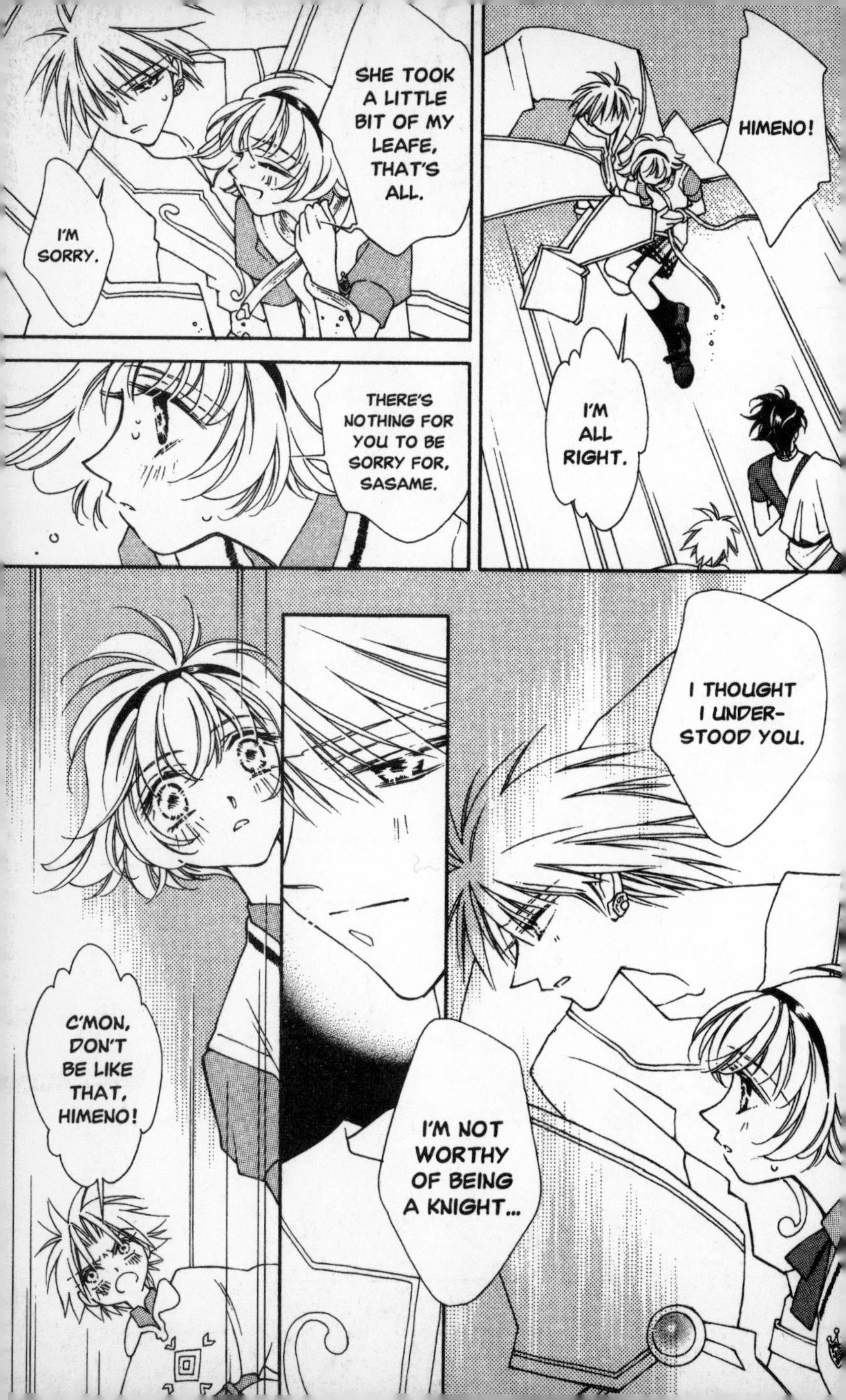
HIMENO!
I'M ALL RIGHT.
SHE TOOK A LITTLE BIT OF MY LEAFE, THAT'S ALL.
I'M SORRY.
THERE'S NOTHING FOR YOU TO BE SORRY FOR, SASAME.
I THOUGHT I UNDER-STOOD YOU.
I'M NOT WORTHY OF BEING A KNIGHT...
C'MON, DON'T BE LIKE THAT, HIMENO!

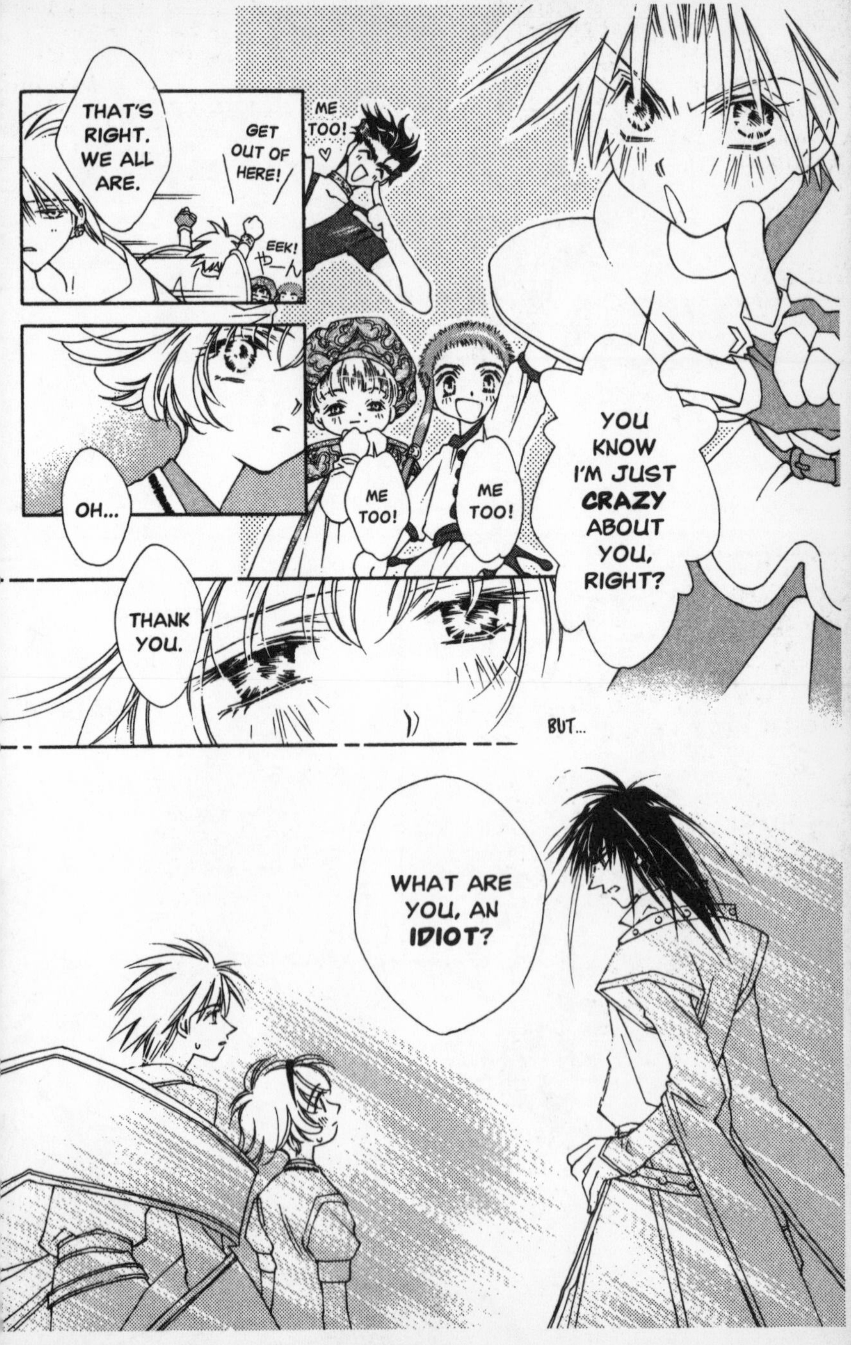
YOU KNOW I'M JUST **CRAZY** ABOUT YOU, RIGHT?
ME TOO! ♡
GET OUT OF HERE!
THAT'S RIGHT. WE ALL ARE.
EEK! やーん
ME TOO!
ME TOO!
OH...
THANK YOU.
BUT...
WHAT ARE YOU, AN **IDIOT**?

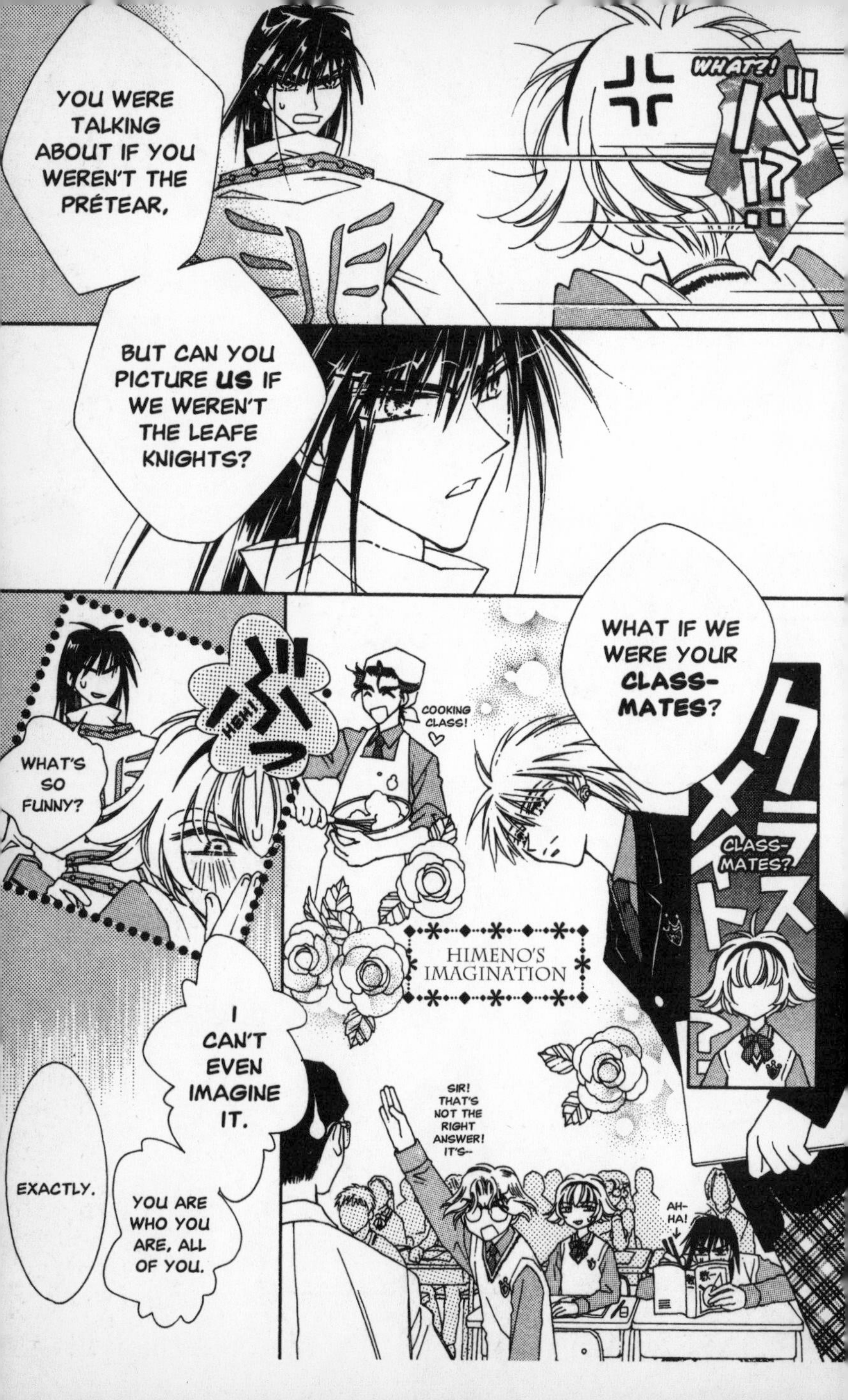
WHAT?!
バ!?!!
YOU WERE TALKING ABOUT IF YOU WEREN'T THE PRÉTEAR,
BUT CAN YOU PICTURE US IF WE WEREN'T THE LEAFE KNIGHTS?
WHAT IF WE WERE YOUR CLASSMATES?
クラスメイト?!
CLASS-MATES?
COOKING CLASS! ♥
HIMENO'S IMAGINATION
SIR! THAT'S NOT THE RIGHT ANSWER! IT'S--
AH-HA!
ぶっ
HEH!
WHAT'S SO FUNNY?
I CAN'T EVEN IMAGINE IT.
YOU ARE WHO YOU ARE, ALL OF YOU.
EXACTLY.

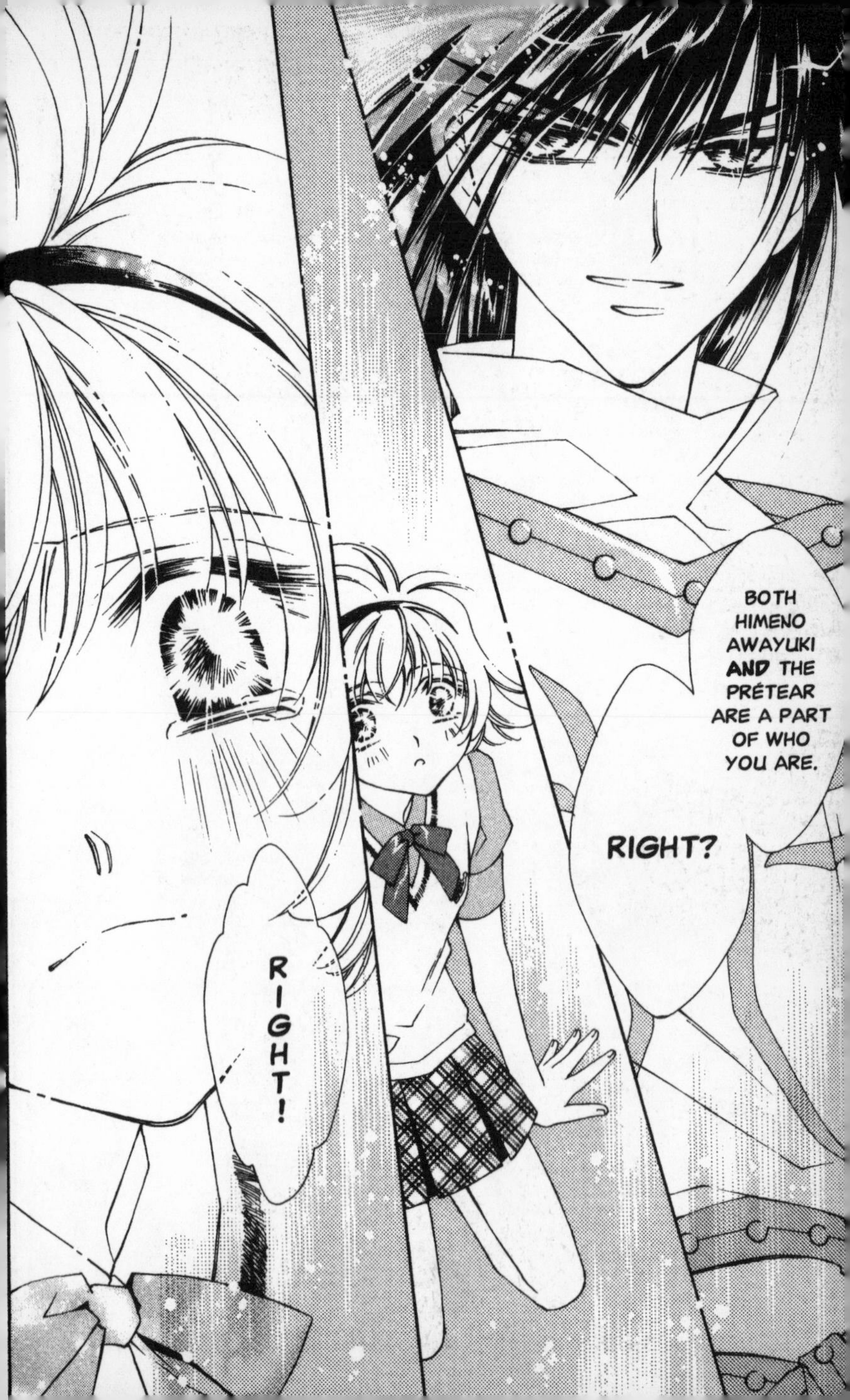
BOTH HIMENO AWAYUKI AND THE PRÉTEAR ARE A PART OF WHO YOU ARE.
RIGHT?
RIGHT!

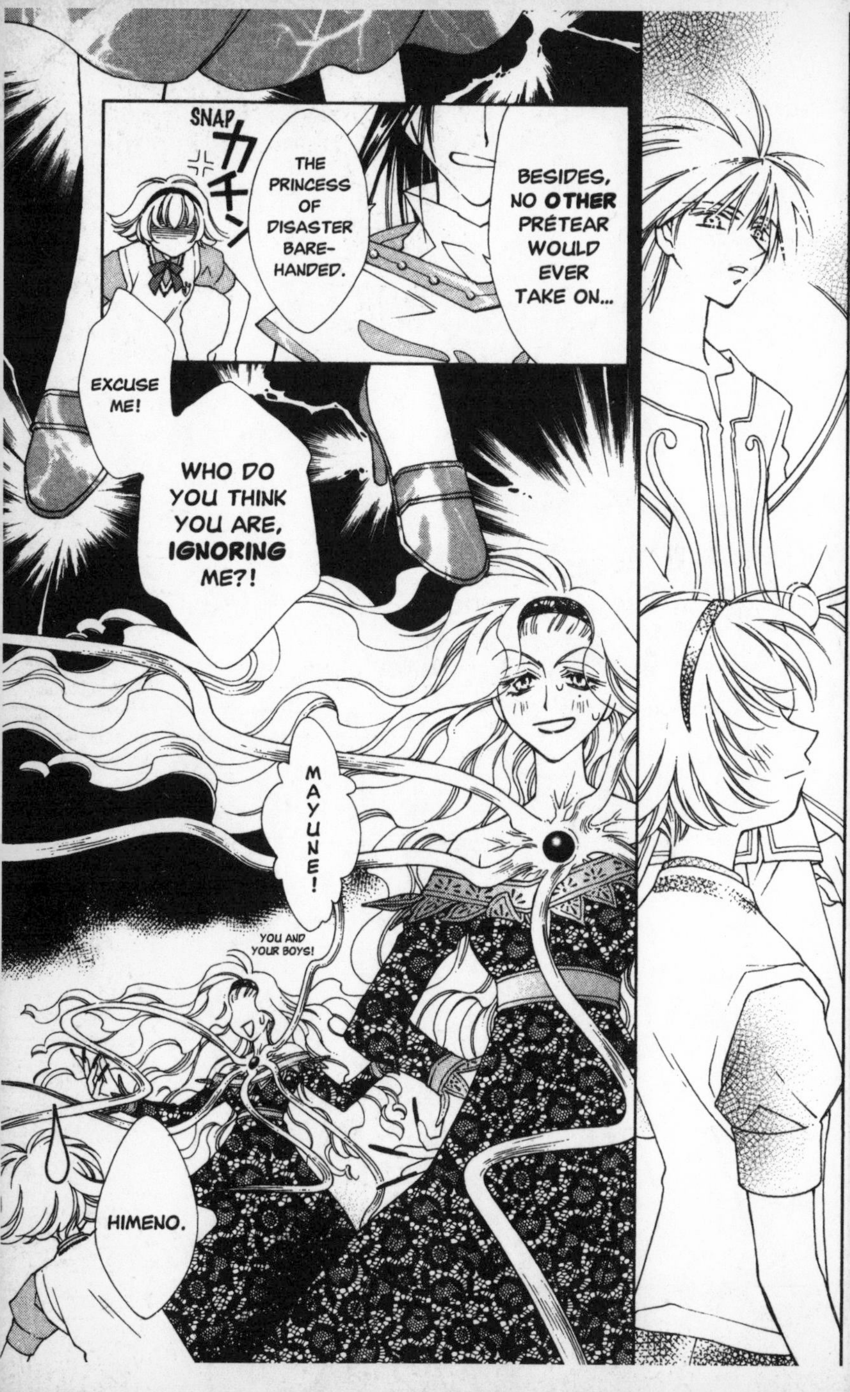

BESIDES, NO OTHER PRÉTEAR WOULD EVER TAKE ON...
THE PRINCESS OF DISASTER BARE-HANDED.
SNAP
カチン
EXCUSE ME!
WHO DO YOU THINK YOU ARE, IGNORING ME?!
MAYUNE!
YOU AND YOUR BOYS!
HIMENO.

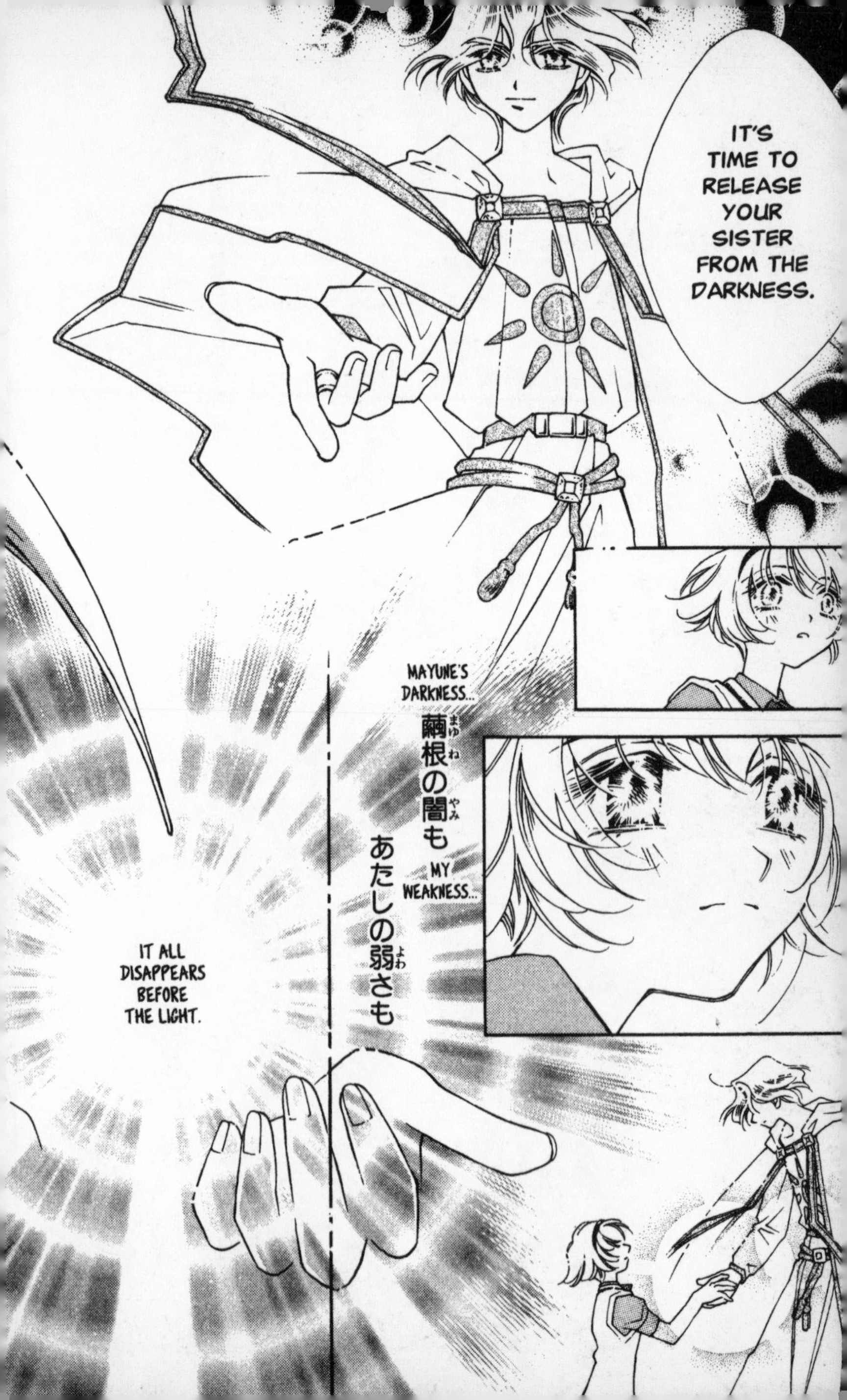
IT'S TIME TO RELEASE YOUR SISTER FROM THE DARKNESS.
MAYUNE'S DARKNESS...
繭根の闇も
MY WEAKNESS...
あたしの弱さも
IT ALL DISAPPEARS BEFORE THE LIGHT.

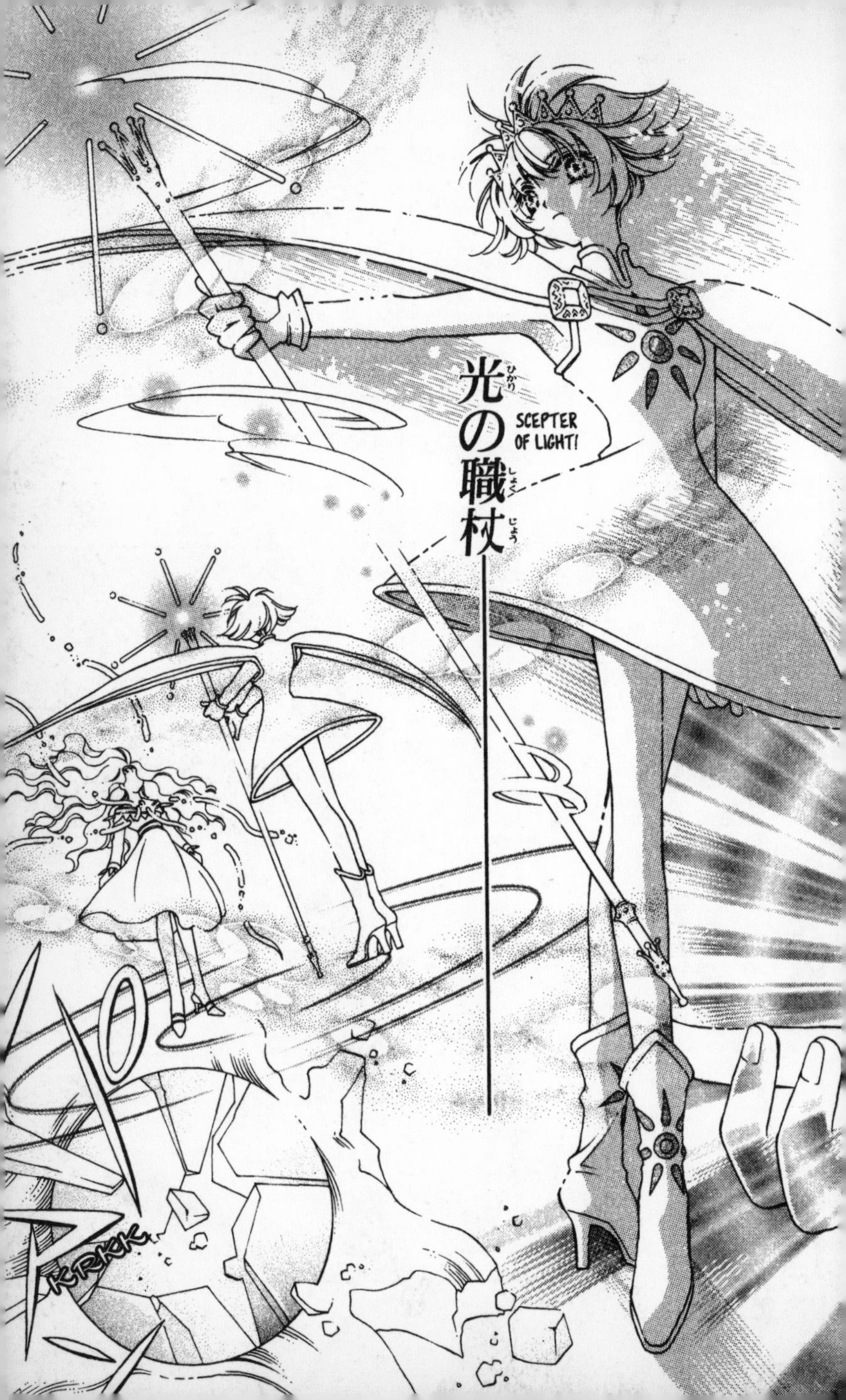
光の職杖
SCEPTER OF LIGHT!
KRKKK

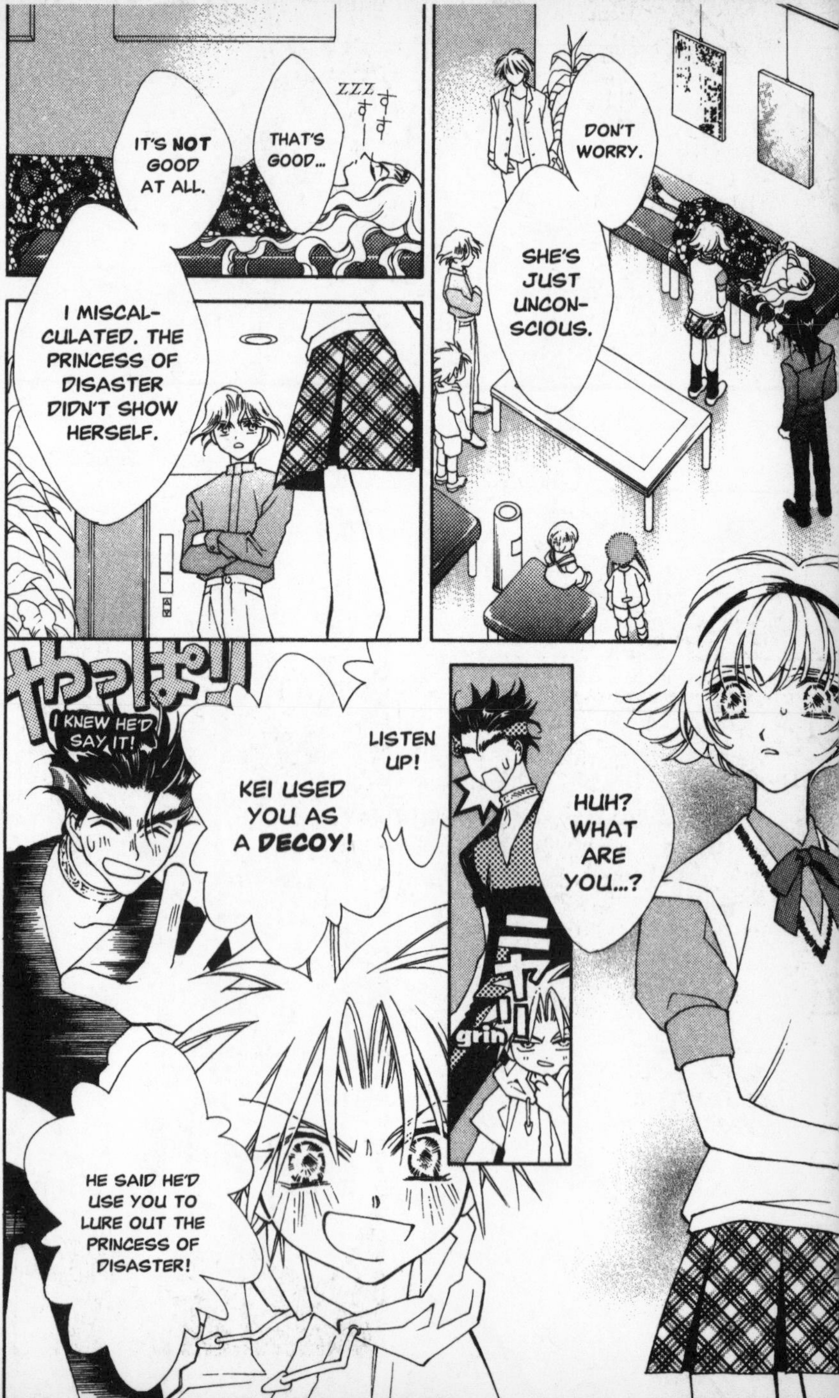
DON'T WORRY.
SHE'S JUST UNCONSCIOUS.
THAT'S GOOD...
ZZZ すーすー
IT'S **NOT** GOOD AT ALL.
I MISCALCULATED. THE PRINCESS OF DISASTER DIDN'T SHOW HERSELF.
HUH? WHAT ARE YOU...?
ニヤリ
grin
LISTEN UP!
KEI USED YOU AS A **DECOY**!
やっぱり
I KNEW HE'D SAY IT!
HE SAID HE'D USE YOU TO LURE OUT THE PRINCESS OF DISASTER!

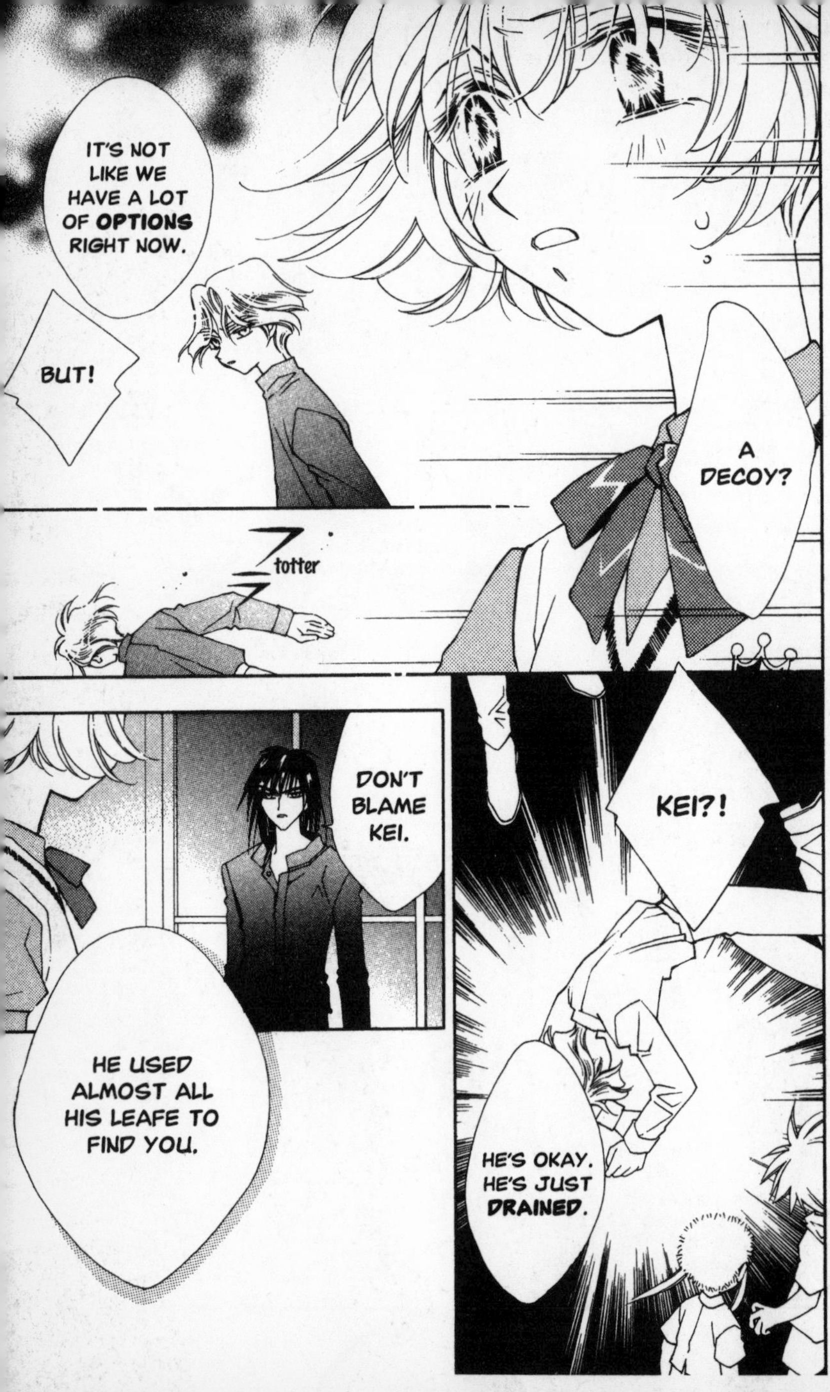
A DECOY?
IT'S NOT LIKE WE HAVE A LOT OF **OPTIONS** RIGHT NOW.
BUT!
totter
KEI?!
HE'S OKAY. HE'S JUST **DRAINED**.
DON'T BLAME KEI.
HE USED ALMOST ALL HIS LEAFE TO FIND YOU.

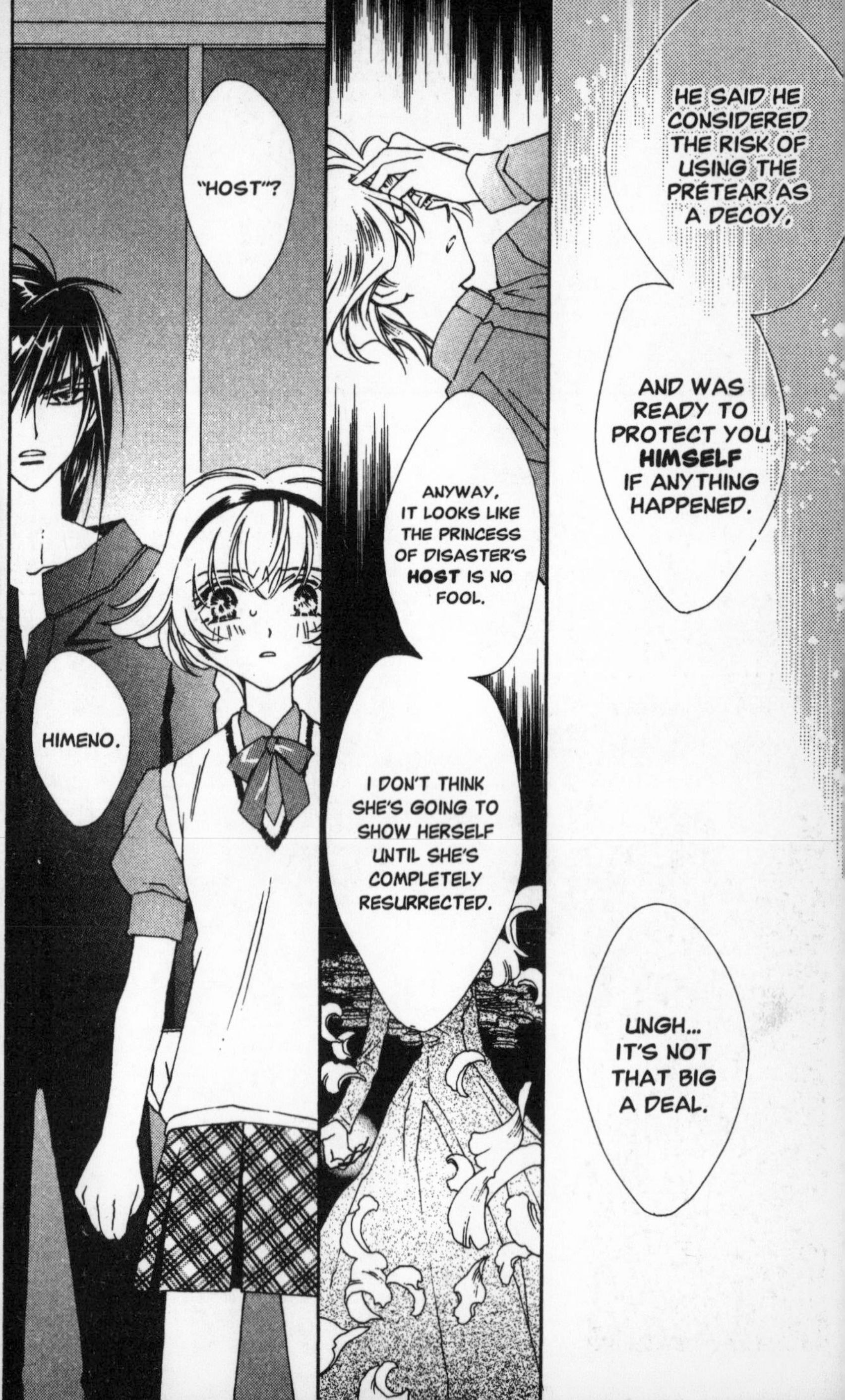
HE SAID HE CONSIDERED THE RISK OF USING THE PRÉTEAR AS A DECOY.
AND WAS READY TO PROTECT YOU **HIMSELF** IF ANYTHING HAPPENED.
UNGH... IT'S NOT THAT BIG A DEAL.
ANYWAY, IT LOOKS LIKE THE PRINCESS OF DISASTER'S **HOST** IS NO FOOL.
I DON'T THINK SHE'S GOING TO SHOW HERSELF UNTIL SHE'S COMPLETELY RESURRECTED.
"HOST"?
HIMENO.

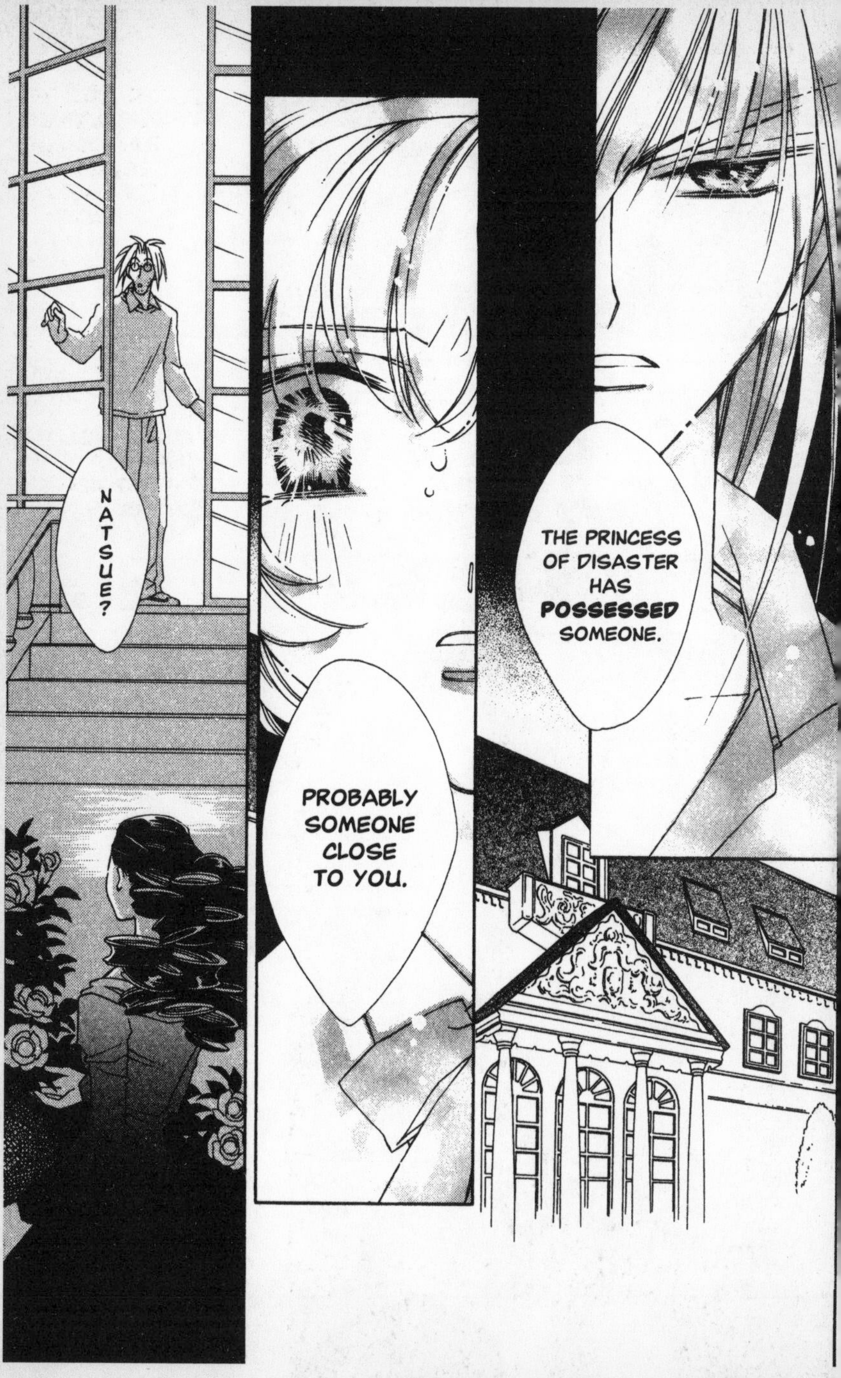
THE PRINCESS OF DISASTER HAS POSSESSED SOMEONE.
PROBABLY SOMEONE CLOSE TO YOU.
NATSUE?

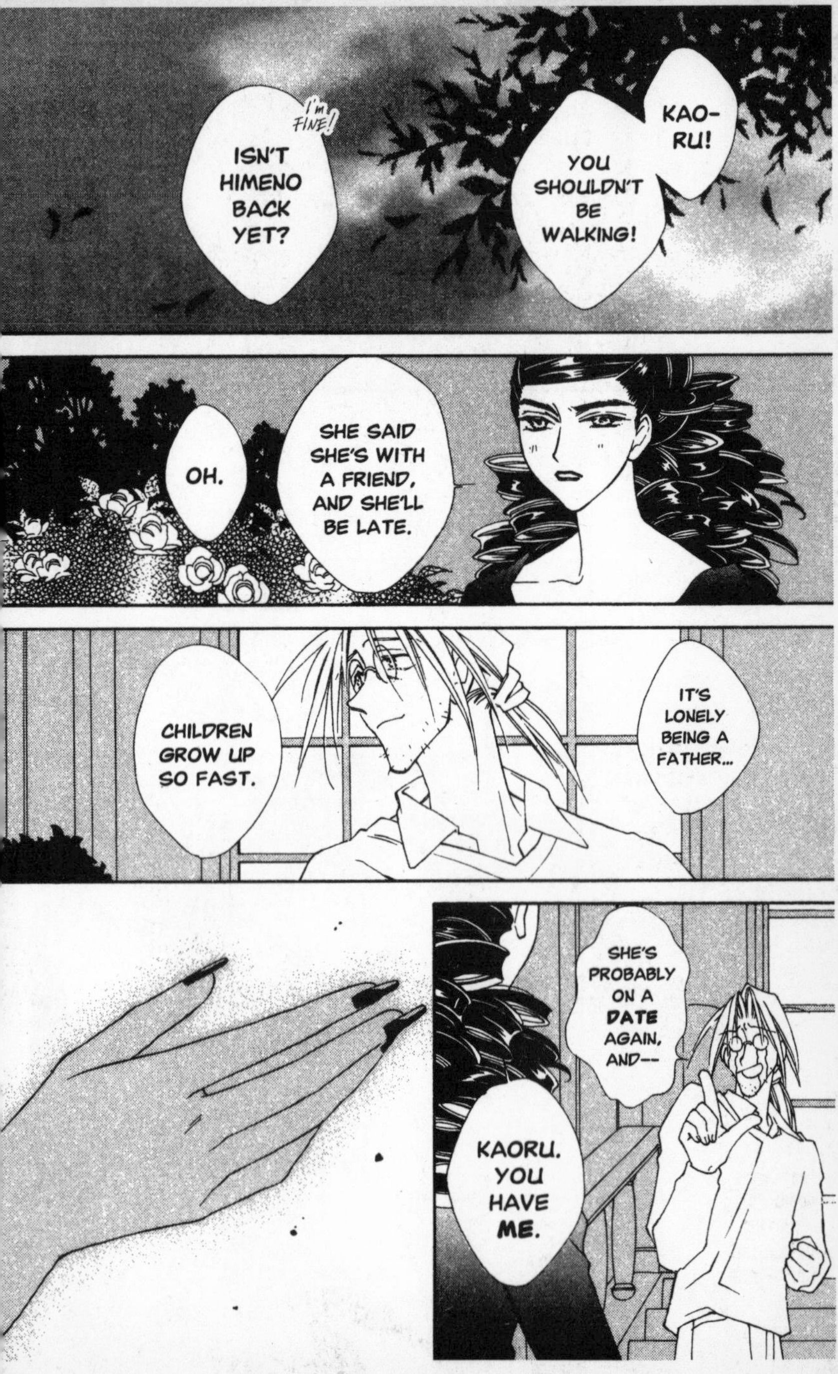
KAO-RU!
YOU SHOULDN'T BE WALKING!
I'm FINE!
ISN'T HIMENO BACK YET?
SHE SAID SHE'S WITH A FRIEND, AND SHE'LL BE LATE.
OH.
IT'S LONELY BEING A FATHER...
CHILDREN GROW UP SO FAST.
SHE'S PROBABLY ON A DATE AGAIN, AND--
KAORU. YOU HAVE ME.

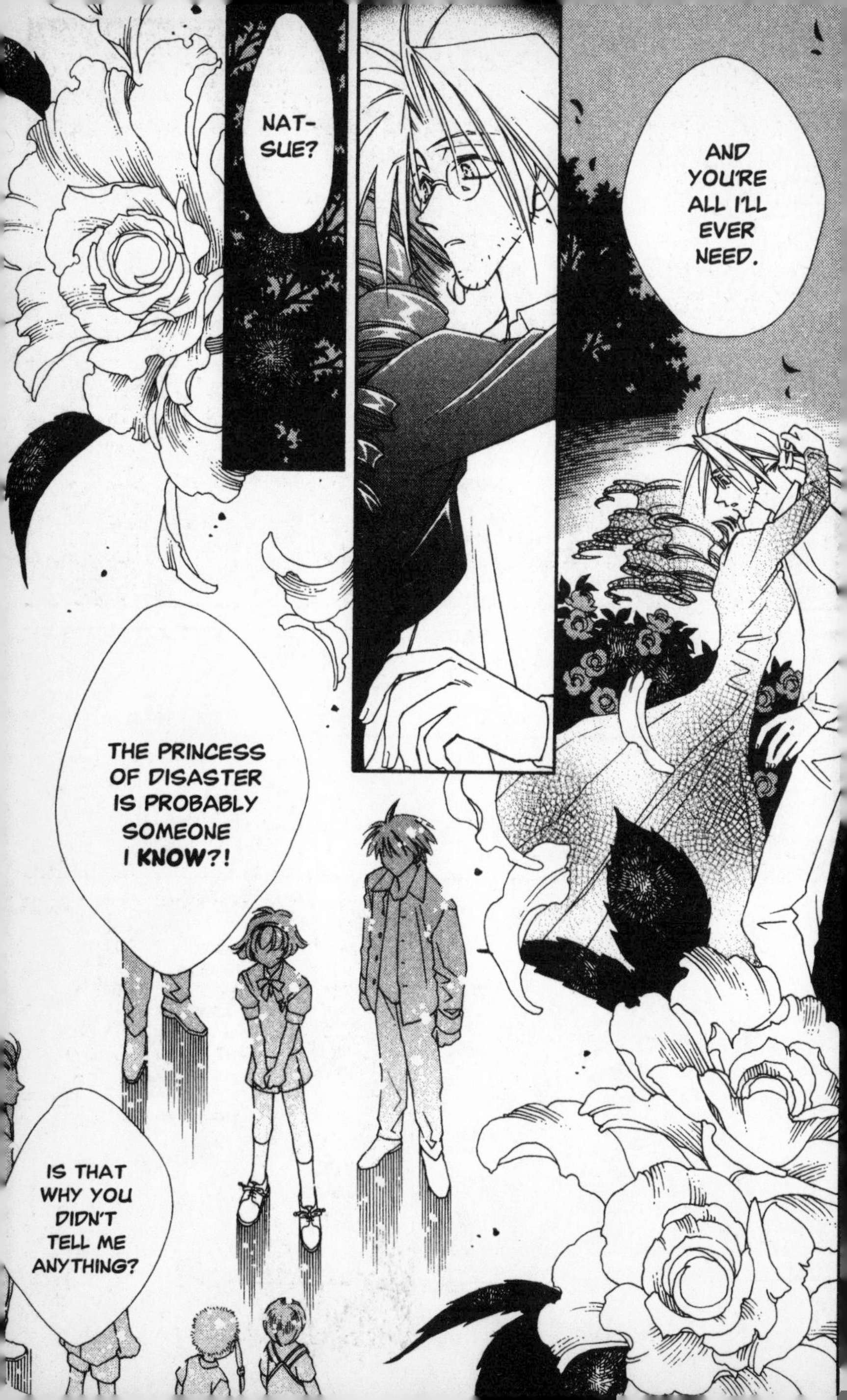
AND YOU'RE ALL I'LL EVER NEED.
NAT-SUE?
THE PRINCESS OF DISASTER IS PROBABLY SOMEONE I **KNOW**?!
IS THAT WHY YOU DIDN'T TELL ME ANYTHING?

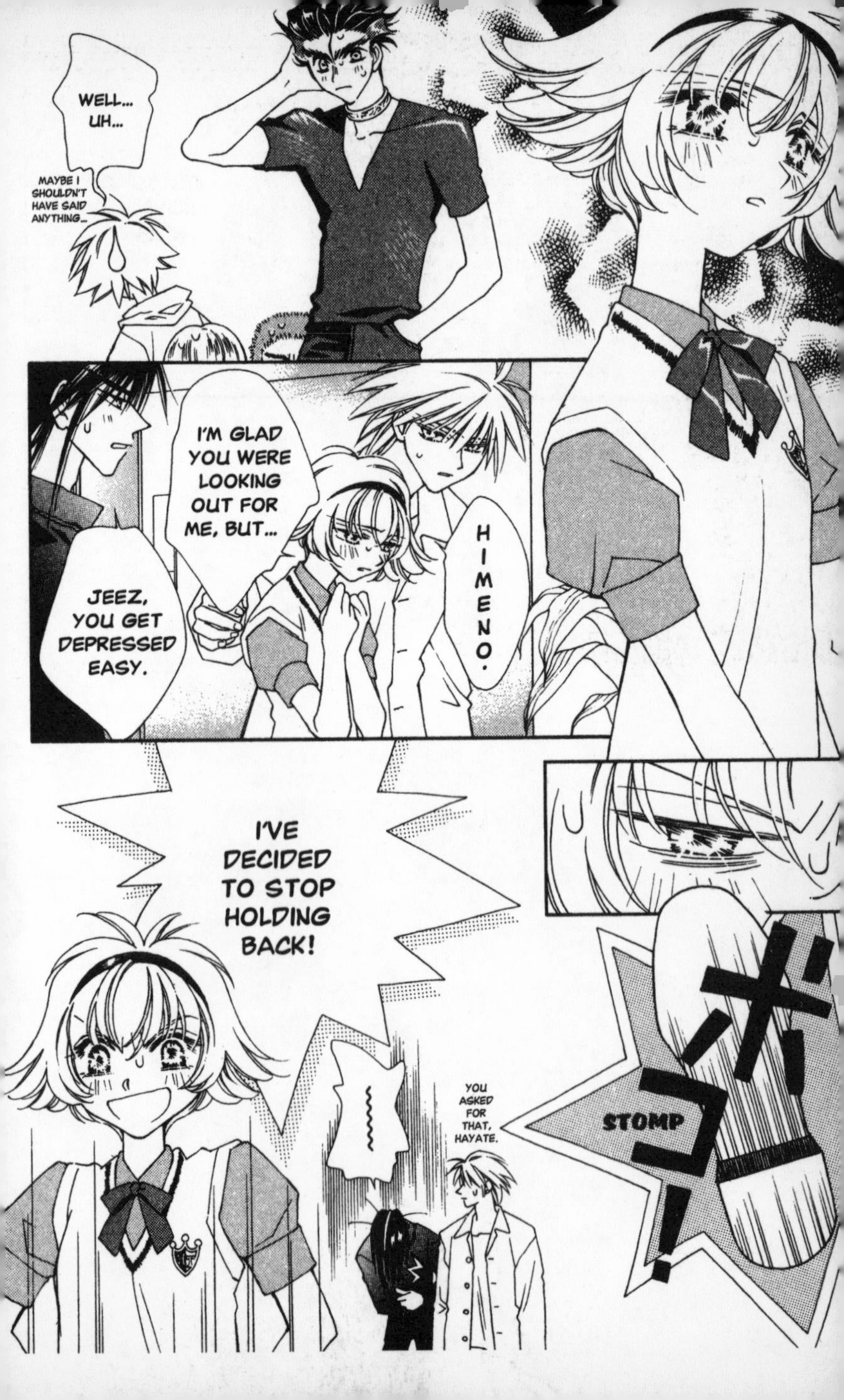
WELL... UH...
MAYBE I SHOULDN'T HAVE SAID ANYTHING...
HIMENO.
I'M GLAD YOU WERE LOOKING OUT FOR ME, BUT...
JEEZ, YOU GET DEPRESSED EASY.
STOMP
I'VE DECIDED TO STOP HOLDING BACK!
YOU ASKED FOR THAT, HAYATE.

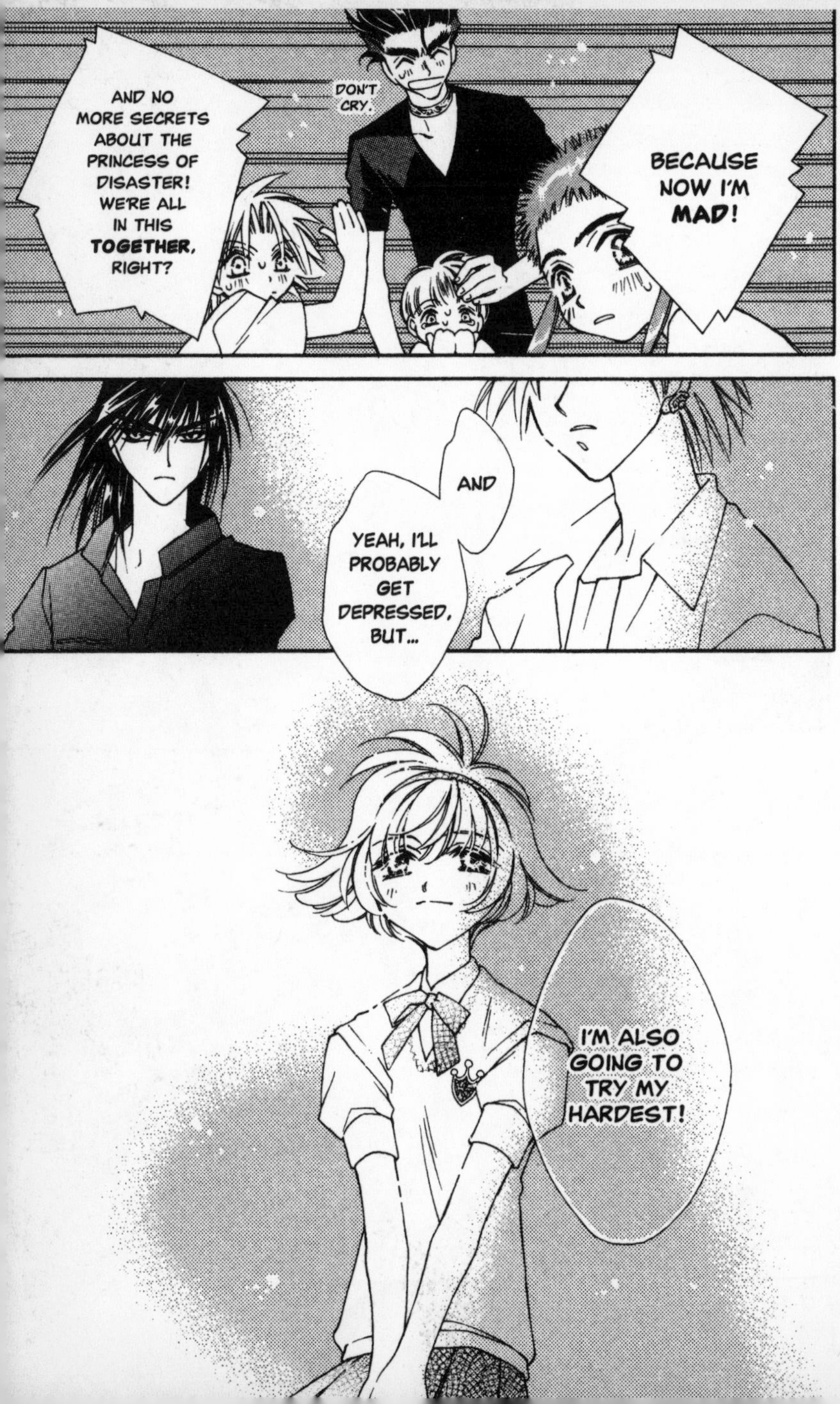
BECAUSE NOW I'M MAD!
DON'T CRY.
AND NO MORE SECRETS ABOUT THE PRINCESS OF DISASTER! WE'RE ALL IN THIS TOGETHER, RIGHT?
AND
YEAH, I'LL PROBABLY GET DEPRESSED, BUT...
I'M ALSO GOING TO TRY MY HARDEST!

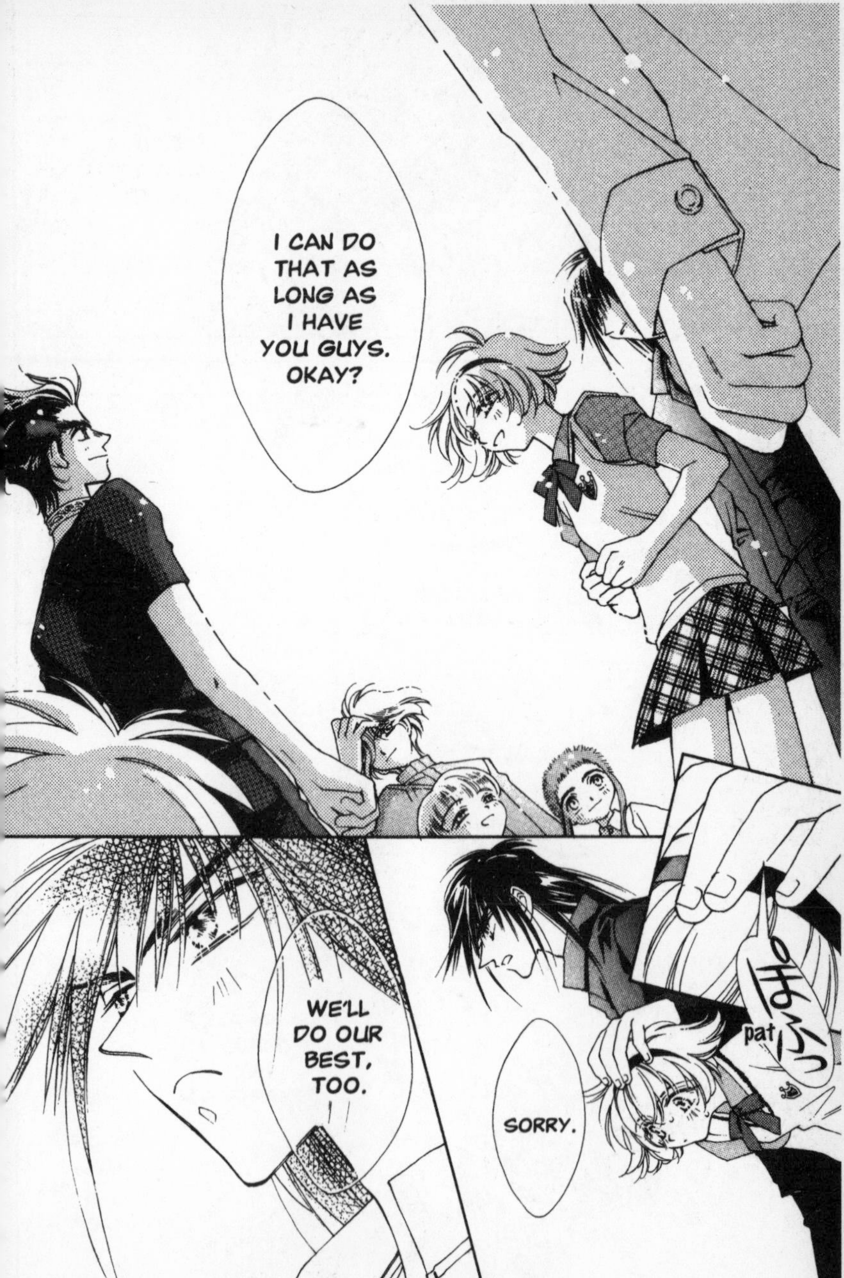
I CAN DO THAT AS LONG AS I HAVE YOU GUYS. OKAY?
ぽふっ
pat
SORRY.
WE'LL DO OUR BEST, TOO.

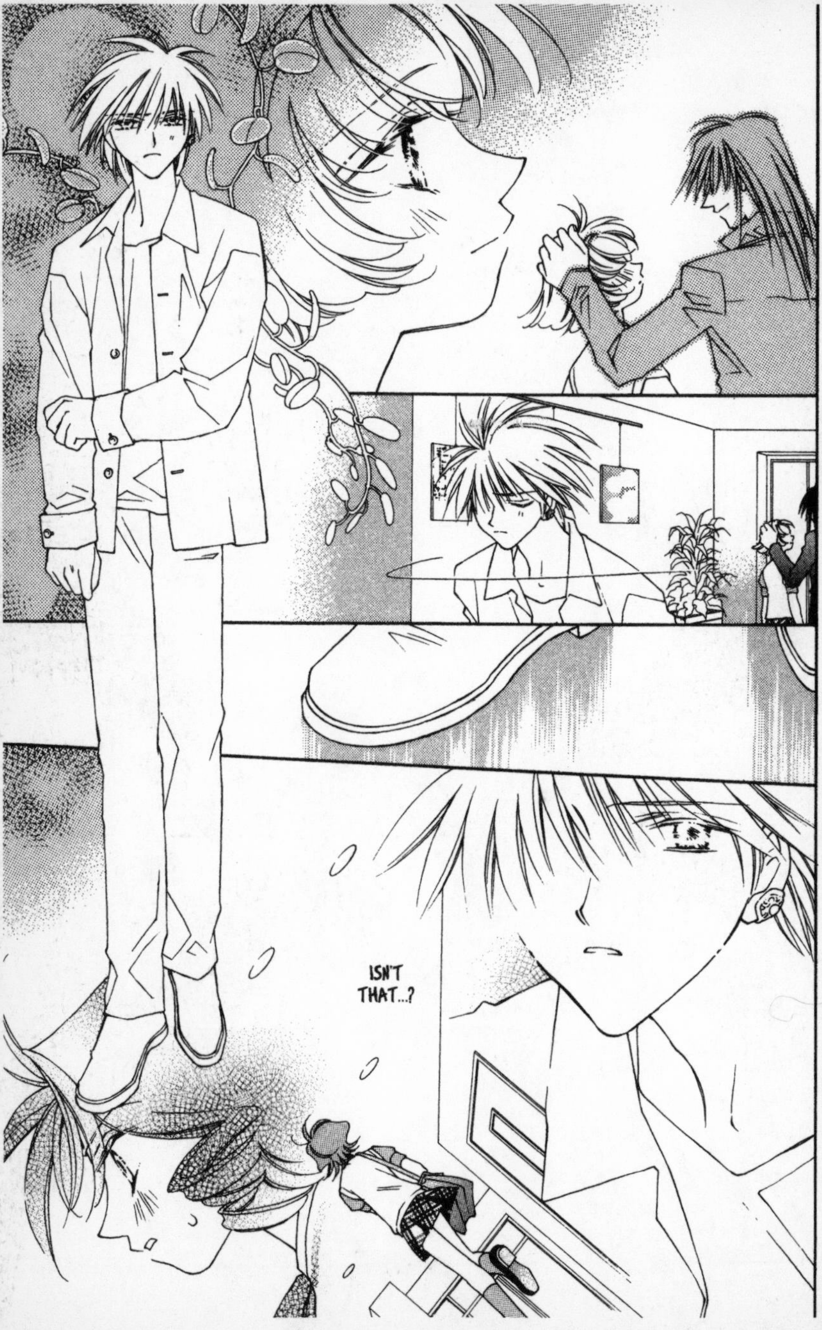
ISN'T THAT...?

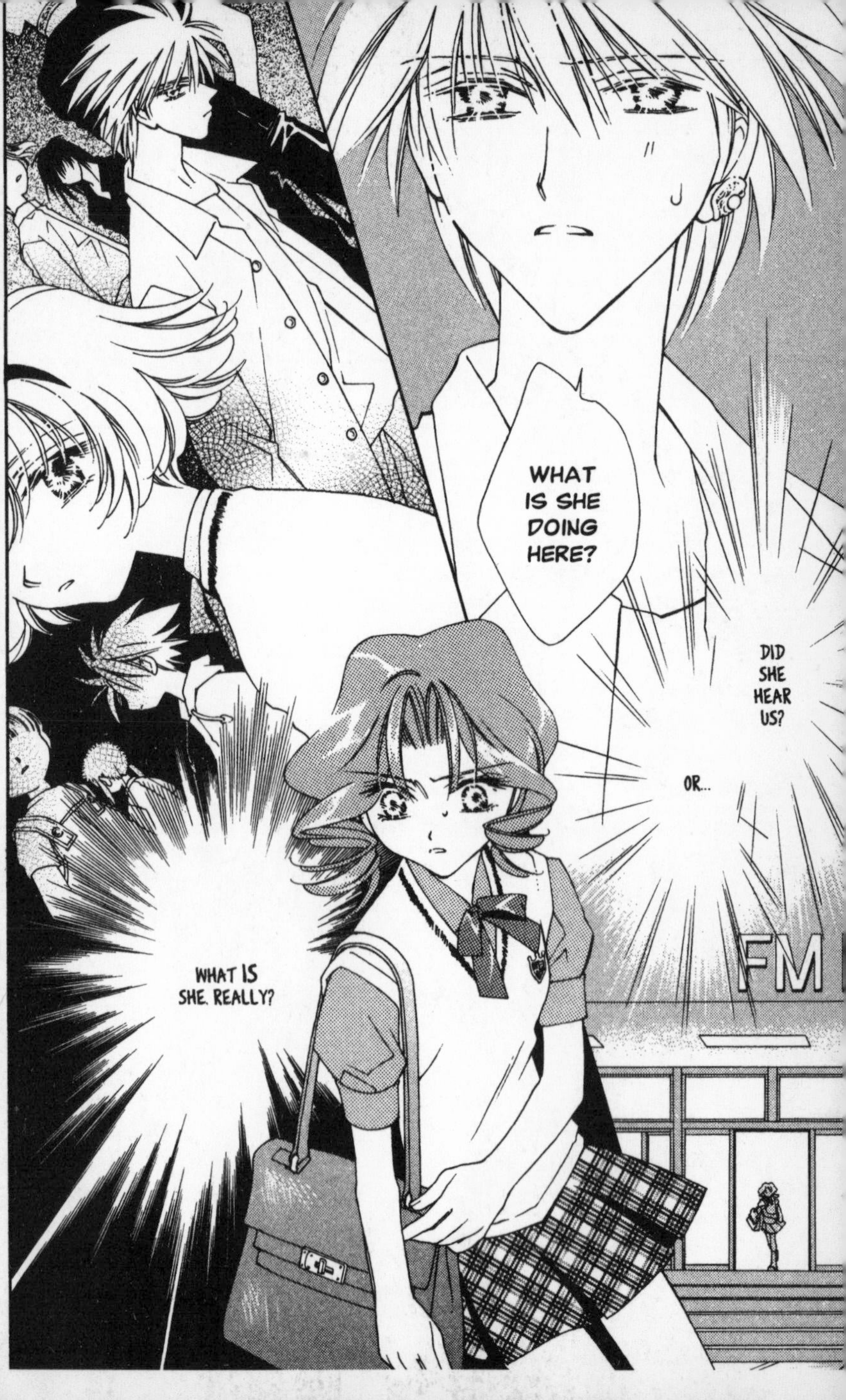
WHAT IS SHE DOING HERE?
DID SHE HEAR US?
OR..
FM
WHAT IS SHE, REALLY?

CHAPTER 15

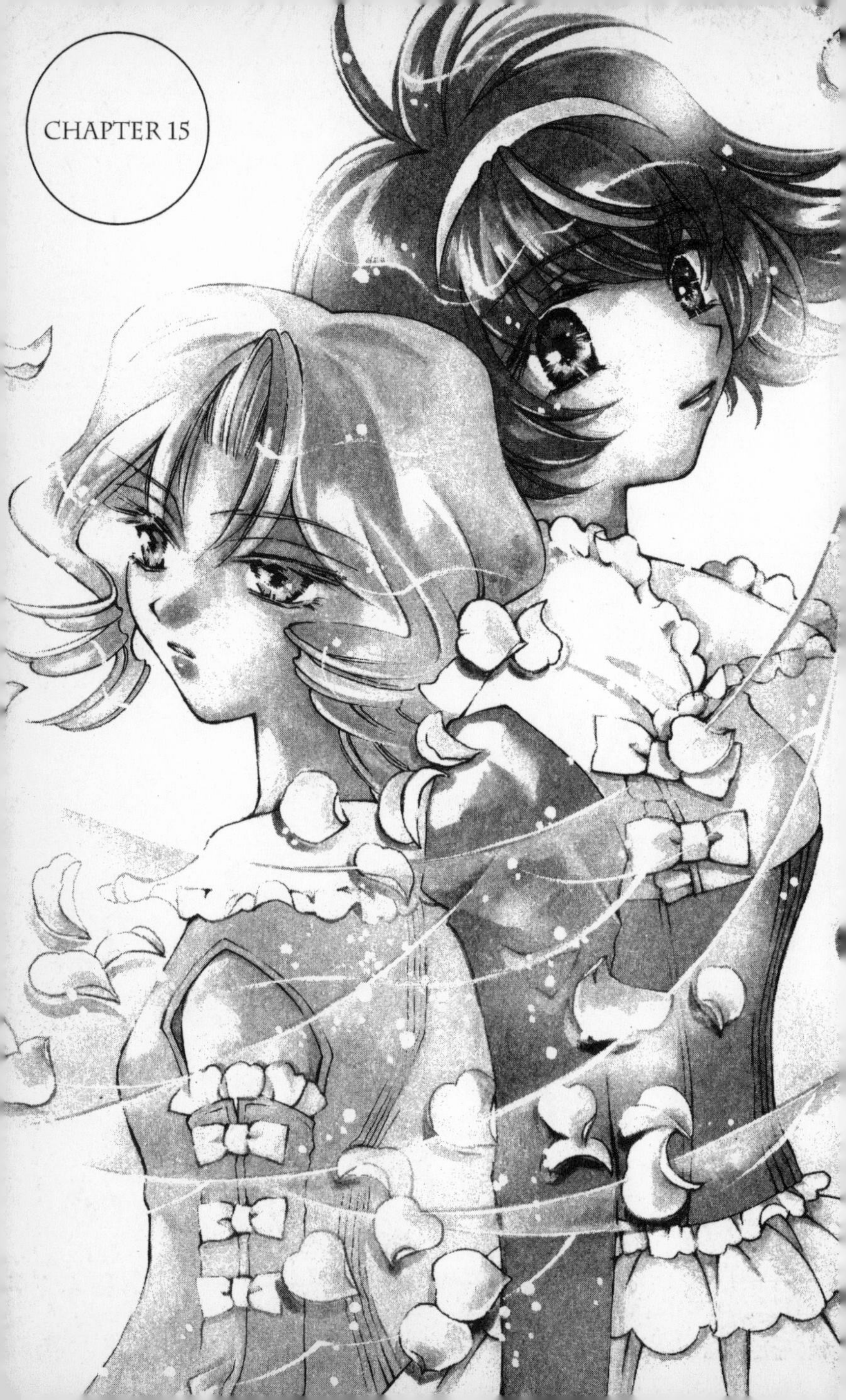

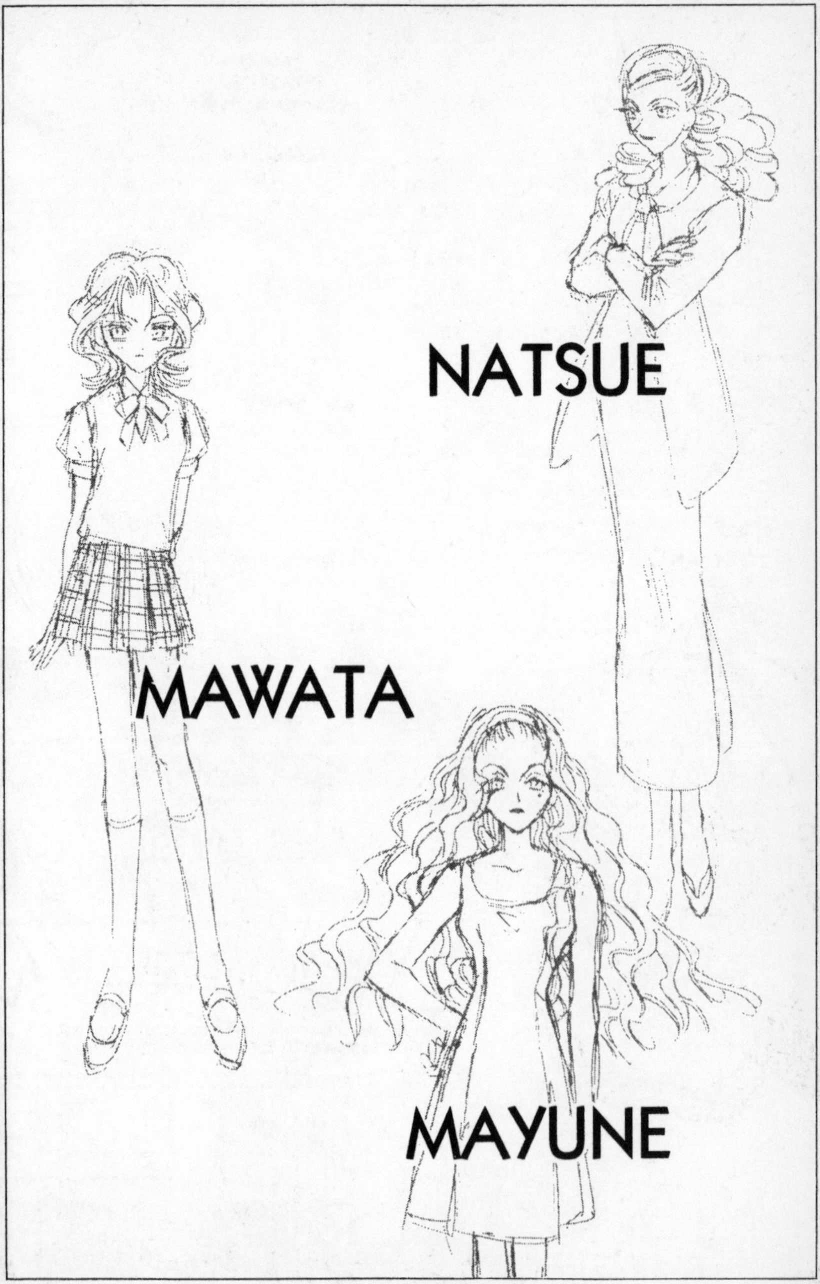
NATSUE
MAWATA
MAYUNE

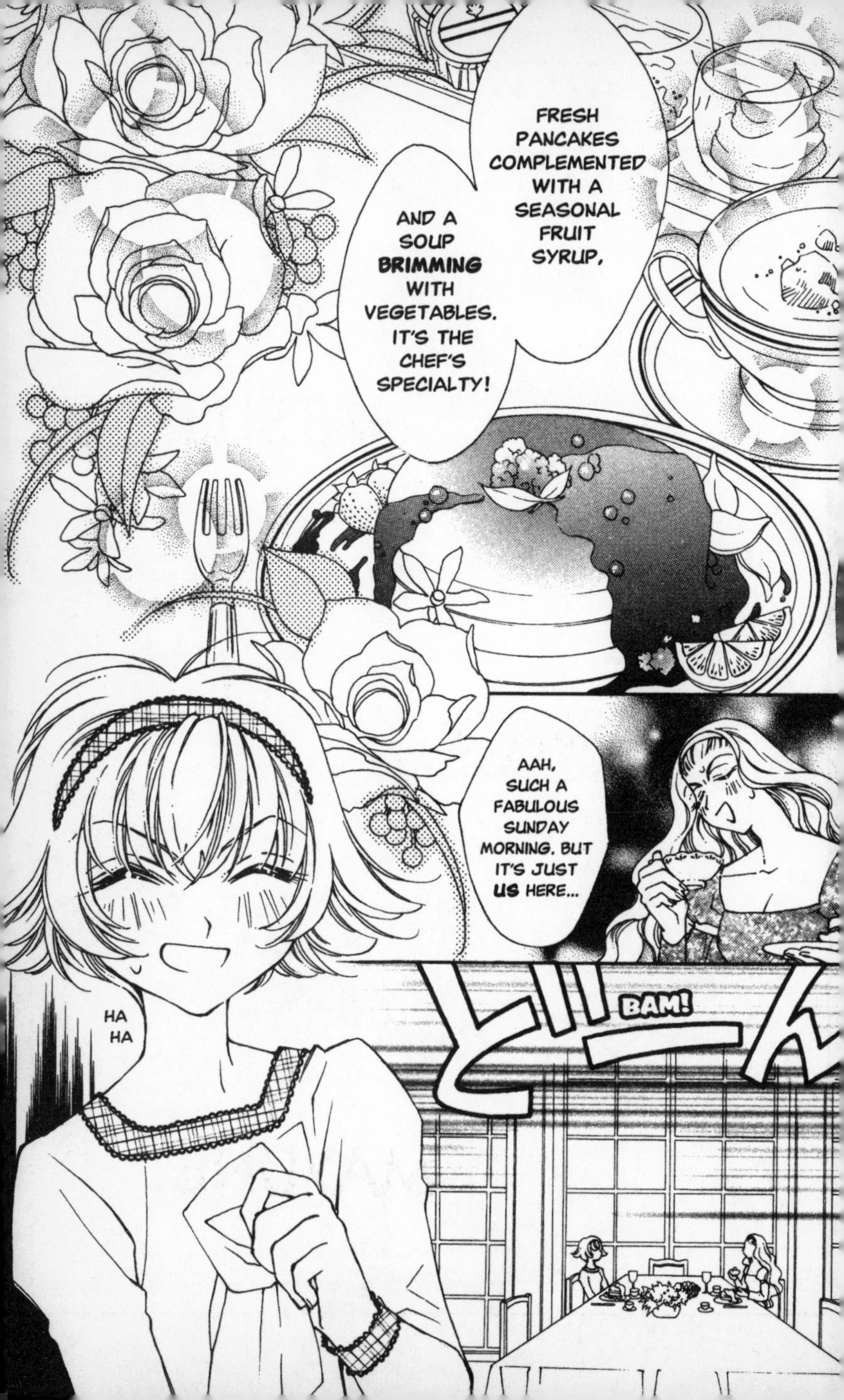
FRESH PANCAKES COMPLEMENTED WITH A SEASONAL FRUIT SYRUP,
AND A SOUP **BRIMMING** WITH VEGETABLES. IT'S THE CHEF'S SPECIALTY!
AAH, SUCH A FABULOUS SUNDAY MORNING. BUT IT'S JUST **US** HERE...
BAM!
HA HA

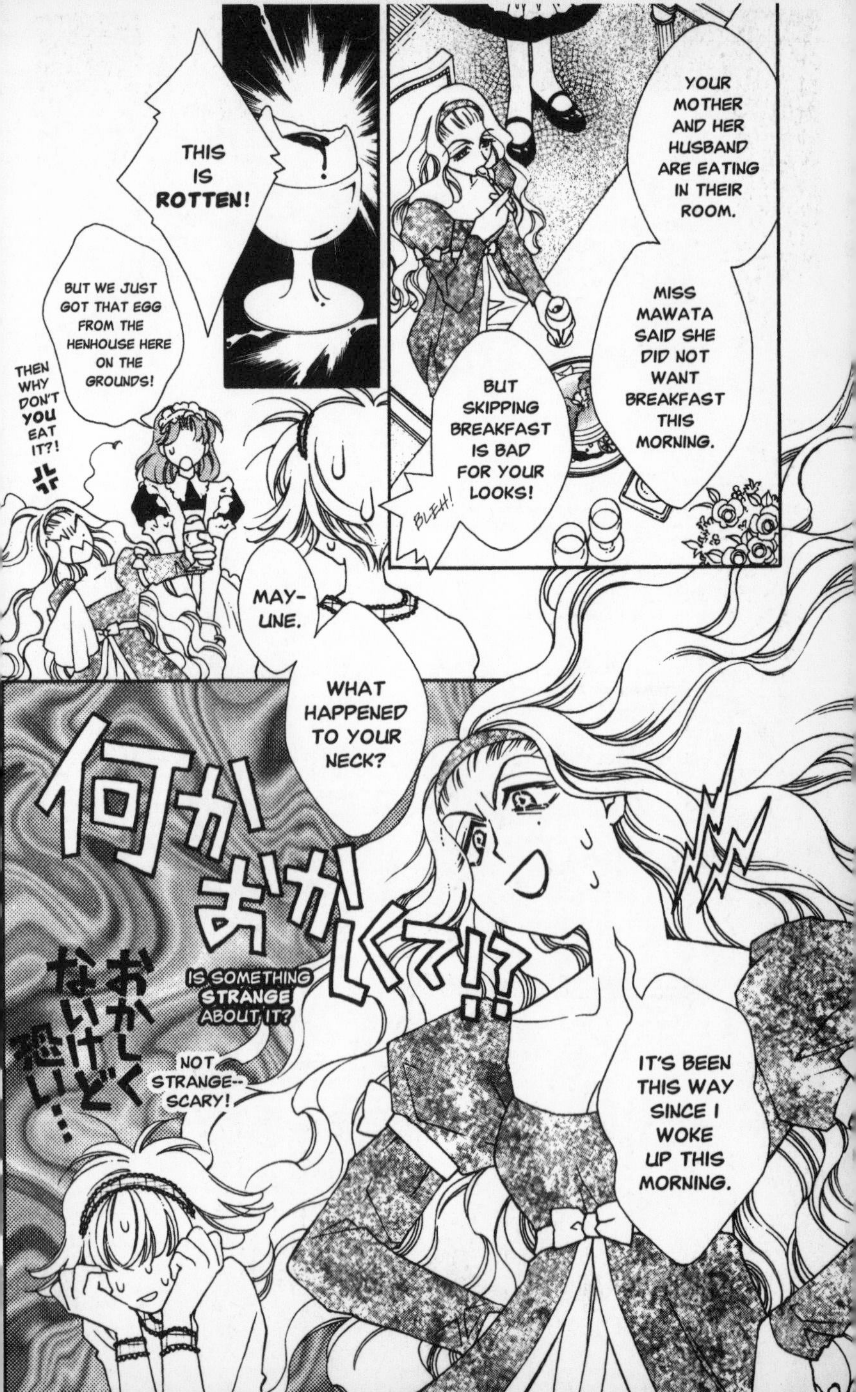
YOUR MOTHER AND HER HUSBAND ARE EATING IN THEIR ROOM.
MISS MAWATA SAID SHE DID NOT WANT BREAKFAST THIS MORNING.
BUT SKIPPING BREAKFAST IS BAD FOR YOUR LOOKS!
BLEH!
THIS IS ROTTEN!
BUT WE JUST GOT THAT EGG FROM THE HENHOUSE HERE ON THE GROUNDS!
THEN WHY DON'T YOU EAT IT?!
MAY-UNE.
WHAT HAPPENED TO YOUR NECK?
IT'S BEEN THIS WAY SINCE I WOKE UP THIS MORNING.
何かおかしくて!?
IS SOMETHING STRANGE ABOUT IT?
おかしくないけど恐い…
NOT STRANGE--SCARY!

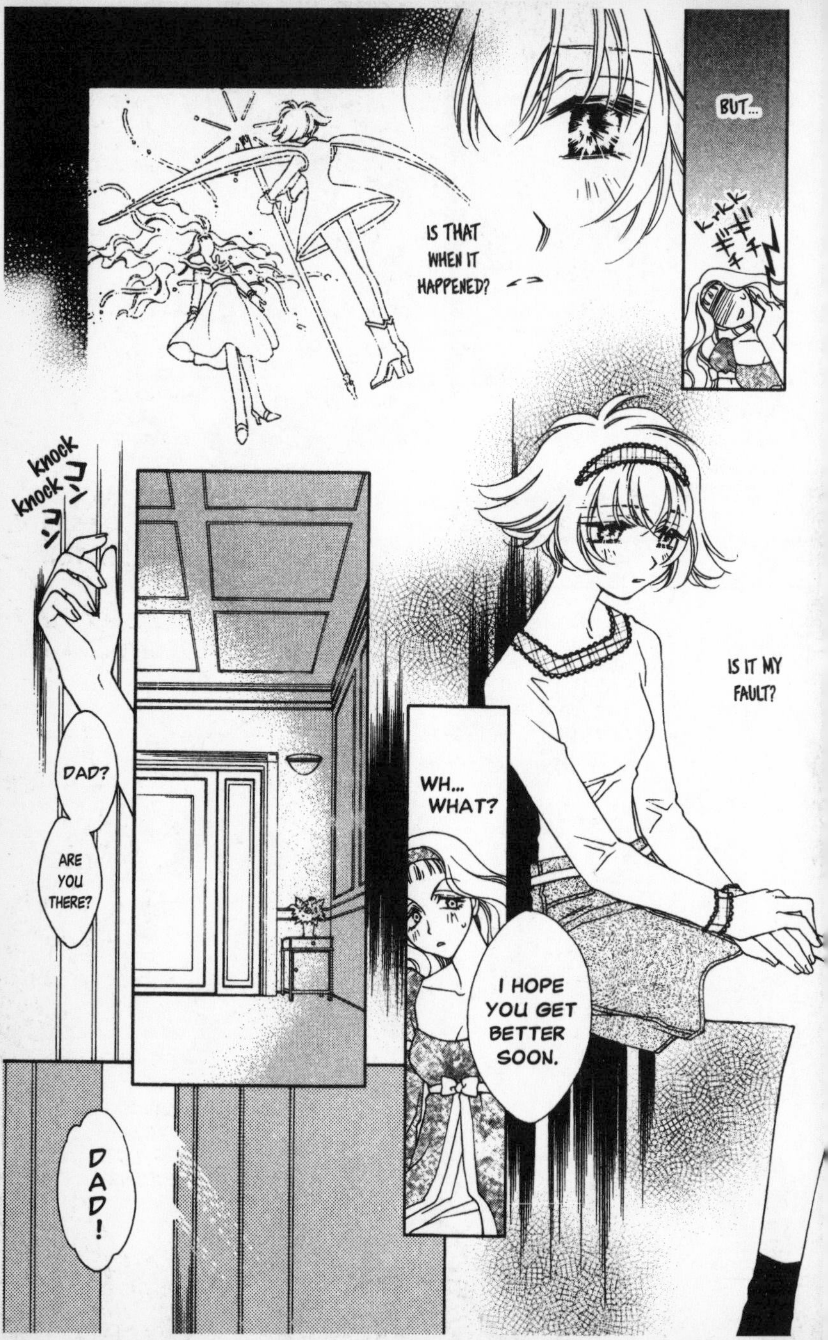
BUT...
k-r-k-k
ギチギチ
IS THAT WHEN IT HAPPENED?
IS IT MY FAULT?
WH... WHAT?
I HOPE YOU GET BETTER SOON.
knock knock
コンコン
DAD?
ARE YOU THERE?
DAD!

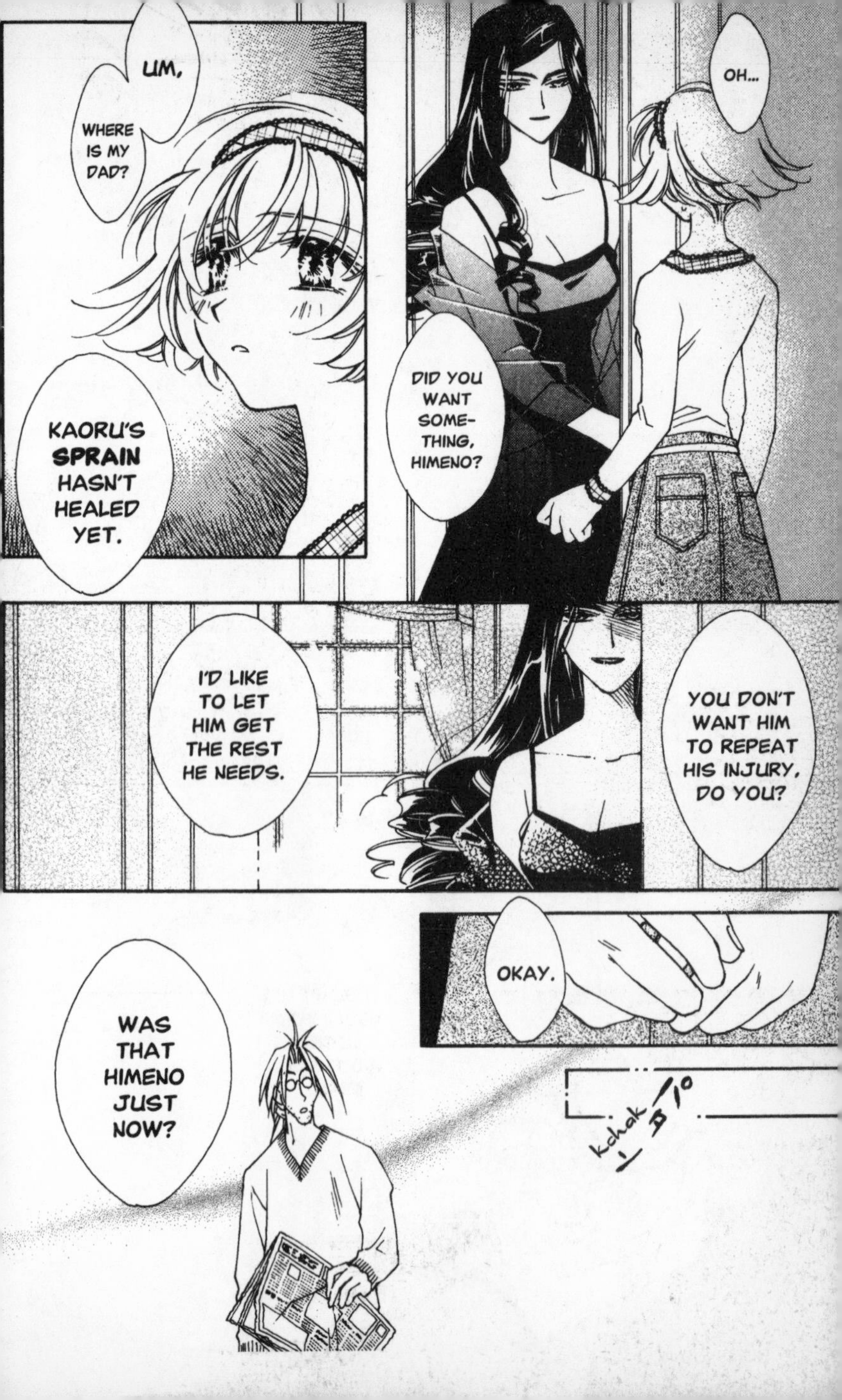

OH...
DID YOU WANT SOMETHING, HIMENO?
UM,
WHERE IS MY DAD?
KAORU'S SPRAIN HASN'T HEALED YET.
I'D LIKE TO LET HIM GET THE REST HE NEEDS.
YOU DON'T WANT HIM TO REPEAT HIS INJURY, DO YOU?
OKAY.
kchak
WAS THAT HIMENO JUST NOW?

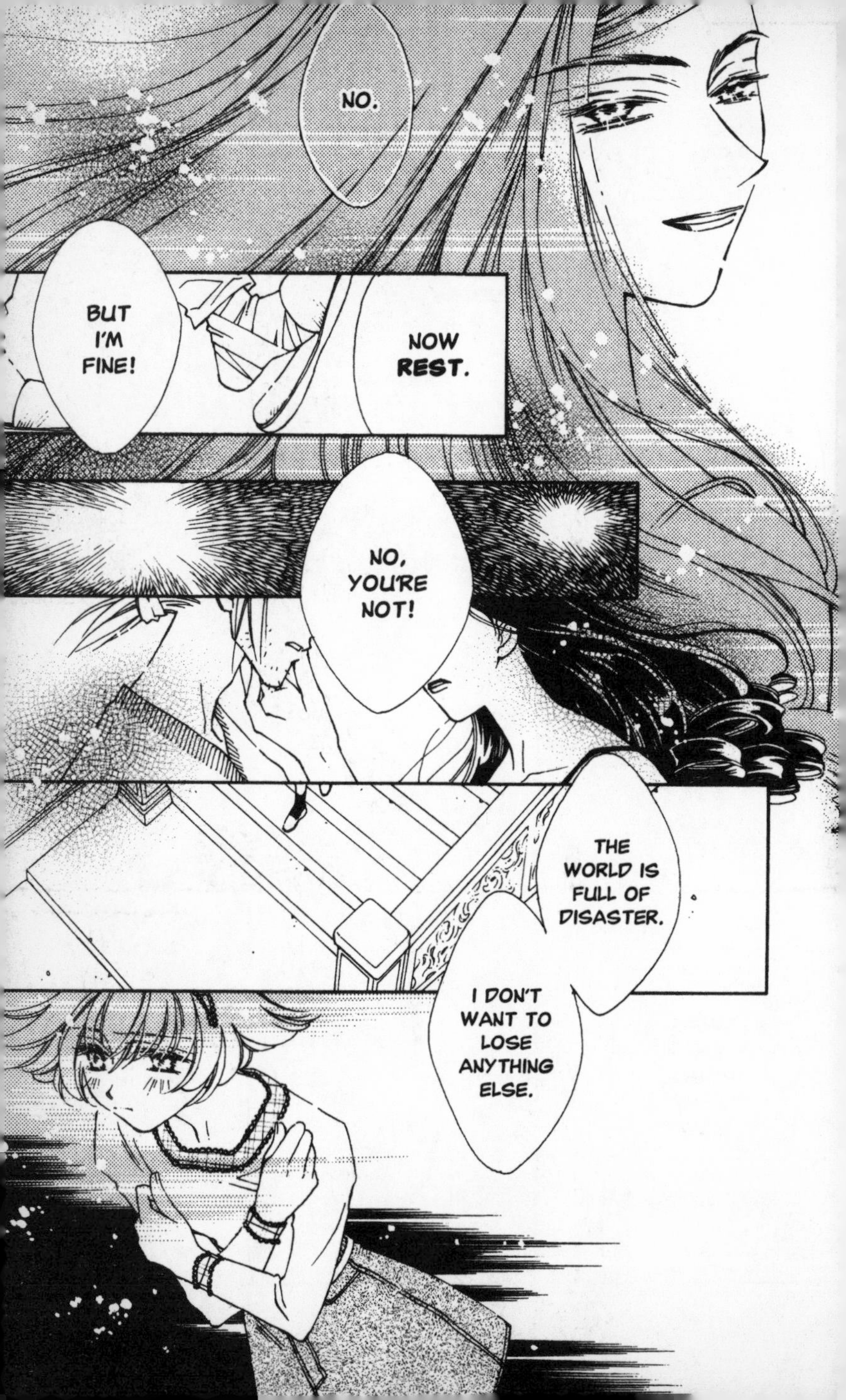
NO.
NOW REST.
BUT I'M FINE!
NO, YOU'RE NOT!
THE WORLD IS FULL OF DISASTER.
I DON'T WANT TO LOSE ANYTHING ELSE.

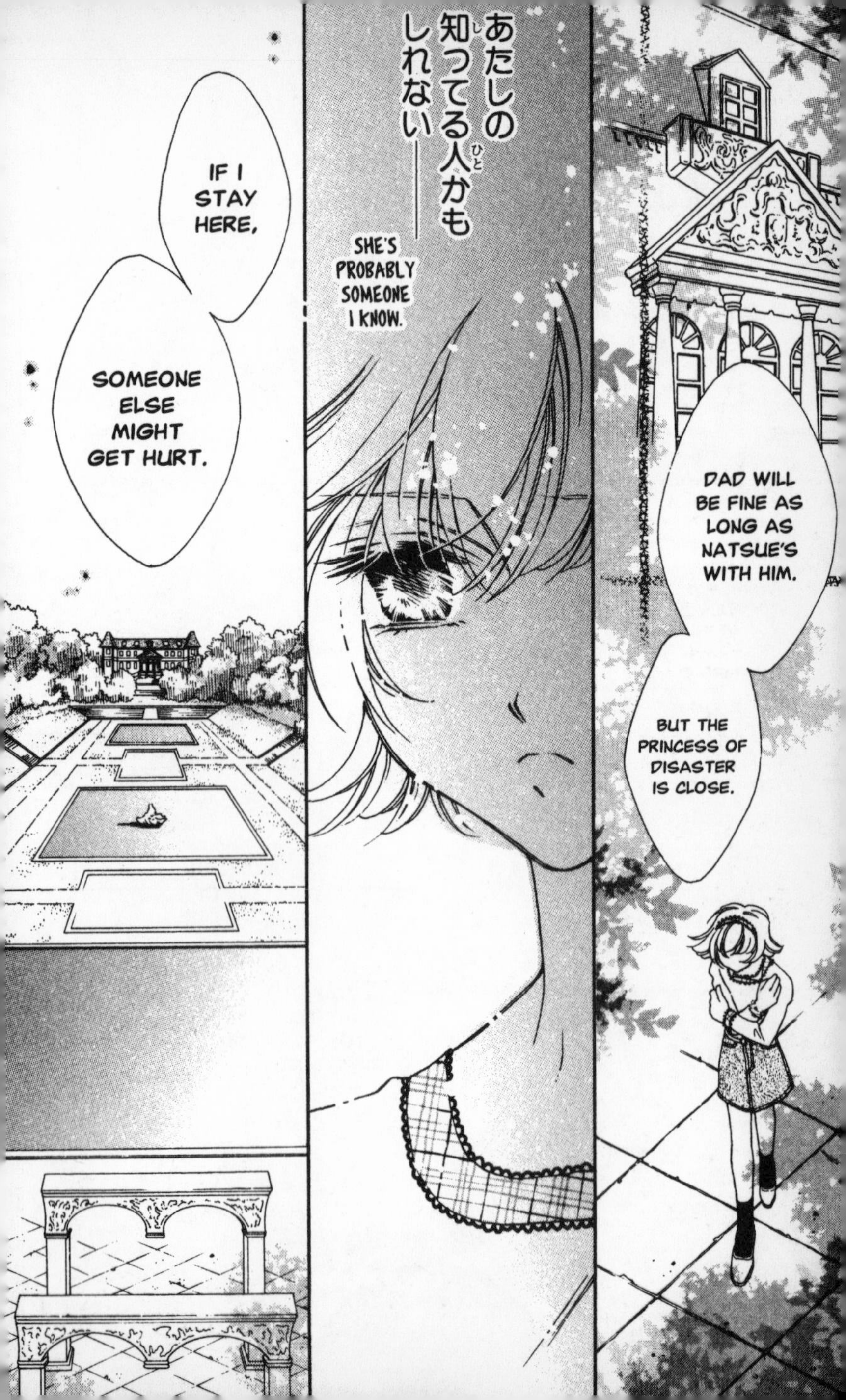
DAD WILL BE FINE AS LONG AS NATSUE'S WITH HIM.
BUT THE PRINCESS OF DISASTER IS CLOSE.
あたしの知ってる人かもしれない——
SHE'S PROBABLY SOMEONE I KNOW.
IF I STAY HERE,
SOMEONE ELSE MIGHT GET HURT.

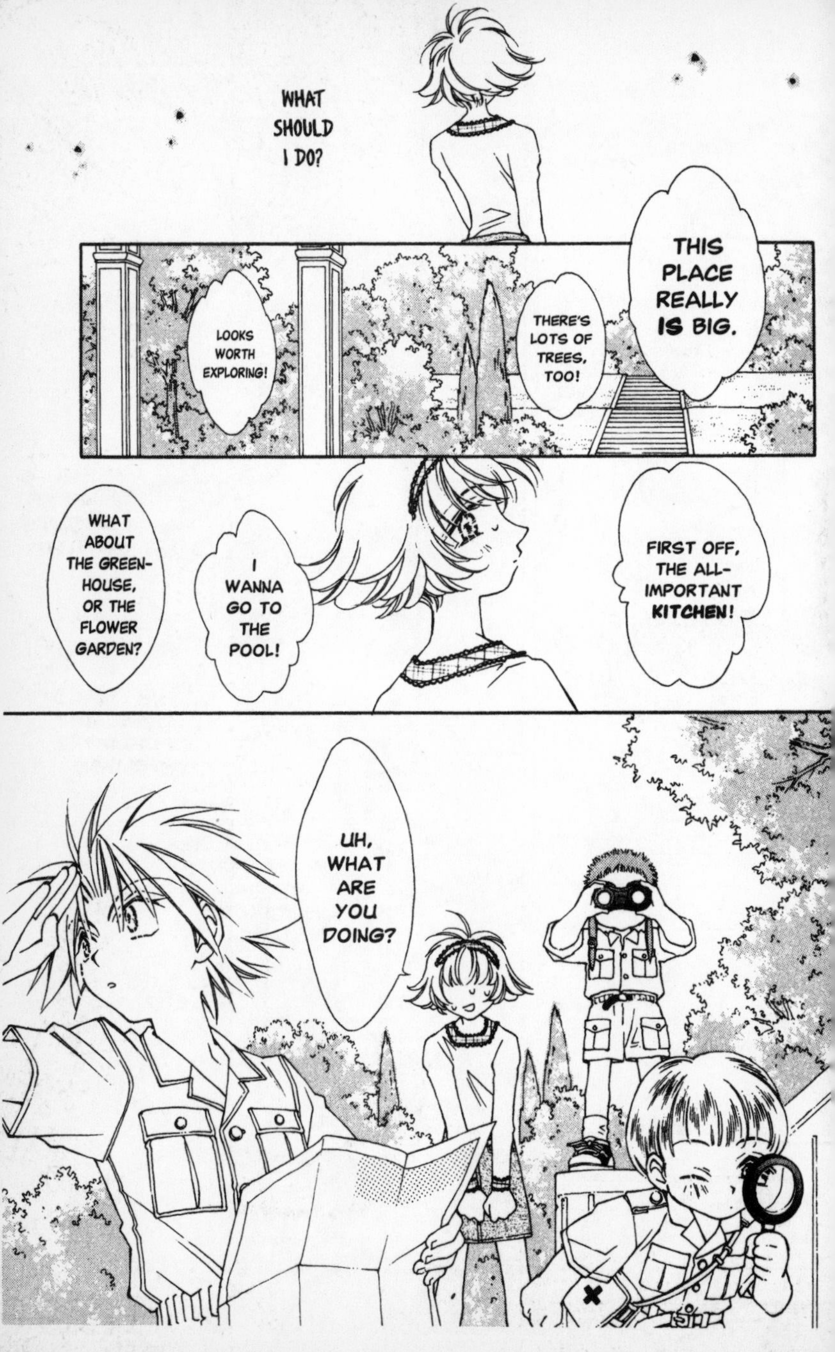
WHAT SHOULD I DO?
THIS PLACE REALLY IS BIG.
THERE'S LOTS OF TREES, TOO!
LOOKS WORTH EXPLORING!
FIRST OFF, THE ALL-IMPORTANT KITCHEN!
I WANNA GO TO THE POOL!
WHAT ABOUT THE GREEN-HOUSE, OR THE FLOWER GARDEN?
UH, WHAT ARE YOU DOING?

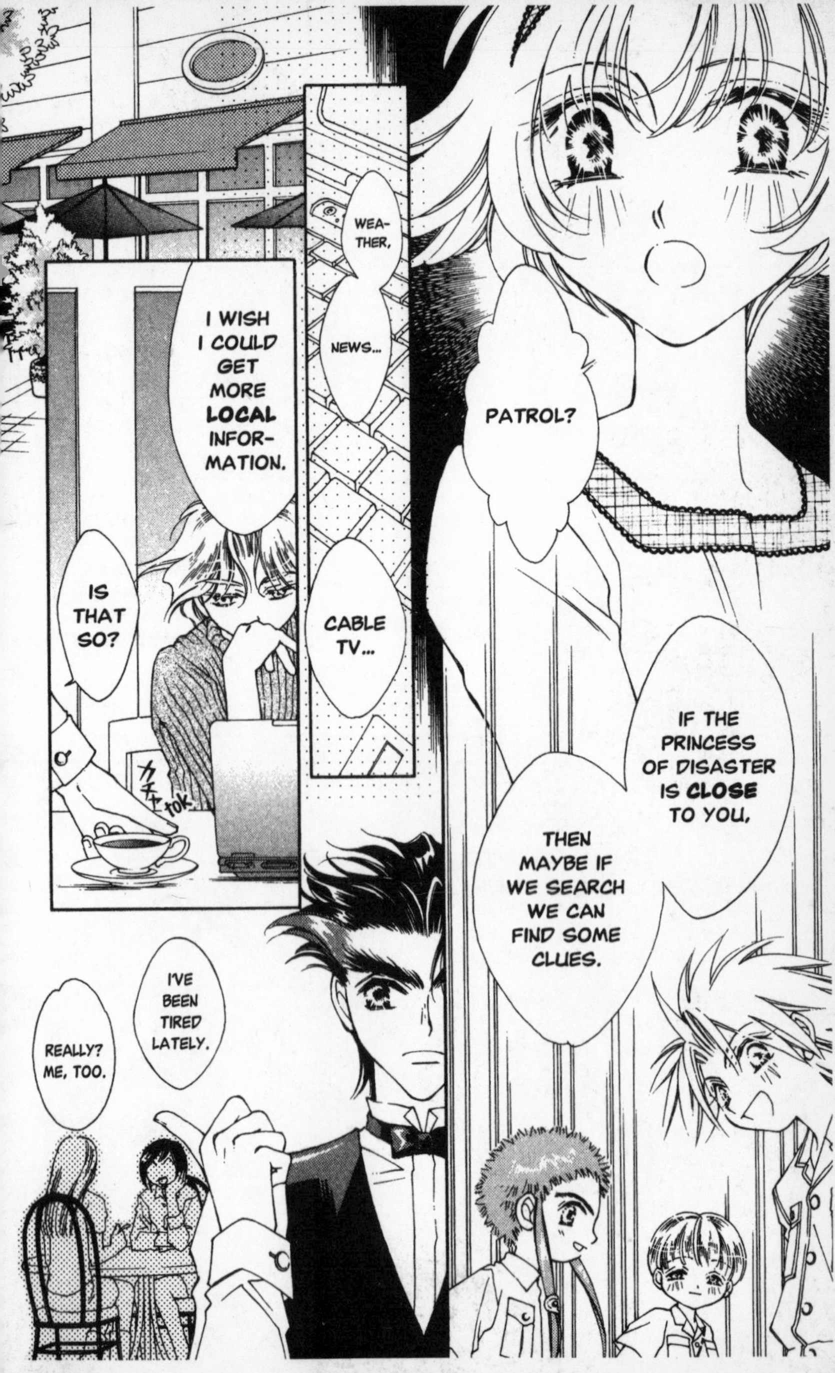
PATROL?
IF THE PRINCESS OF DISASTER IS CLOSE TO YOU,
THEN MAYBE IF WE SEARCH WE CAN FIND SOME CLUES.
WEA-THER,
NEWS...
CABLE TV...
I WISH I COULD GET MORE LOCAL INFOR-MATION.
IS THAT SO?
tok
I'VE BEEN TIRED LATELY.
REALLY? ME, TOO.

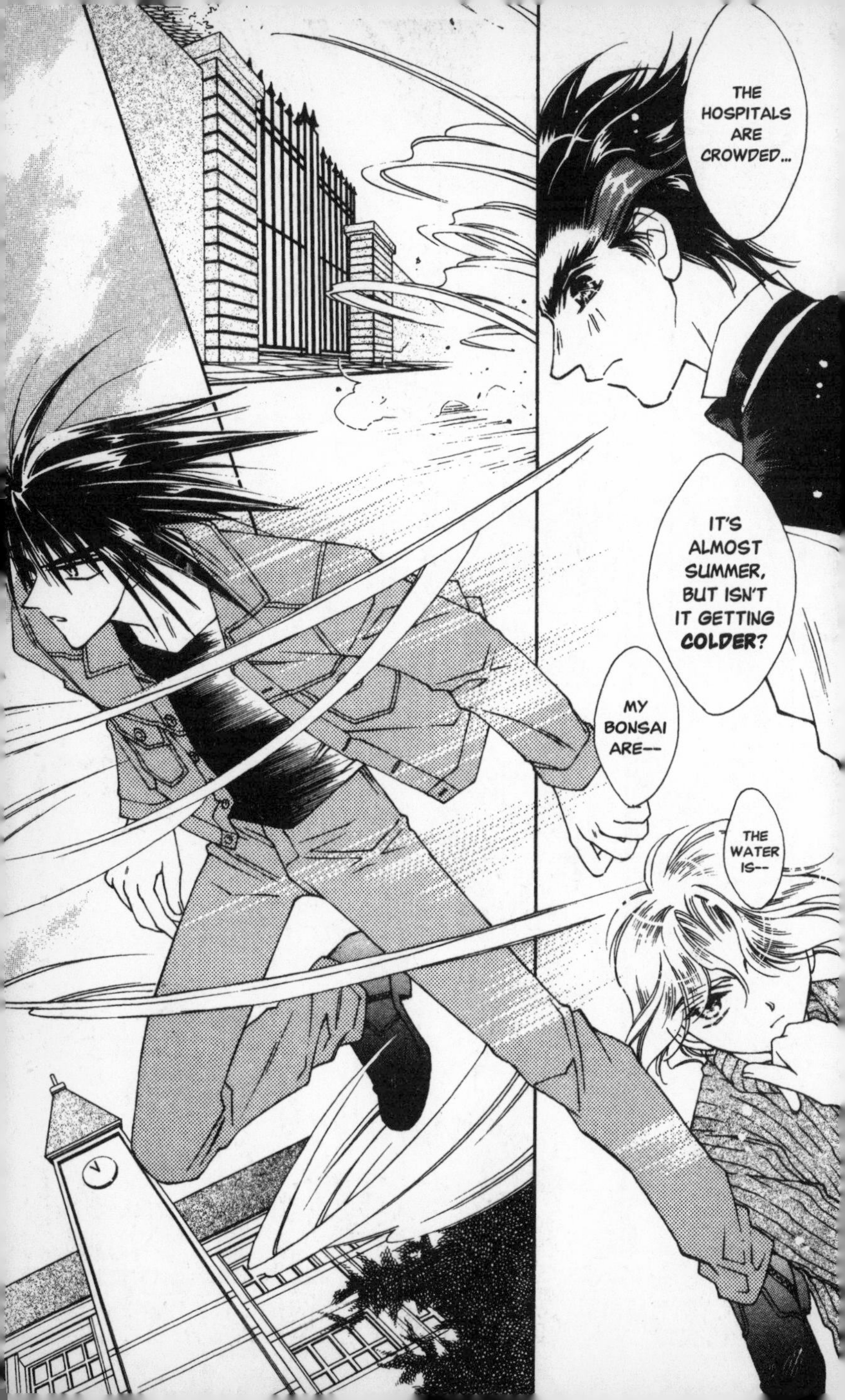
THE HOSPITALS ARE CROWDED...
IT'S ALMOST SUMMER, BUT ISN'T IT GETTING **COLDER**?
MY BONSAI ARE--
THE WATER IS--

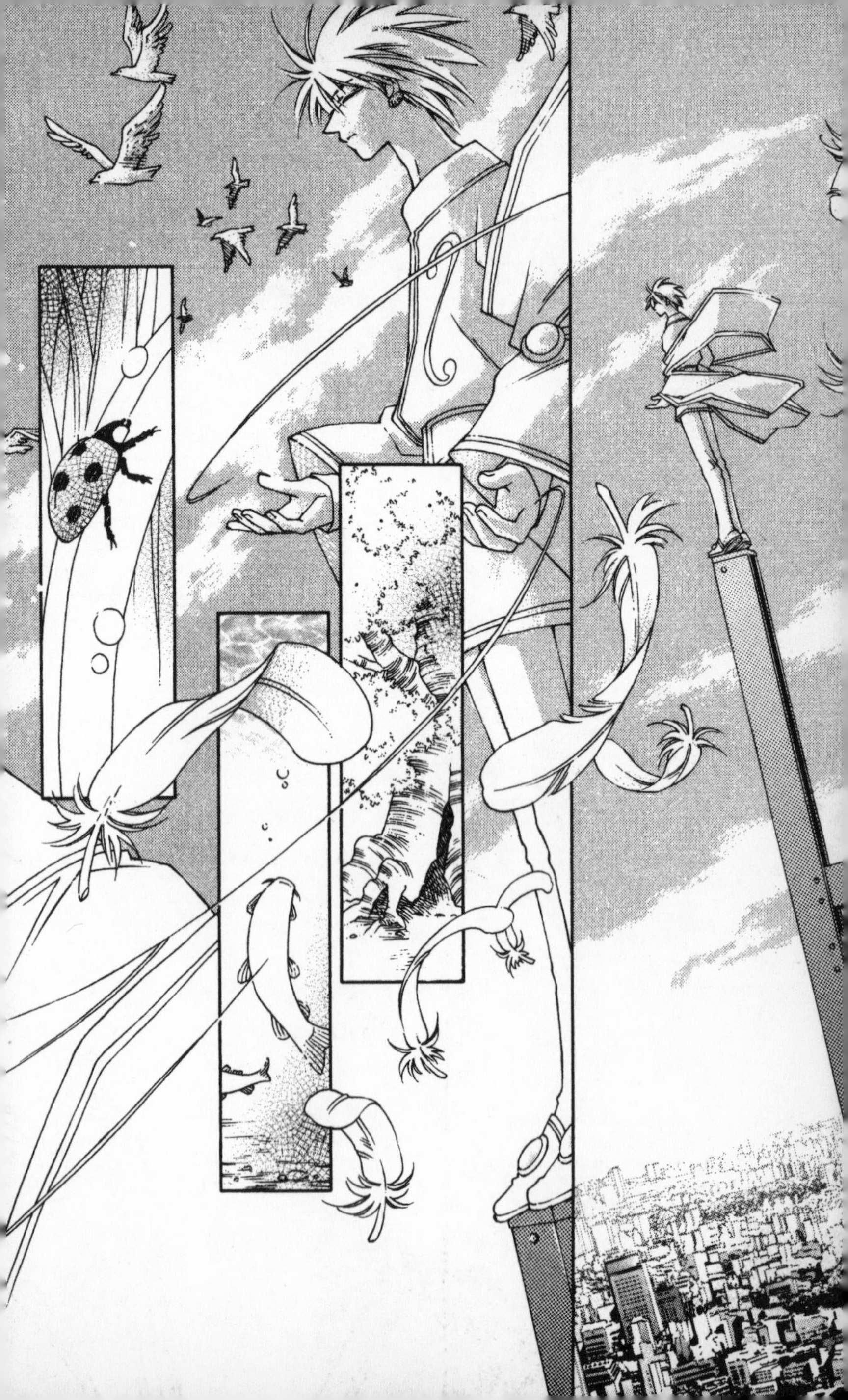

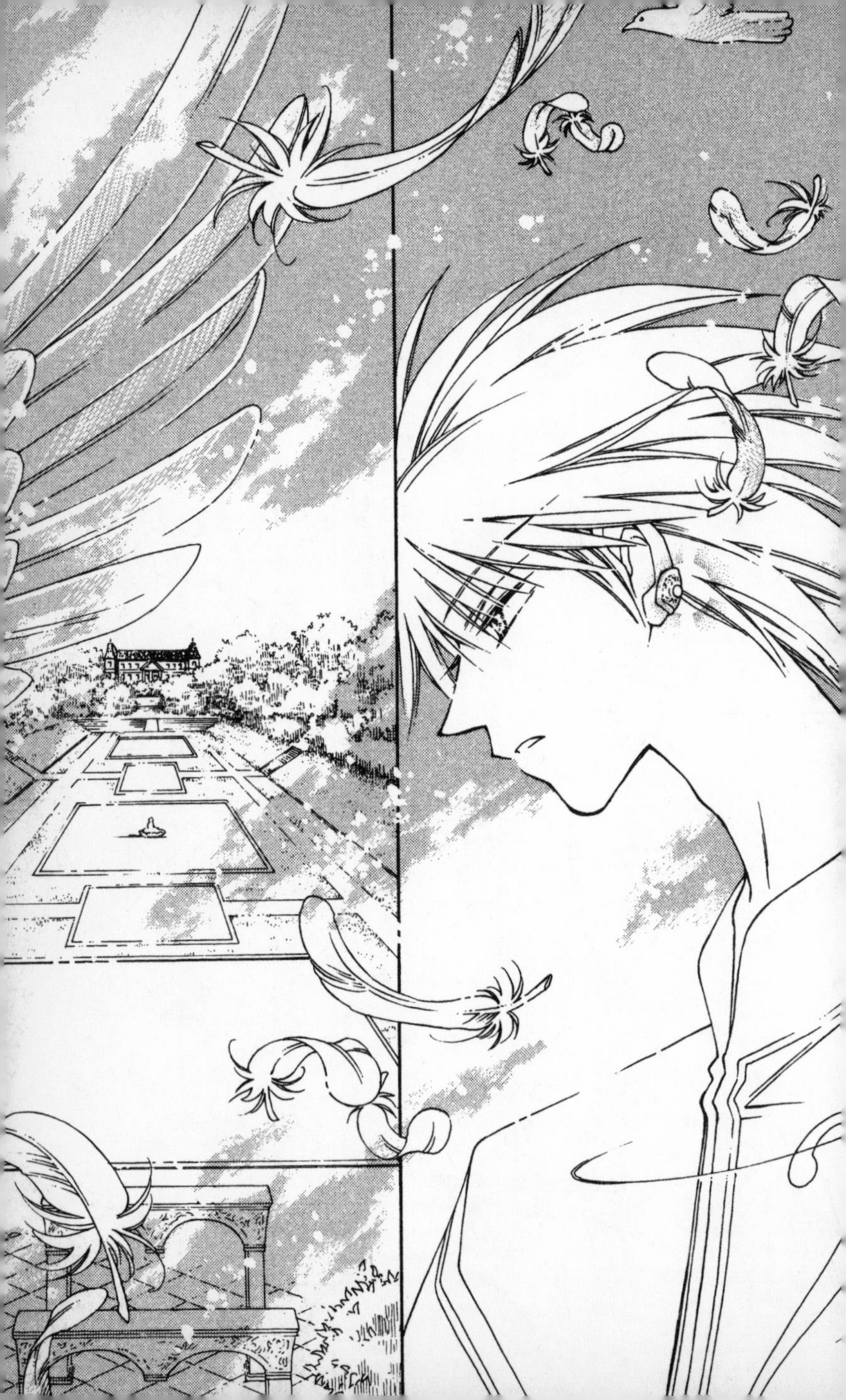

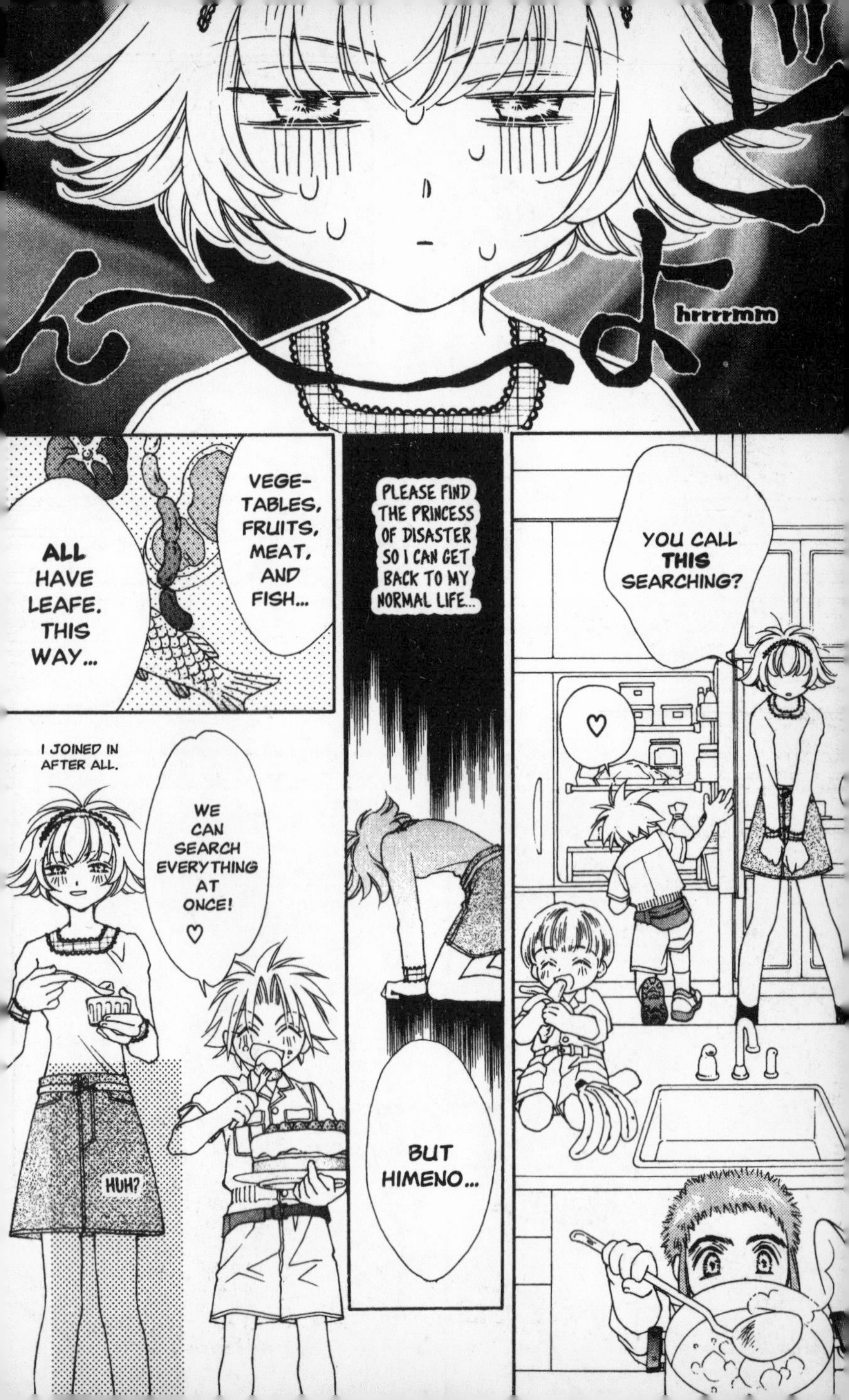
hrrrrmm
YOU CALL THIS SEARCHING?
♡
PLEASE FIND THE PRINCESS OF DISASTER SO I CAN GET BACK TO MY NORMAL LIFE...
BUT HIMENO...
VEGE-TABLES, FRUITS, MEAT, AND FISH...
ALL HAVE LEAFE. THIS WAY...
I JOINED IN AFTER ALL.
WE CAN SEARCH EVERYTHING AT ONCE! ♡
HUH?

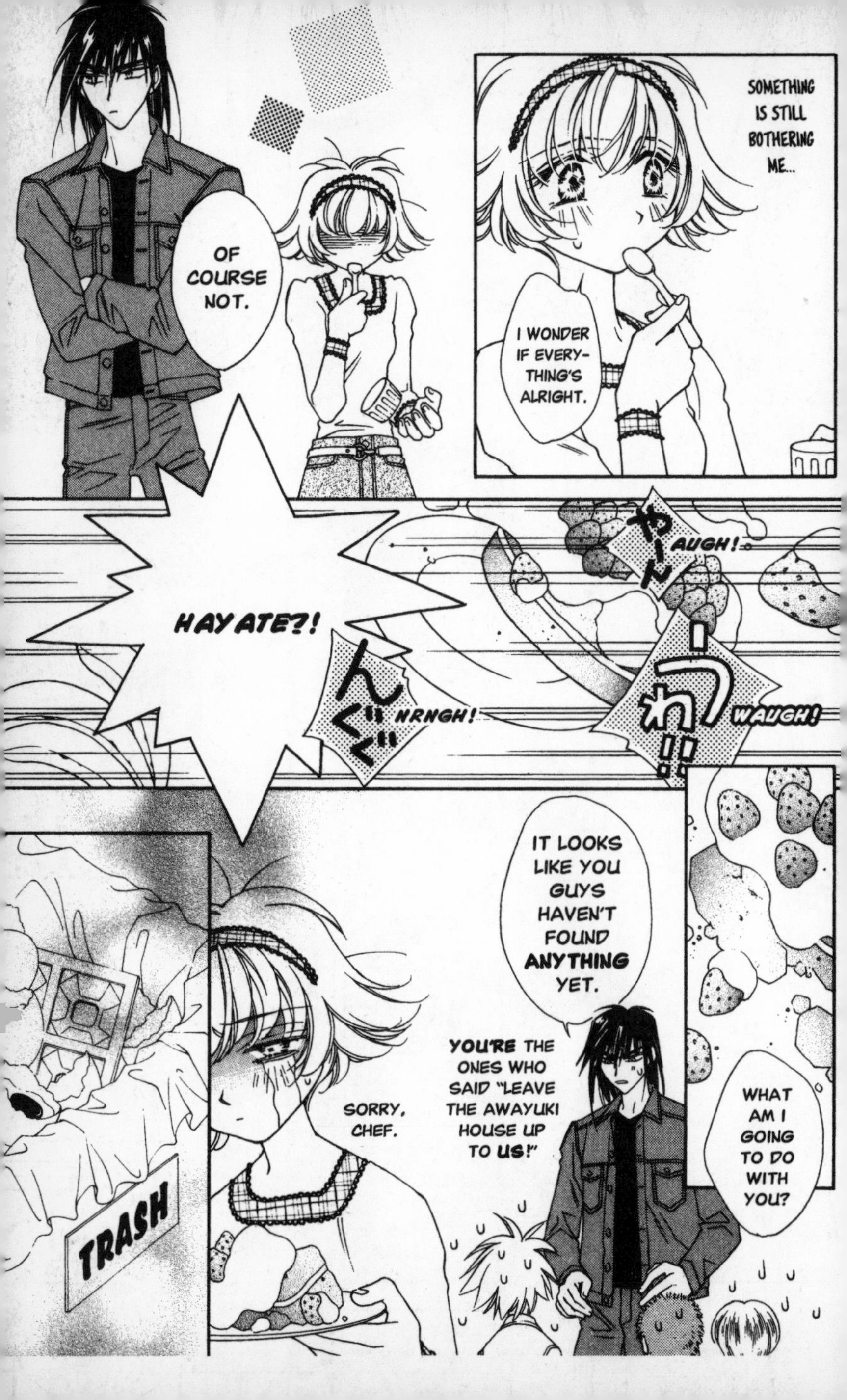
SOMETHING IS STILL BOTHERING ME...
I WONDER IF EVERY-THING'S ALRIGHT.
OF COURSE NOT.
やーん
AUGH!
うわ!!
WAUGH!
HAYATE?!
んぐぐ
NRNGH!
WHAT AM I GOING TO DO WITH YOU?
IT LOOKS LIKE YOU GUYS HAVEN'T FOUND ANYTHING YET.
YOU'RE THE ONES WHO SAID "LEAVE THE AWAYUKI HOUSE UP TO US!"
SORRY, CHEF.
TRASH

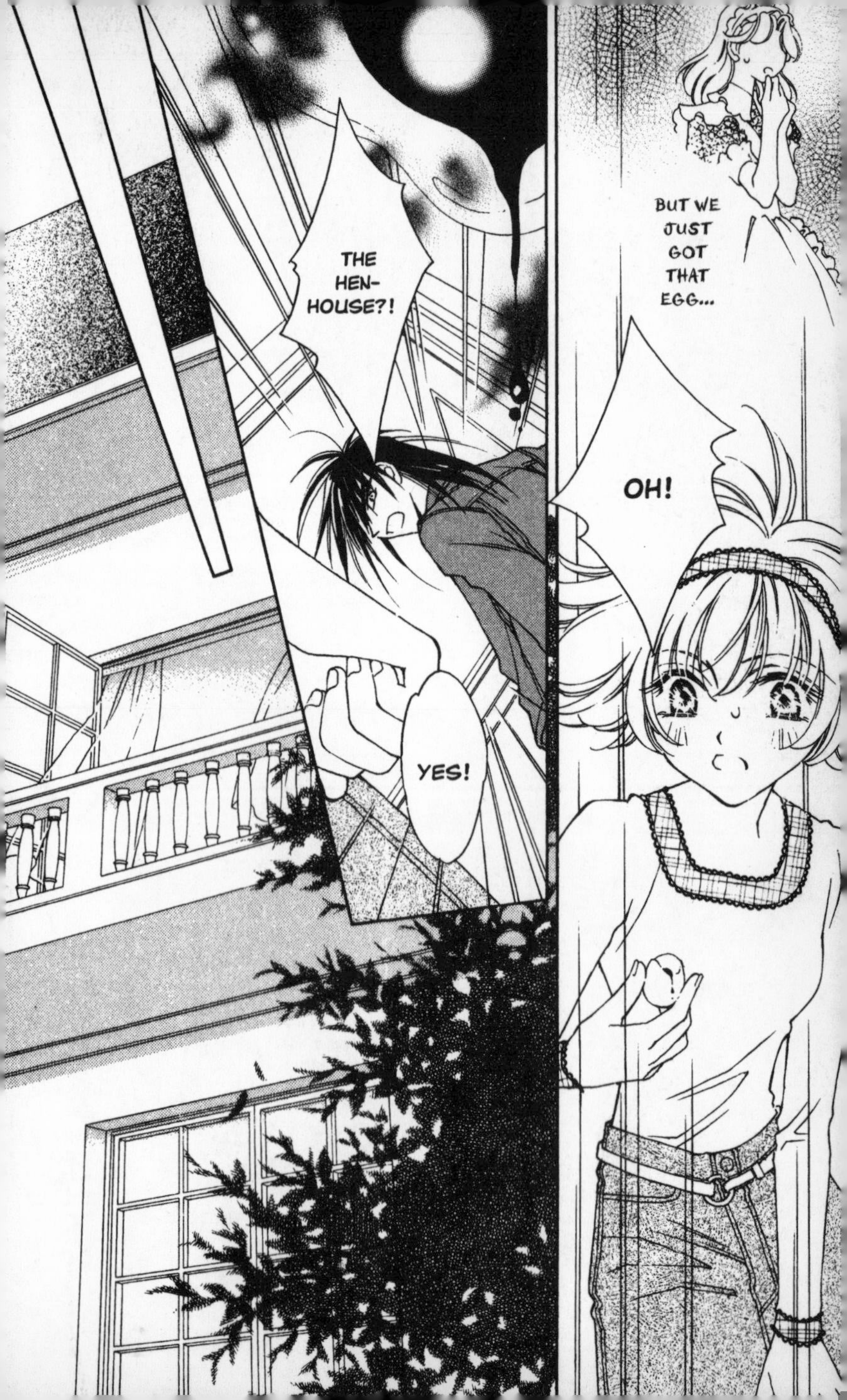
BUT WE JUST GOT THAT EGG...
OH!
THE HEN-HOUSE?!
YES!

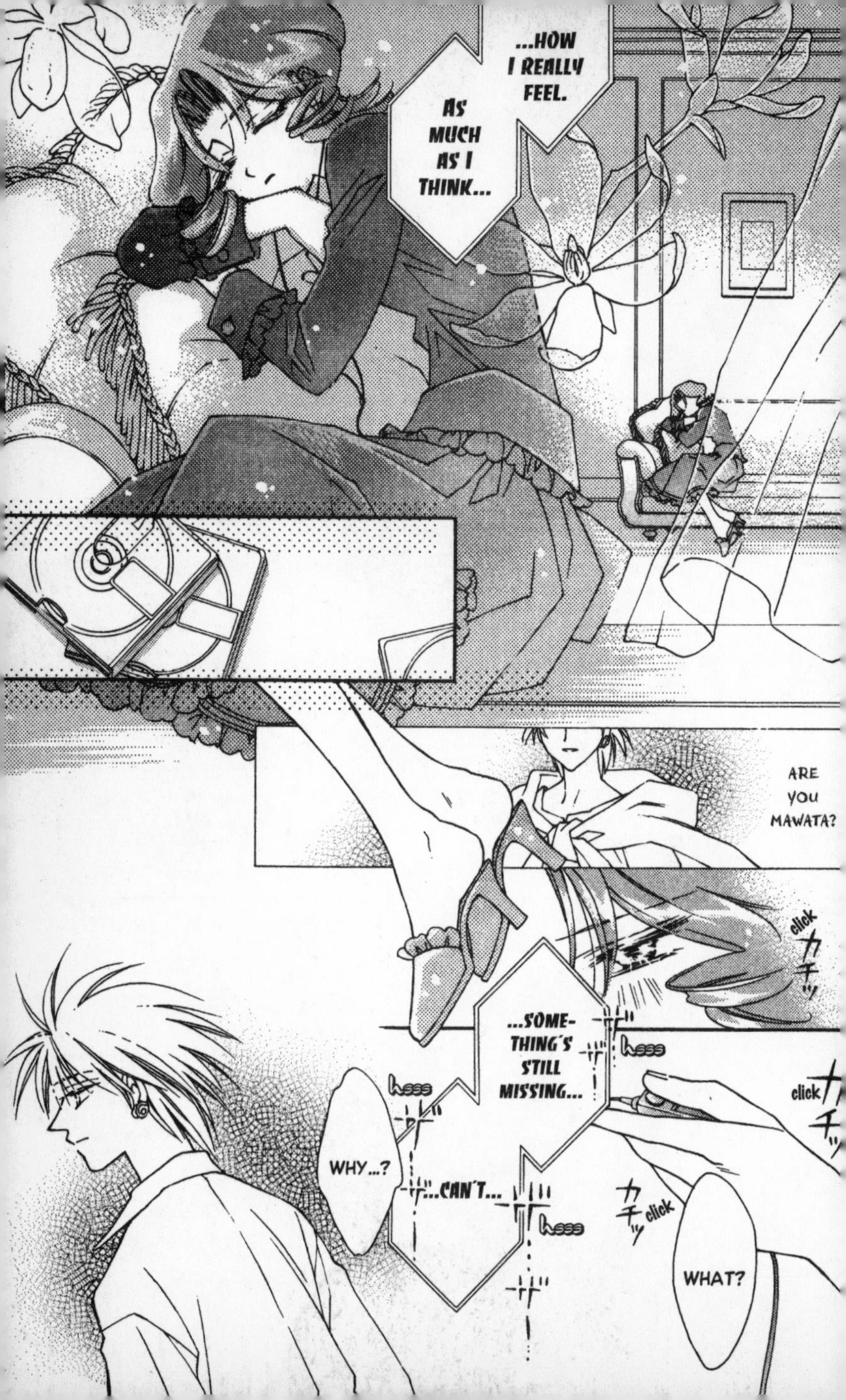
AS MUCH AS I THINK... ...HOW I REALLY FEEL.
ARE YOU MAWATA?
click カチッ
click カチッ
...SOME-THING'S STILL MISSING...
hsss
WHAT?
カチッ click
hsss
...CAN'T...
hsss
WHY...?

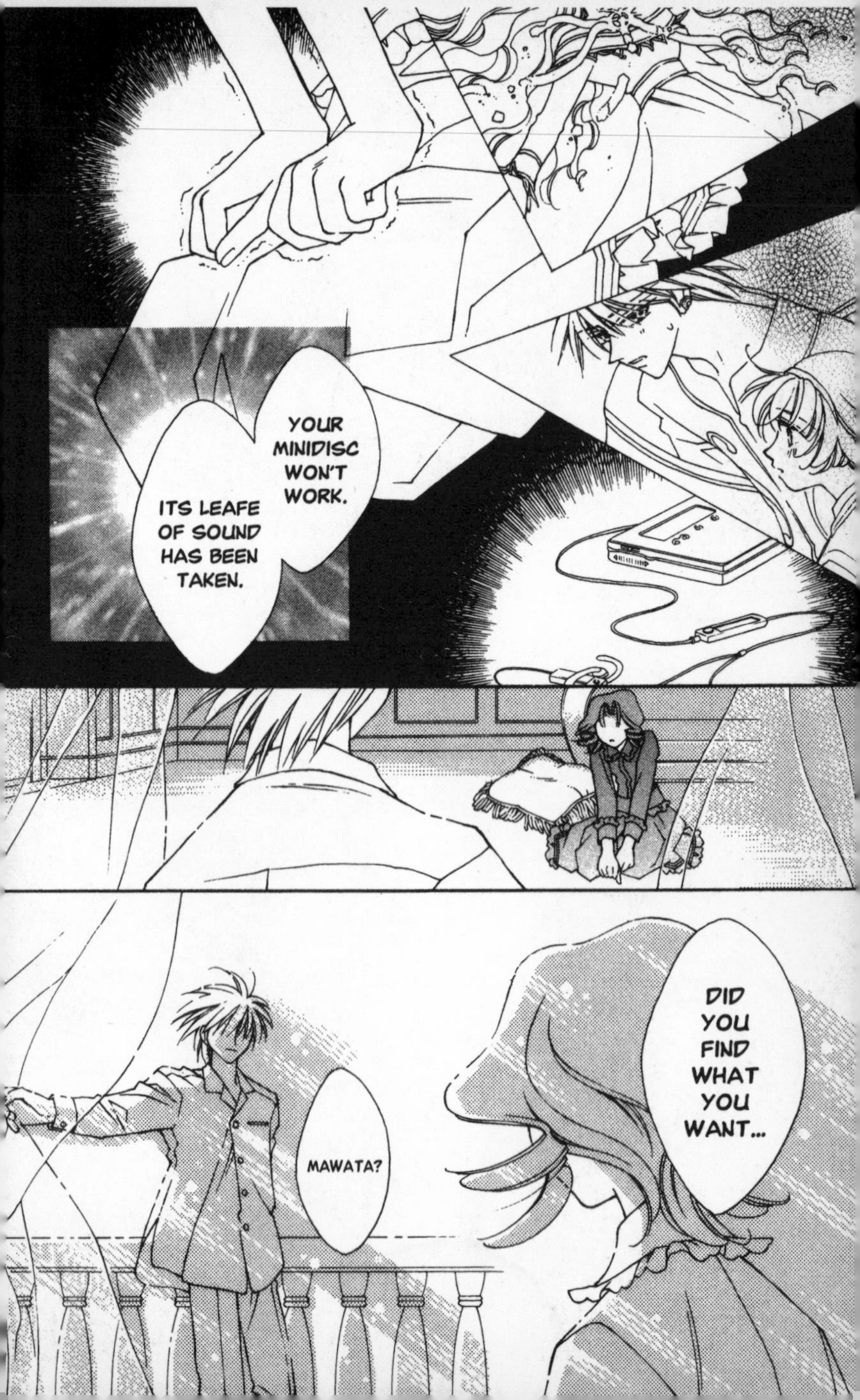
YOUR MINIDISC WON'T WORK.
ITS LEAFE OF SOUND HAS BEEN TAKEN.
DID YOU FIND WHAT YOU WANT...
MAWATA?

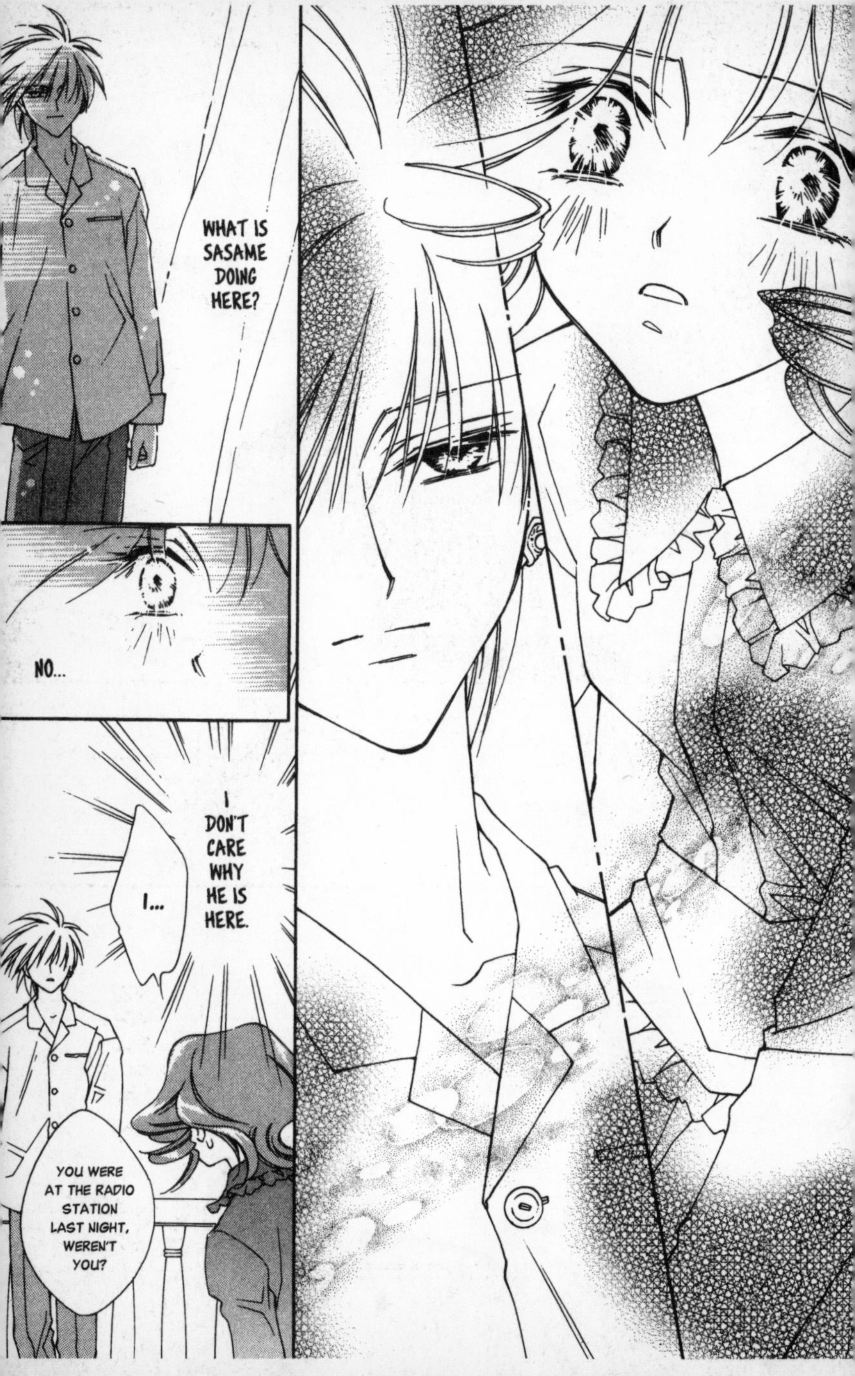
WHAT IS SASAME DOING HERE?
NO...
I DON'T CARE WHY HE IS HERE.
I...
YOU WERE AT THE RADIO STATION LAST NIGHT, WEREN'T YOU?

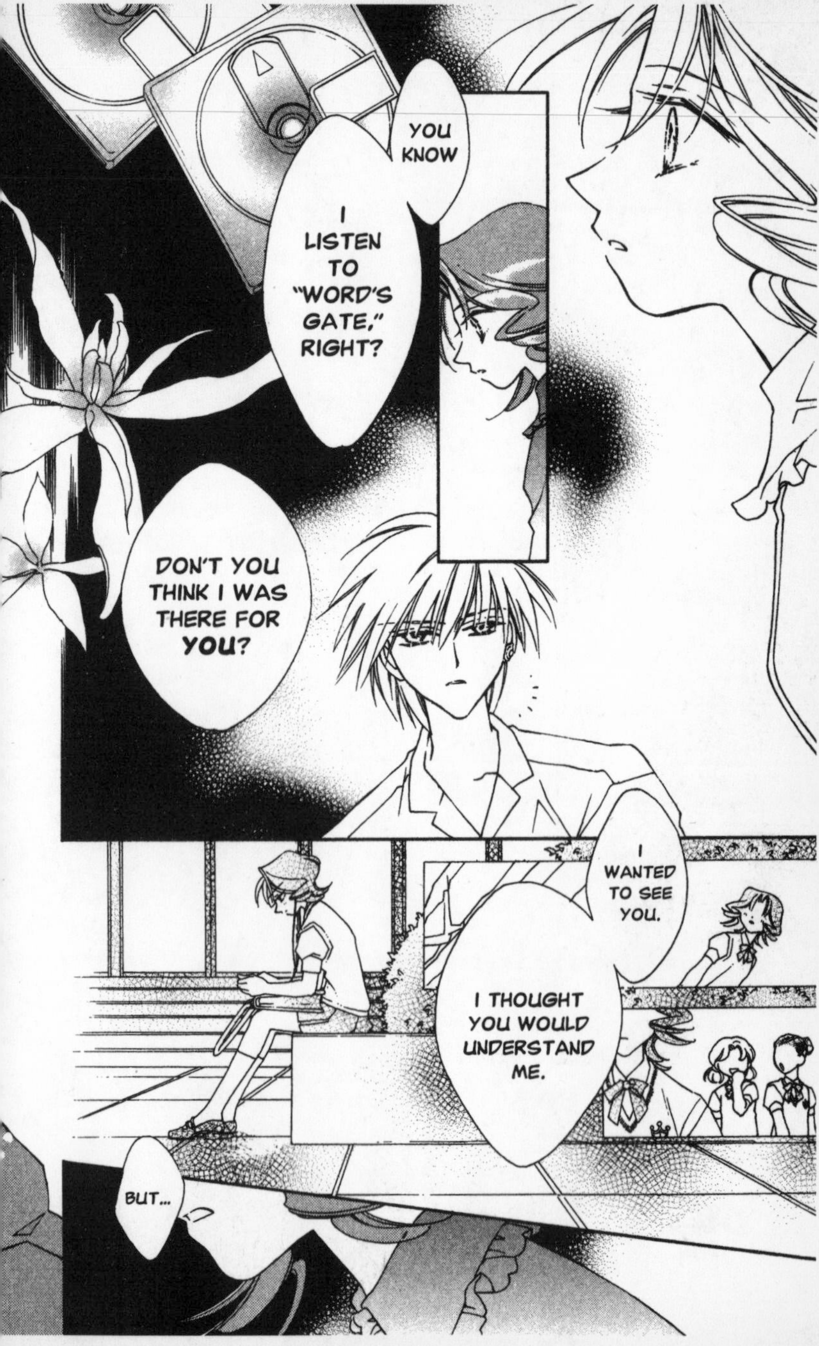
YOU KNOW
I LISTEN TO "WORD'S GATE," RIGHT?
DON'T YOU THINK I WAS THERE FOR YOU?
I WANTED TO SEE YOU.
I THOUGHT YOU WOULD UNDERSTAND ME.
BUT...

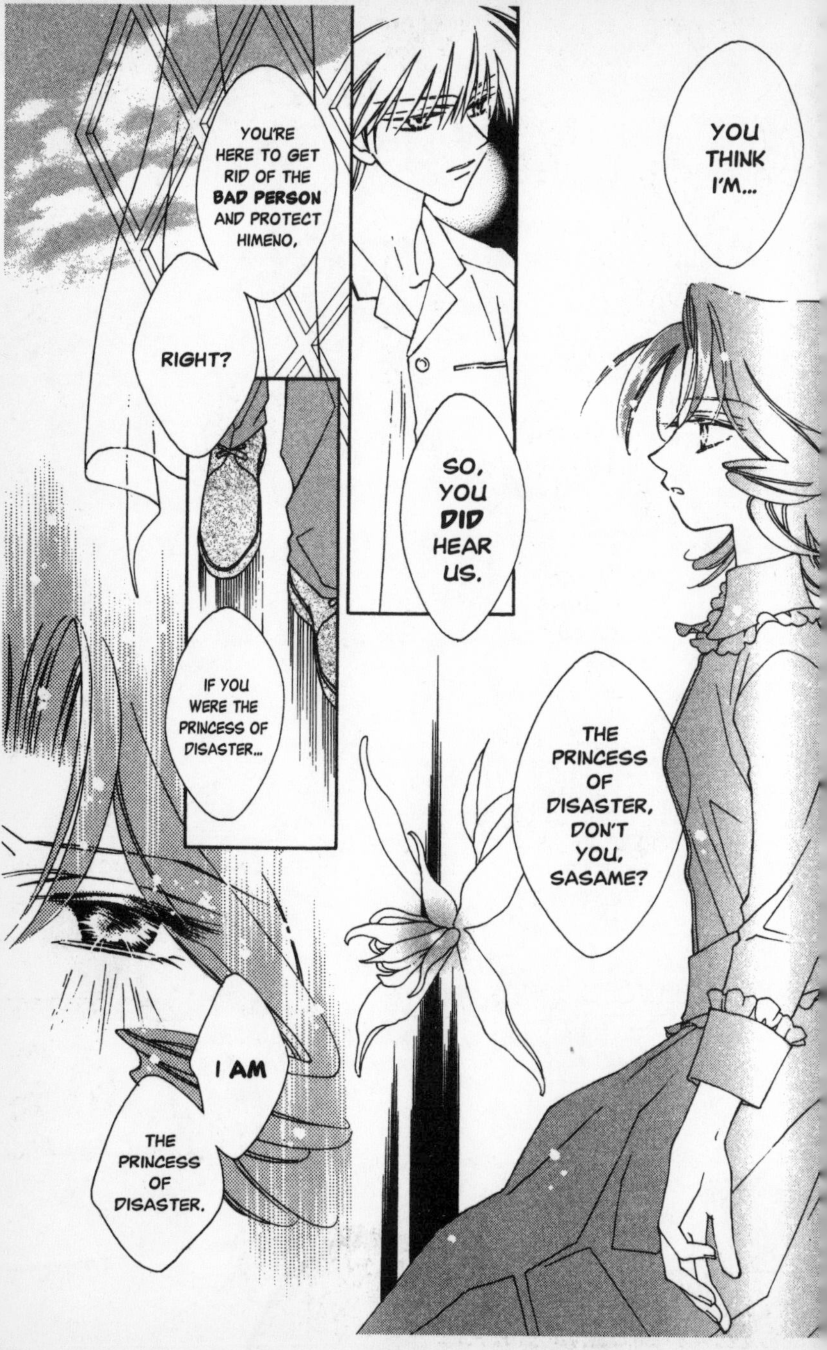
YOU THINK I'M...
THE PRINCESS OF DISASTER, DON'T YOU, SASAME?
SO, YOU **DID** HEAR US.
YOU'RE HERE TO GET RID OF THE **BAD PERSON** AND PROTECT HIMENO,
RIGHT?
IF YOU WERE THE PRINCESS OF DISASTER...
I AM
THE PRINCESS OF DISASTER.

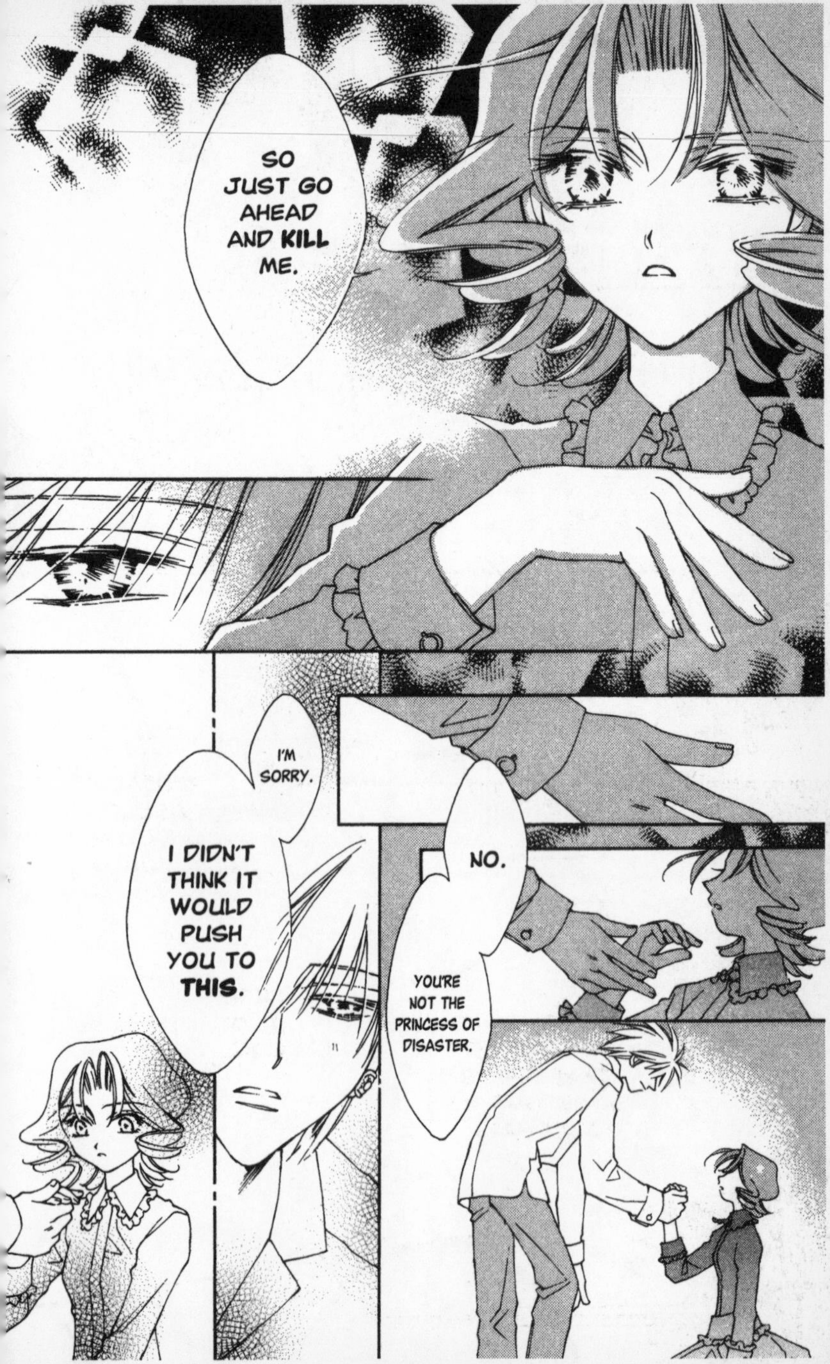
SO JUST GO AHEAD AND KILL ME.
NO.
YOU'RE NOT THE PRINCESS OF DISASTER.
I'M SORRY.
I DIDN'T THINK IT WOULD PUSH YOU TO THIS.

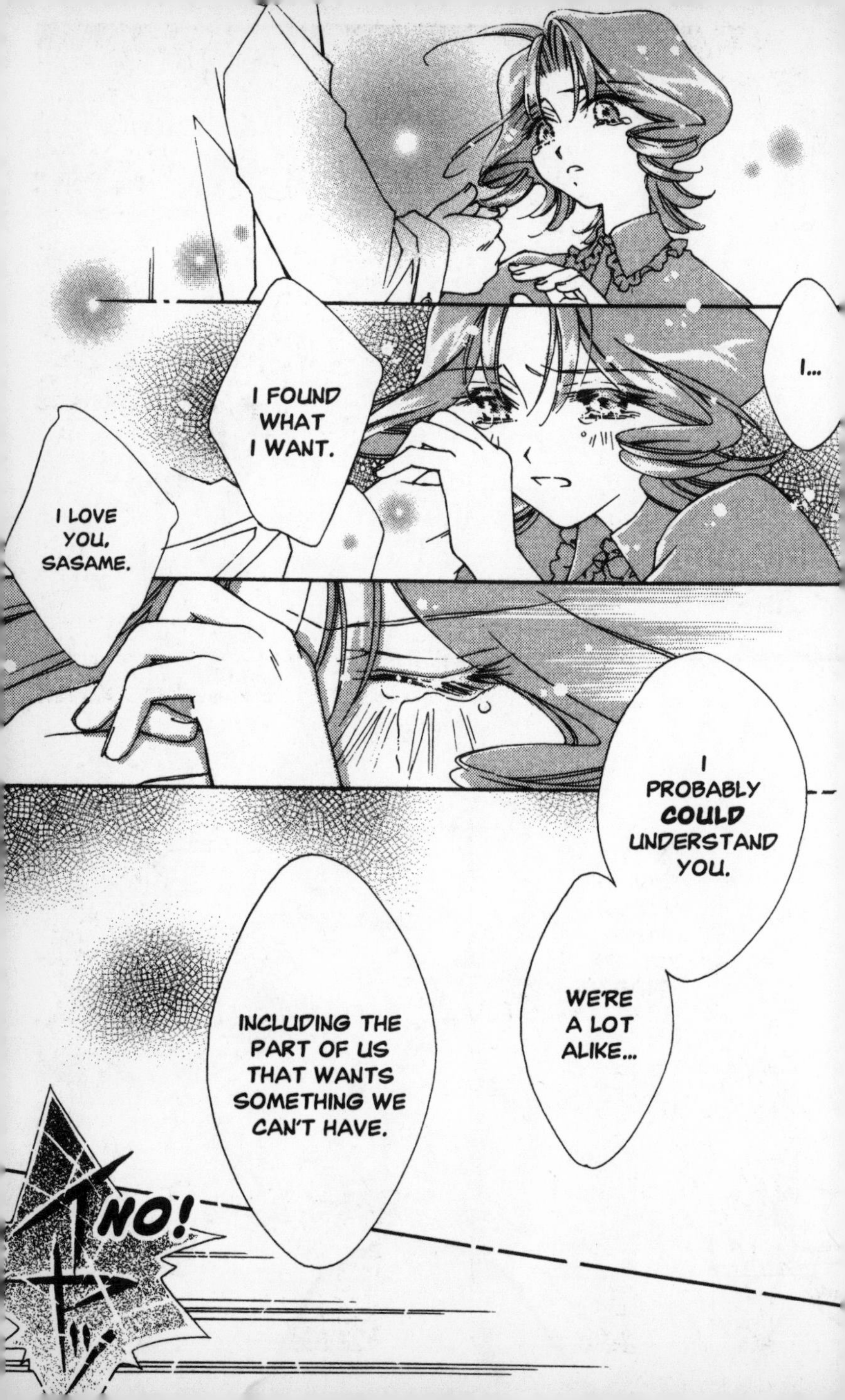
I...
I FOUND WHAT I WANT.
I LOVE YOU, SASAME.
I PROBABLY **COULD** UNDERSTAND YOU.
WE'RE A LOT ALIKE...
INCLUDING THE PART OF US THAT WANTS SOMETHING WE CAN'T HAVE.
NO!

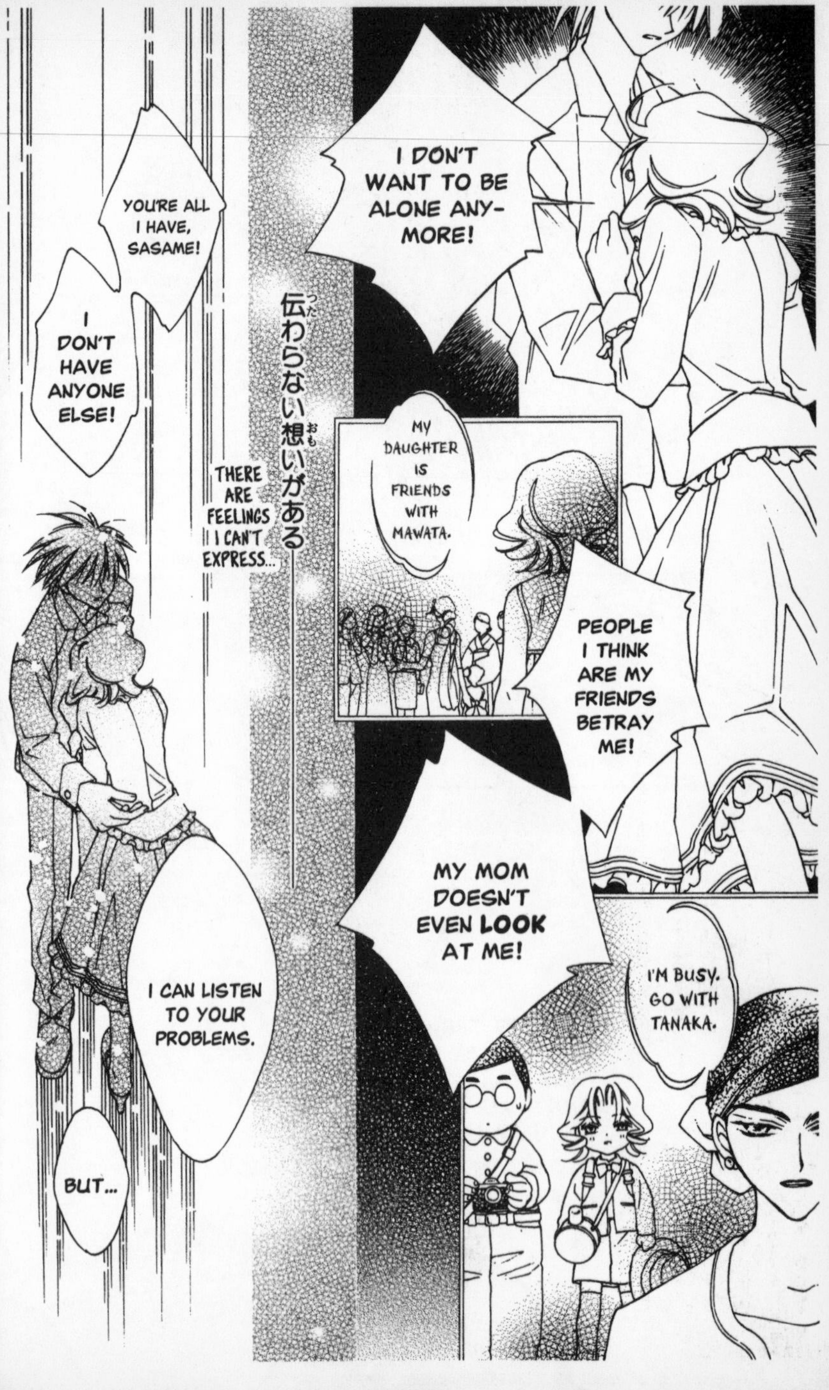

I DON'T WANT TO BE ALONE ANY-MORE!
MY DAUGHTER IS FRIENDS WITH MAWATA.
PEOPLE I THINK ARE MY FRIENDS BETRAY ME!
MY MOM DOESN'T EVEN **LOOK** AT ME!
I'M BUSY. GO WITH TANAKA.
伝わらない想いがある
THERE ARE FEELINGS I CAN'T EXPRESS...
YOU'RE ALL I HAVE, SASAME!
I DON'T HAVE ANYONE ELSE!
I CAN LISTEN TO YOUR PROBLEMS.
BUT...

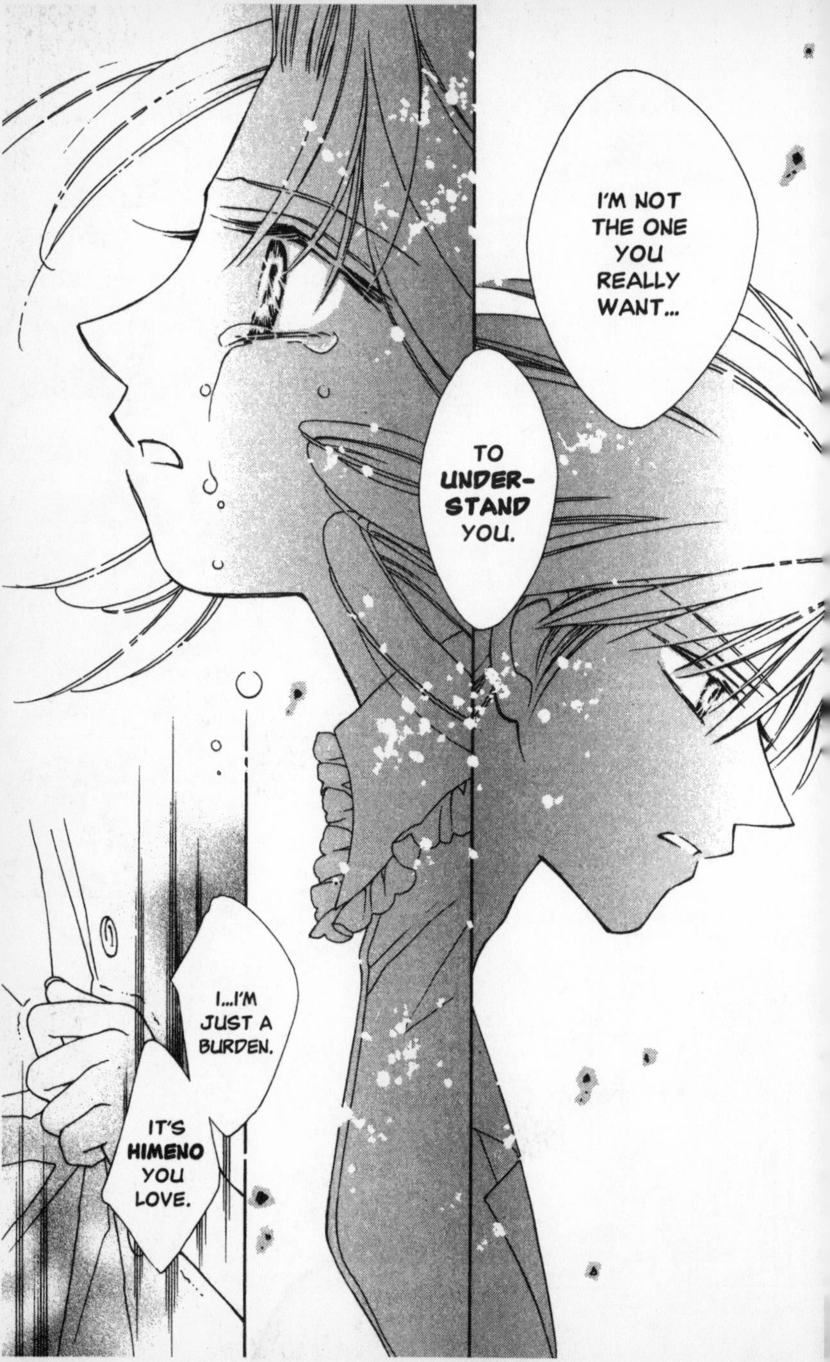
I'M NOT THE ONE YOU REALLY WANT...
TO UNDER-STAND YOU.
I...I'M JUST A BURDEN.
IT'S HIMENO YOU LOVE.

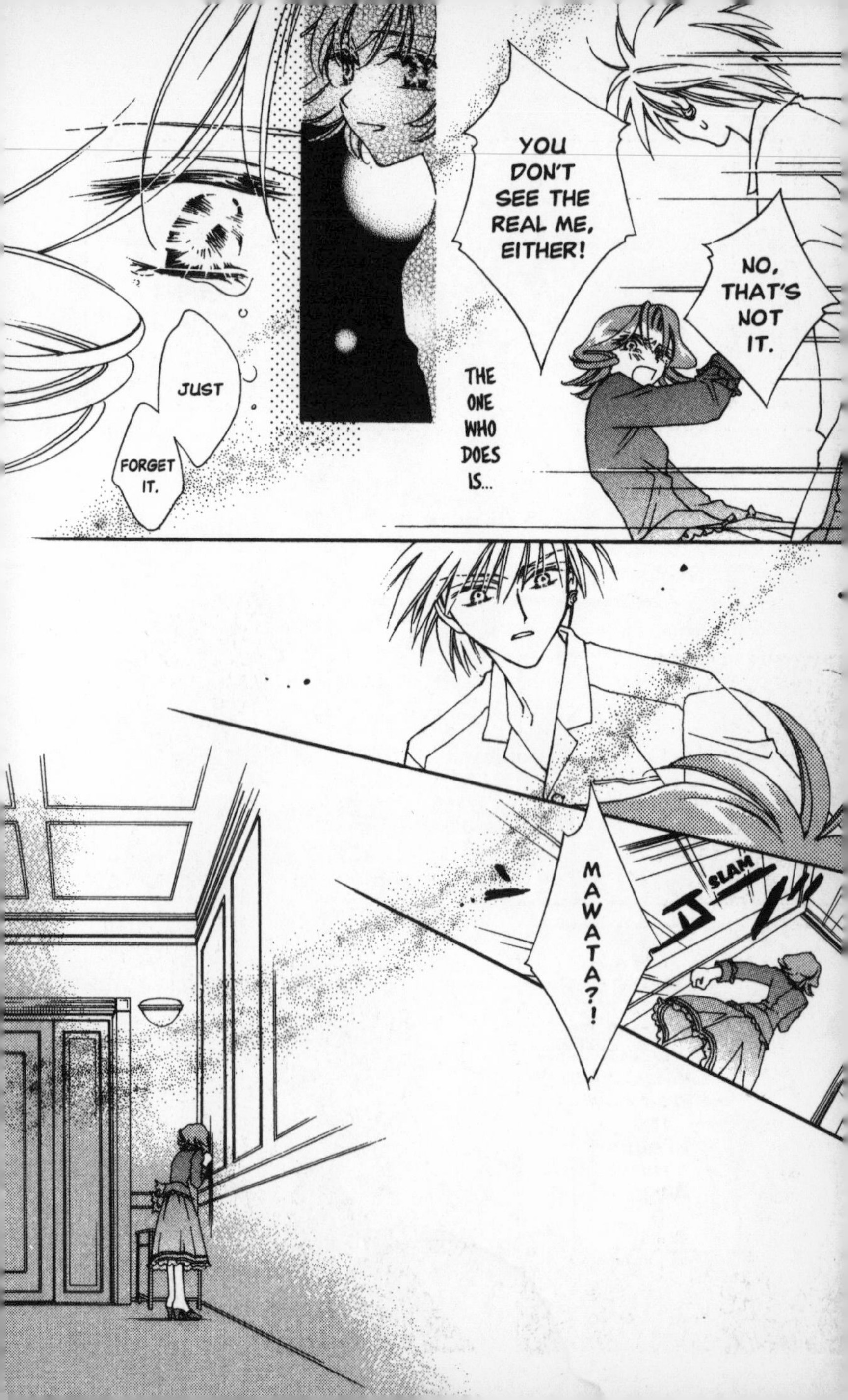

YOU DON'T SEE THE REAL ME, EITHER!
NO, THAT'S NOT IT.
THE ONE WHO DOES IS...
JUST FORGET IT.
SLAM
MAWATA?!

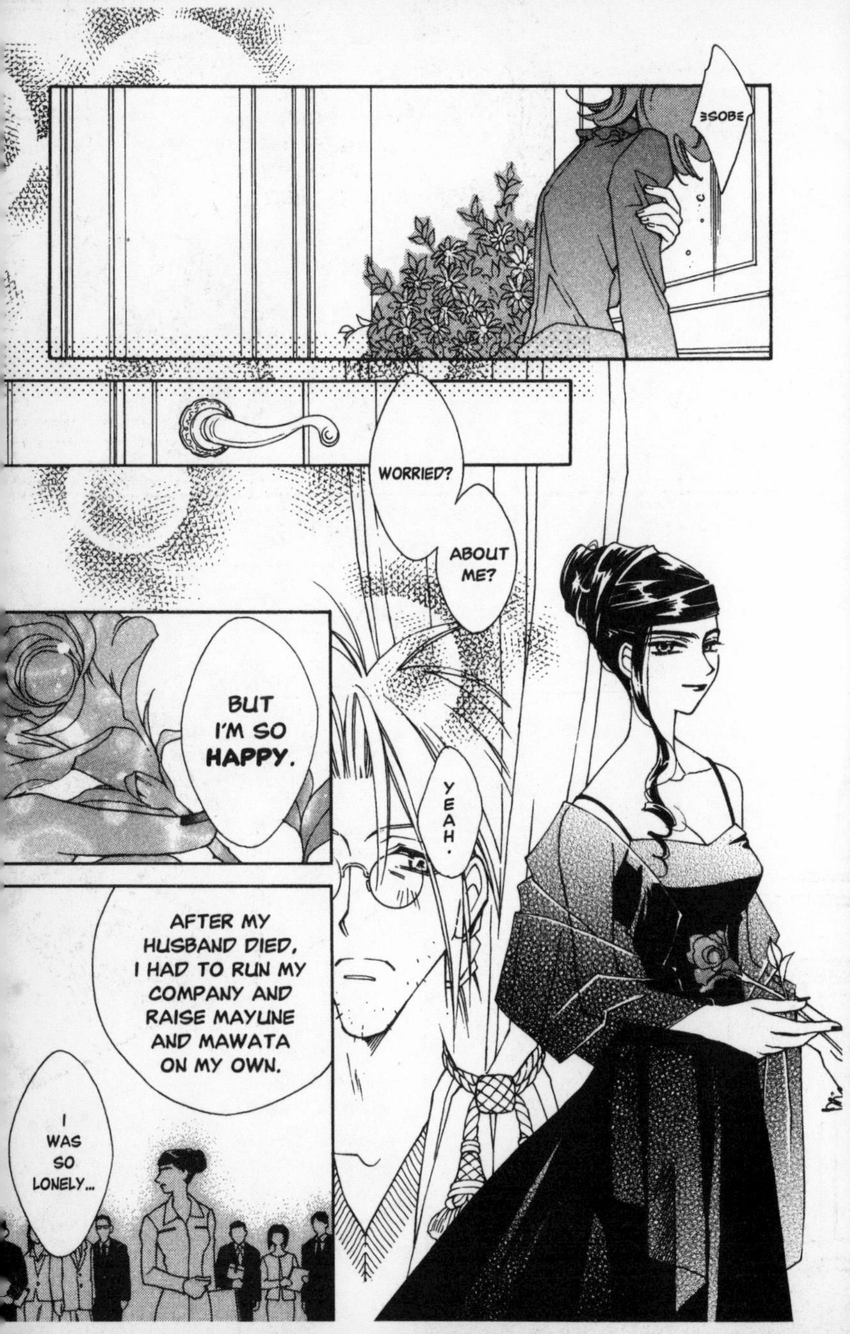
SOB
WORRIED?
ABOUT ME?
YEAH.
BUT I'M SO **HAPPY**.
AFTER MY HUSBAND DIED, I HAD TO RUN MY COMPANY AND RAISE MAYUNE AND MAWATA ON MY OWN.
I WAS SO LONELY...

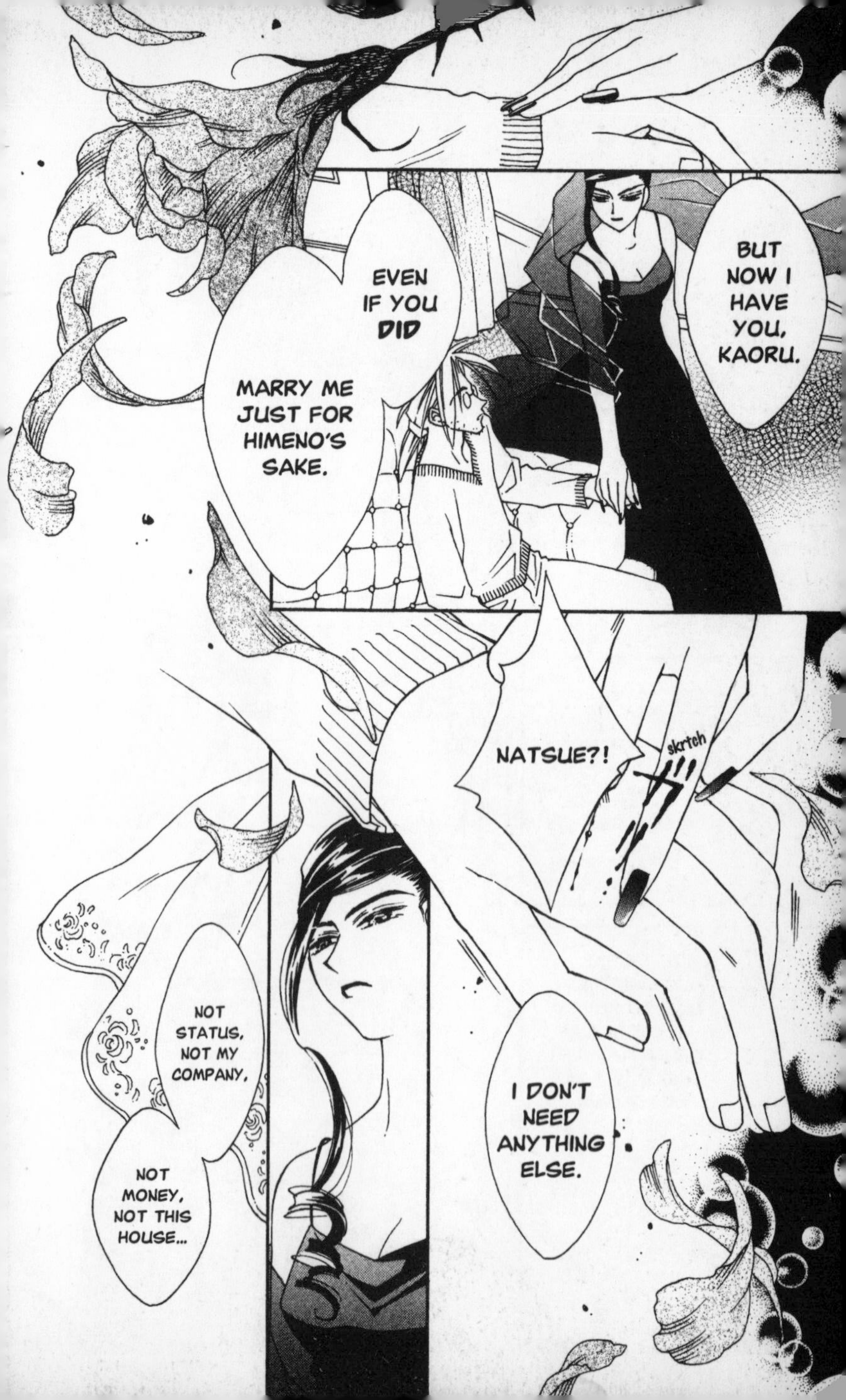
BUT NOW I HAVE YOU, KAORU.
EVEN IF YOU DID
MARRY ME JUST FOR HIMENO'S SAKE.
NATSUE?!
skrtch
NOT STATUS, NOT MY COMPANY,
NOT MONEY, NOT THIS HOUSE...
I DON'T NEED ANYTHING ELSE.

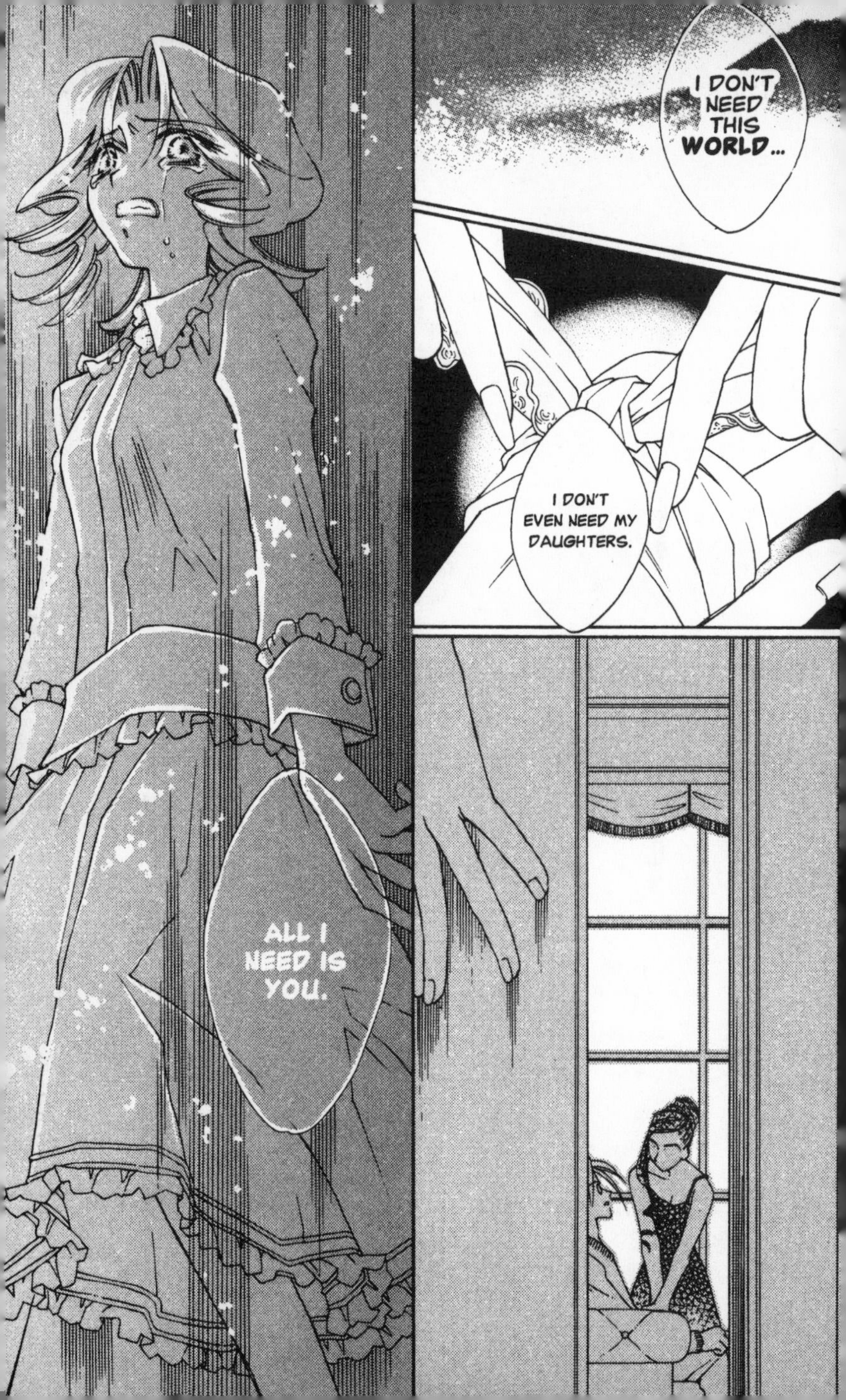
I DON'T NEED THIS WORLD...
I DON'T EVEN NEED MY DAUGHTERS.
ALL I NEED IS YOU.

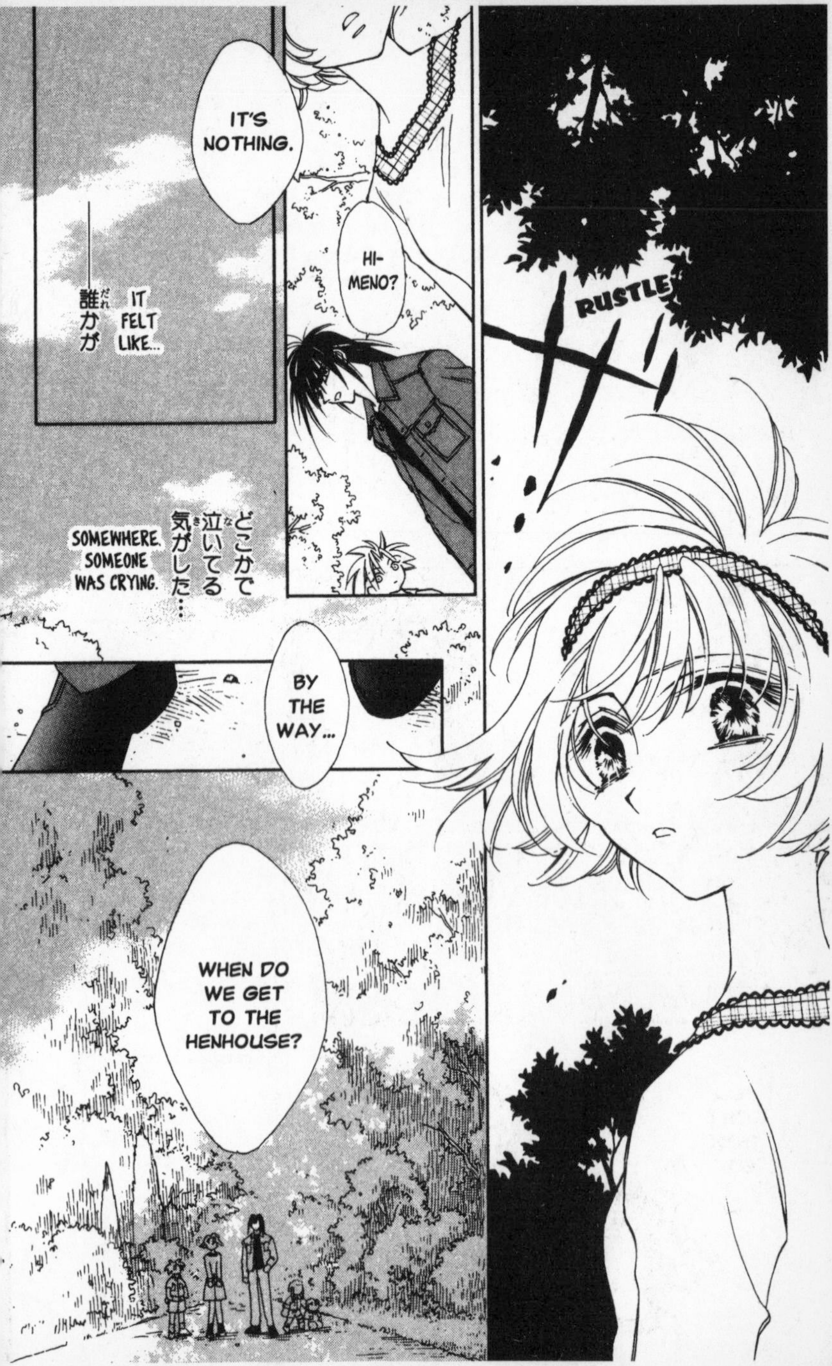
RUSTLE
HI-MENO?
IT'S NOTHING.
誰かが
IT FELT LIKE...
どこかで泣いてる気がした…
SOMEWHERE, SOMEONE WAS CRYING.
BY THE WAY...
WHEN DO WE GET TO THE HENHOUSE?

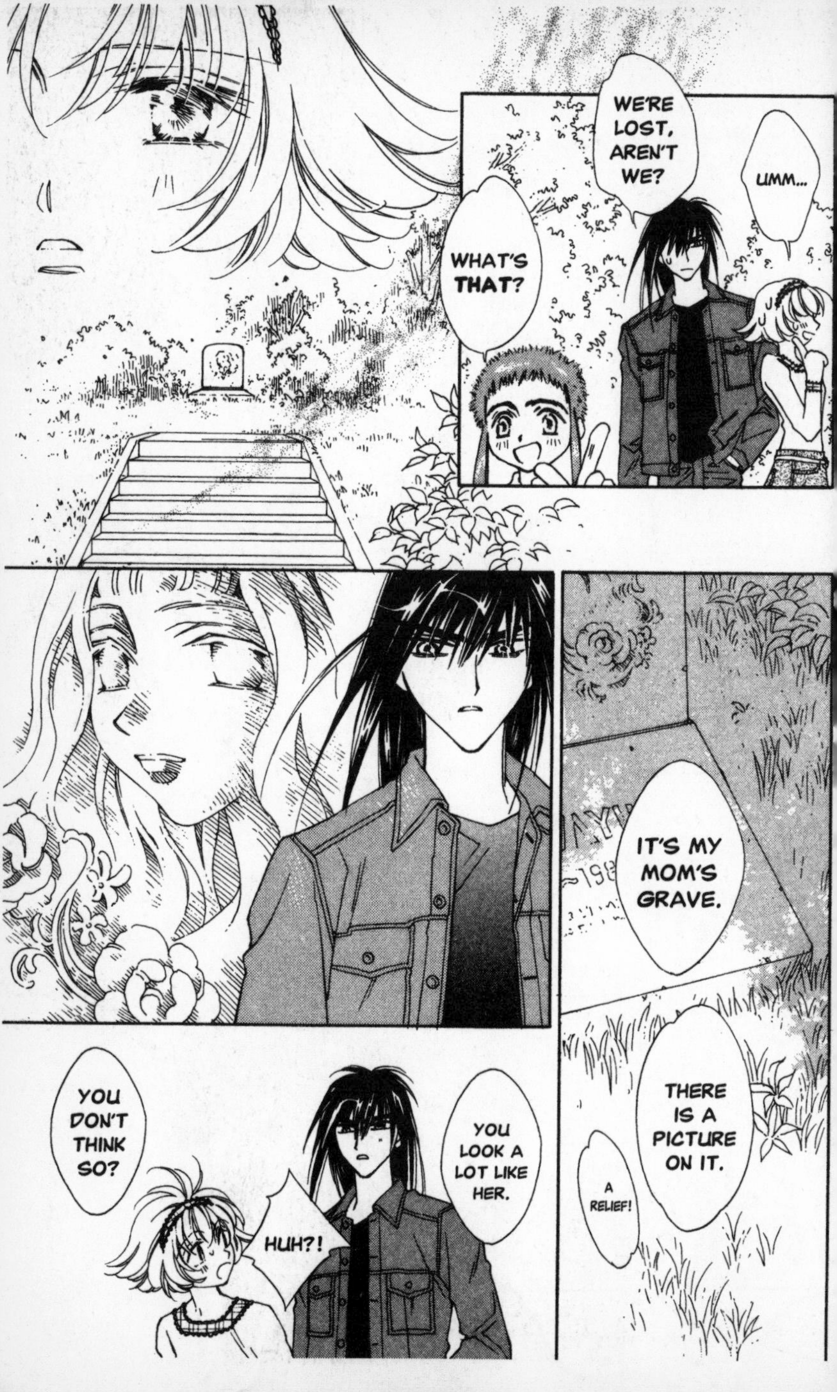
WE'RE LOST, AREN'T WE?
UMM...
WHAT'S THAT?
IT'S MY MOM'S GRAVE.
THERE IS A PICTURE ON IT.
A RELIEF!
YOU LOOK A LOT LIKE HER.
HUH?!
YOU DON'T THINK SO?

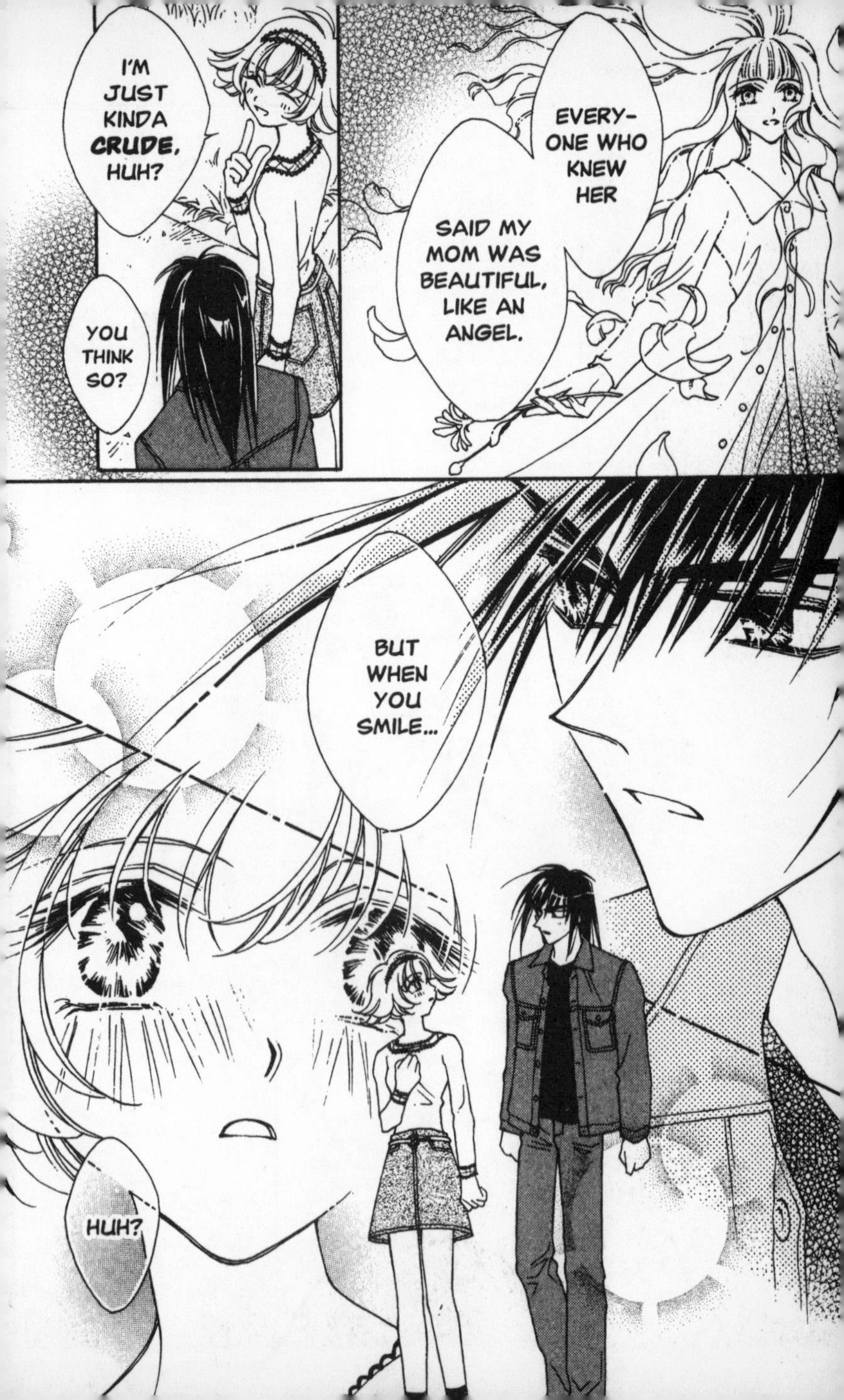
EVERY-ONE WHO KNEW HER
SAID MY MOM WAS BEAUTIFUL, LIKE AN ANGEL.
I'M JUST KINDA **CRUDE**, HUH?
YOU THINK SO?
BUT WHEN YOU SMILE...
HUH?

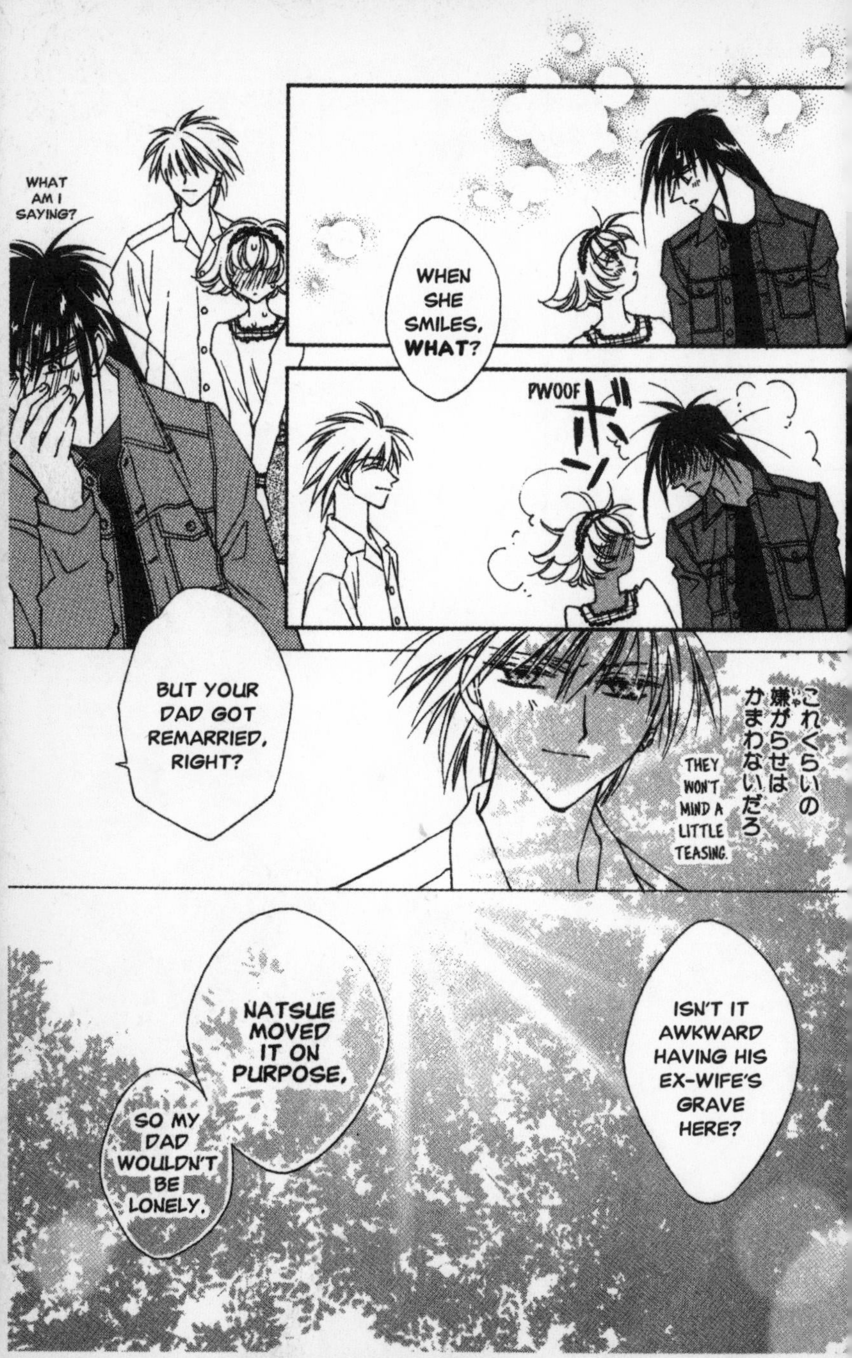
WHEN SHE SMILES, **WHAT**?
PWOOF
ボン
WHAT AM I SAYING?
これくらいの嫌がらせはかまわないだろ
THEY WON'T MIND A LITTLE TEASING.
BUT YOUR DAD GOT REMARRIED, RIGHT?
ISN'T IT AWKWARD HAVING HIS EX-WIFE'S GRAVE HERE?
NATSUE MOVED IT ON PURPOSE,
SO MY DAD WOULDN'T BE LONELY.

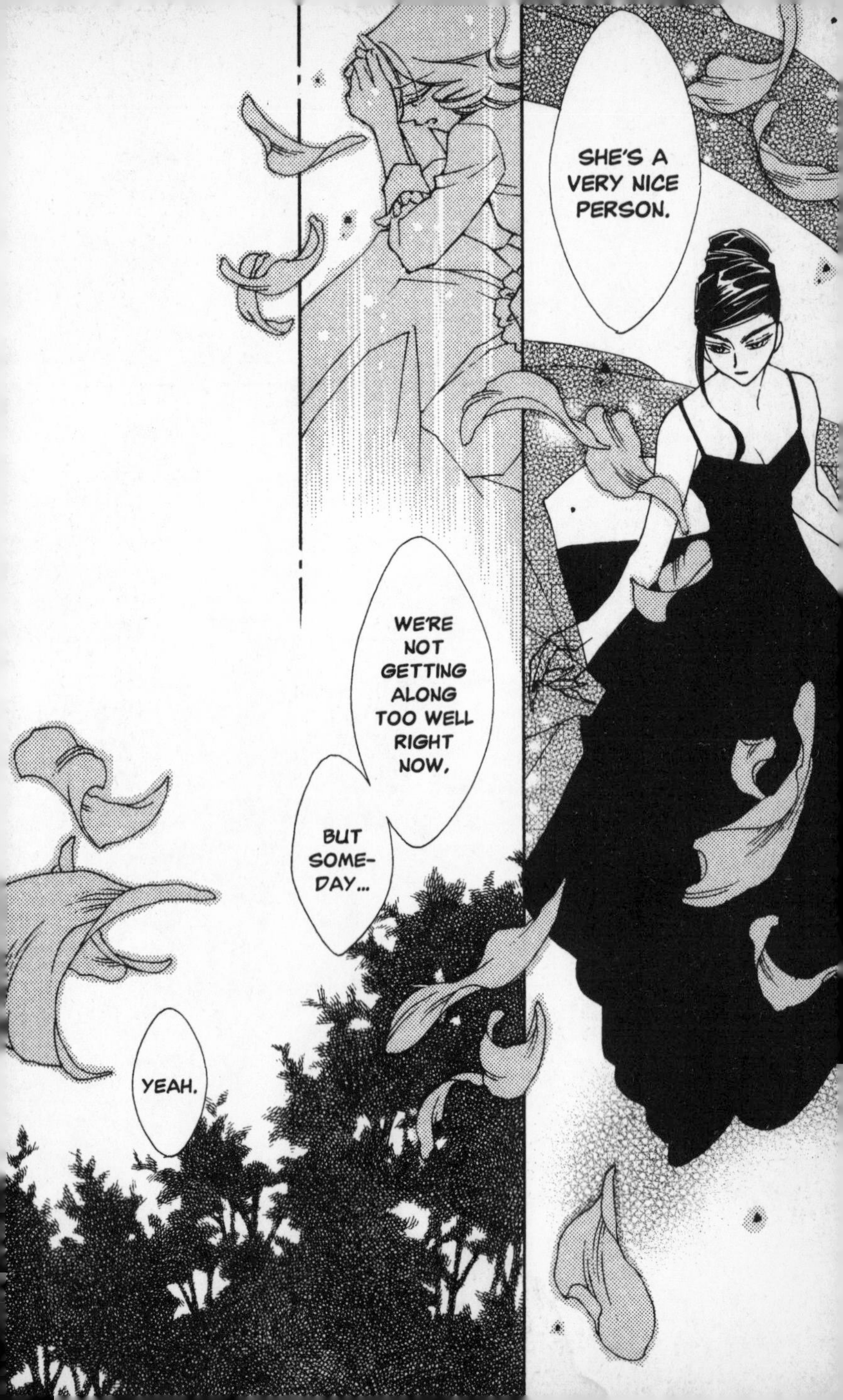
SHE'S A VERY NICE PERSON.
WE'RE NOT GETTING ALONG TOO WELL RIGHT NOW,
BUT SOME-DAY...
YEAH.

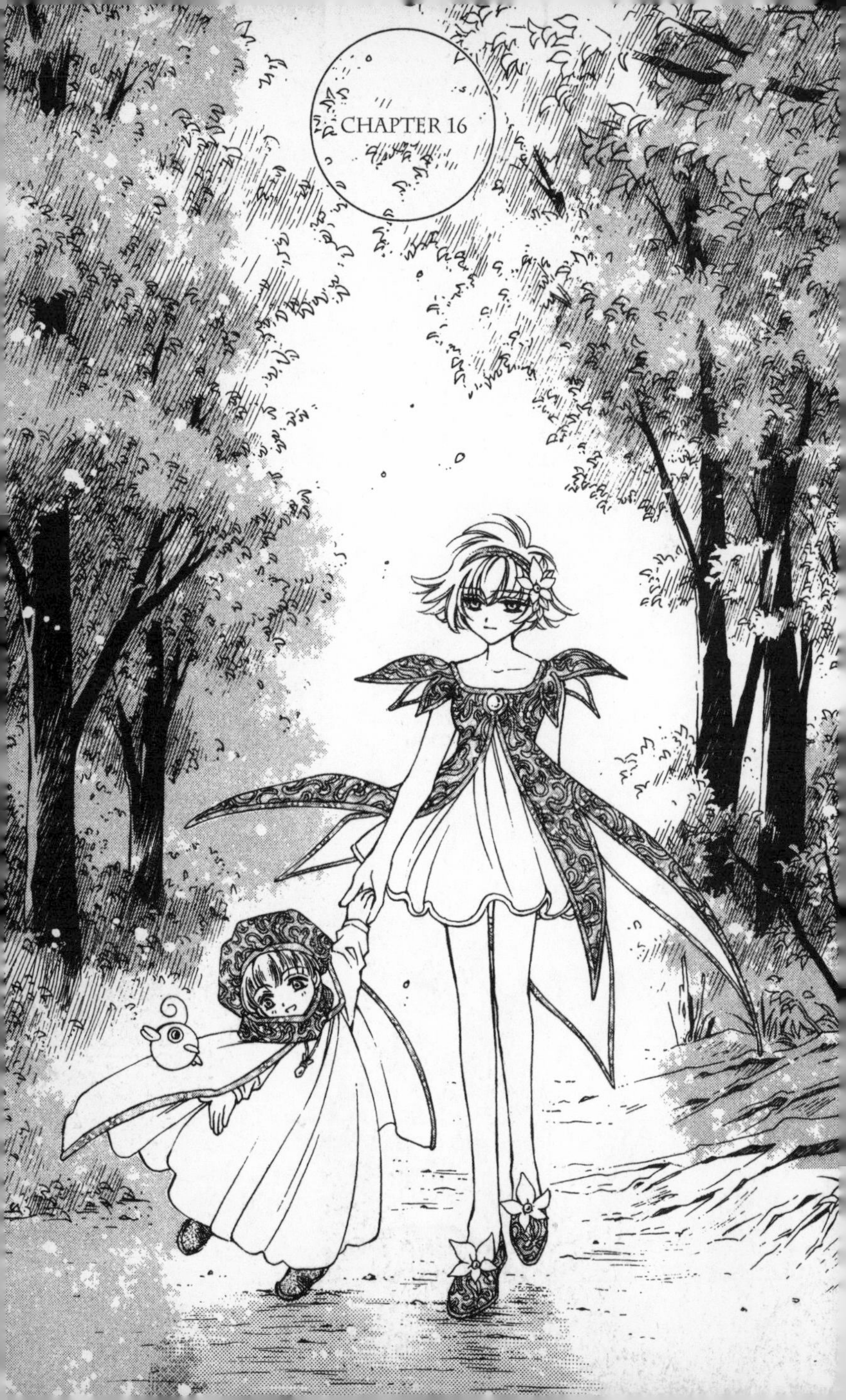
CHAPTER 16

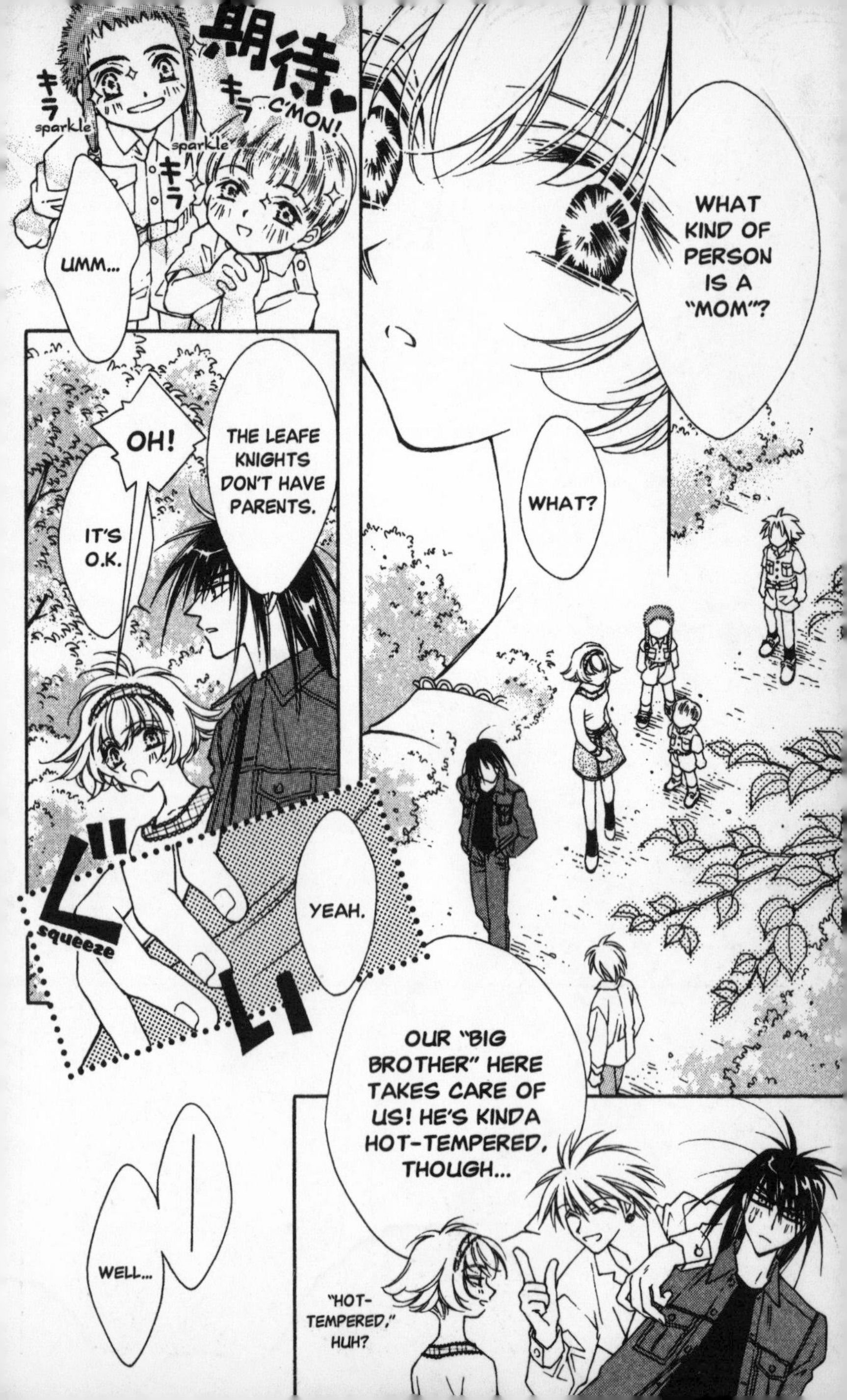
WHAT KIND OF PERSON IS A "MOM"?
WHAT?
期待
キラ
sparkle
キラ
sparkle
キラ
C'MON!
UMM...
THE LEAFE KNIGHTS DON'T HAVE PARENTS.
OH!
IT'S O.K.
ぎゅ
squeeze
YEAH.
OUR "BIG BROTHER" HERE TAKES CARE OF US! HE'S KINDA HOT-TEMPERED, THOUGH...
"HOT-TEMPERED," HUH?
WELL...

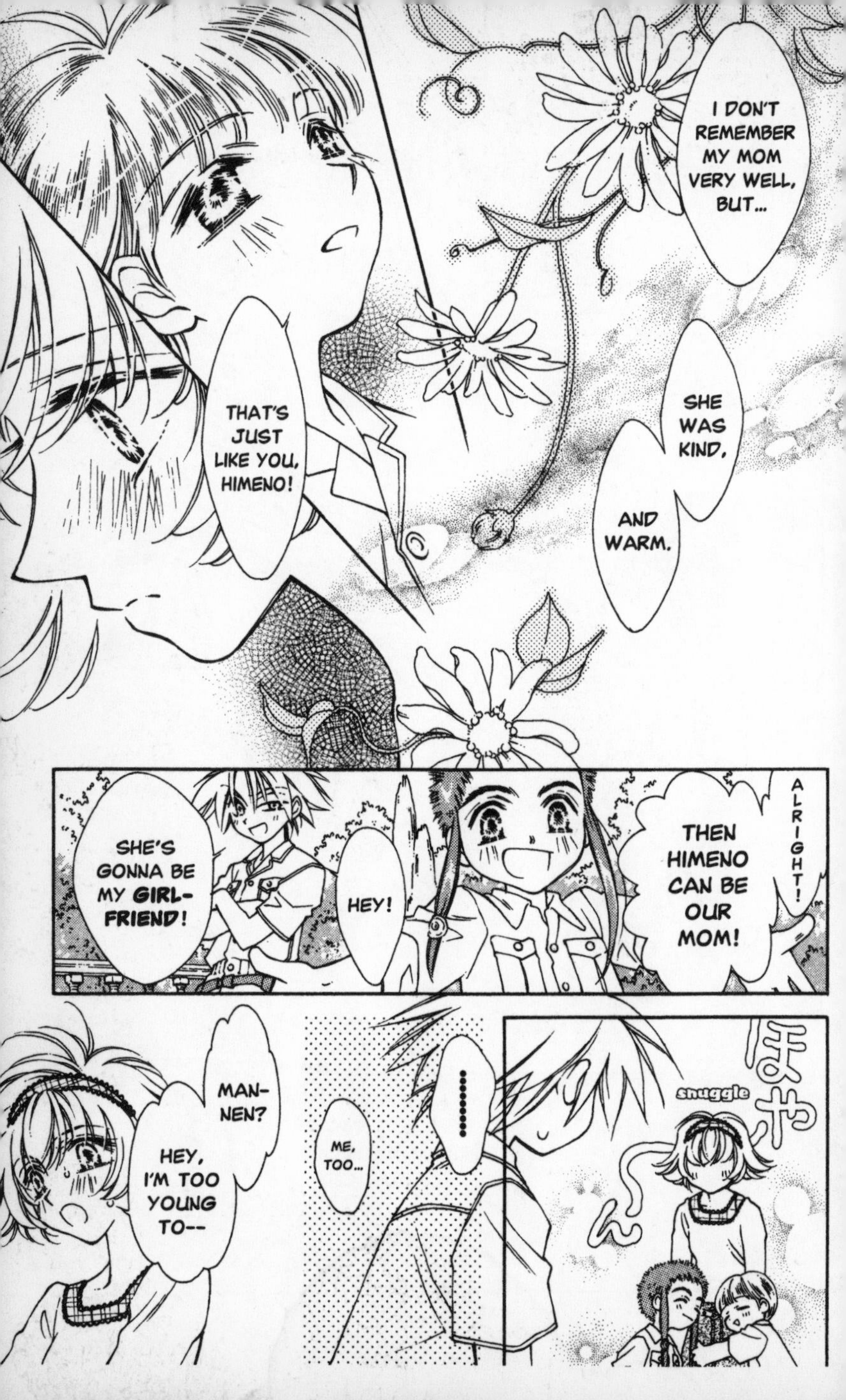
I DON'T REMEMBER MY MOM VERY WELL, BUT...
SHE WAS KIND,
AND WARM.
THAT'S JUST LIKE YOU, HIMENO!
ALRIGHT!
THEN HIMENO CAN BE OUR MOM!
HEY!
SHE'S GONNA BE MY **GIRL-FRIEND**!
ほやん
snuggle
....
ME, TOO...
MAN-NEN?
HEY, I'M TOO YOUNG TO--

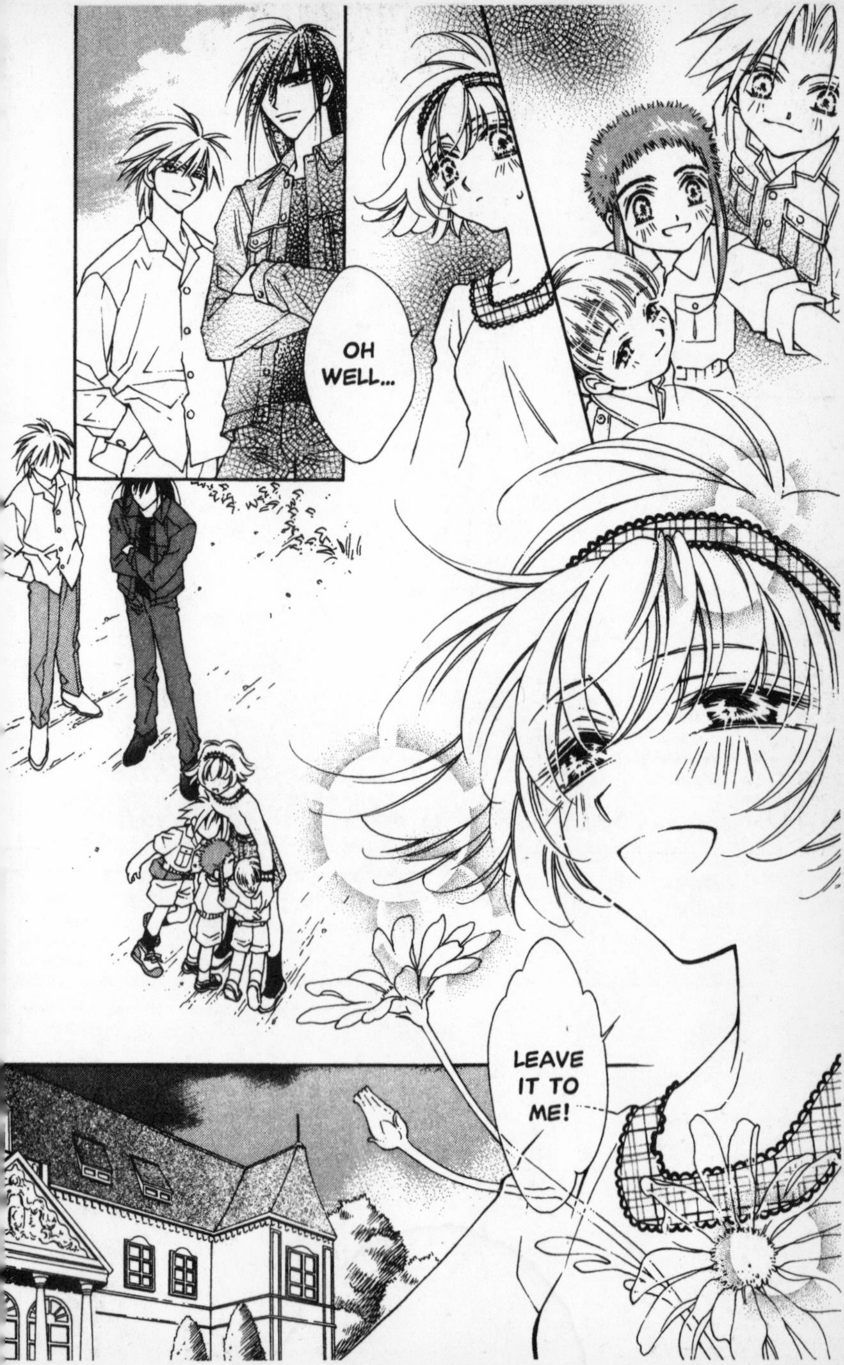
OH WELL...
LEAVE IT TO ME!

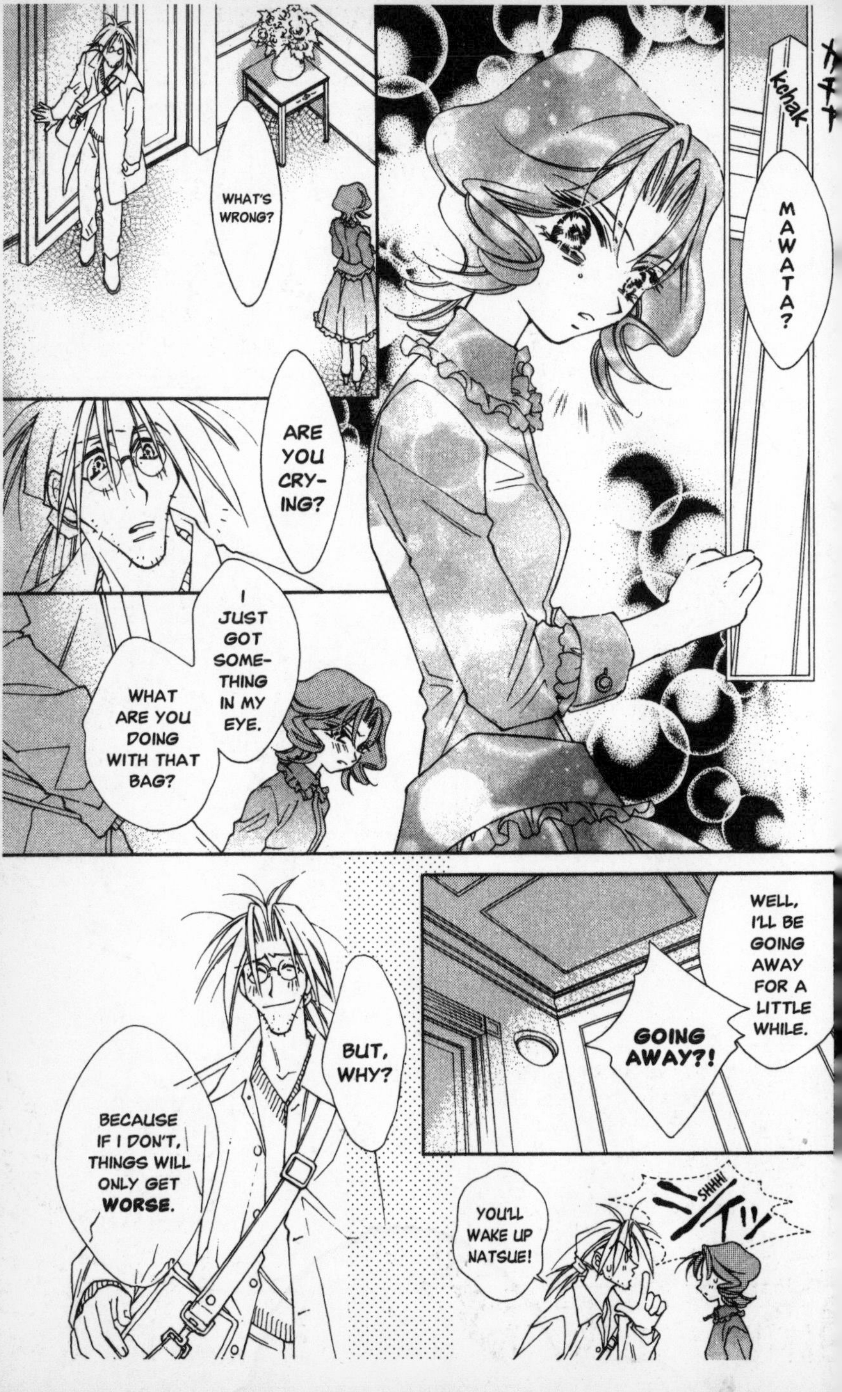
kchak
MAWATA?
WHAT'S WRONG?
ARE YOU CRY-ING?
I JUST GOT SOME-THING IN MY EYE.
WHAT ARE YOU DOING WITH THAT BAG?
WELL, I'LL BE GOING AWAY FOR A LITTLE WHILE.
GOING AWAY?!
SHHH!
YOU'LL WAKE UP NATSUE!
BUT, WHY?
BECAUSE IF I DON'T, THINGS WILL ONLY GET **WORSE**.

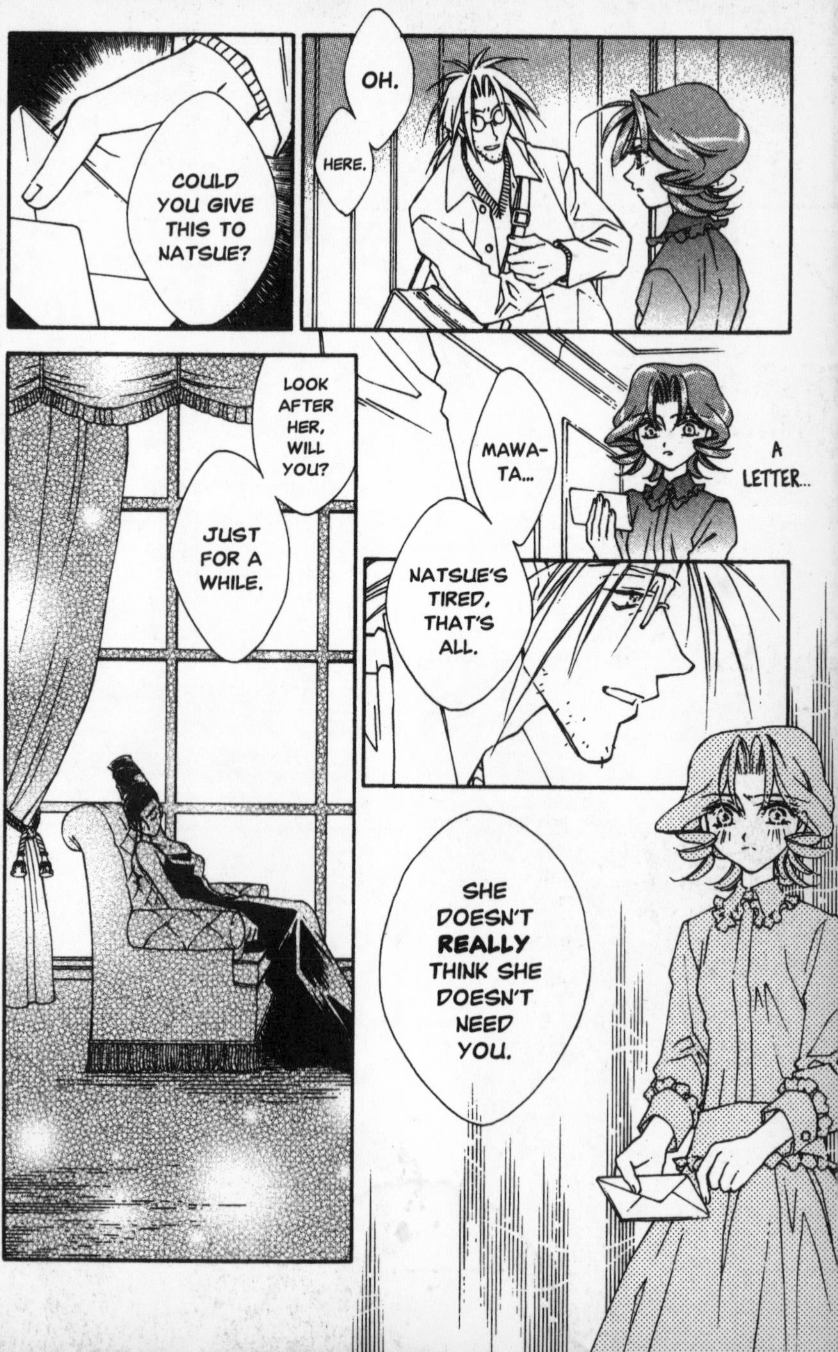
OH.
HERE.
COULD YOU GIVE THIS TO NATSUE?
A LETTER...
MAWA-TA...
NATSUE'S TIRED, THAT'S ALL.
LOOK AFTER HER, WILL YOU?
JUST FOR A WHILE.
SHE DOESN'T **REALLY** THINK SHE DOESN'T NEED YOU.

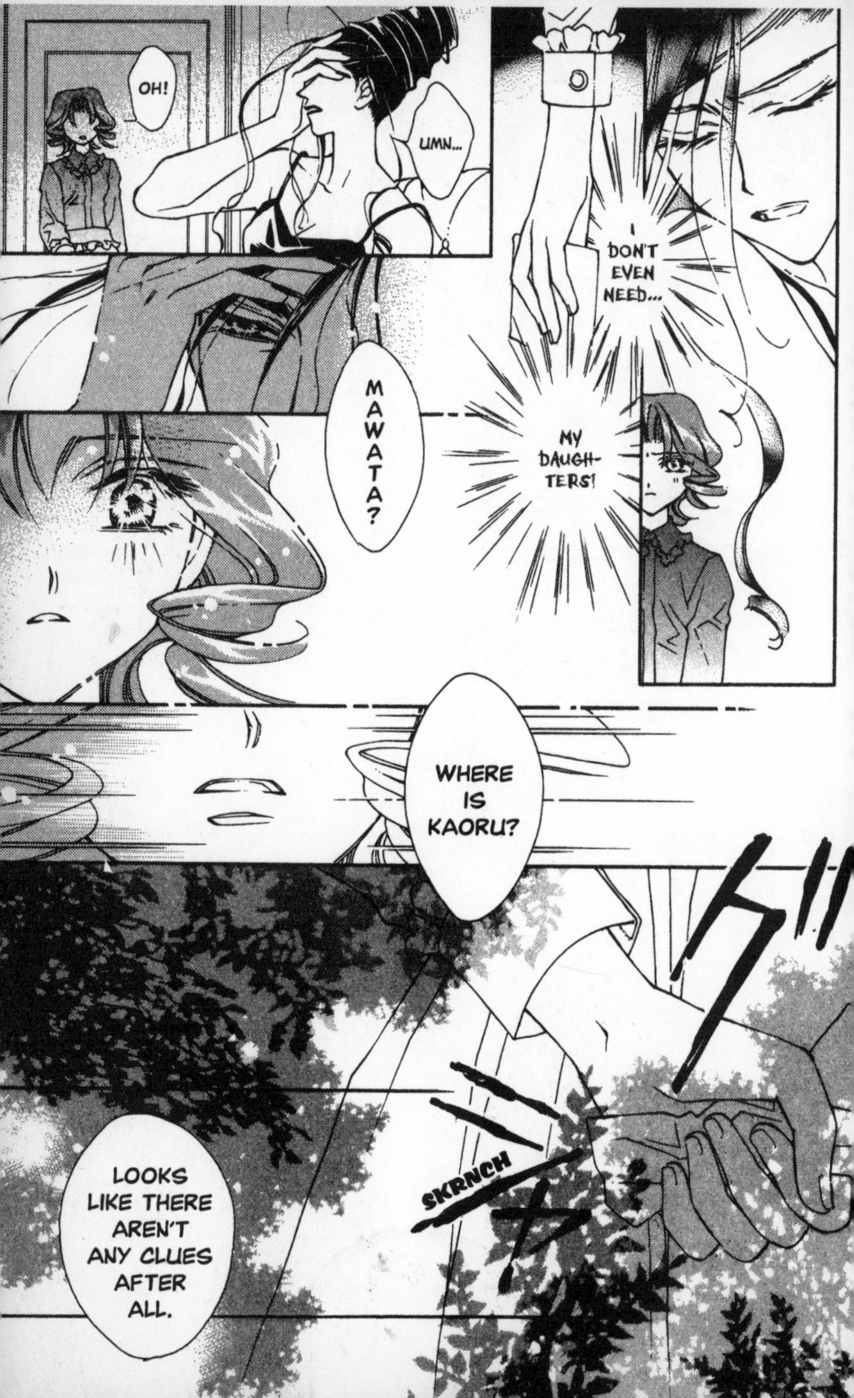
I DON'T EVEN NEED...
MY DAUGHTERS!
OH!
UMN...
MAWATA?
WHERE IS KAORU?
SKRNCH
LOOKS LIKE THERE AREN'T ANY CLUES AFTER ALL.

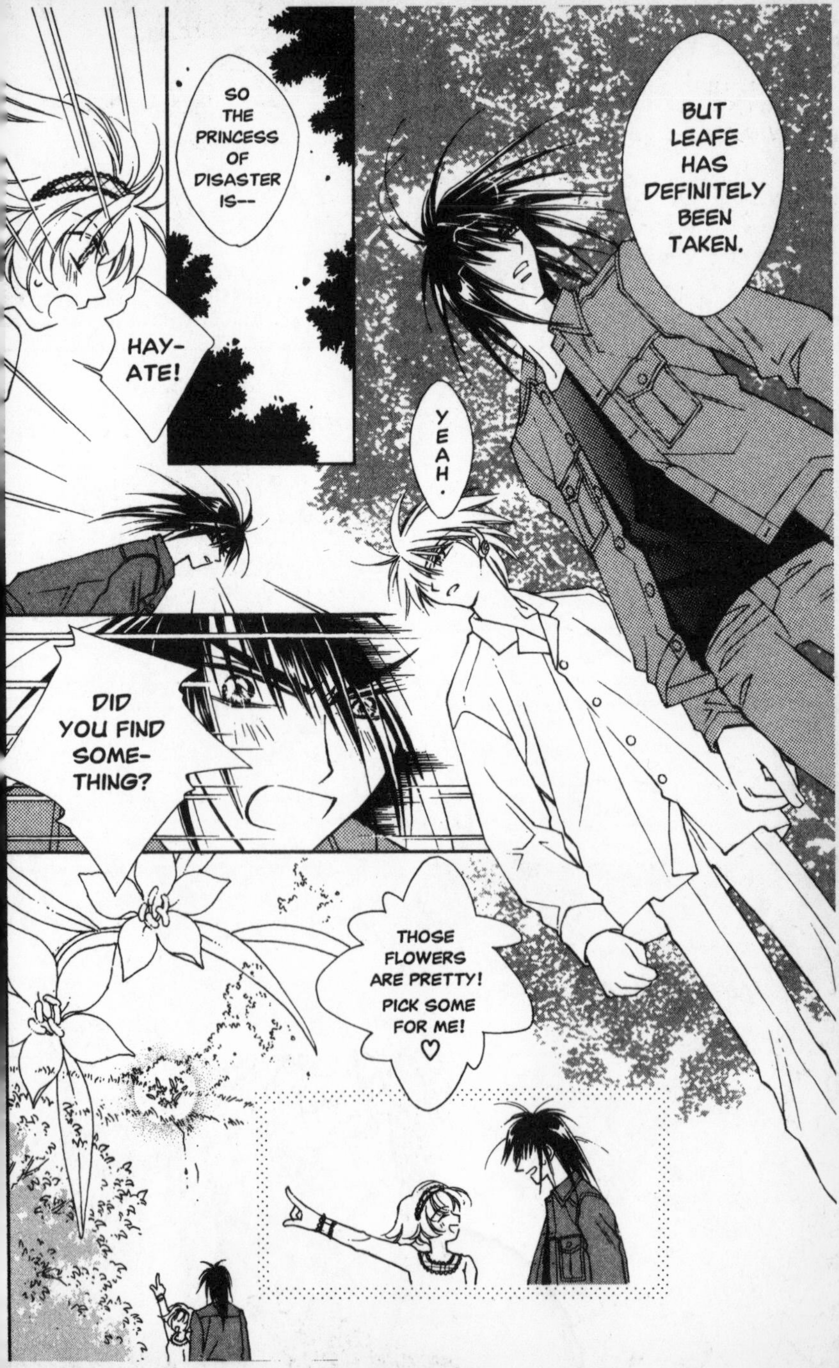
BUT LEAFE HAS DEFINITELY BEEN TAKEN.
YEAH.
SO THE PRINCESS OF DISASTER IS--
HAY-ATE!
DID YOU FIND SOME-THING?
THOSE FLOWERS ARE PRETTY! PICK SOME FOR ME! ♡

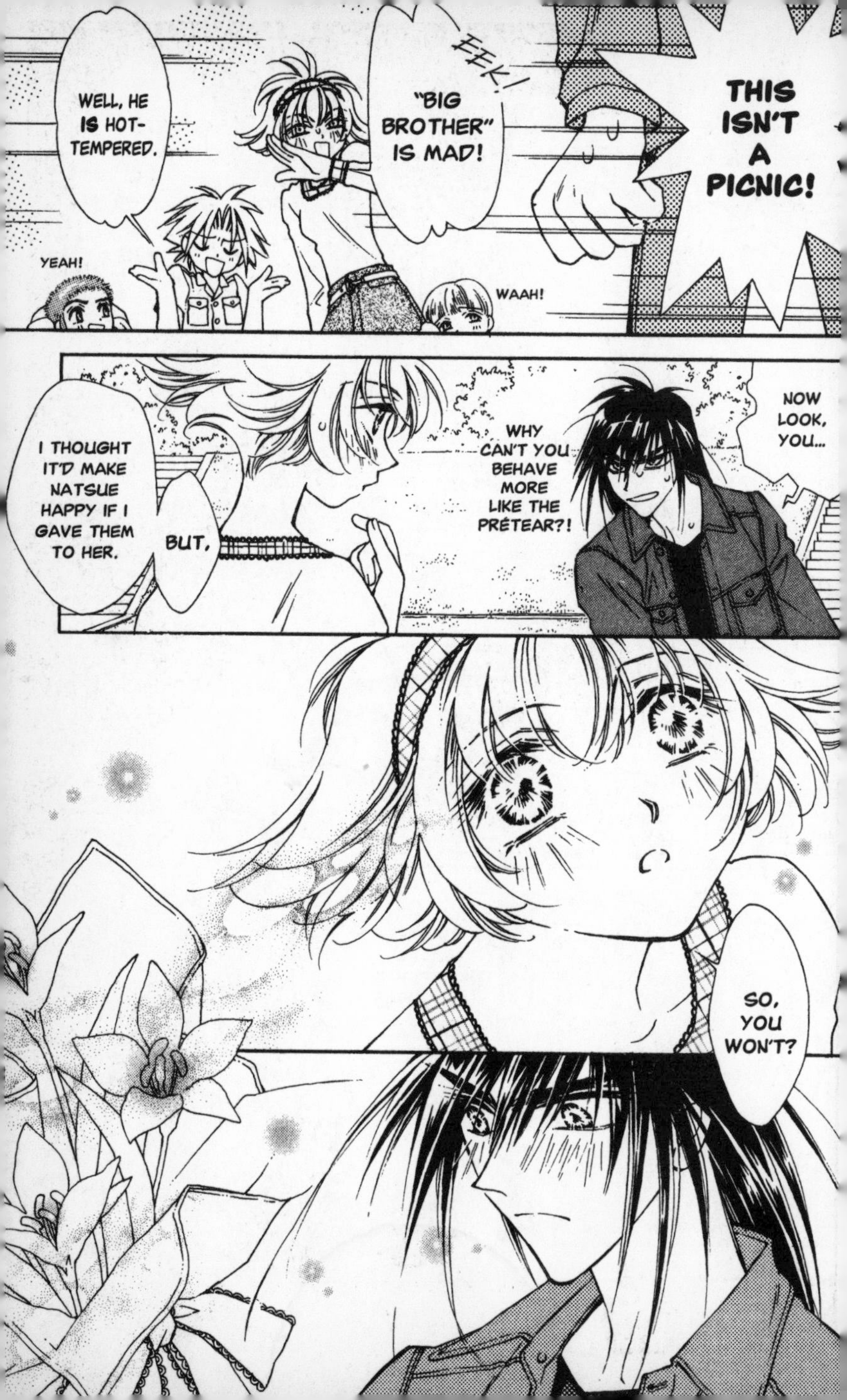
THIS ISN'T A PICNIC!
EEK!
"BIG BROTHER" IS MAD!
WELL, HE IS HOT-TEMPERED.
WAAH!
YEAH!
NOW LOOK, YOU...
WHY CAN'T YOU BEHAVE MORE LIKE THE PRÉTEAR?!
BUT,
I THOUGHT IT'D MAKE NATSUE HAPPY IF I GAVE THEM TO HER.
SO, YOU WON'T?

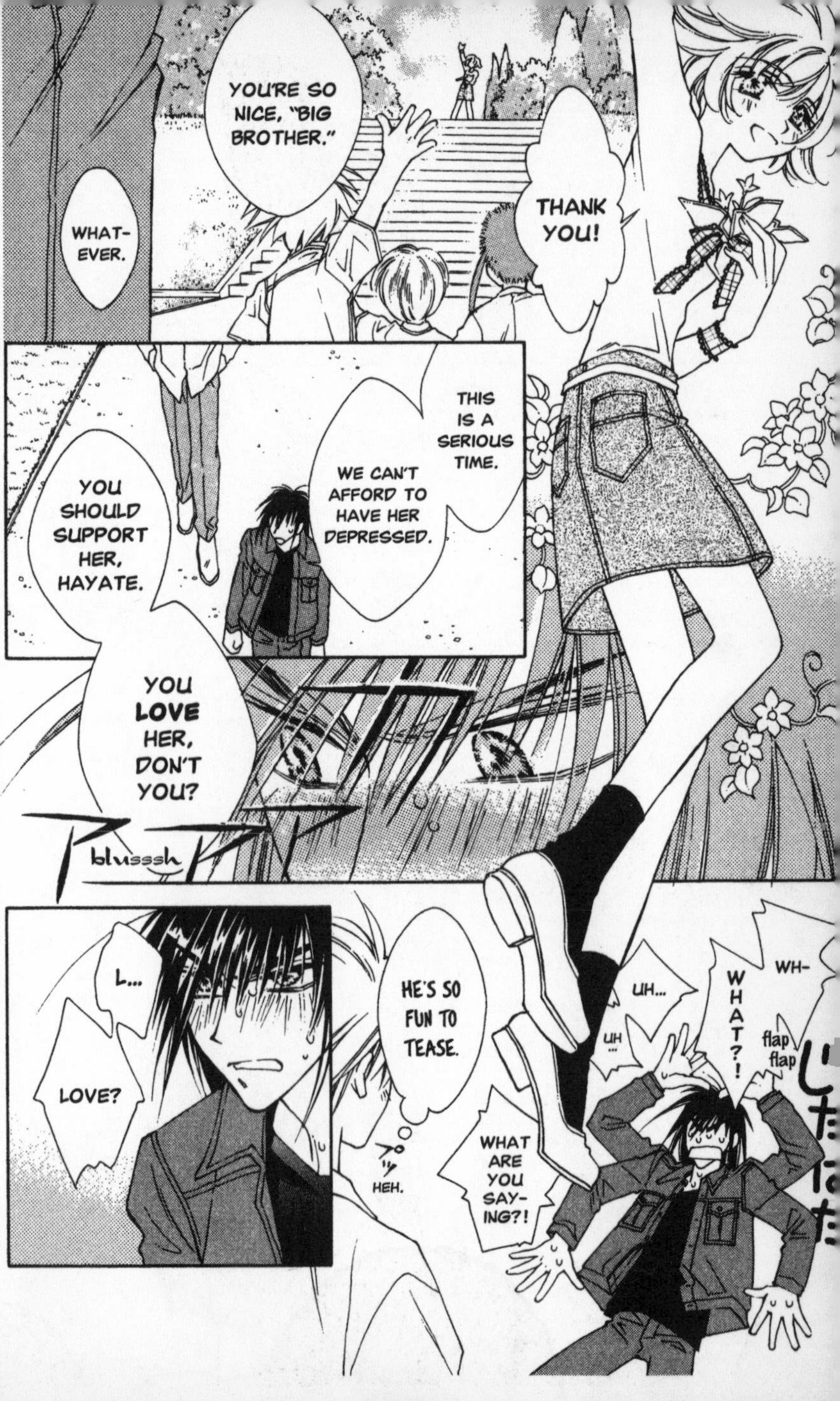
THANK YOU!
YOU'RE SO NICE, "BIG BROTHER."
WHAT-EVER.
THIS IS A SERIOUS TIME.
WE CAN'T AFFORD TO HAVE HER DEPRESSED.
YOU SHOULD SUPPORT HER, HAYATE.
YOU **LOVE** HER, DON'T YOU?
blusssh
WH-
WHAT?!
flap flap
じたばた
UH...
UH...
WHAT ARE YOU SAY-ING?!
HE'S SO FUN TO TEASE.
HEH.
L...
LOVE?

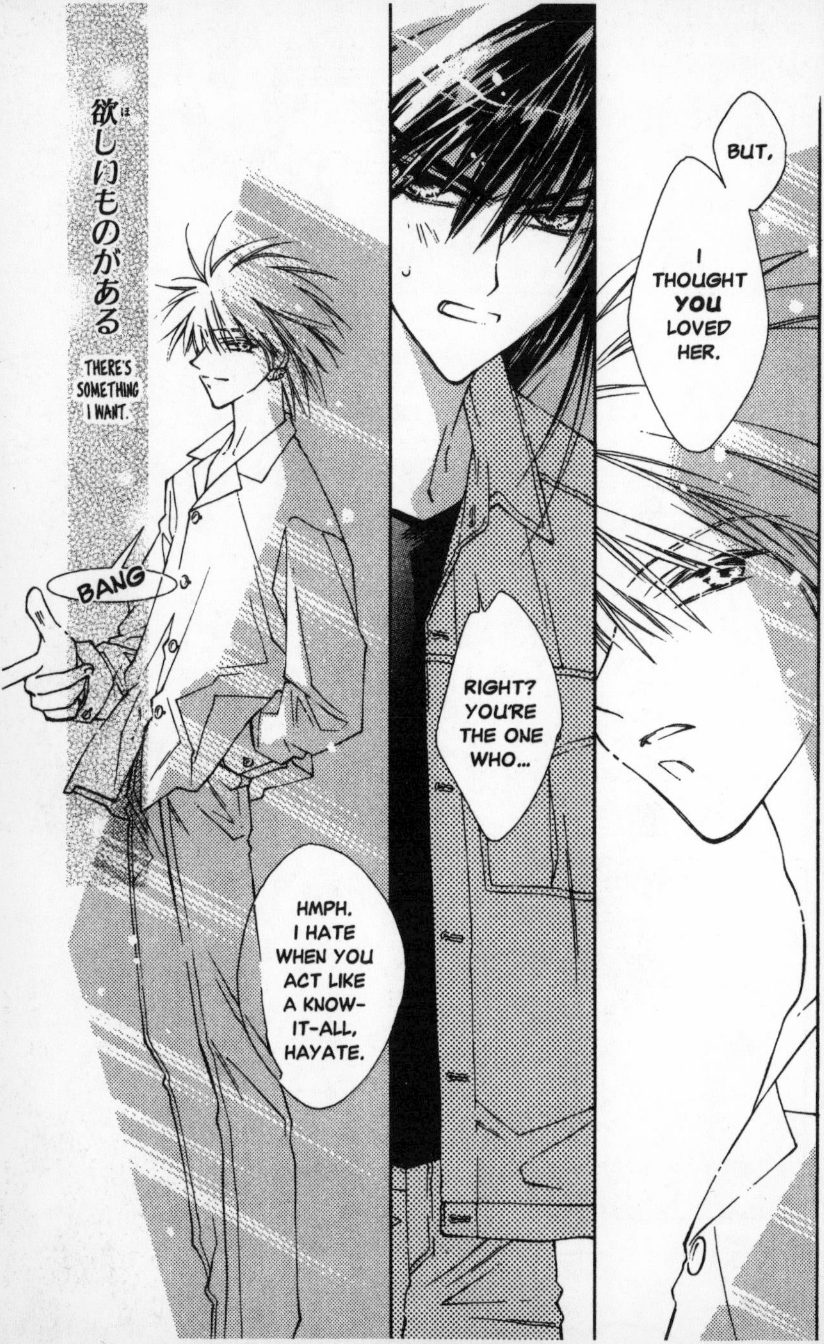
BUT,
I THOUGHT YOU LOVED HER.
RIGHT? YOU'RE THE ONE WHO...
欲しいものがある
THERE'S SOMETHING I WANT.
BANG
HMPH. I HATE WHEN YOU ACT LIKE A KNOW-IT-ALL, HAYATE.

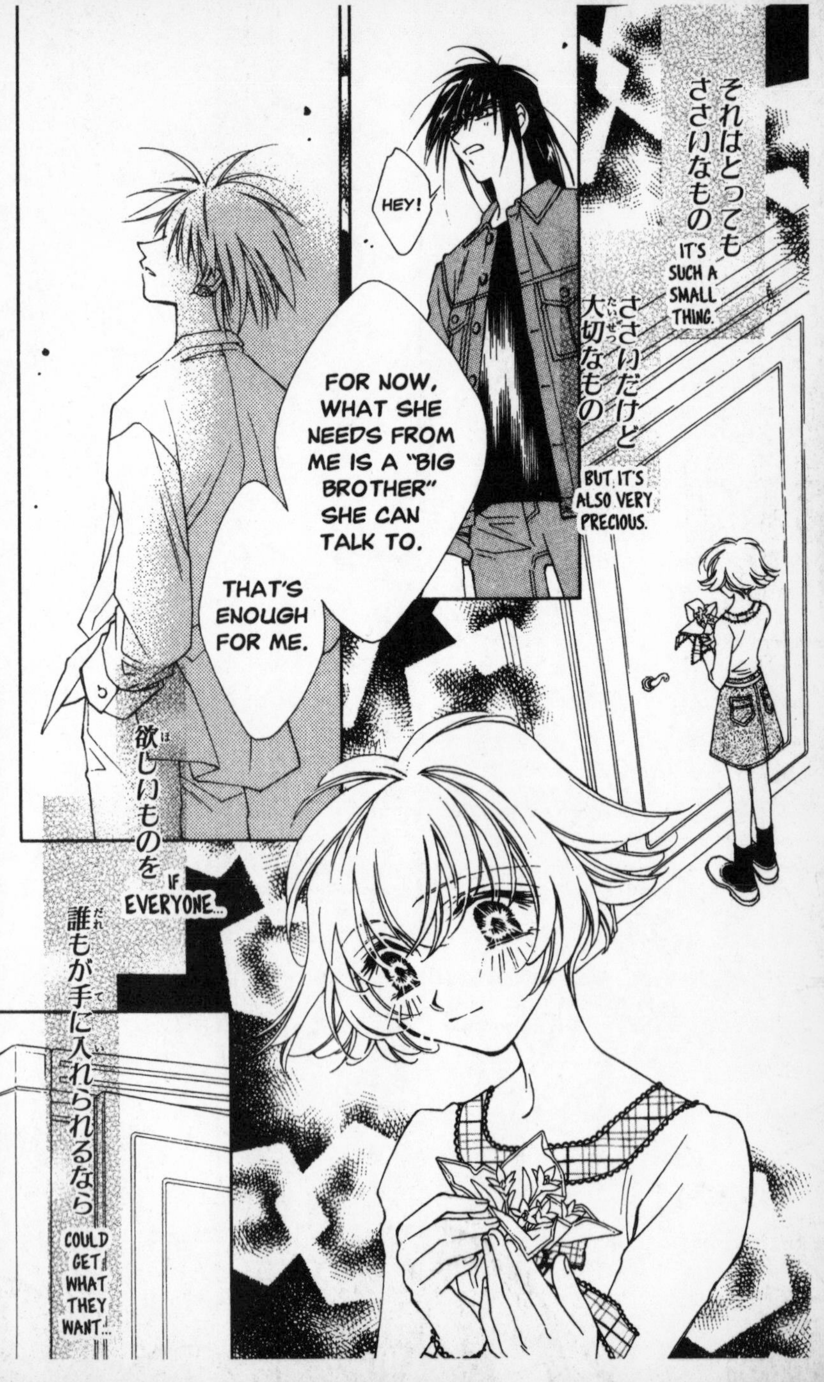
それはとってもささいなもの
IT'S SUCH A SMALL THING.
ささいだけど大切なもの
BUT IT'S ALSO VERY PRECIOUS.
HEY!
FOR NOW, WHAT SHE NEEDS FROM ME IS A "BIG BROTHER" SHE CAN TALK TO.
THAT'S ENOUGH FOR ME.
欲しいものを
IF EVERYONE...
誰もが手に入れられるなら
COULD GET WHAT THEY WANT...

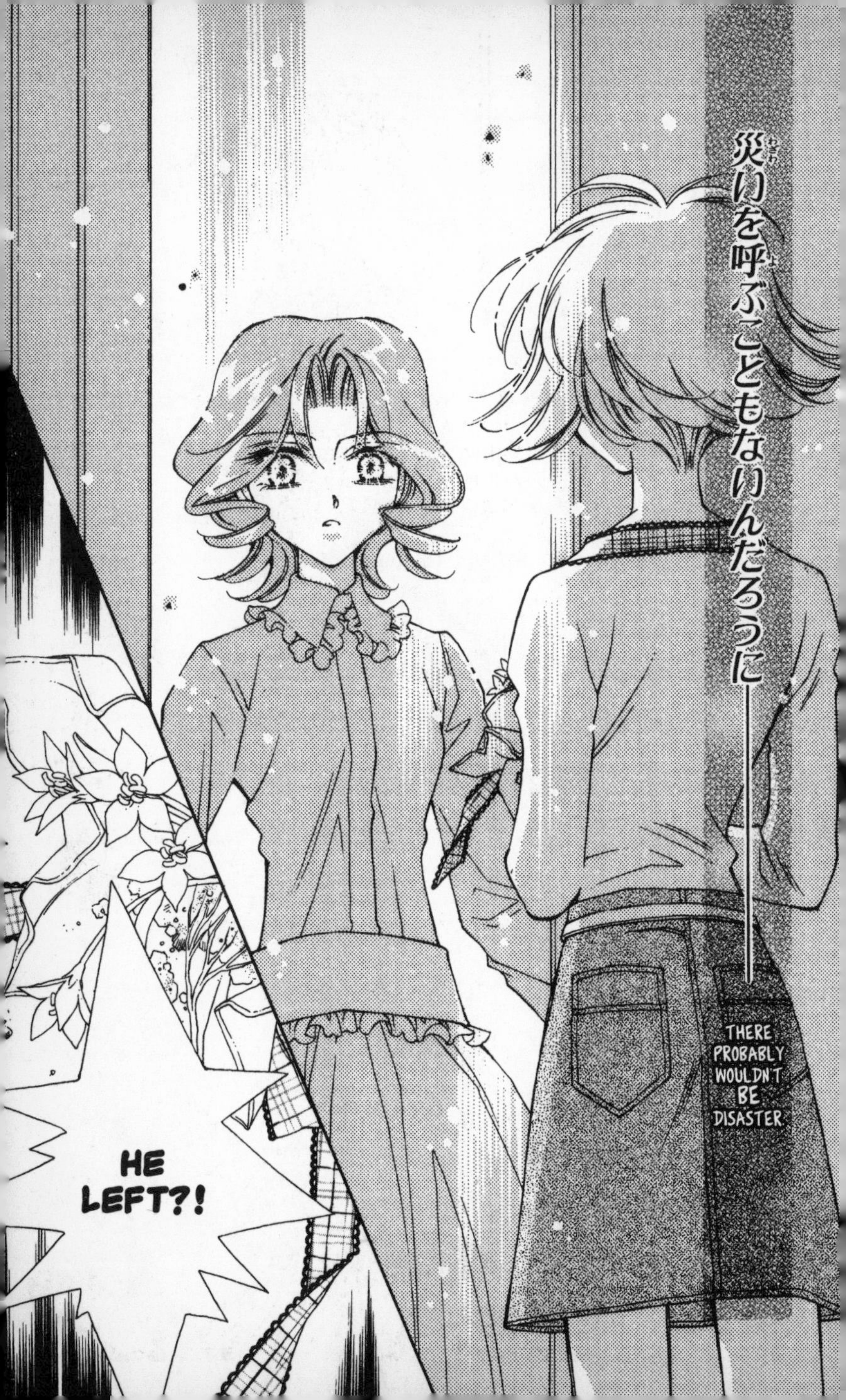
災いを呼ぶこともないんだろうに——
THERE PROBABLY WOULDN'T BE DISASTER.
HE LEFT?!

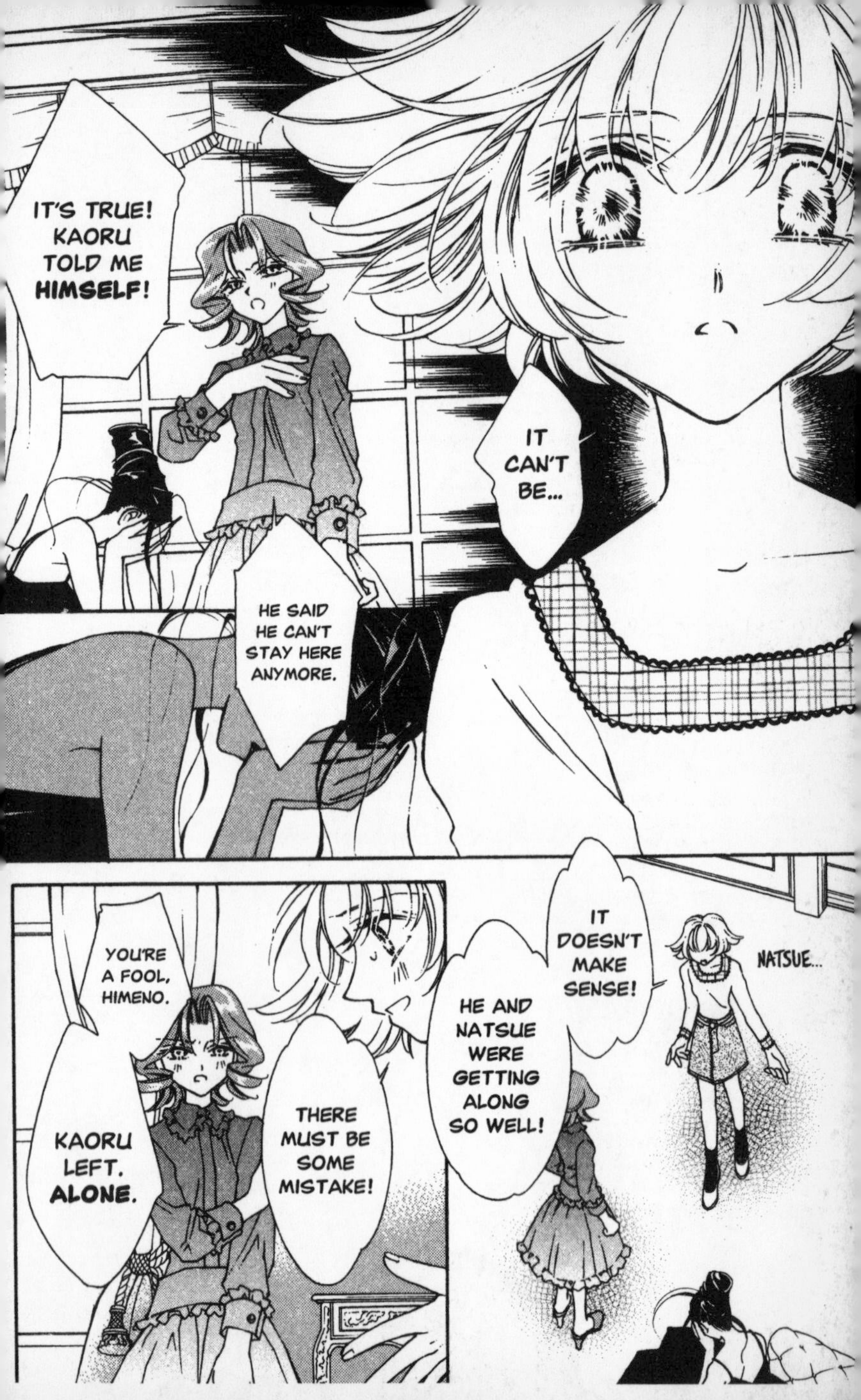

IT CAN'T BE...
IT'S TRUE! KAORU TOLD ME HIMSELF!
HE SAID HE CAN'T STAY HERE ANYMORE.
NATSUE...
IT DOESN'T MAKE SENSE!
HE AND NATSUE WERE GETTING ALONG SO WELL!
THERE MUST BE SOME MISTAKE!
YOU'RE A FOOL, HIMENO.
KAORU LEFT. ALONE.

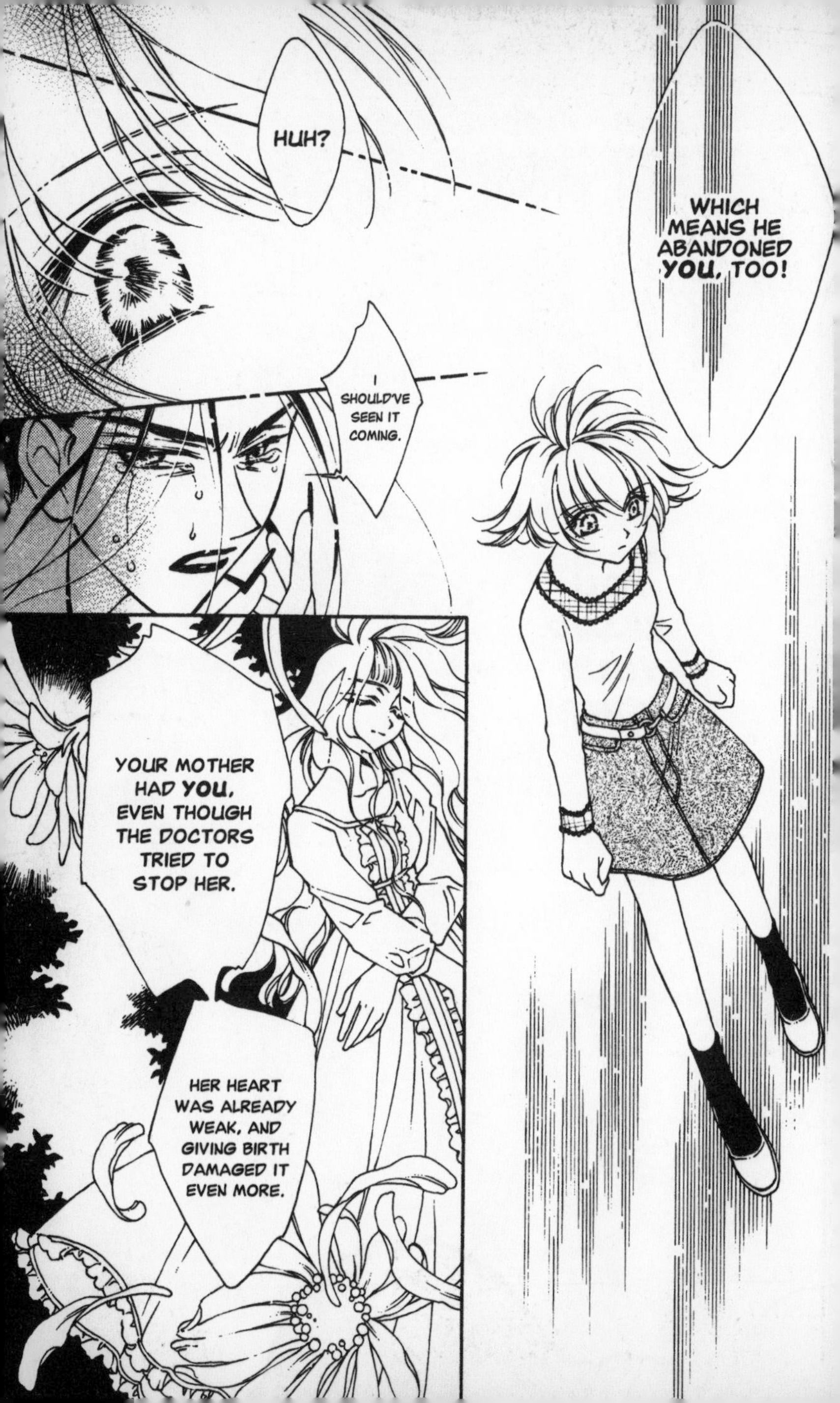
WHICH MEANS HE ABANDONED **YOU**, TOO!
HUH?
I SHOULD'VE SEEN IT COMING.
YOUR MOTHER HAD **YOU**, EVEN THOUGH THE DOCTORS TRIED TO STOP HER.
HER HEART WAS ALREADY WEAK, AND GIVING BIRTH DAMAGED IT EVEN MORE.

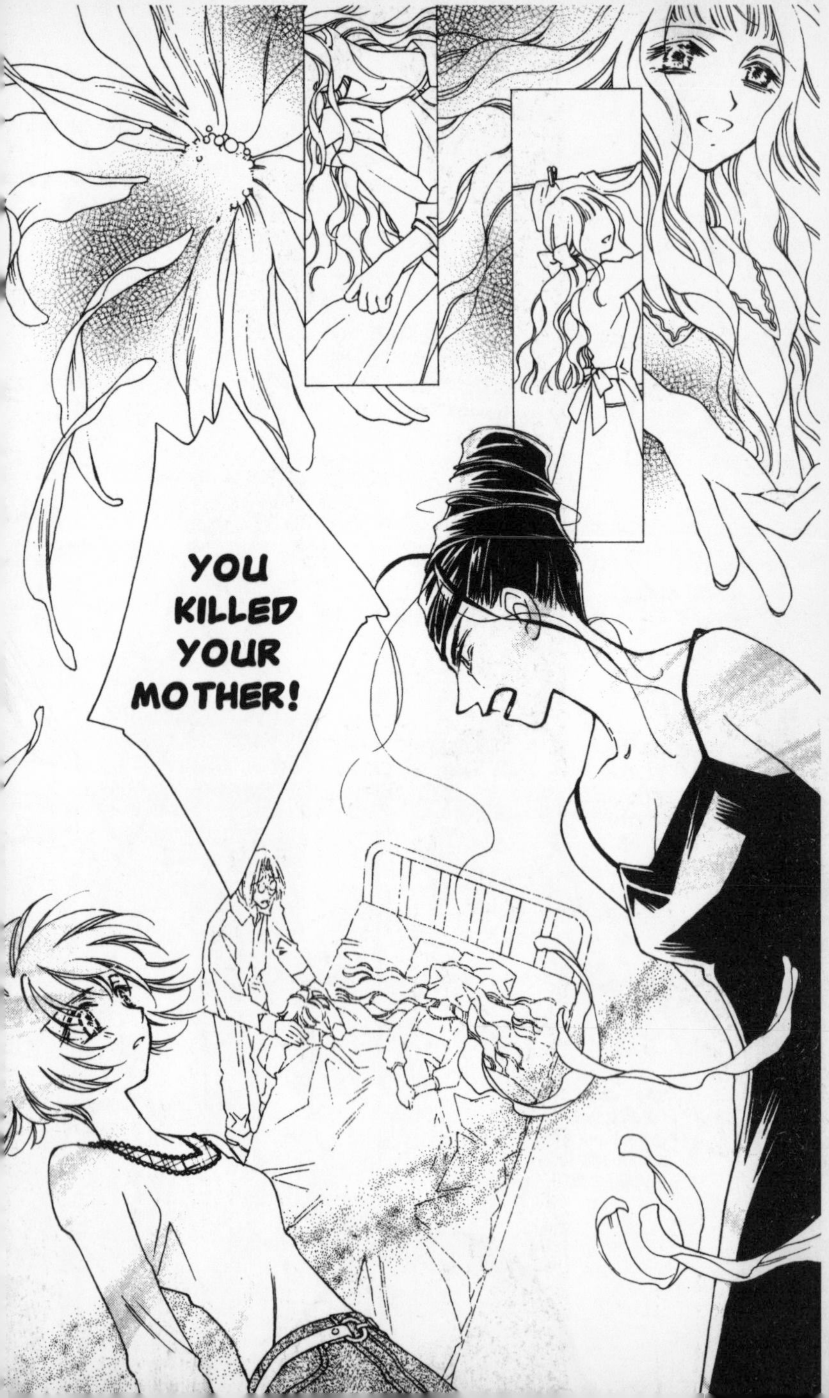
YOU KILLED YOUR MOTHER!

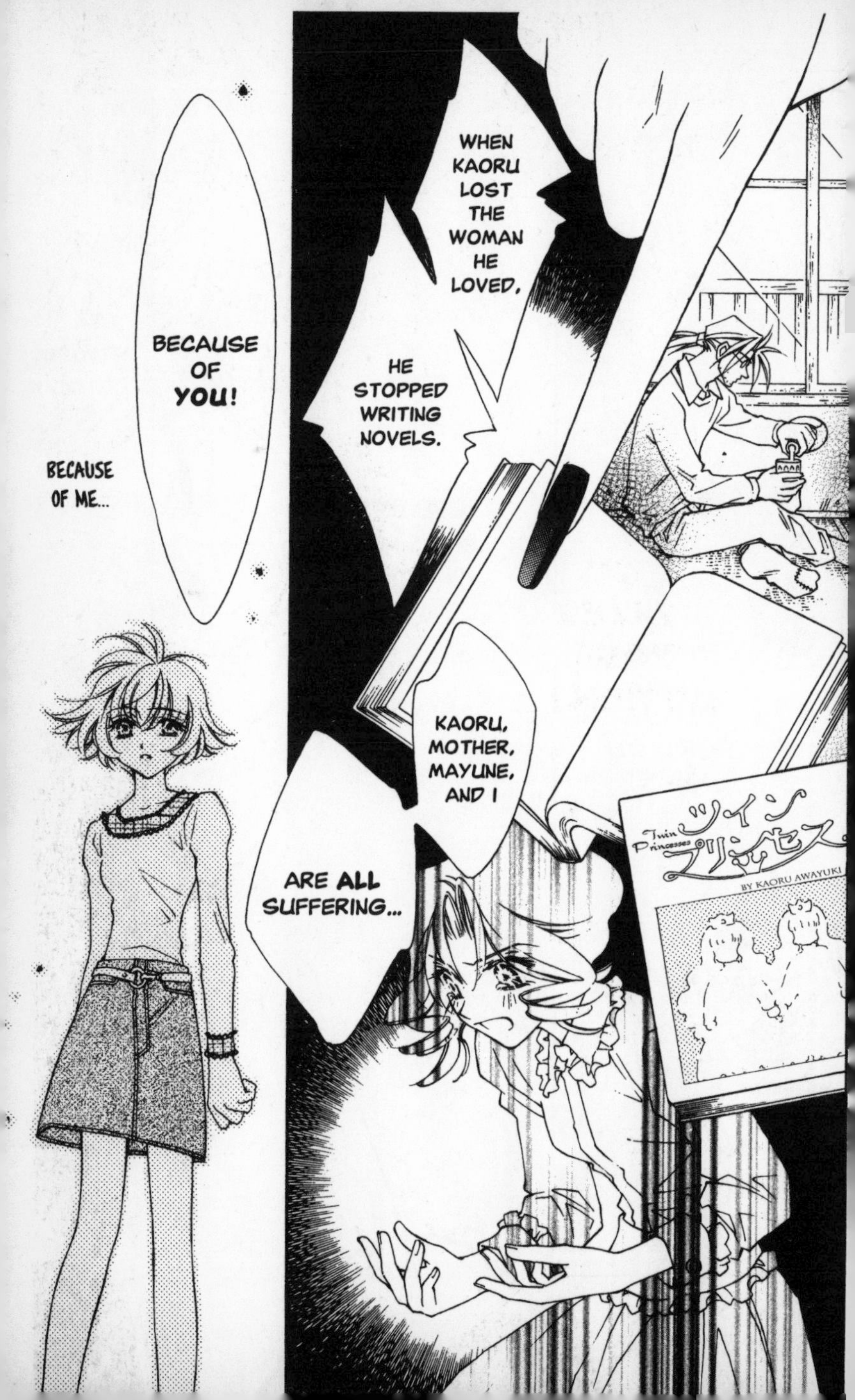
WHEN KAORU LOST THE WOMAN HE LOVED,
HE STOPPED WRITING NOVELS.
KAORU, MOTHER, MAYUNE, AND I
ARE ALL SUFFERING...
Twin Princesses
ツインプリンセス
BY KAORU AWAYUKI
BECAUSE OF YOU!
BECAUSE OF ME...

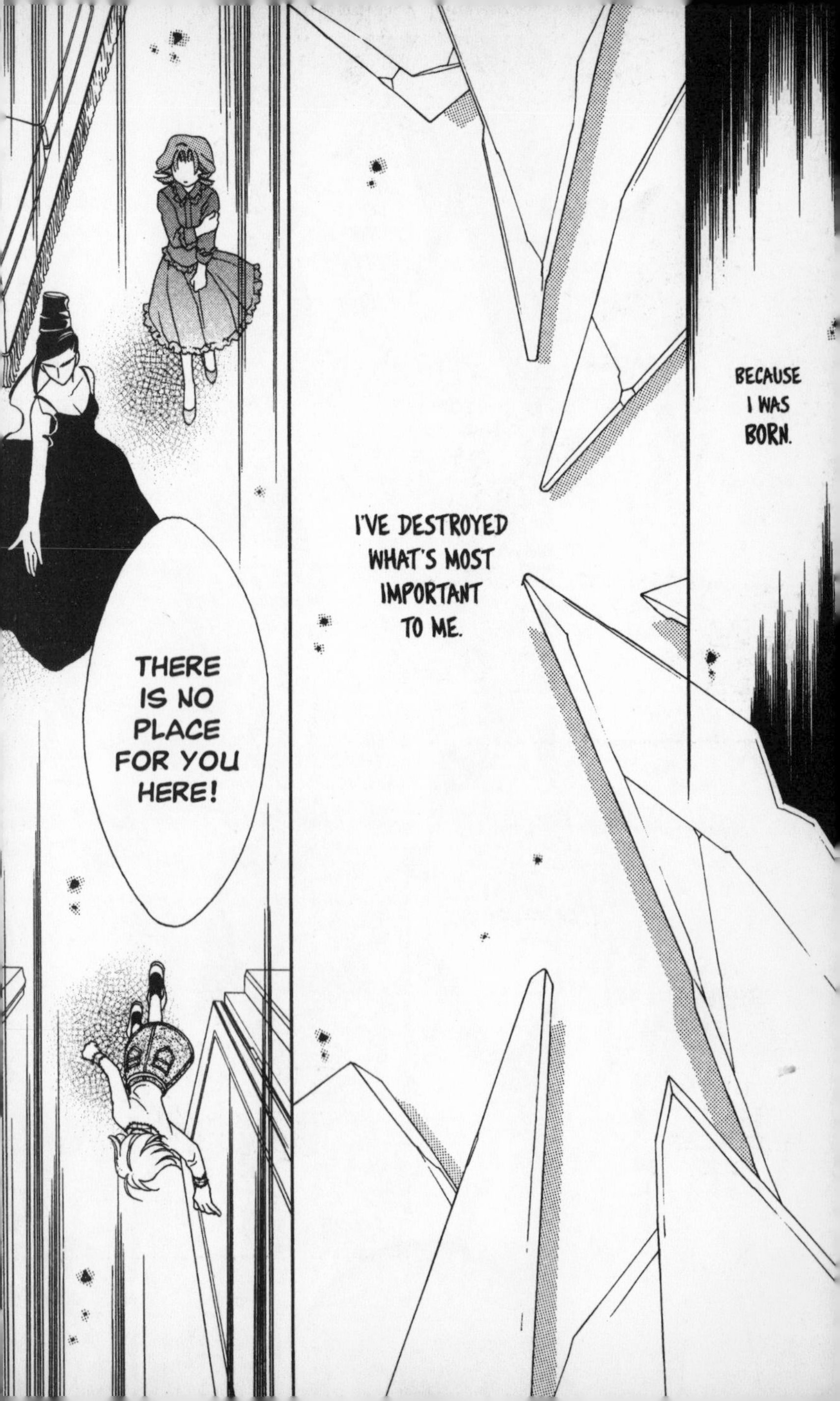
BECAUSE I WAS BORN.
I'VE DESTROYED WHAT'S MOST IMPORTANT TO ME.
THERE IS NO PLACE FOR YOU HERE!

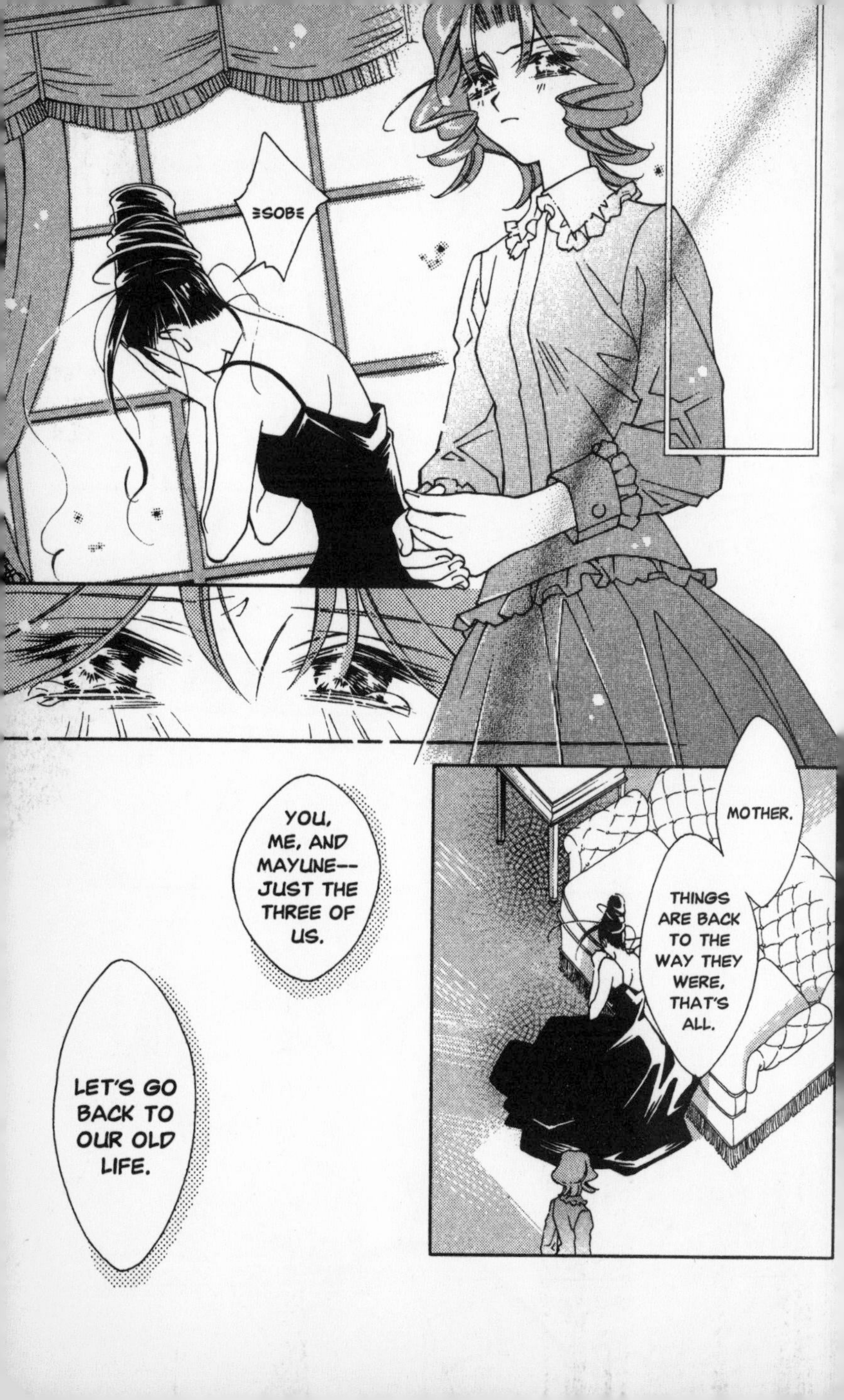
SOB
MOTHER.
THINGS ARE BACK TO THE WAY THEY WERE, THAT'S ALL.
YOU, ME, AND MAYUNE--JUST THE THREE OF US.
LET'S GO BACK TO OUR OLD LIFE.

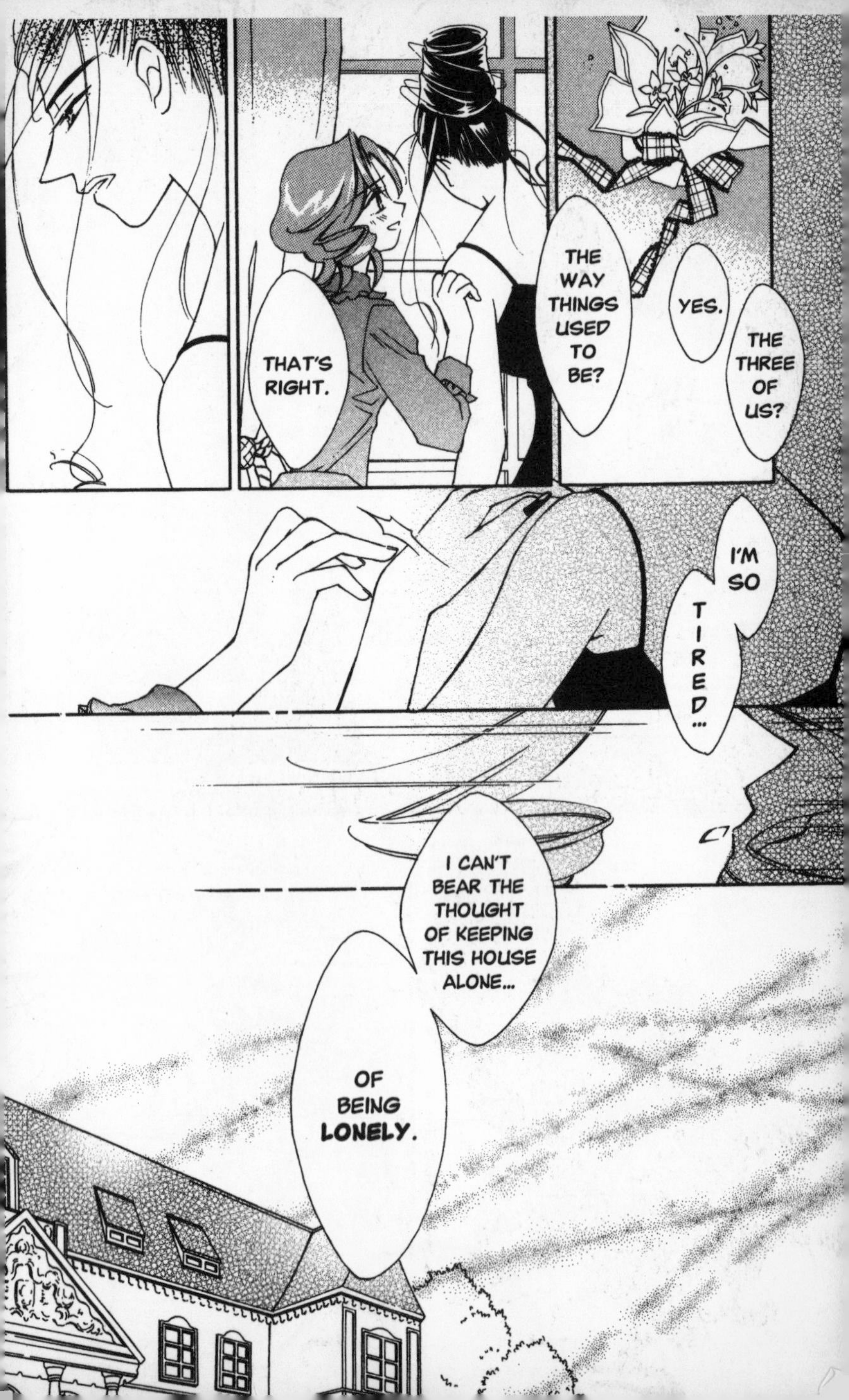
THE THREE OF US?
YES.
THE WAY THINGS USED TO BE?
THAT'S RIGHT.
I'M SO TIRED...
I CAN'T BEAR THE THOUGHT OF KEEPING THIS HOUSE ALONE...
OF BEING **LONELY**.

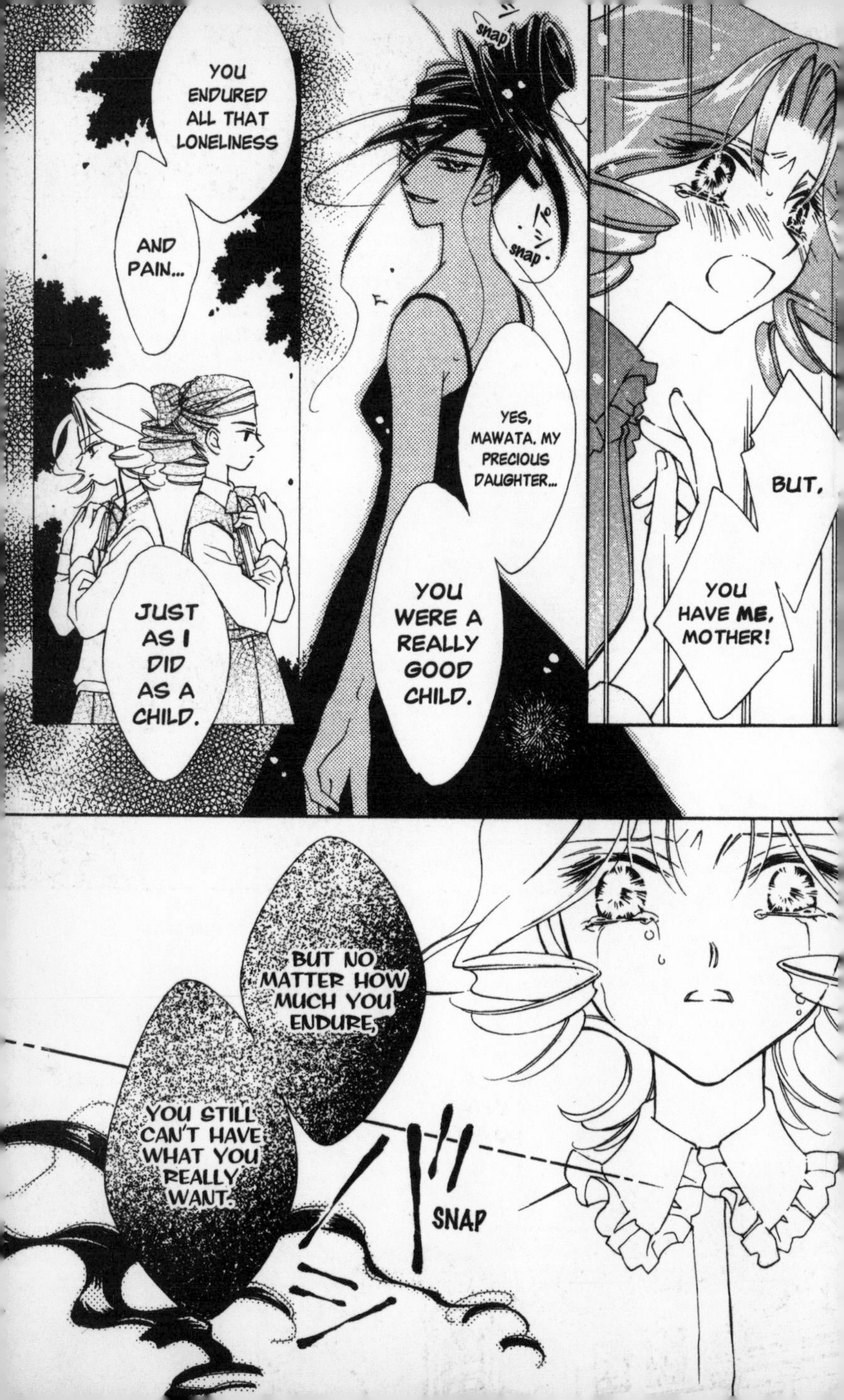
BUT,
YOU HAVE ME, MOTHER!
snap
snap
YES, MAWATA. MY PRECIOUS DAUGHTER...
YOU WERE A REALLY GOOD CHILD.
YOU ENDURED ALL THAT LONELINESS
AND PAIN...
JUST AS I DID AS A CHILD.
BUT NO MATTER HOW MUCH YOU ENDURE,
YOU STILL CAN'T HAVE WHAT YOU REALLY WANT.
SNAP

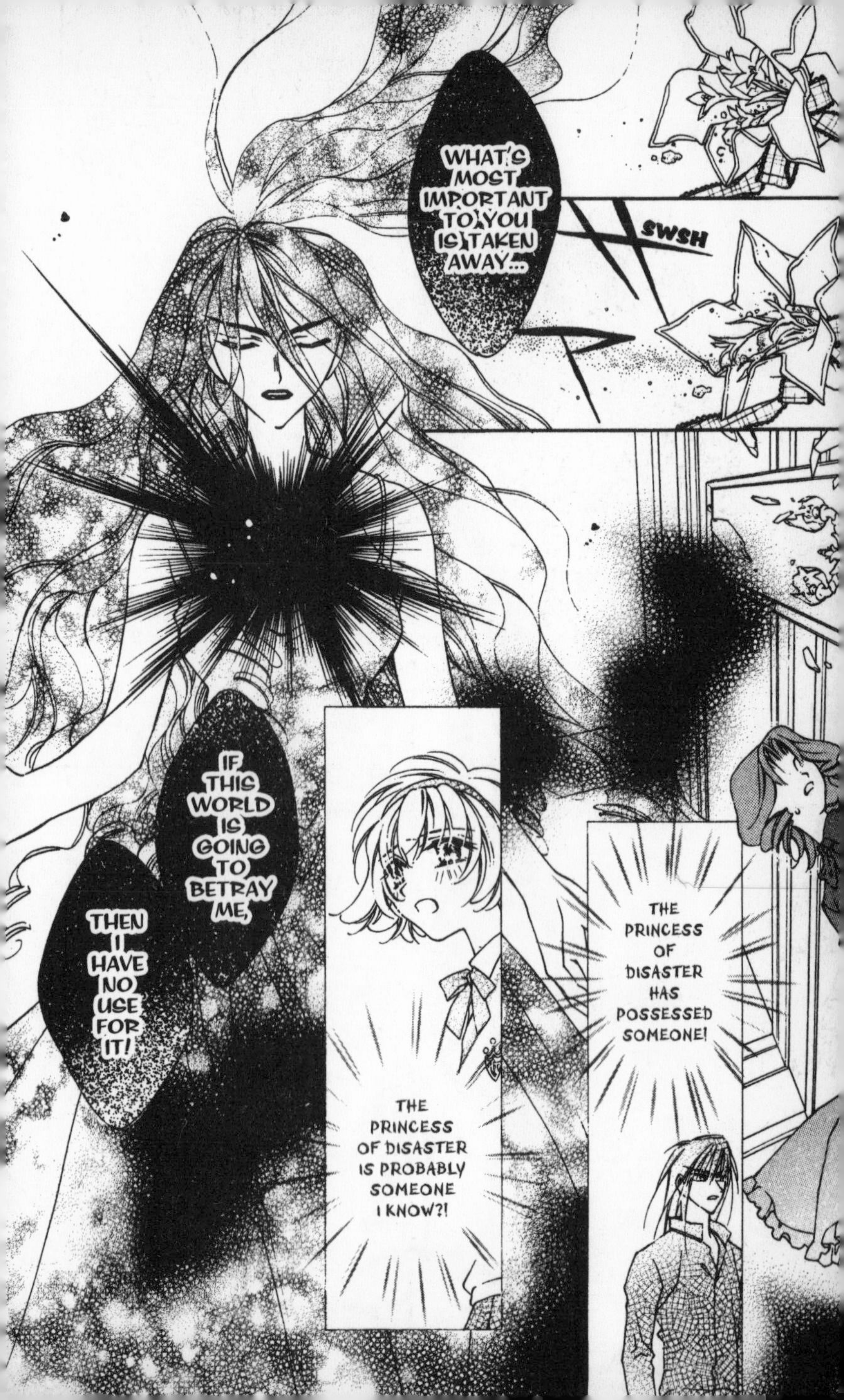
SWSH
THE PRINCESS OF DISASTER HAS POSSESSED SOMEONE!
THE PRINCESS OF DISASTER IS PROBABLY SOMEONE I KNOW?!
WHAT'S MOST IMPORTANT TO YOU IS TAKEN AWAY...
IF THIS WORLD IS GOING TO BETRAY ME,
THEN I HAVE NO USE FOR IT!

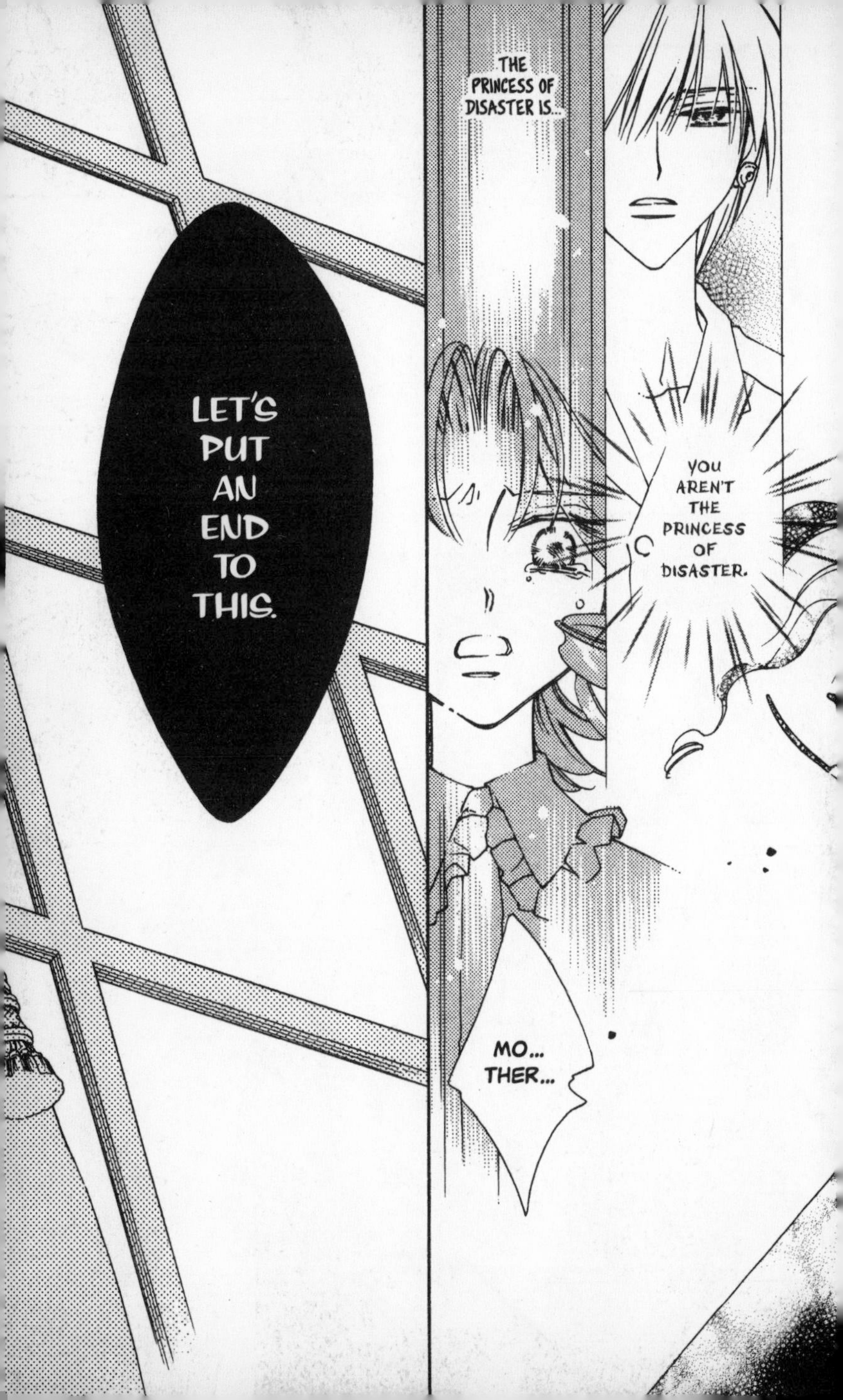
THE PRINCESS OF DISASTER IS...
YOU AREN'T THE PRINCESS OF DISASTER.
MO... THER...
LET'S PUT AN END TO THIS.

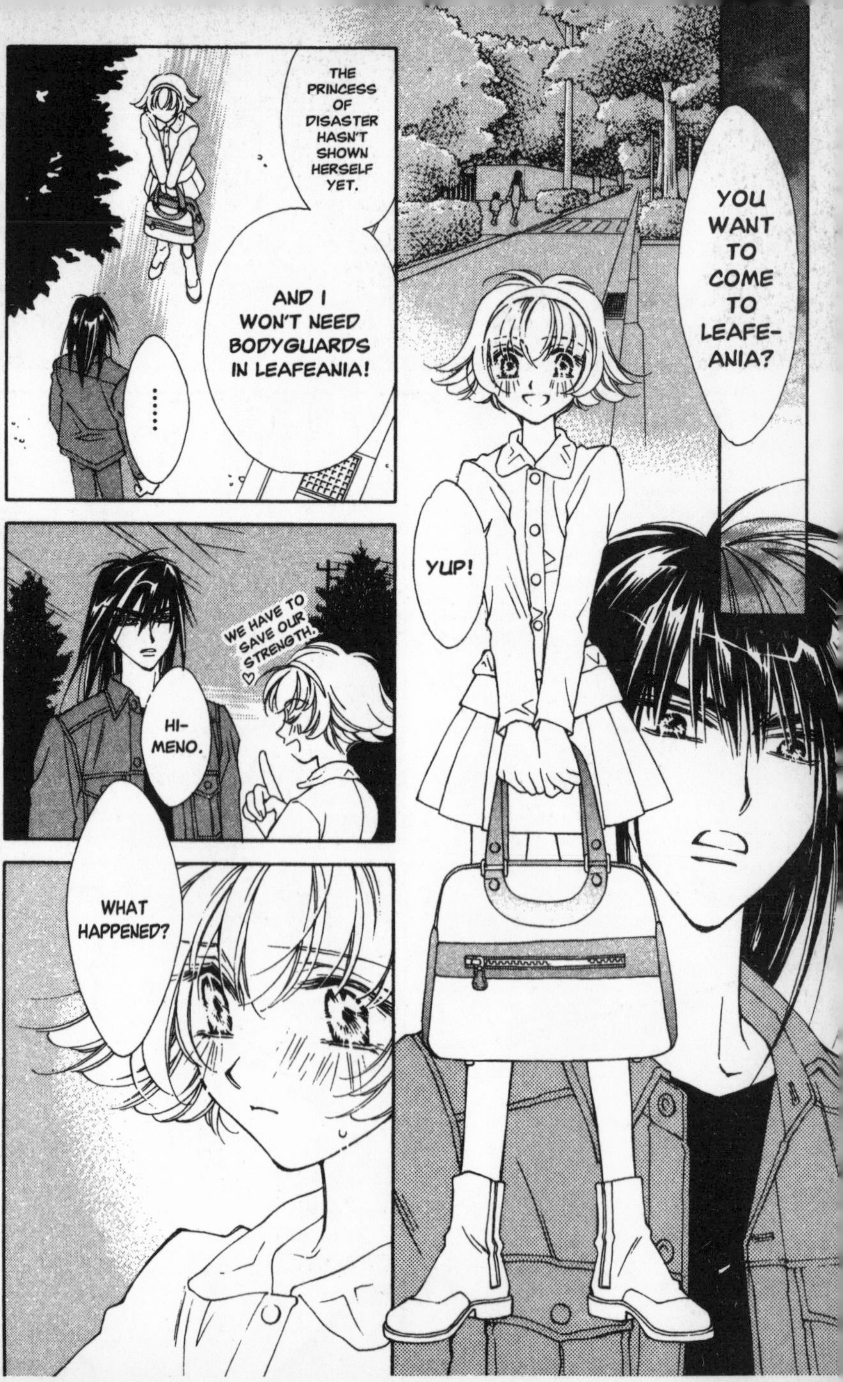
YOU WANT TO COME TO LEAFE-ANIA?
YUP!
THE PRINCESS OF DISASTER HASN'T SHOWN HERSELF YET.
AND I WON'T NEED BODYGUARDS IN LEAFEANIA!
......
WE HAVE TO SAVE OUR STRENGTH. ♡
HI-MENO.
WHAT HAPPENED?

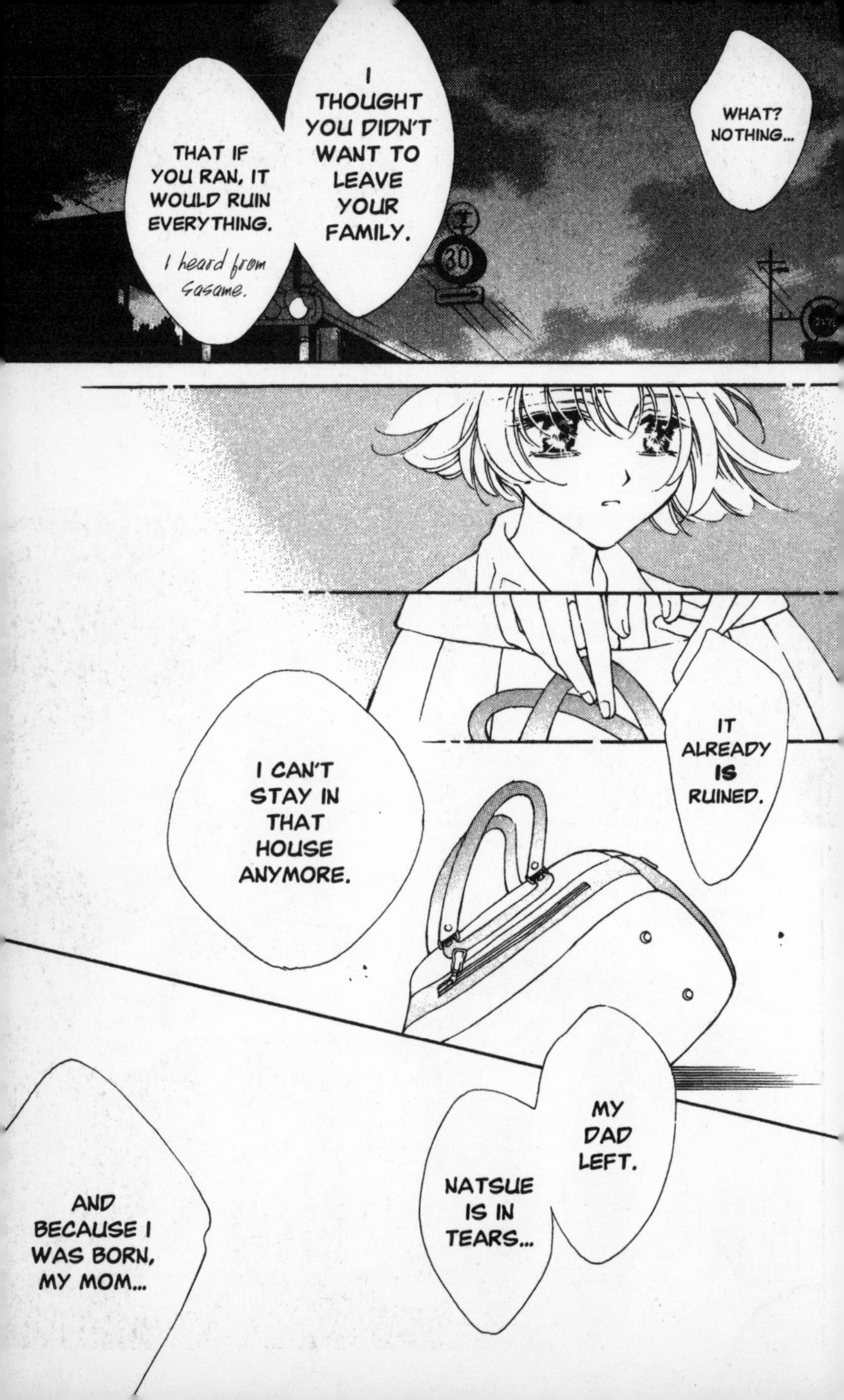
WHAT? NOTHING...
I THOUGHT YOU DIDN'T WANT TO LEAVE YOUR FAMILY.
THAT IF YOU RAN, IT WOULD RUIN EVERYTHING.
I heard from Sasame.
IT ALREADY IS RUINED.
I CAN'T STAY IN THAT HOUSE ANYMORE.
MY DAD LEFT.
NATSUE IS IN TEARS...
AND BECAUSE I WAS BORN, MY MOM...

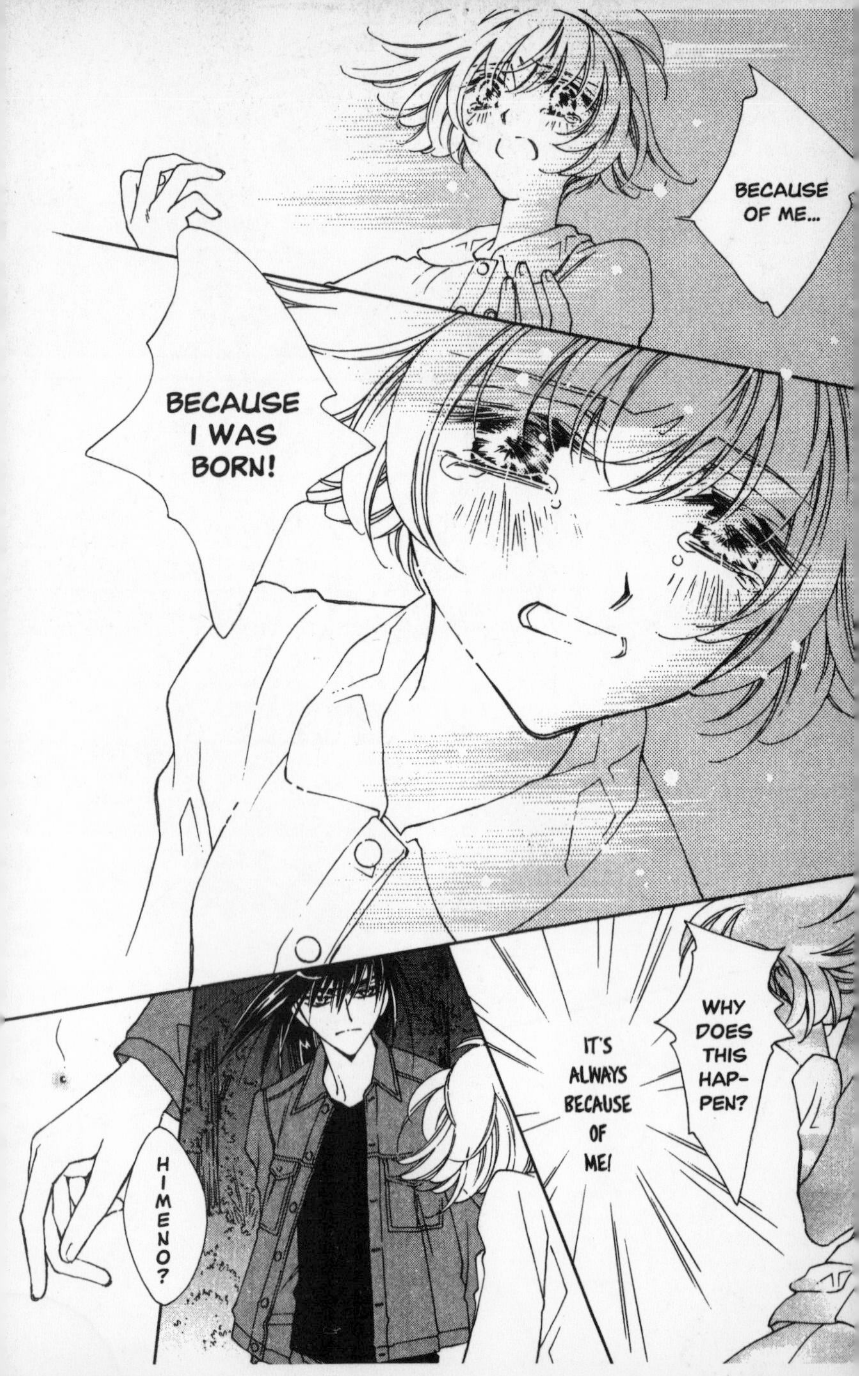
BECAUSE OF ME...
BECAUSE I WAS BORN!
WHY DOES THIS HAP-PEN?
IT'S ALWAYS BECAUSE OF ME!
HIMENO?

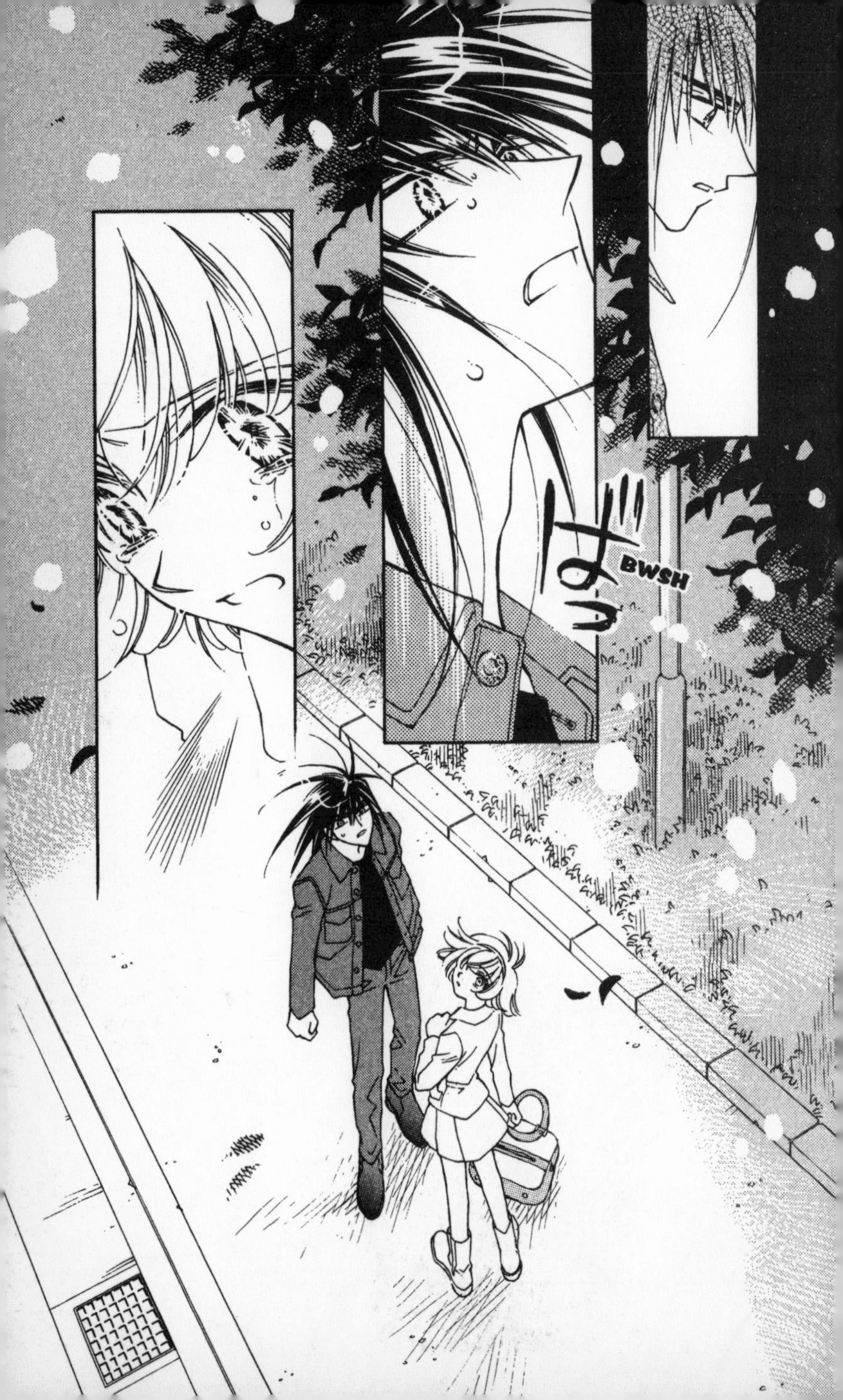
ばっ
BWSH

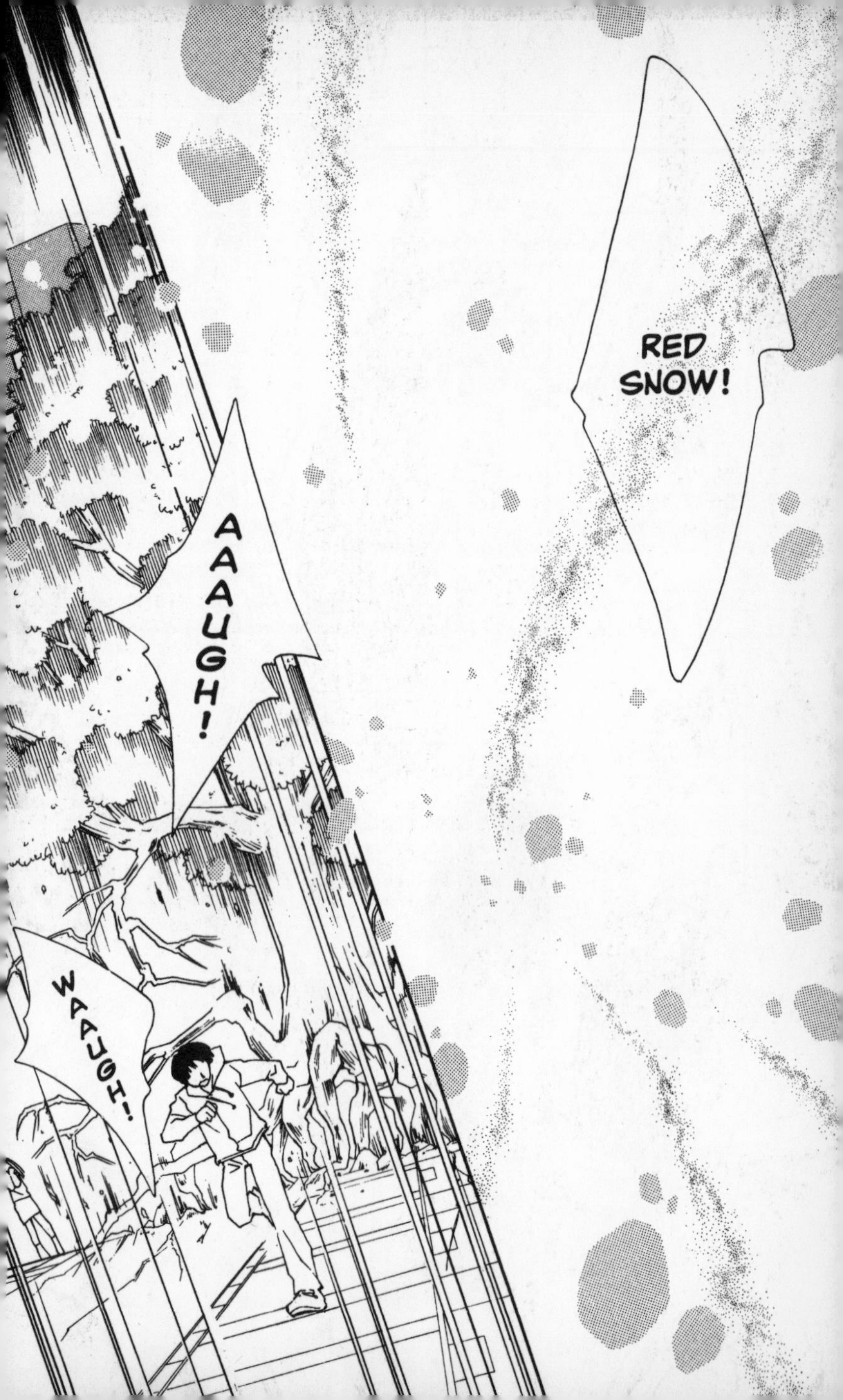
RED SNOW!
AAAUGH!
WAAUGH!

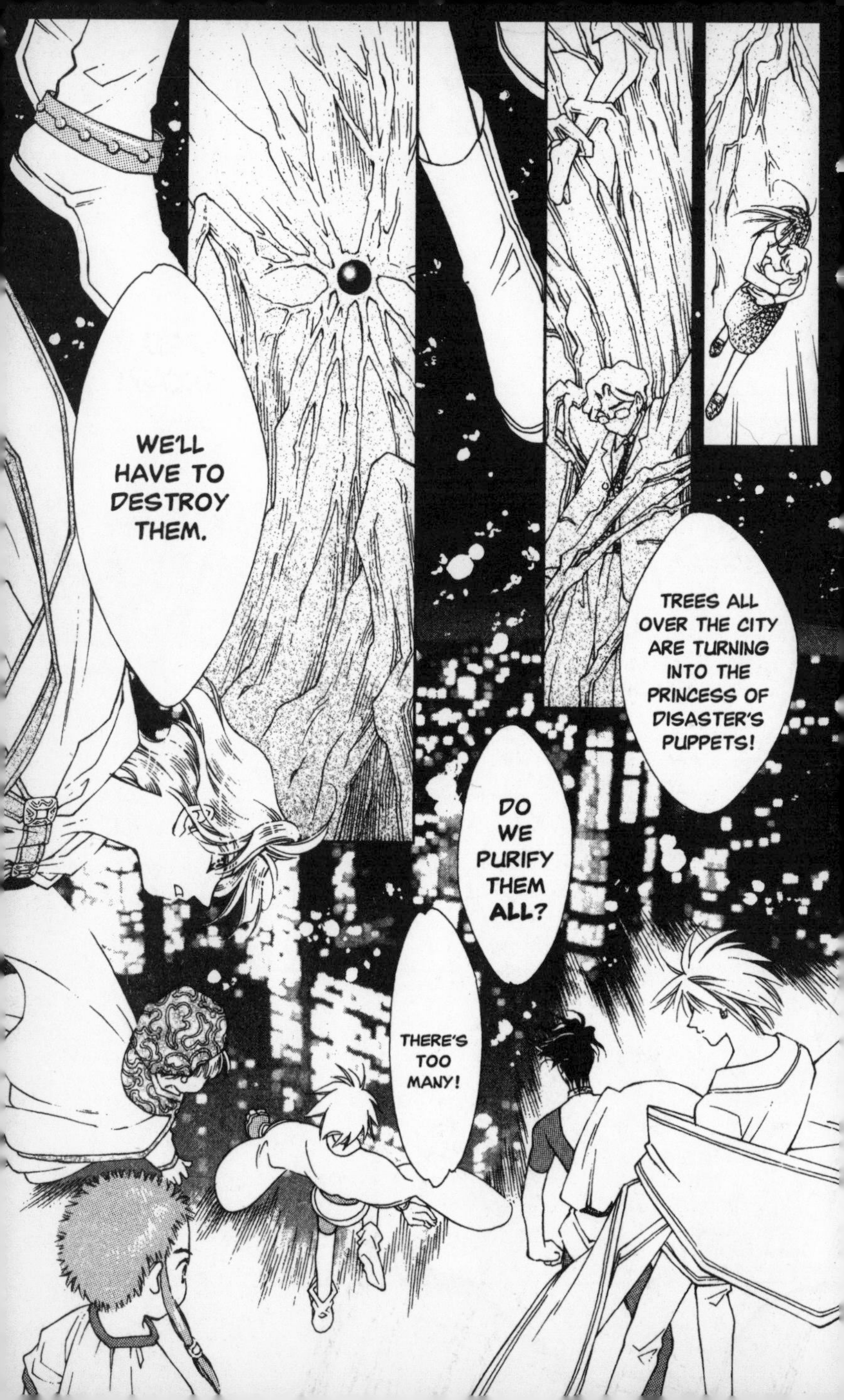
TREES ALL OVER THE CITY ARE TURNING INTO THE PRINCESS OF DISASTER'S PUPPETS!
DO WE PURIFY THEM ALL?
THERE'S TOO MANY!
WE'LL HAVE TO DESTROY THEM.

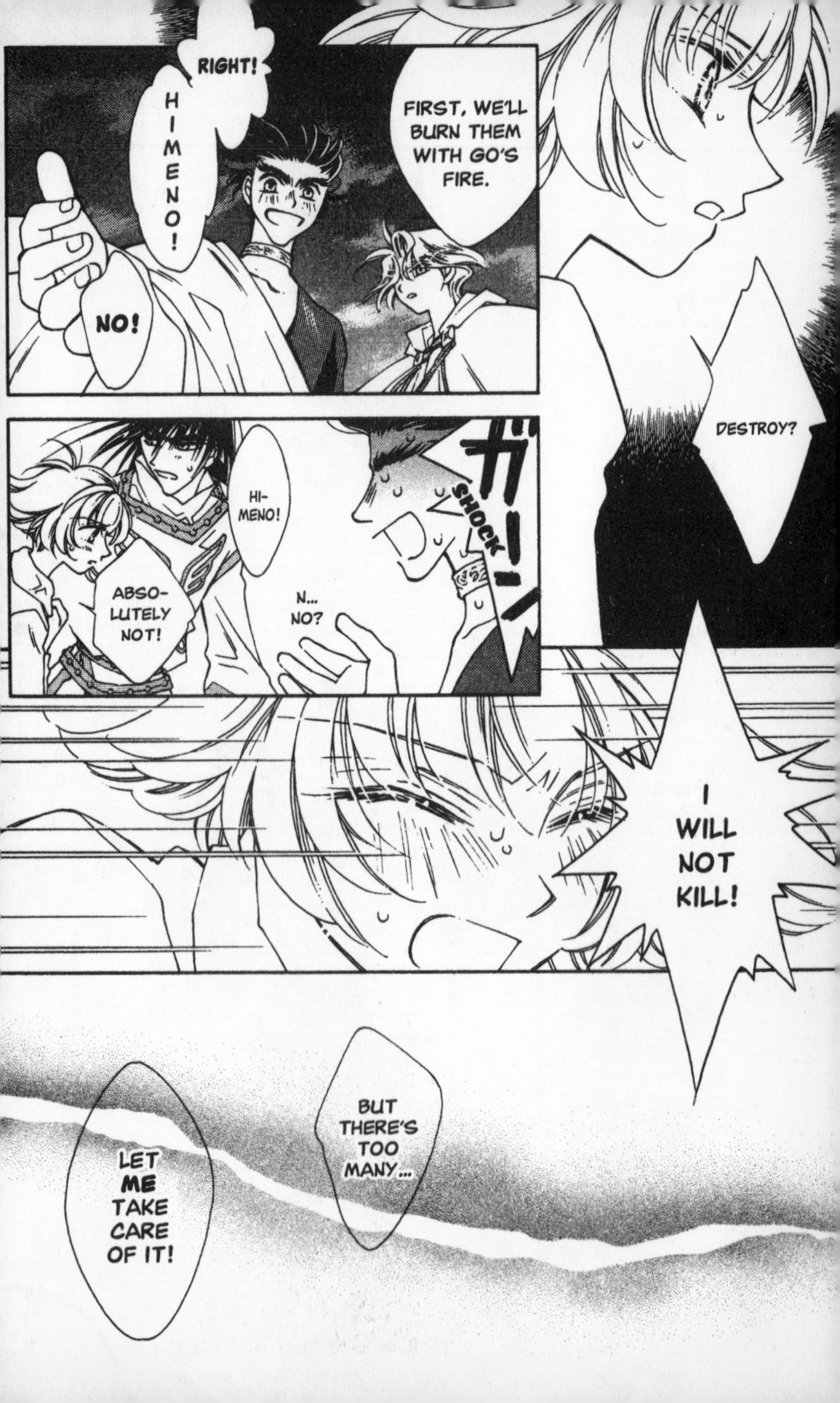
DESTROY?
FIRST, WE'LL BURN THEM WITH GO'S FIRE.
RIGHT!
HIMENO!
NO!
SHOCK
HI-MENO!
N... NO?
ABSO-LUTELY NOT!
I WILL NOT KILL!
BUT THERE'S TOO MANY...
LET ME TAKE CARE OF IT!

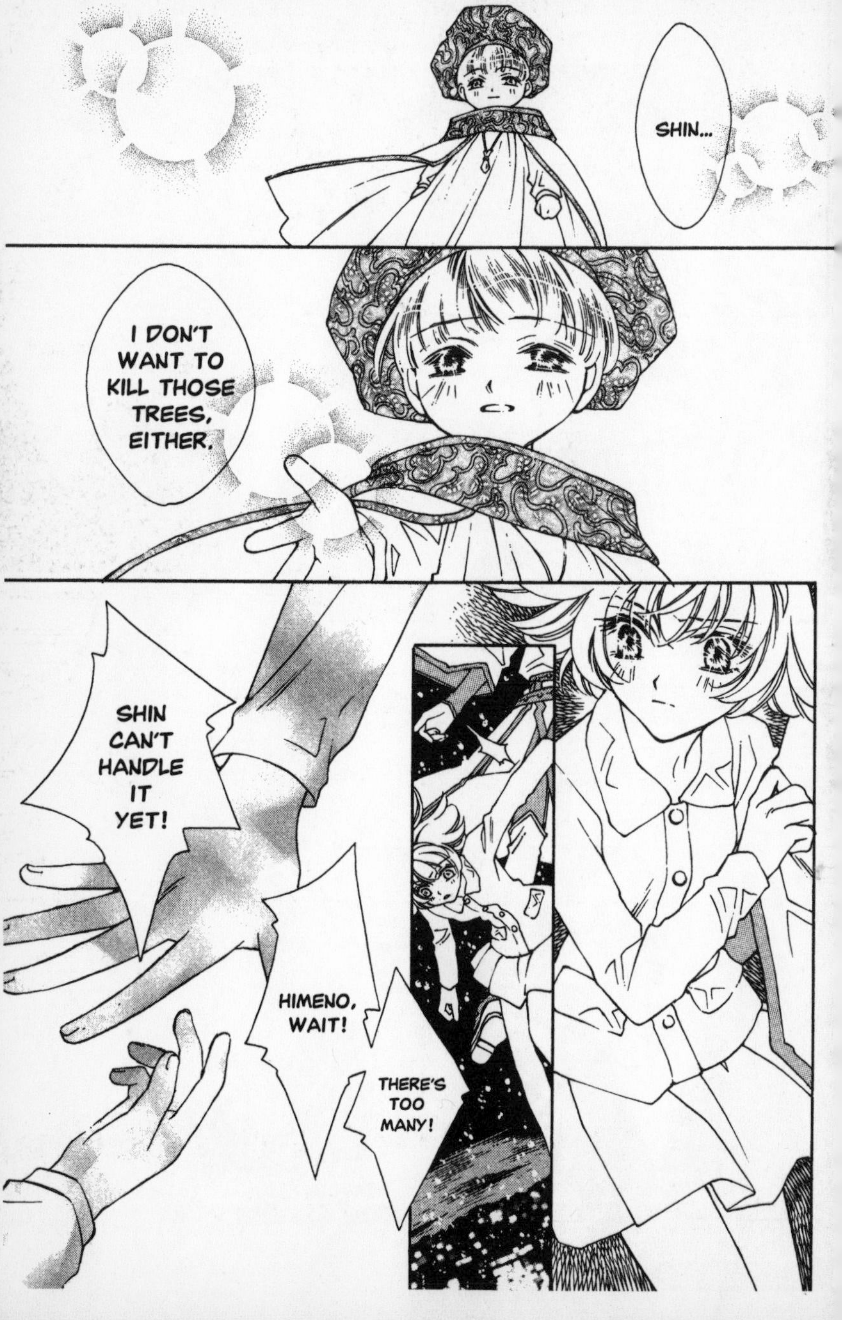
SHIN...
I DON'T WANT TO KILL THOSE TREES, EITHER.
THERE'S TOO MANY!
HIMENO, WAIT!
SHIN CAN'T HANDLE IT YET!

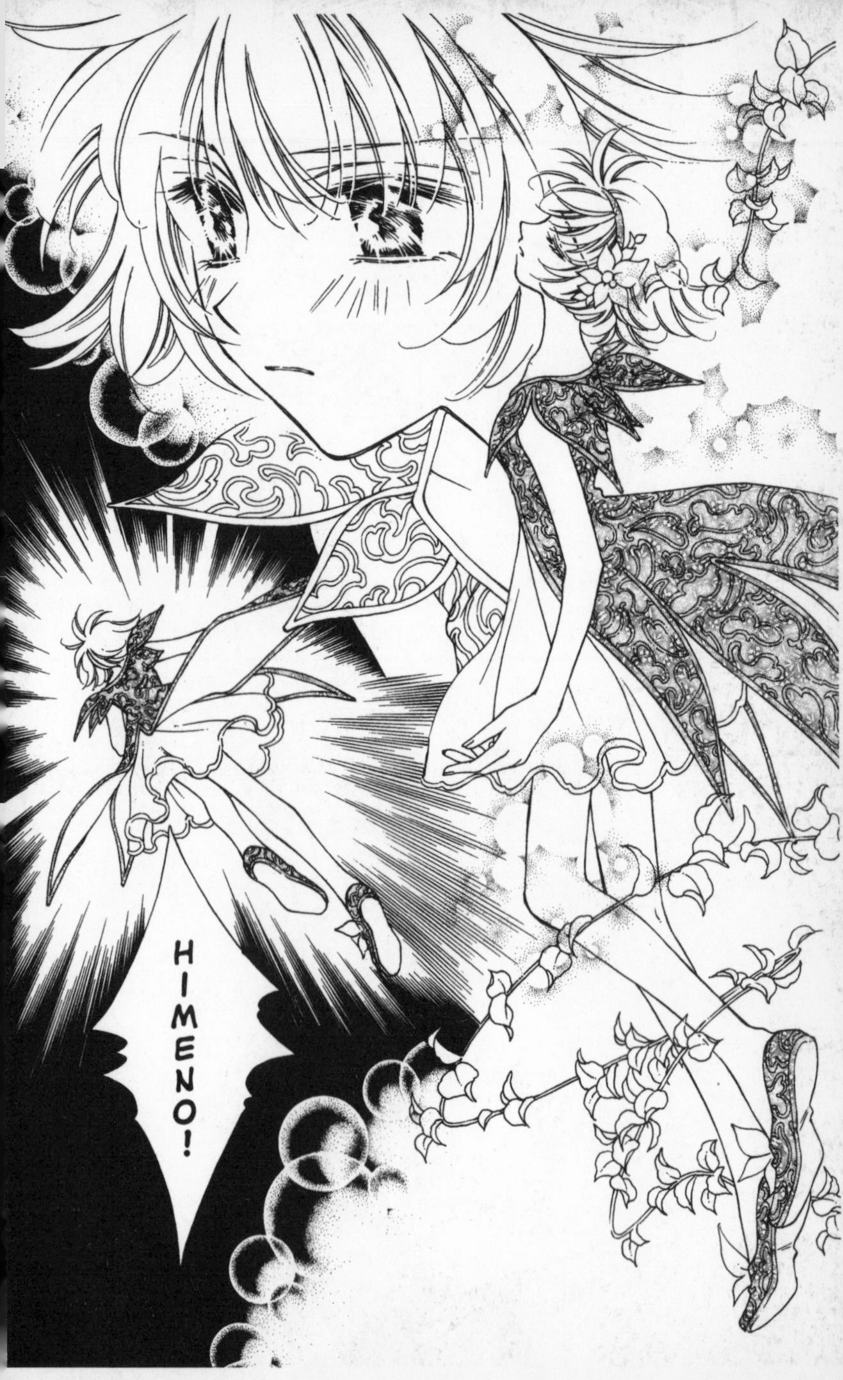
HIMENO!

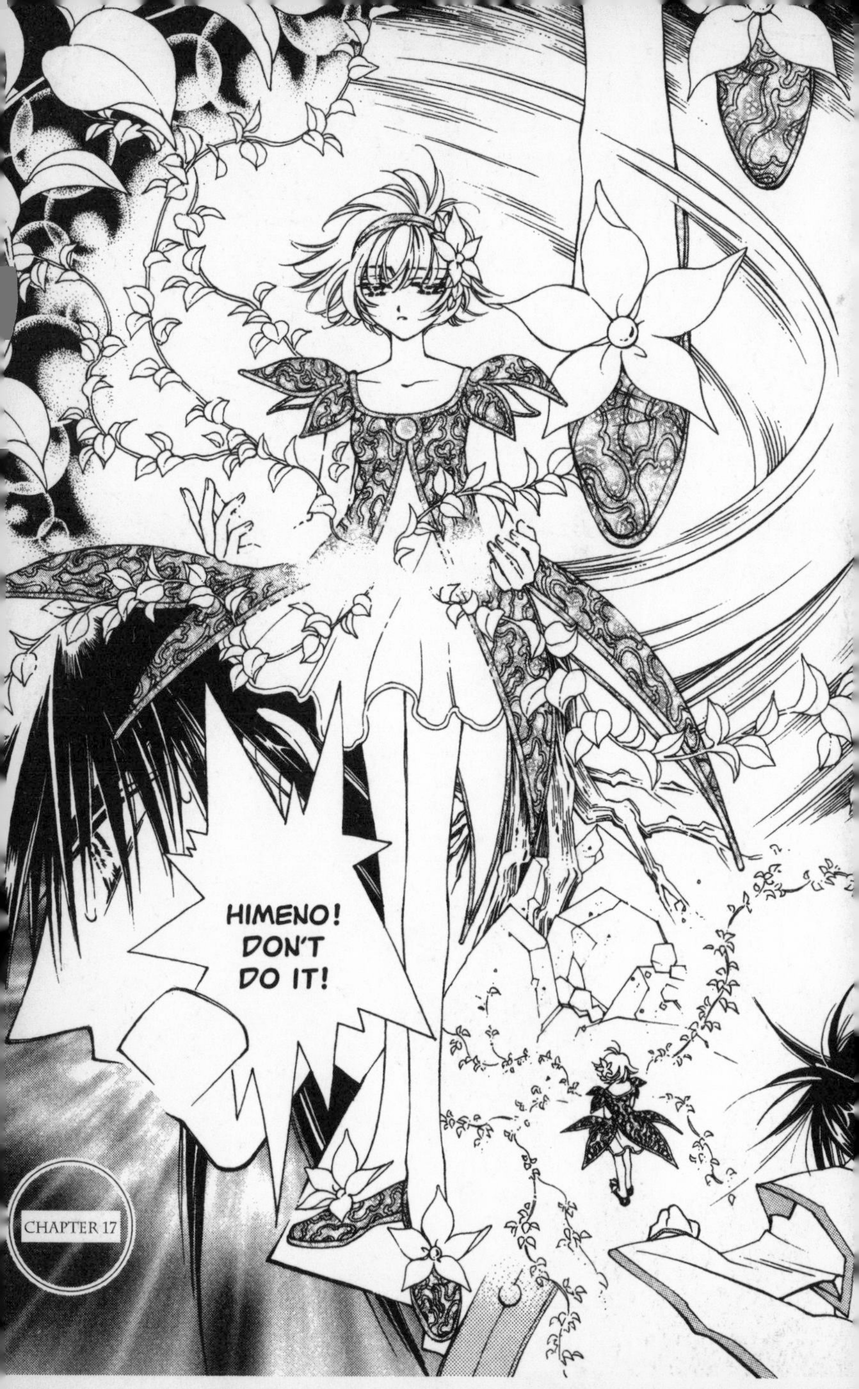
HIMENO! DON'T DO IT!
CHAPTER 17

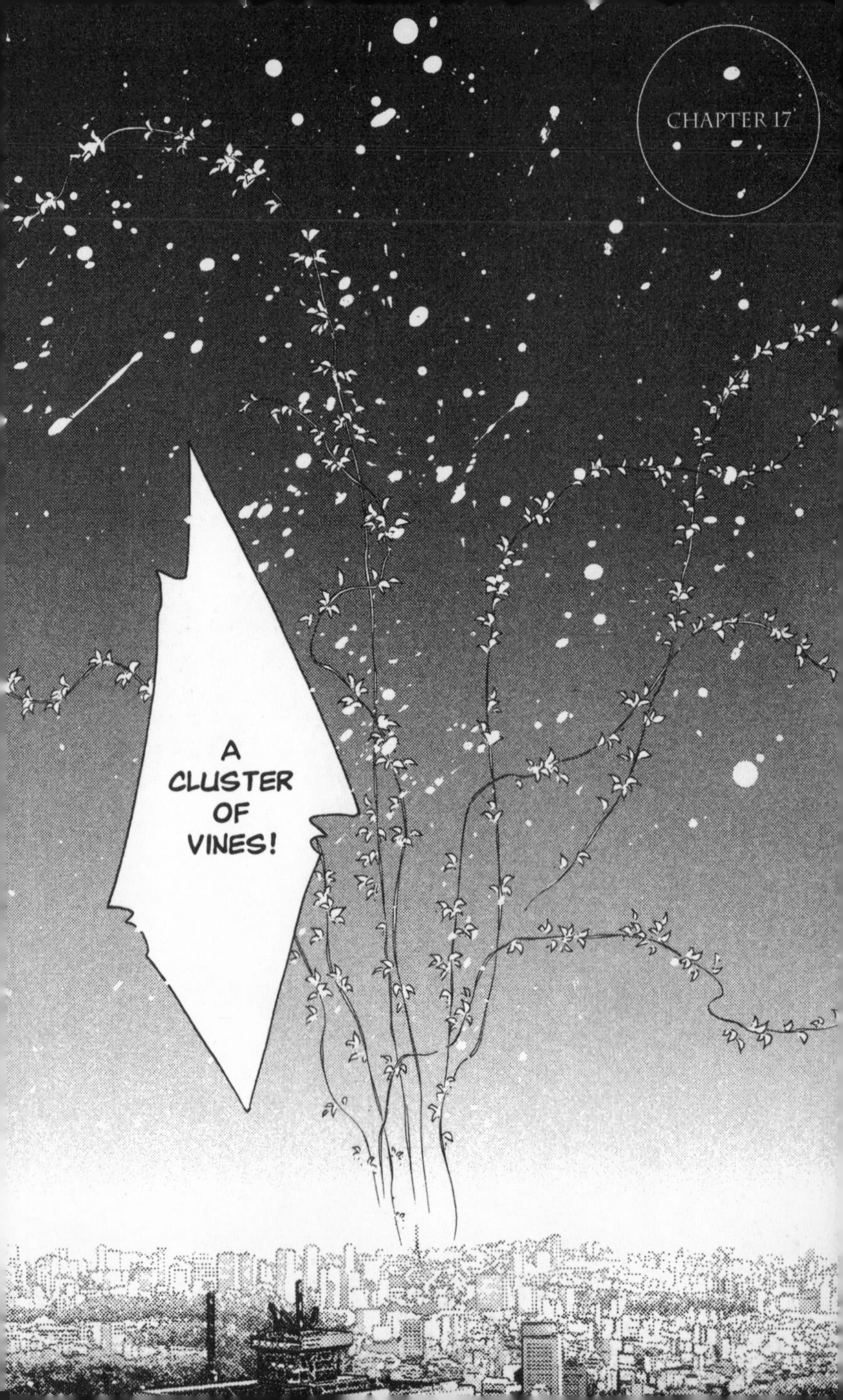
CHAPTER 17
A CLUSTER OF VINES!

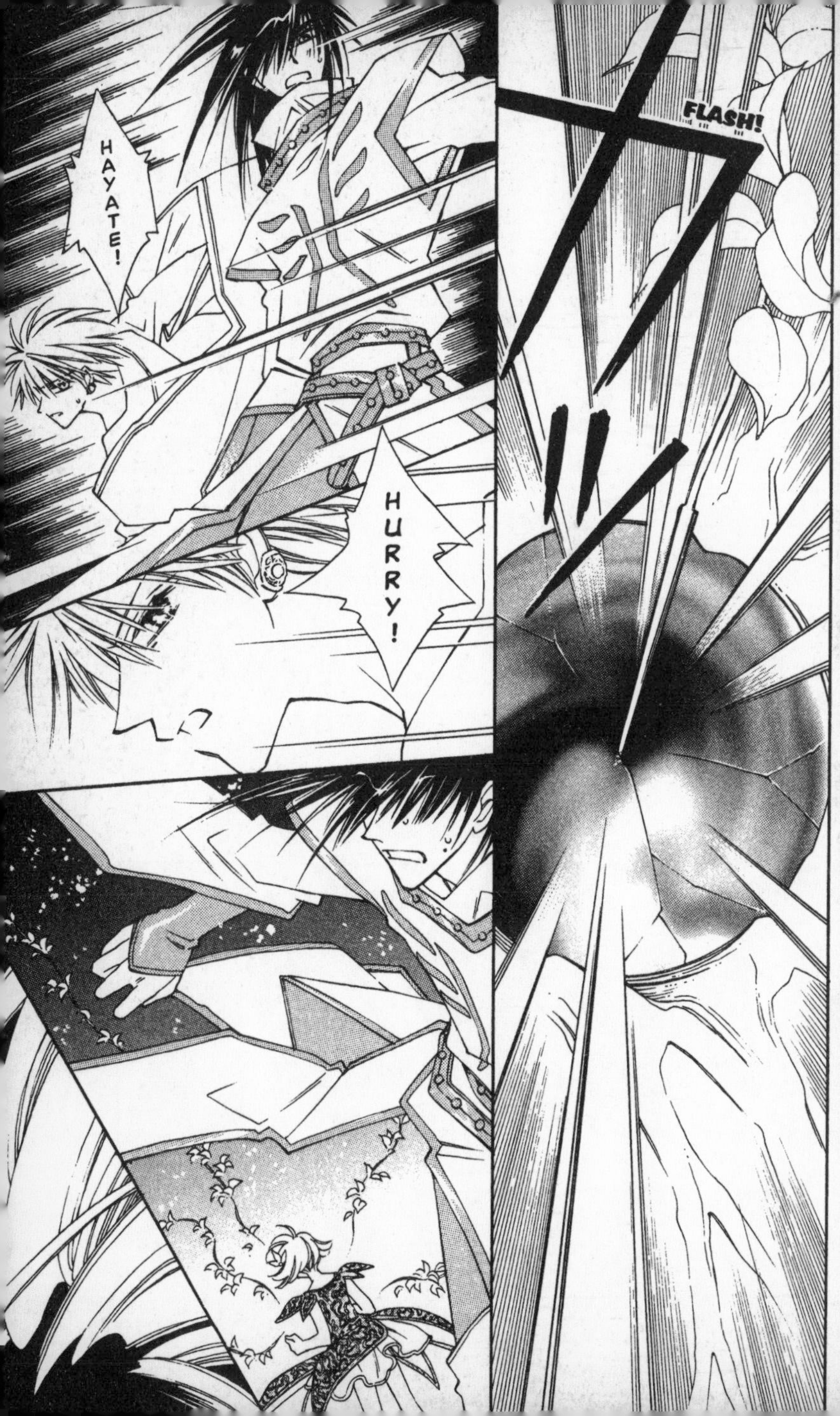
FLASH!
HAYATE!
HURRY!

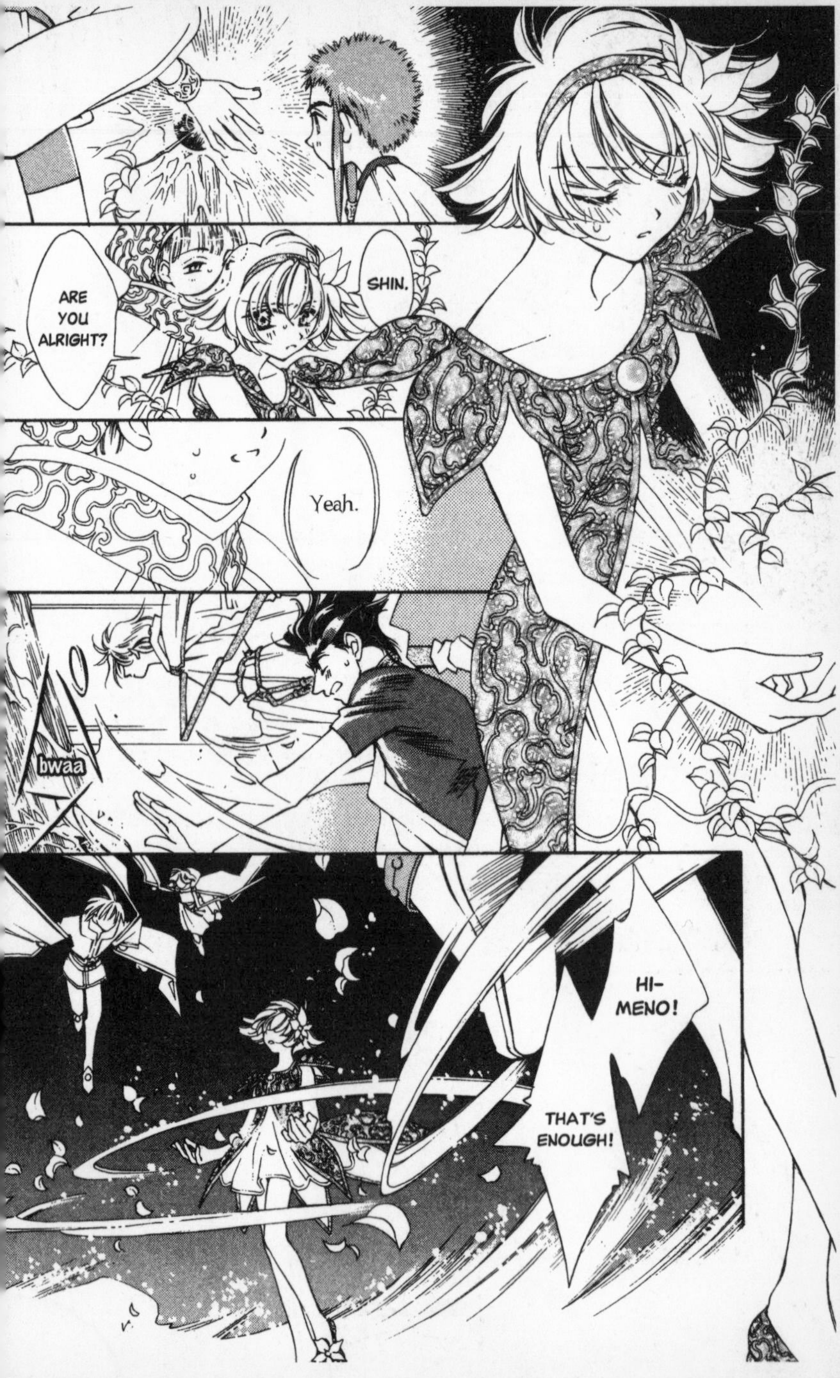
SHIN.
ARE YOU ALRIGHT?
Yeah.
bwaa
HI-MENO!
THAT'S ENOUGH!

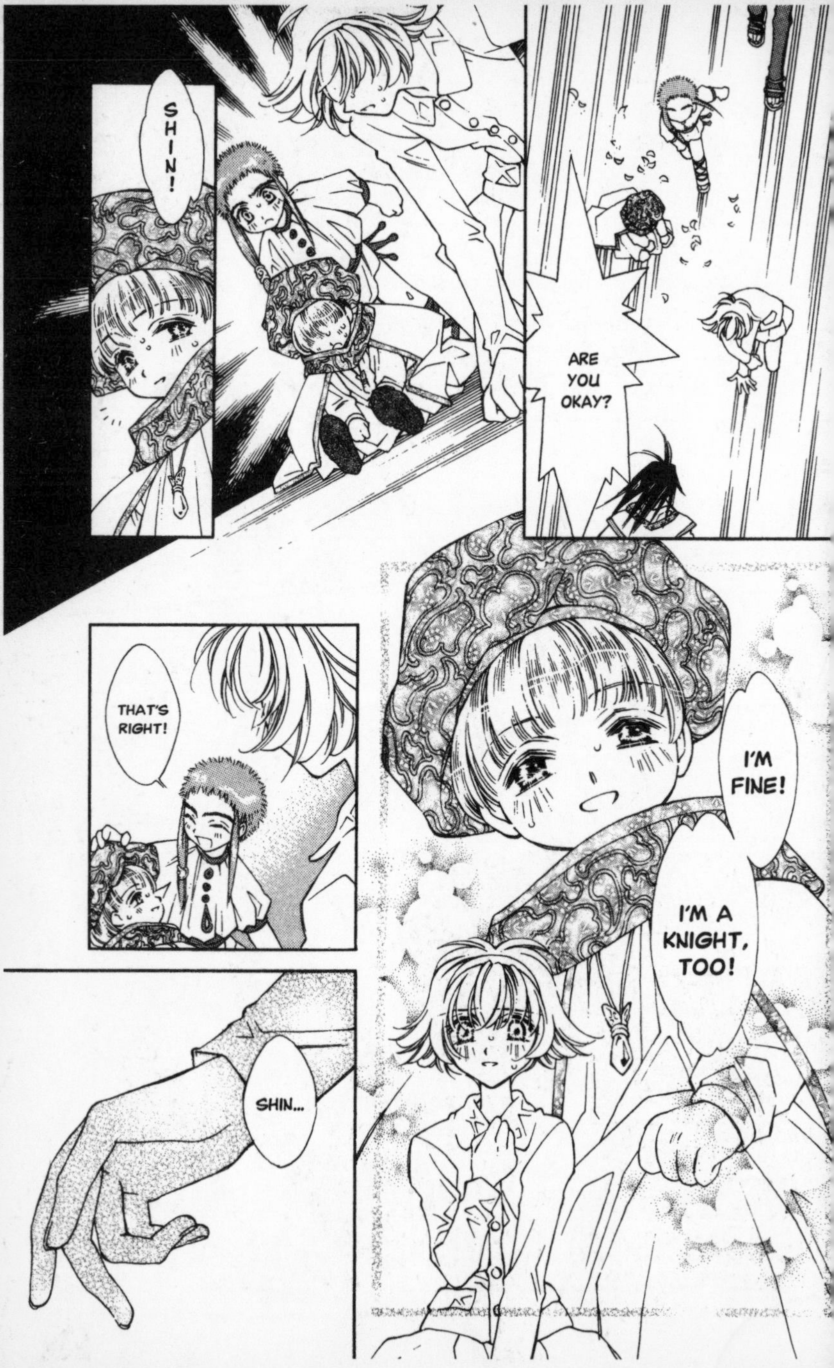
ARE YOU OKAY?
SHIN!
I'M FINE!
I'M A KNIGHT, TOO!
THAT'S RIGHT!
SHIN...

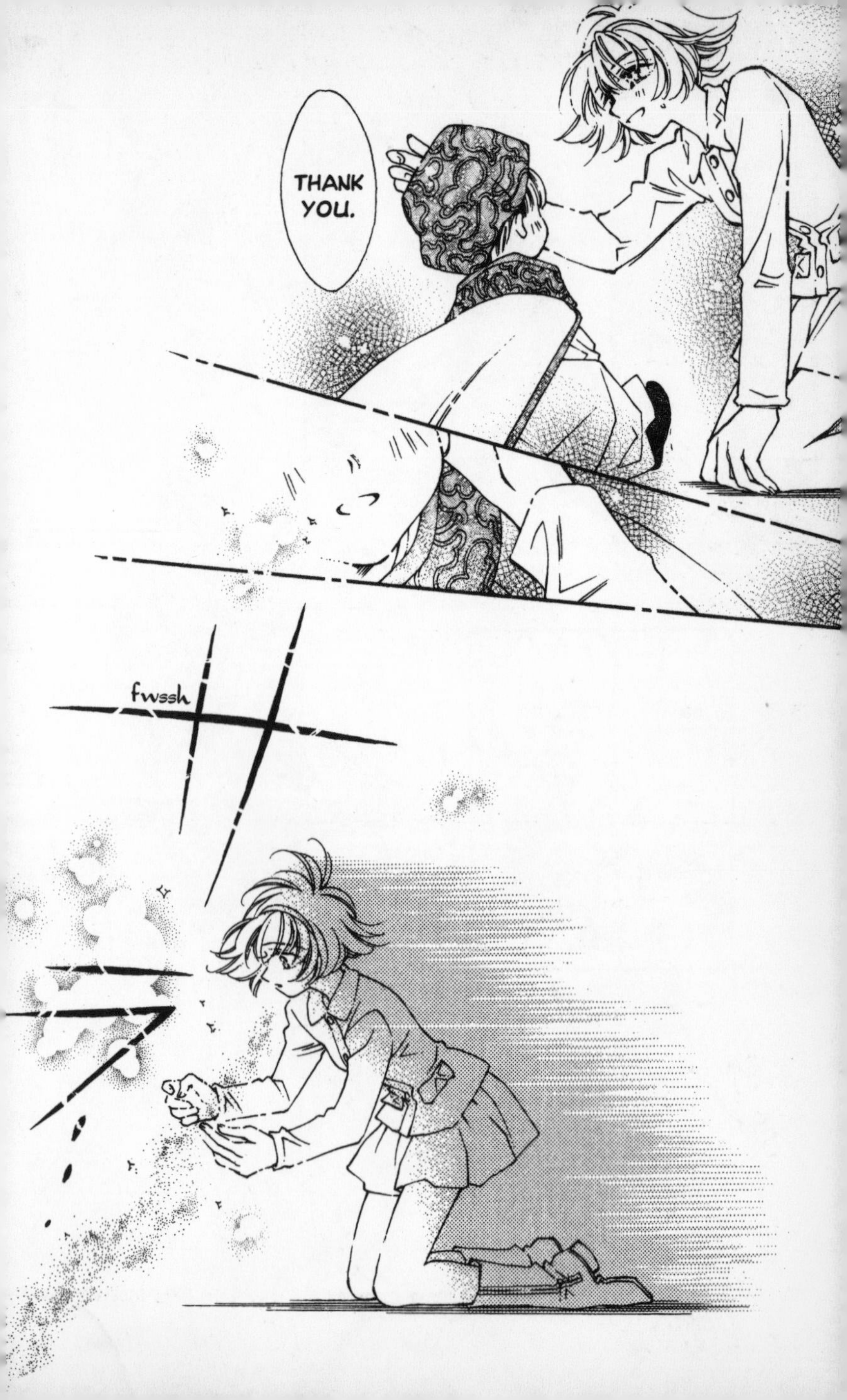
THANK YOU.
fwssh

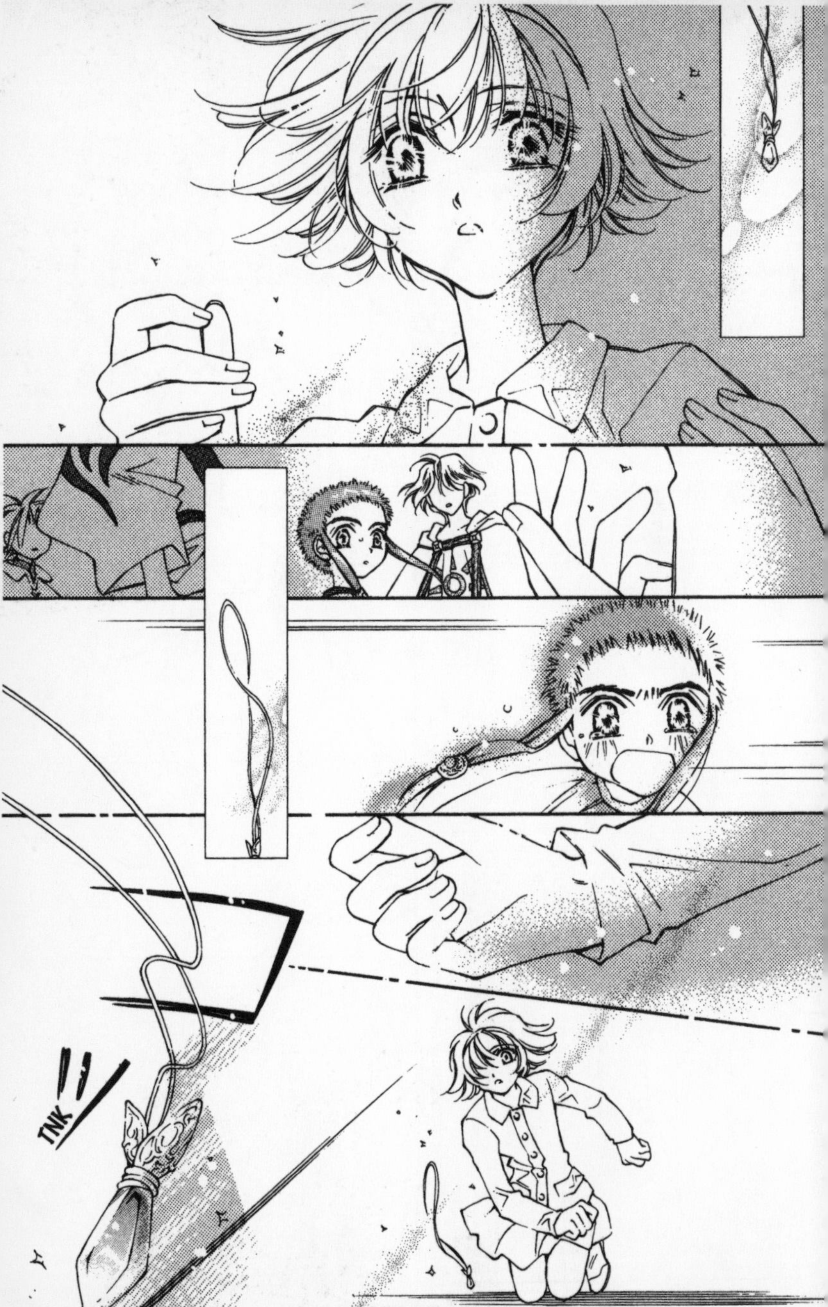
TNK!!

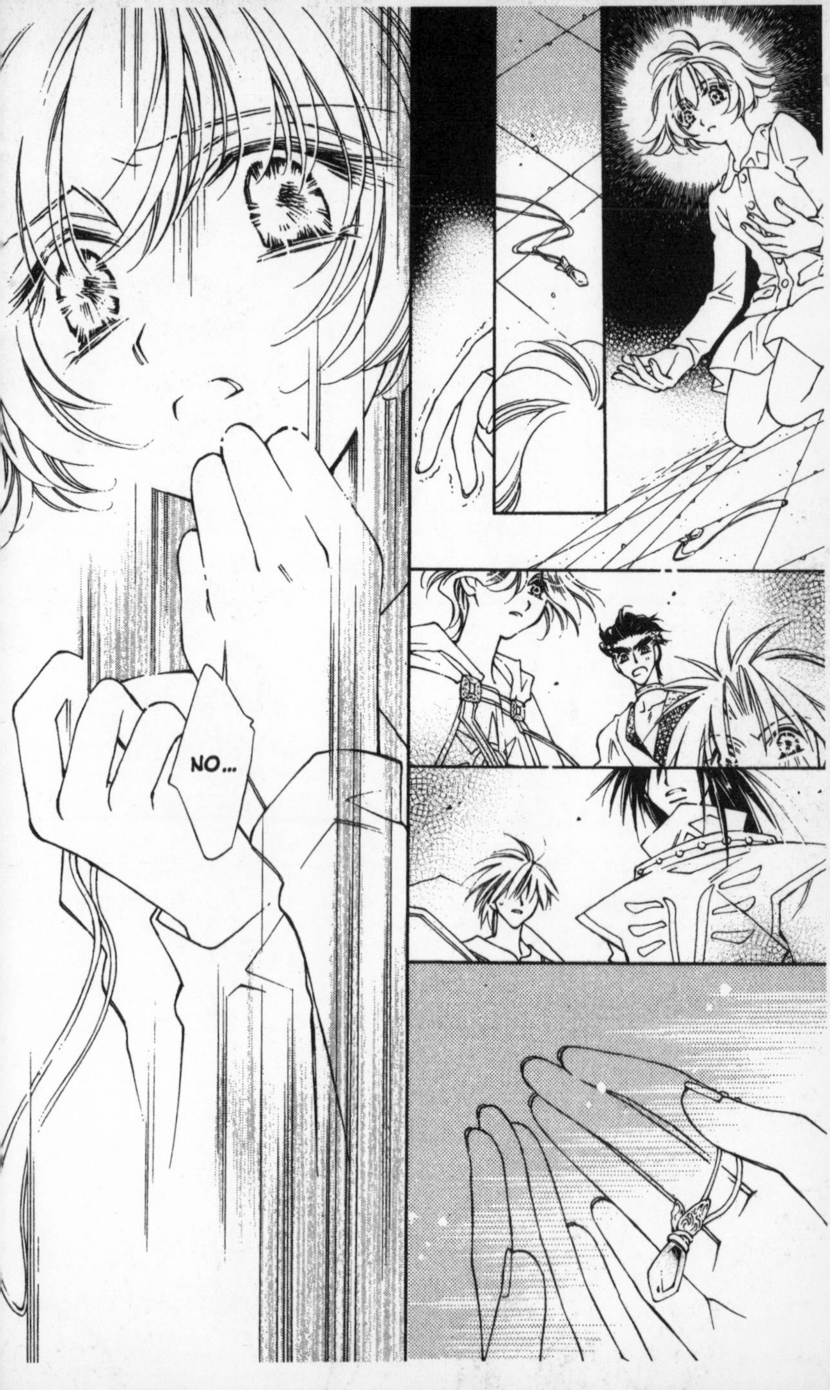
NO...

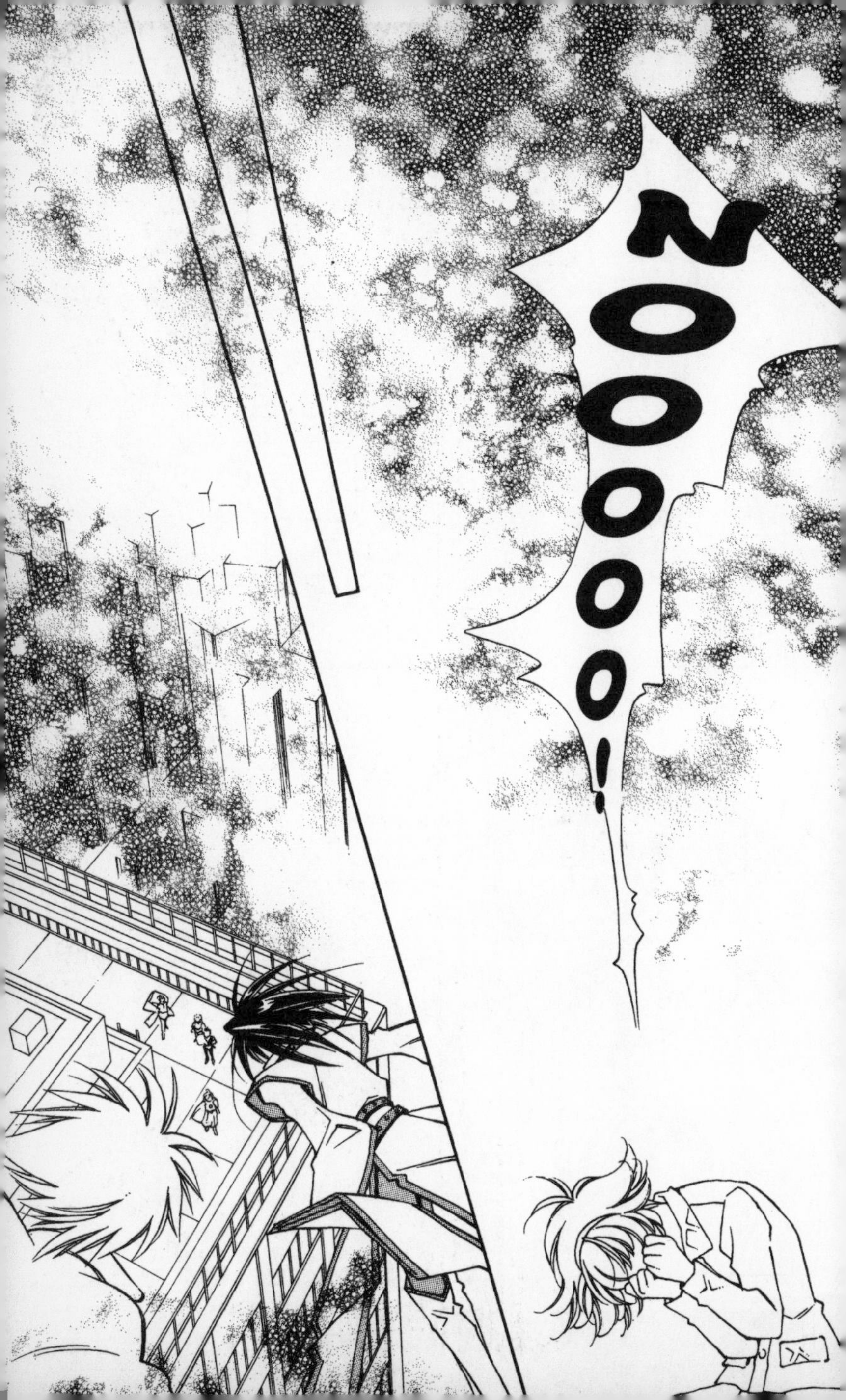
NOOOOOO!

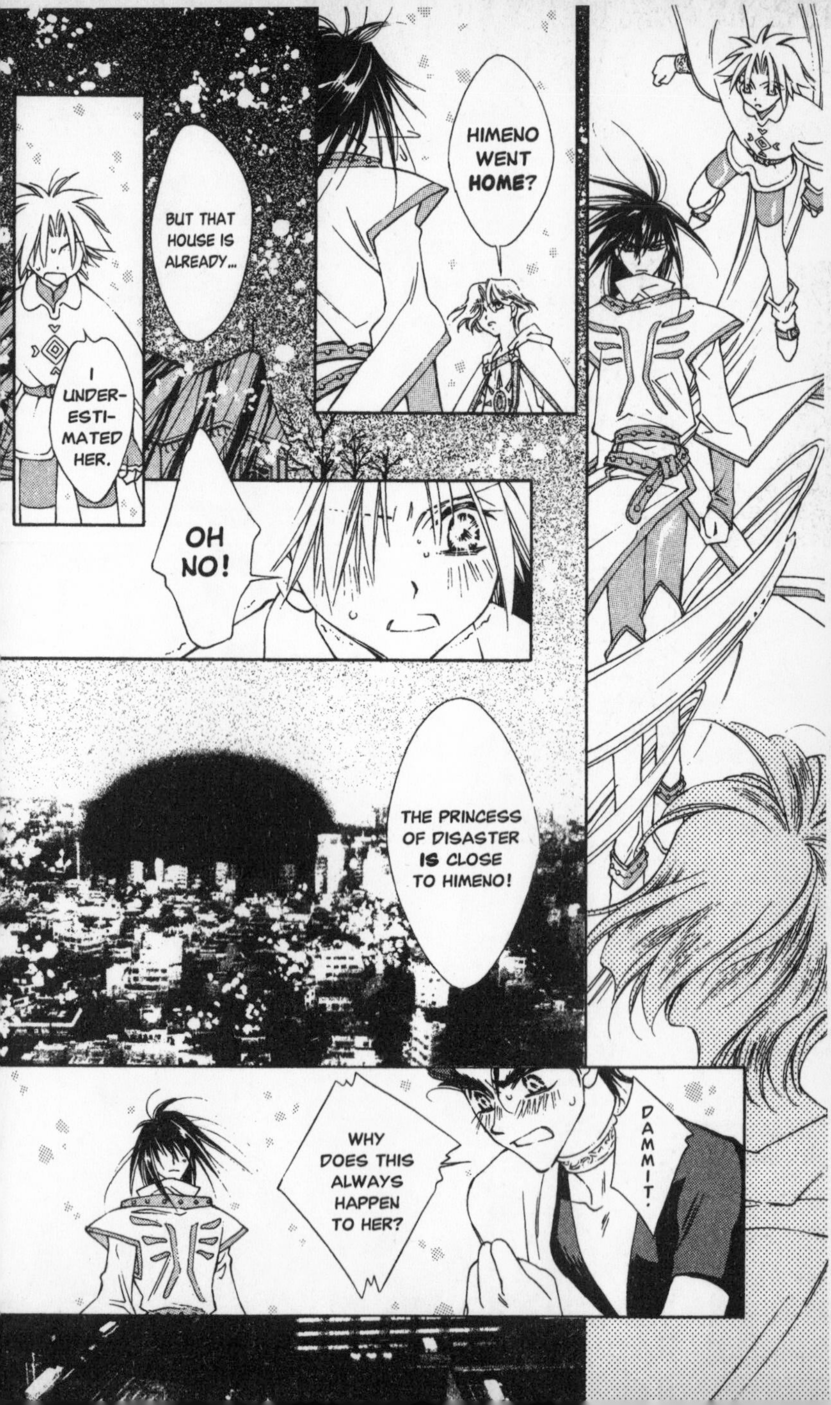
HIMENO WENT **HOME**?
BUT THAT HOUSE IS ALREADY...
I UNDER-ESTI-MATED HER.
OH NO!
THE PRINCESS OF DISASTER **IS** CLOSE TO HIMENO!
DAMMIT.
WHY DOES THIS ALWAYS HAPPEN TO HER?

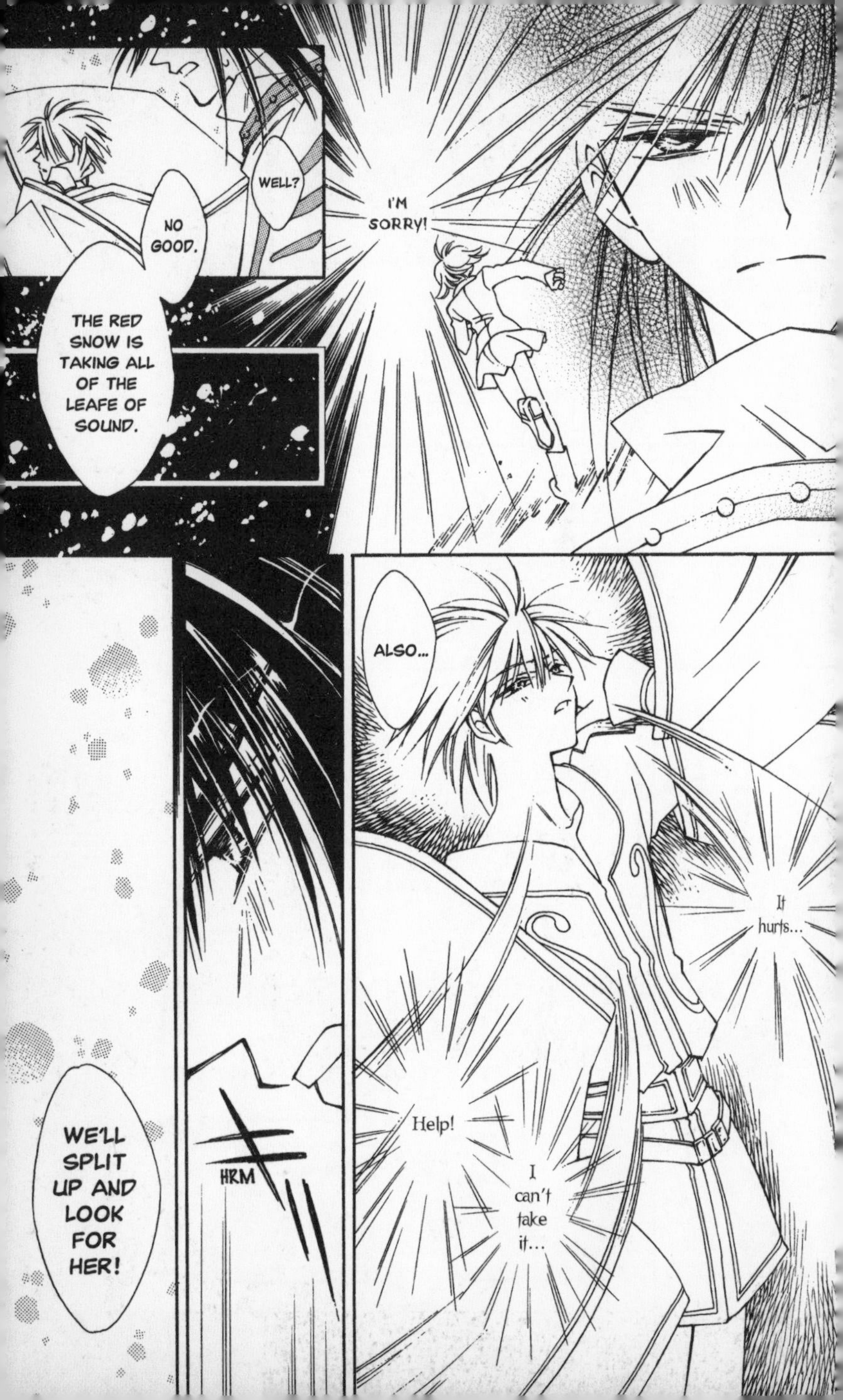
I'M SORRY!
WELL?
NO GOOD.
THE RED SNOW IS TAKING ALL OF THE LEAFE OF SOUND.
ALSO...
It hurts...
Help!
I can't take it...
HRM
WE'LL SPLIT UP AND LOOK FOR HER!

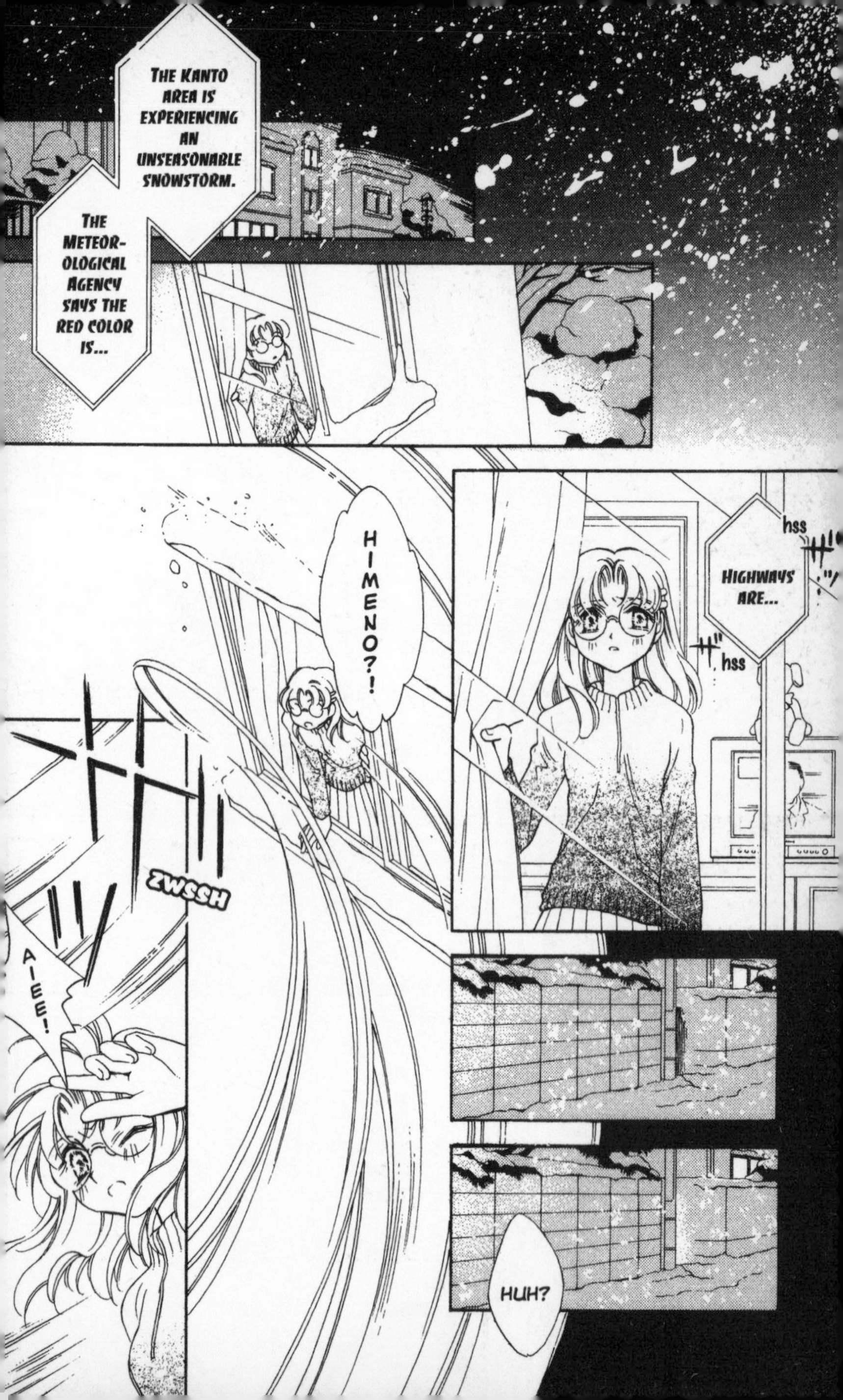
THE KANTO AREA IS EXPERIENCING AN UNSEASONABLE SNOWSTORM.
THE METEOR-OLOGICAL AGENCY SAYS THE RED COLOR IS...
hss
HIGHWAYS ARE...
hss
HUH?
HIMENO?!
ZWSSH
AIEEE!

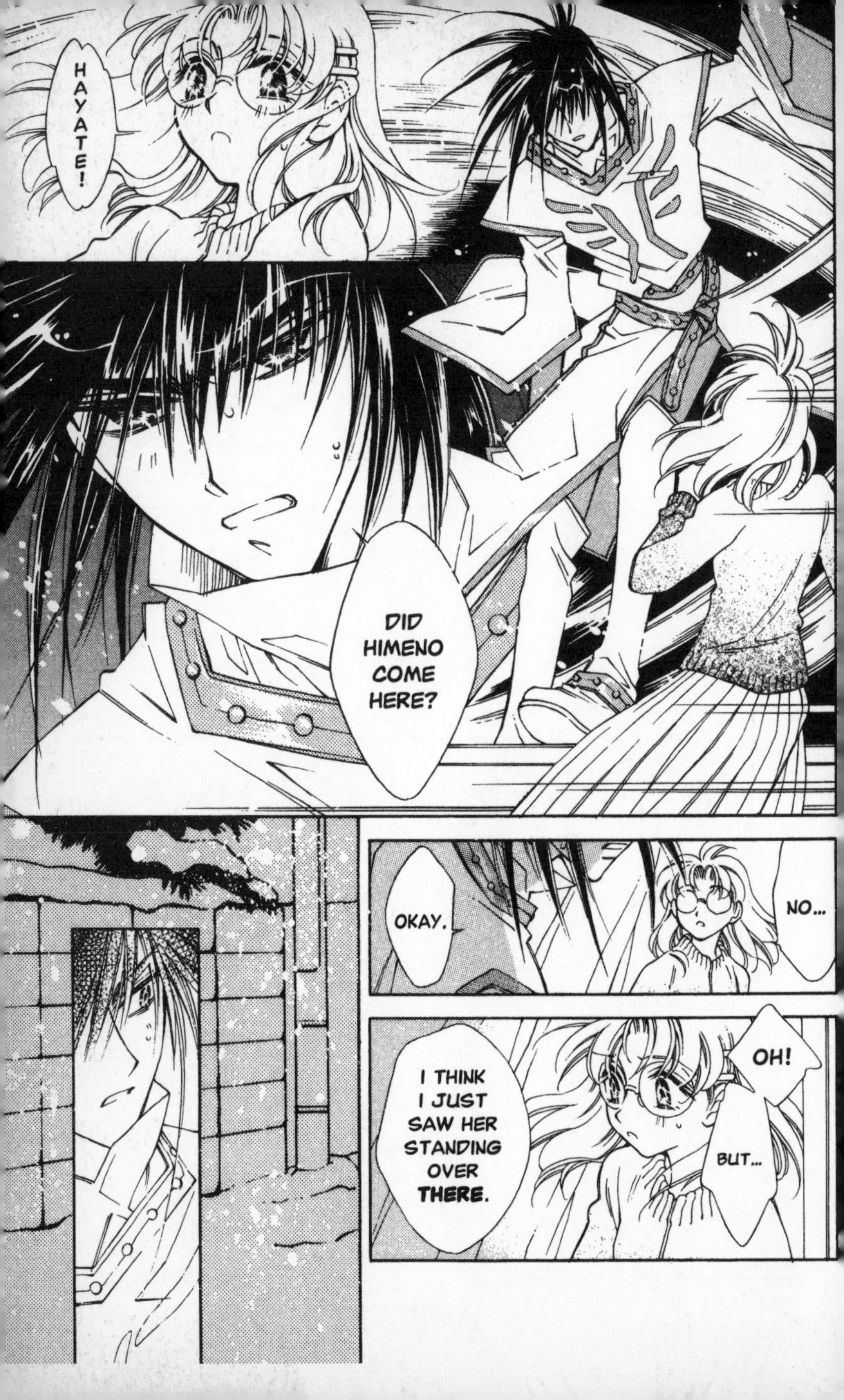
HAYATE!
DID HIMENO COME HERE?
NO...
OKAY.
OH!
BUT...
I THINK I JUST SAW HER STANDING OVER THERE.

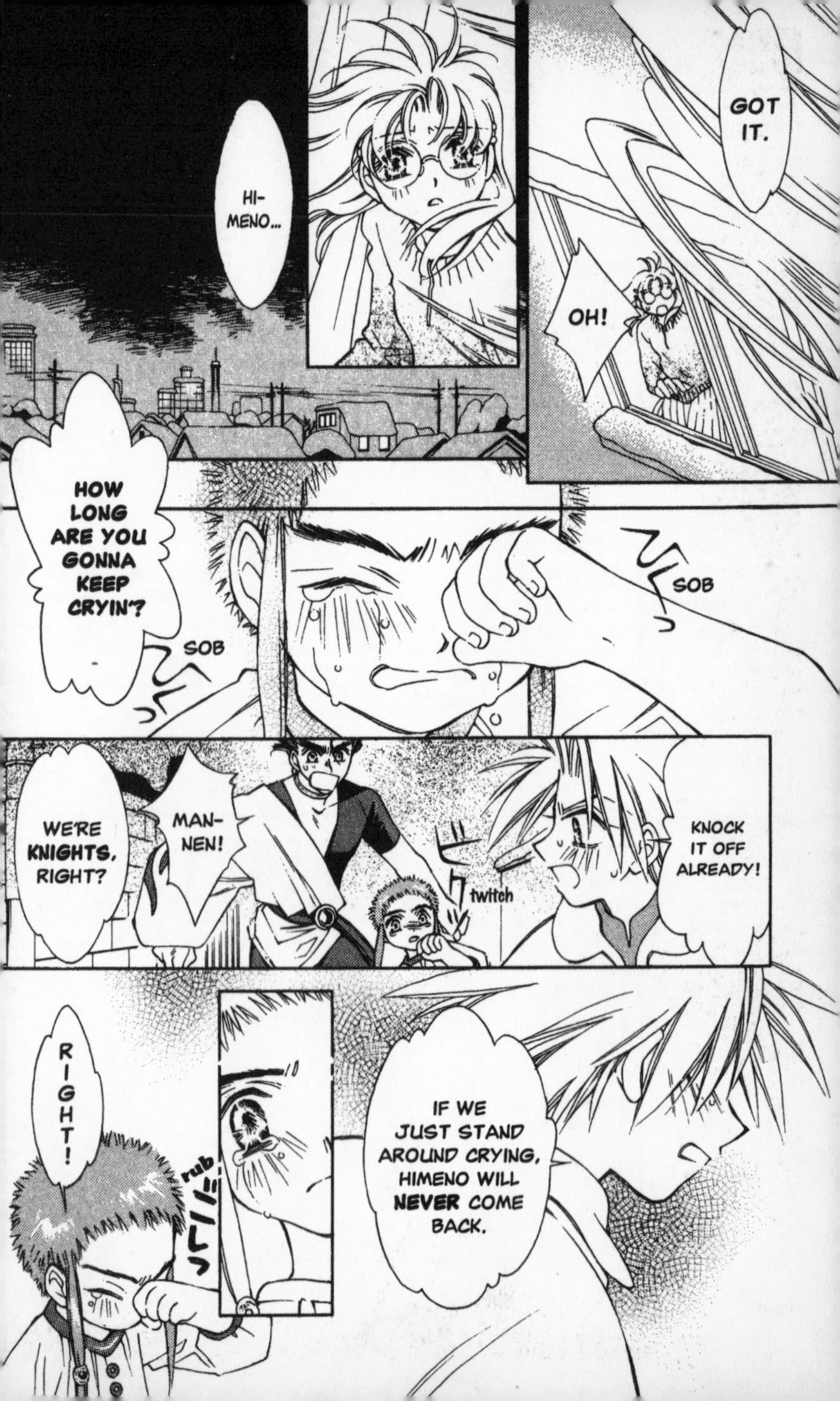

GOT IT.
OH!
HI-MENO...
SOB
HOW LONG ARE YOU GONNA KEEP CRYIN'?
SOB
KNOCK IT OFF ALREADY!
twitch
MAN-NEN!
WE'RE KNIGHTS, RIGHT?
IF WE JUST STAND AROUND CRYING, HIMENO WILL NEVER COME BACK.
rub
RIGHT!

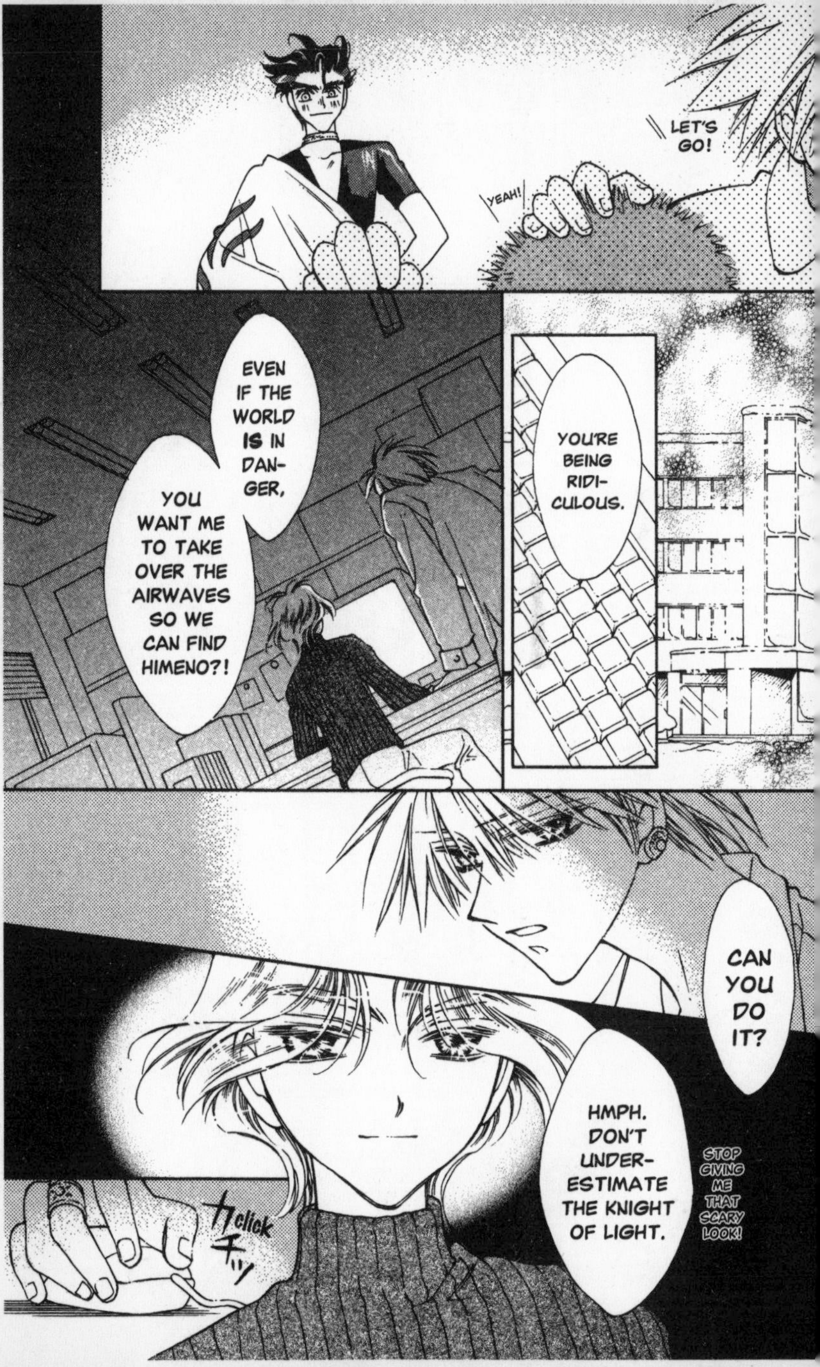
LET'S GO!
YEAH!
YOU'RE BEING RIDICULOUS.
EVEN IF THE WORLD IS IN DANGER,
YOU WANT ME TO TAKE OVER THE AIRWAVES SO WE CAN FIND HIMENO?!
CAN YOU DO IT?
HMPH. DON'T UNDERESTIMATE THE KNIGHT OF LIGHT.
STOP GIVING ME THAT SCARY LOOK!
click

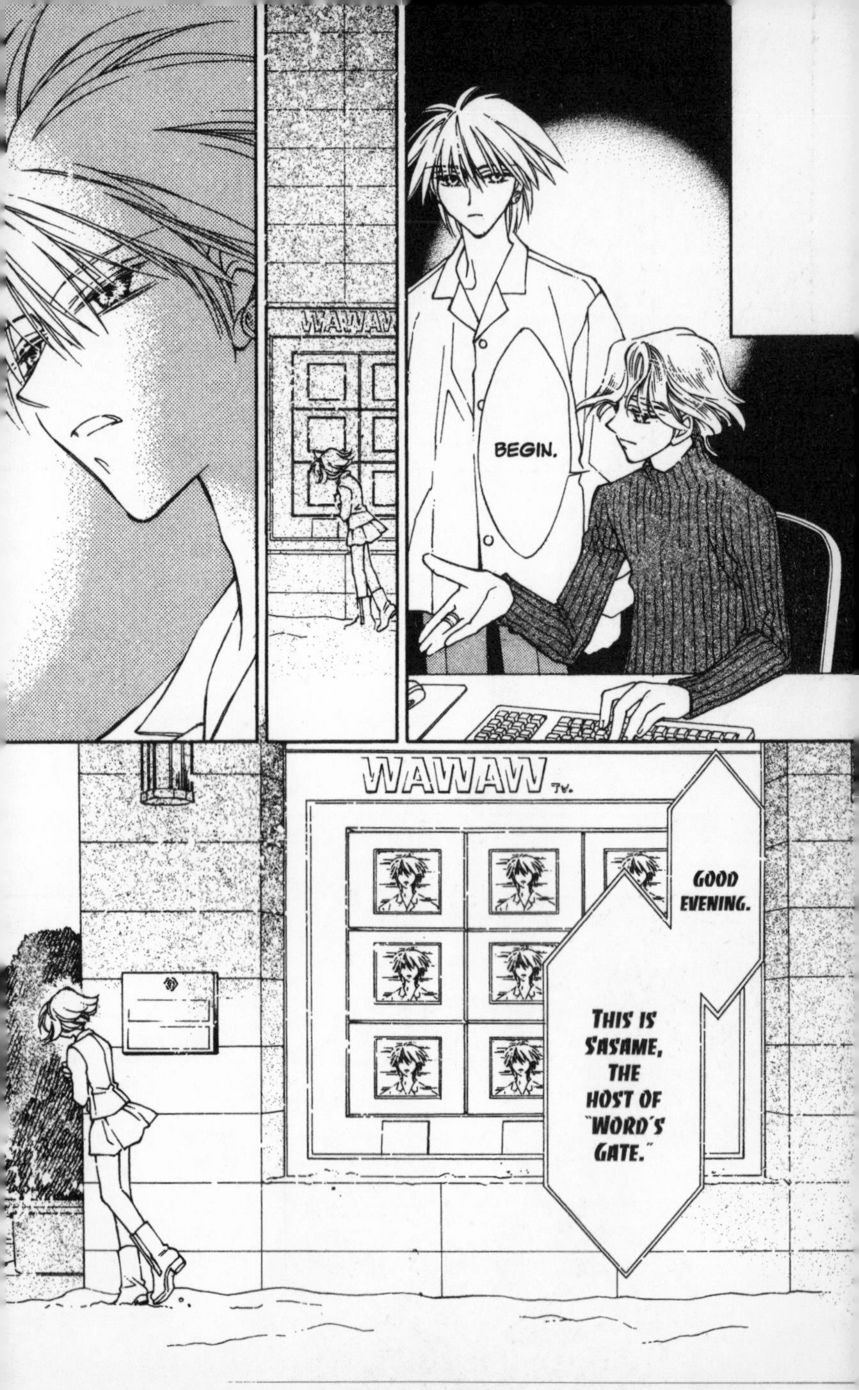
BEGIN.
WAWAW
WAWAW TV.
GOOD EVENING.
THIS IS SASAME, THE HOST OF "WORD'S GATE."

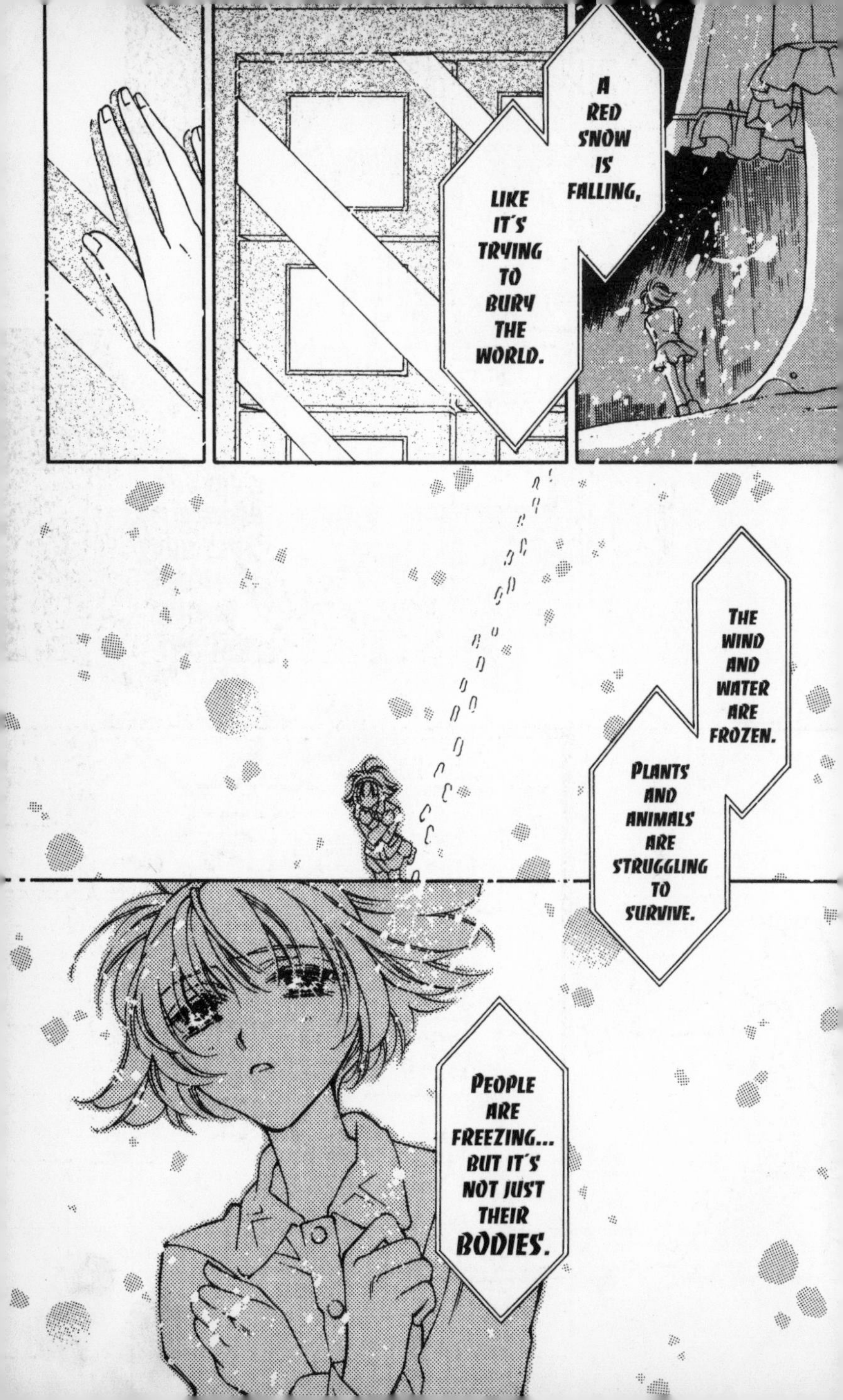
A RED SNOW IS FALLING,
LIKE IT'S TRYING TO BURY THE WORLD.
THE WIND AND WATER ARE FROZEN.
PLANTS AND ANIMALS ARE STRUGGLING TO SURVIVE.
PEOPLE ARE FREEZING... BUT IT'S NOT JUST THEIR BODIES.

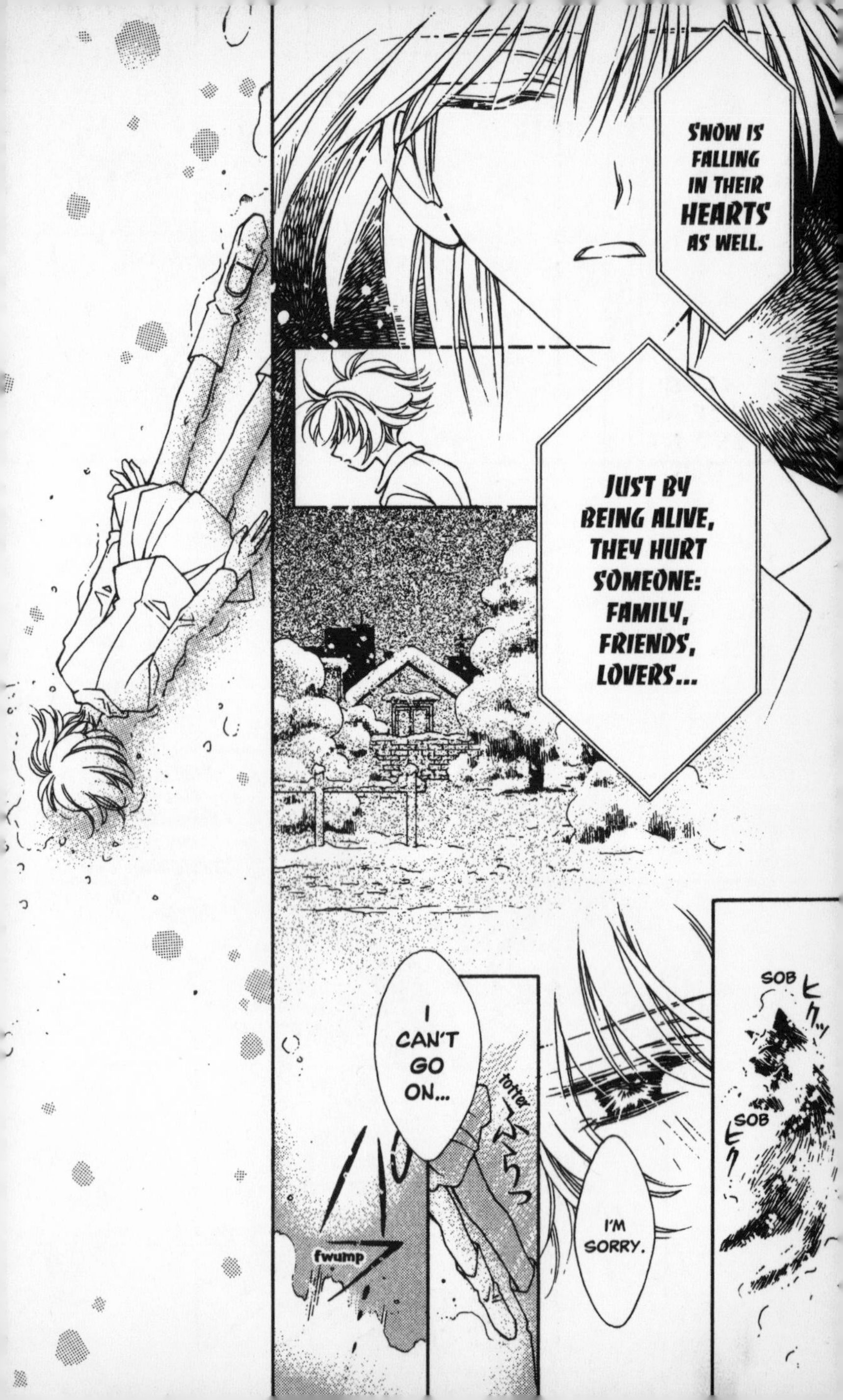

Snow is falling in their HEARTS as well.
Just by being alive, they hurt someone: family, friends, lovers...
SOB
SOB
I'M SORRY.
I CAN'T GO ON...
totter
fwump

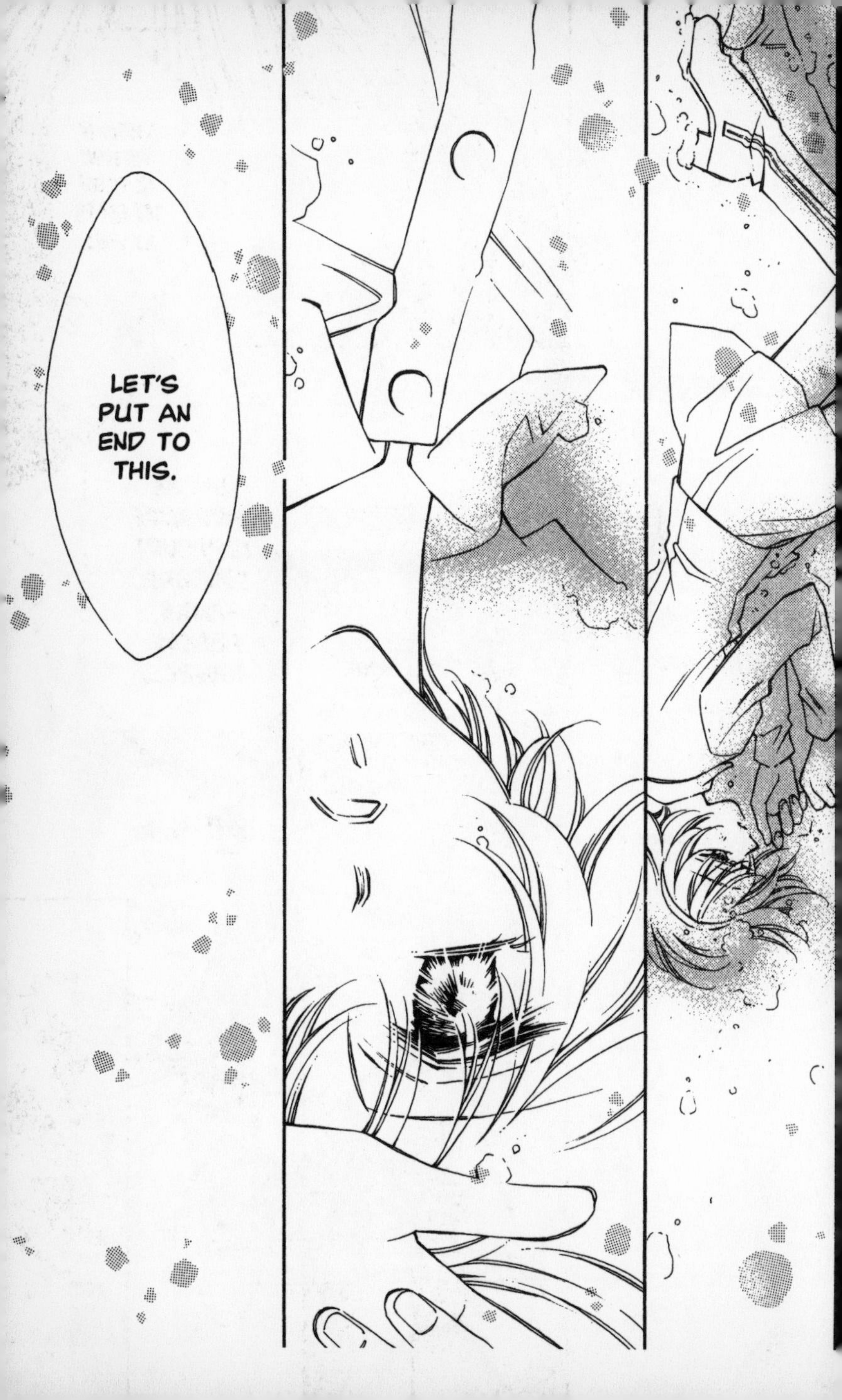
LET'S PUT AN END TO THIS.

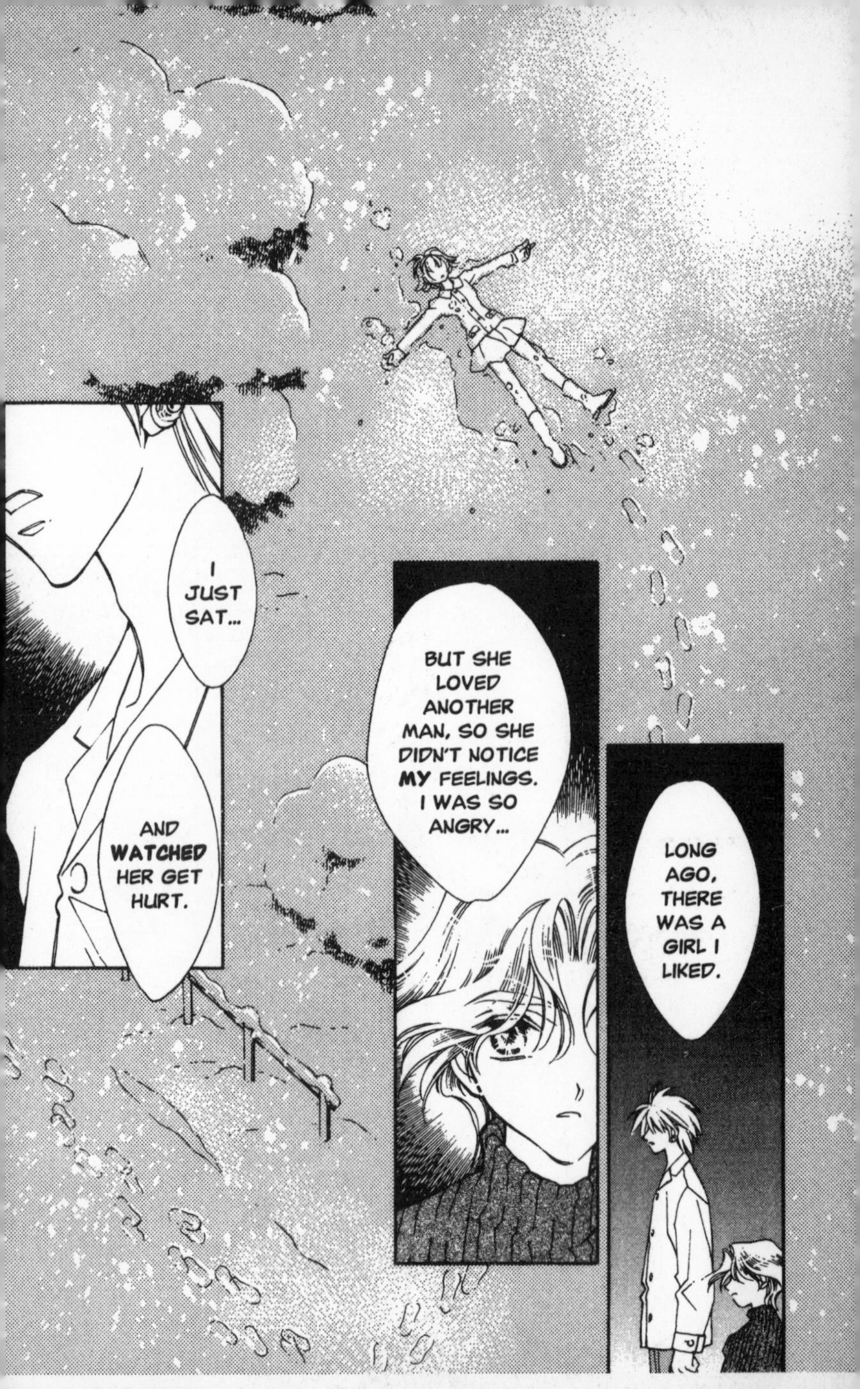
LONG AGO, THERE WAS A GIRL I LIKED.
BUT SHE LOVED ANOTHER MAN, SO SHE DIDN'T NOTICE **MY** FEELINGS. I WAS SO ANGRY...
I JUST SAT...
AND **WATCHED** HER GET HURT.

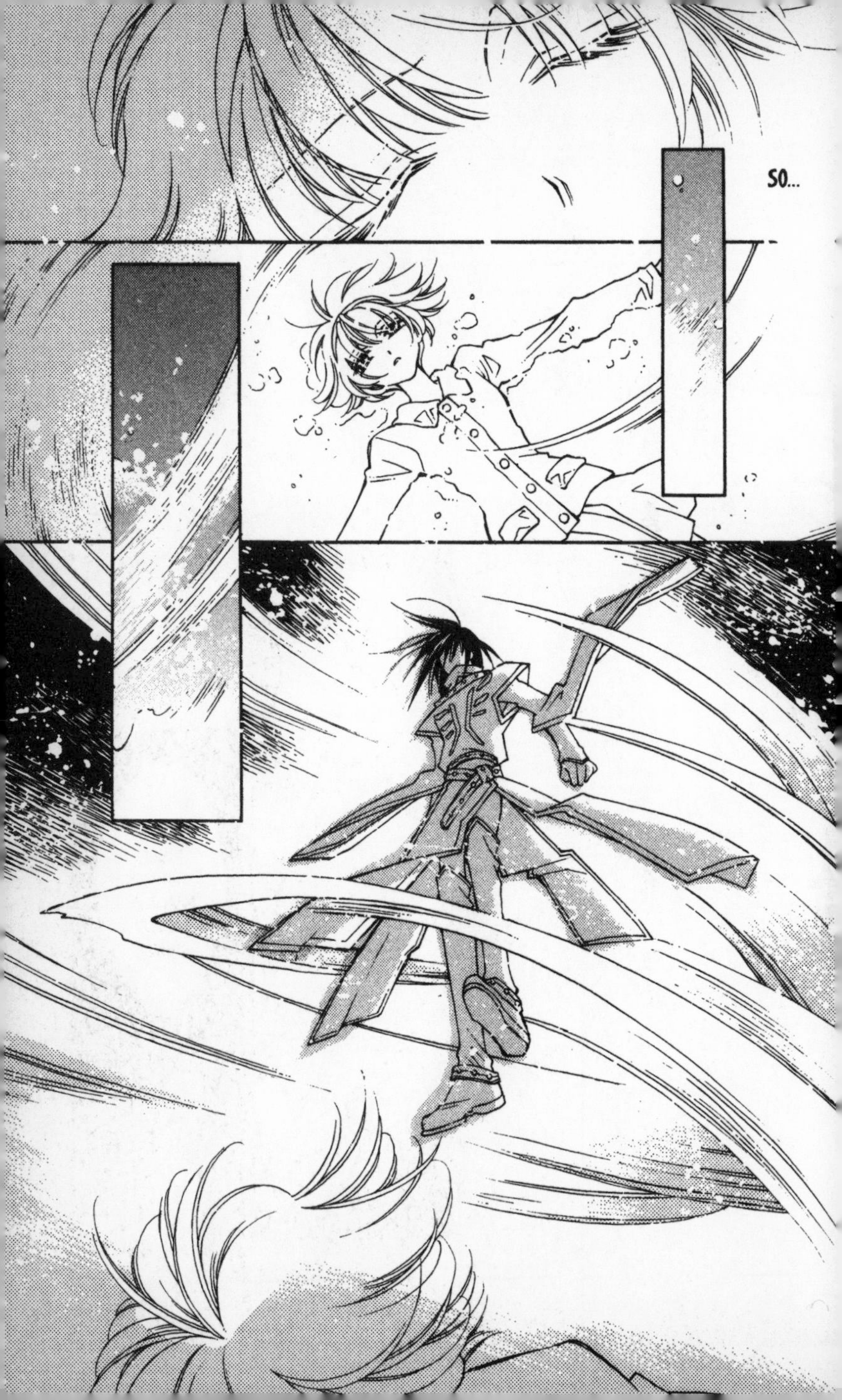
SO...

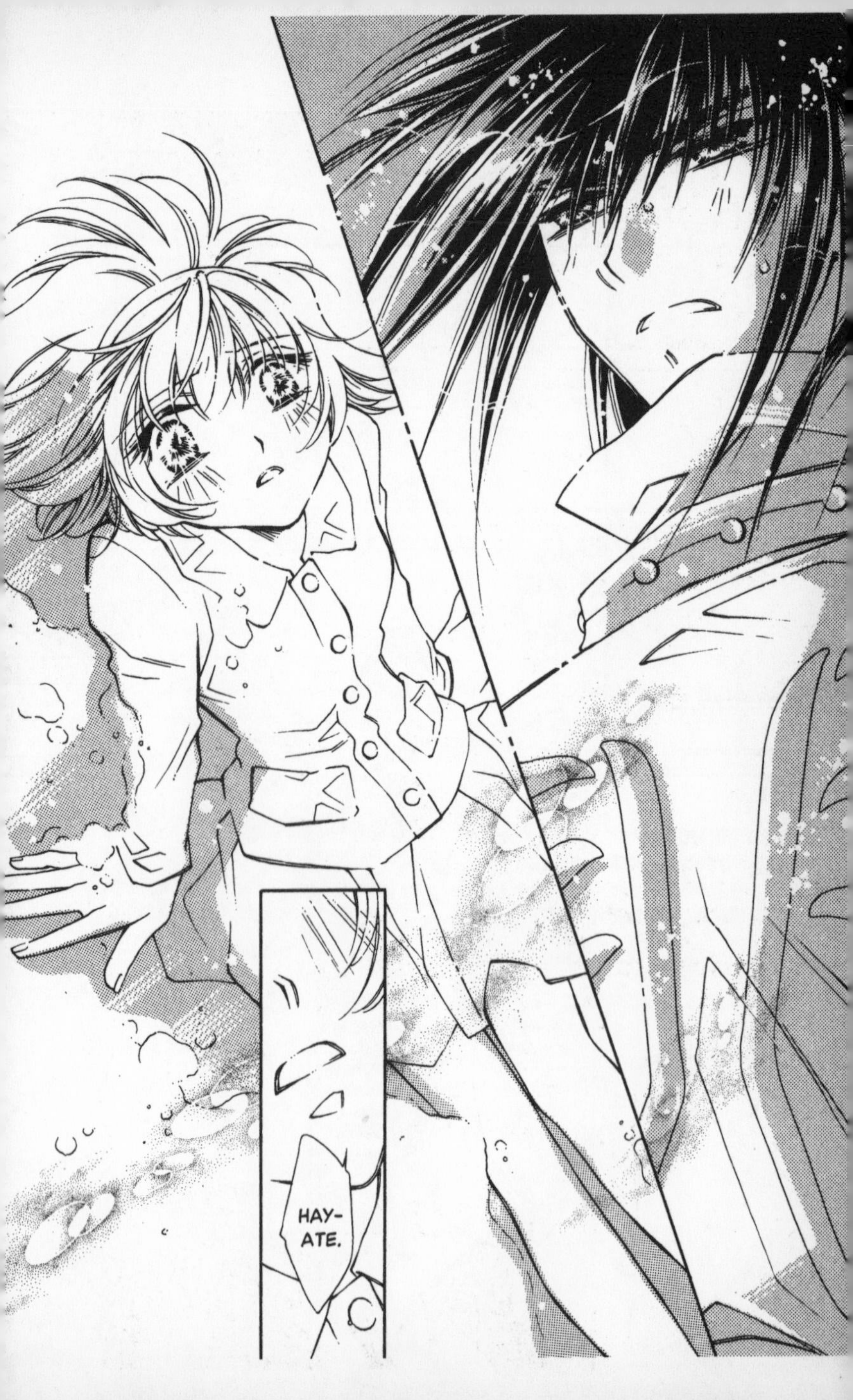
HAY-ATE.

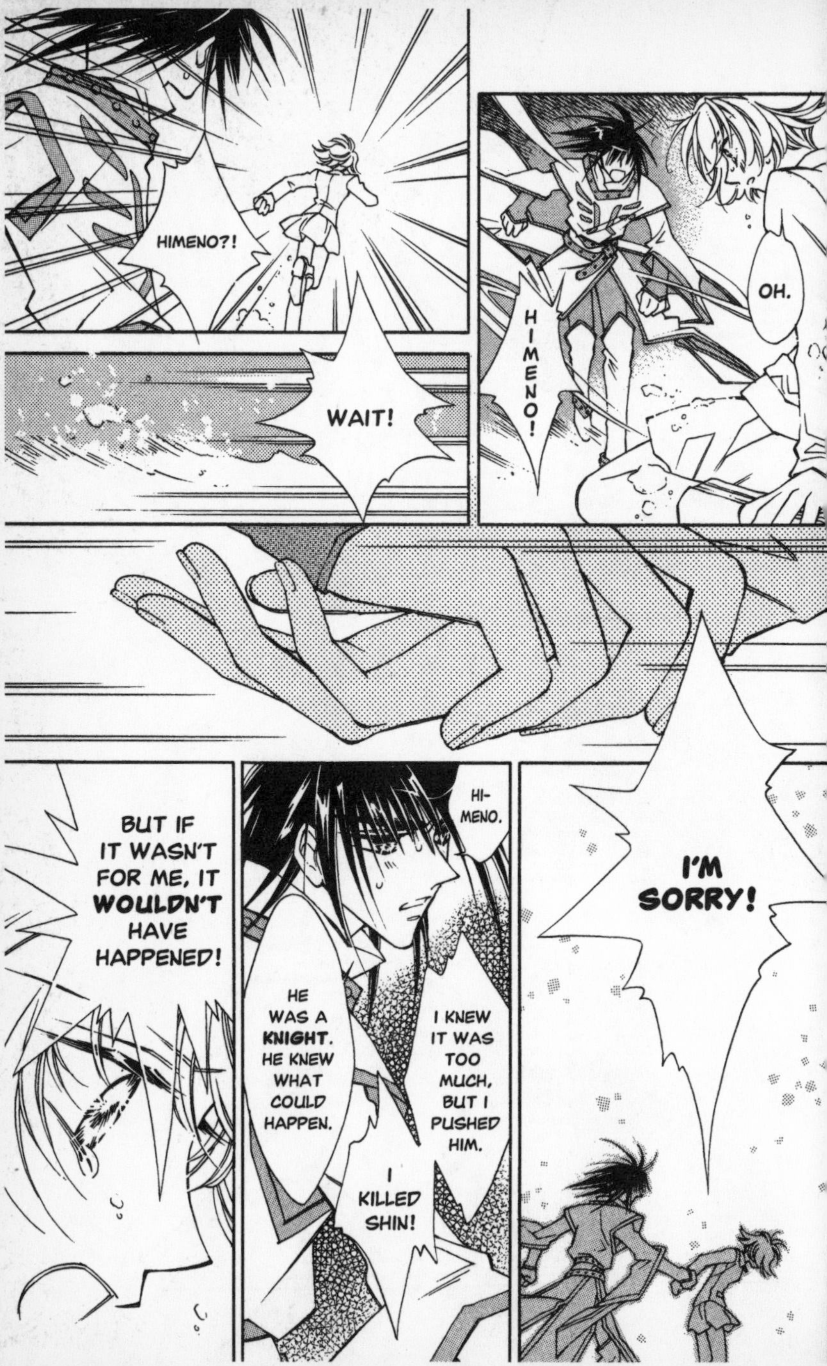
OH.
HIMENO!
HIMENO?!
WAIT!
I'M SORRY!
HI-MENO.
I KNEW IT WAS TOO MUCH, BUT I PUSHED HIM.
HE WAS A KNIGHT. HE KNEW WHAT COULD HAPPEN.
I KILLED SHIN!
BUT IF IT WASN'T FOR ME, IT WOULDN'T HAVE HAPPENED!

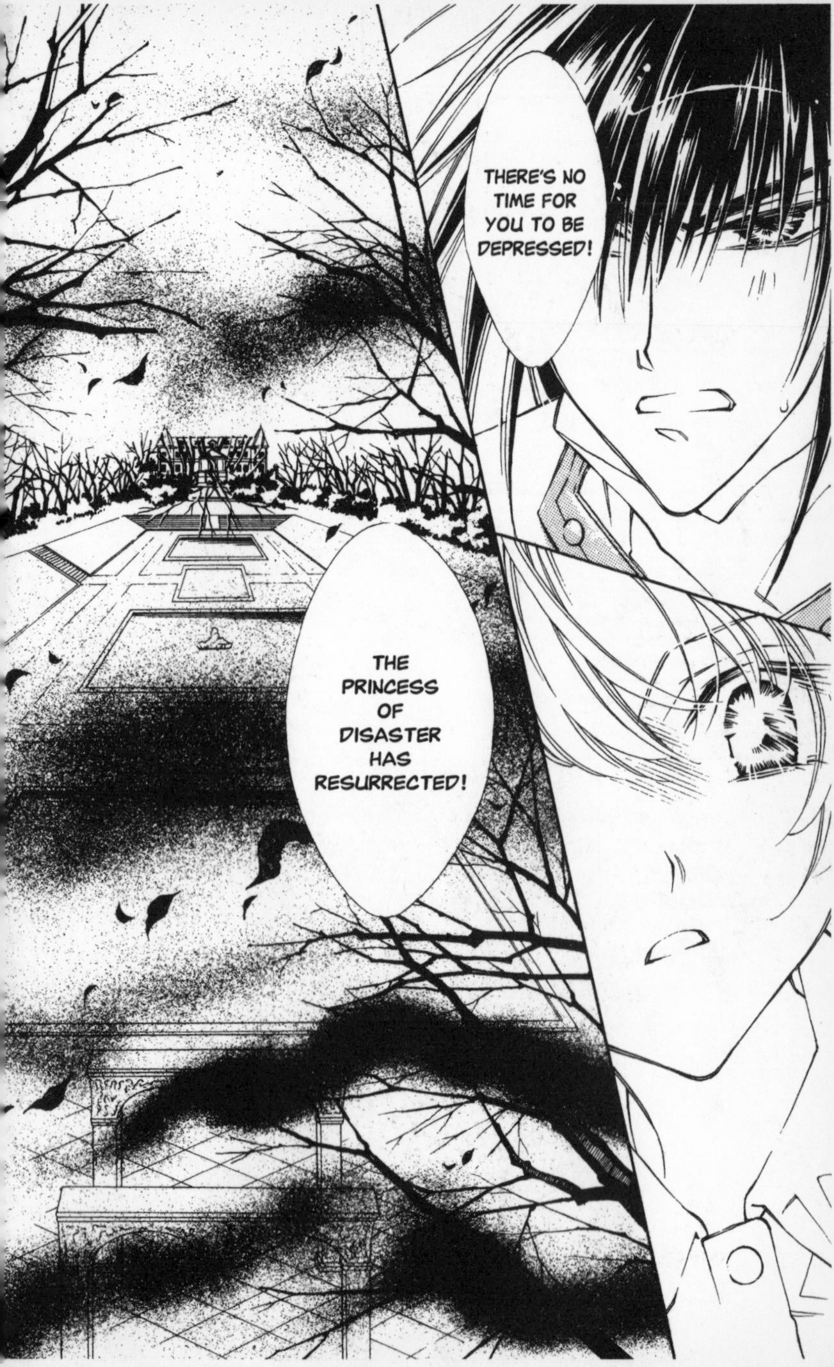
THERE'S NO TIME FOR YOU TO BE DEPRESSED!
THE PRINCESS OF DISASTER HAS RESURRECTED!

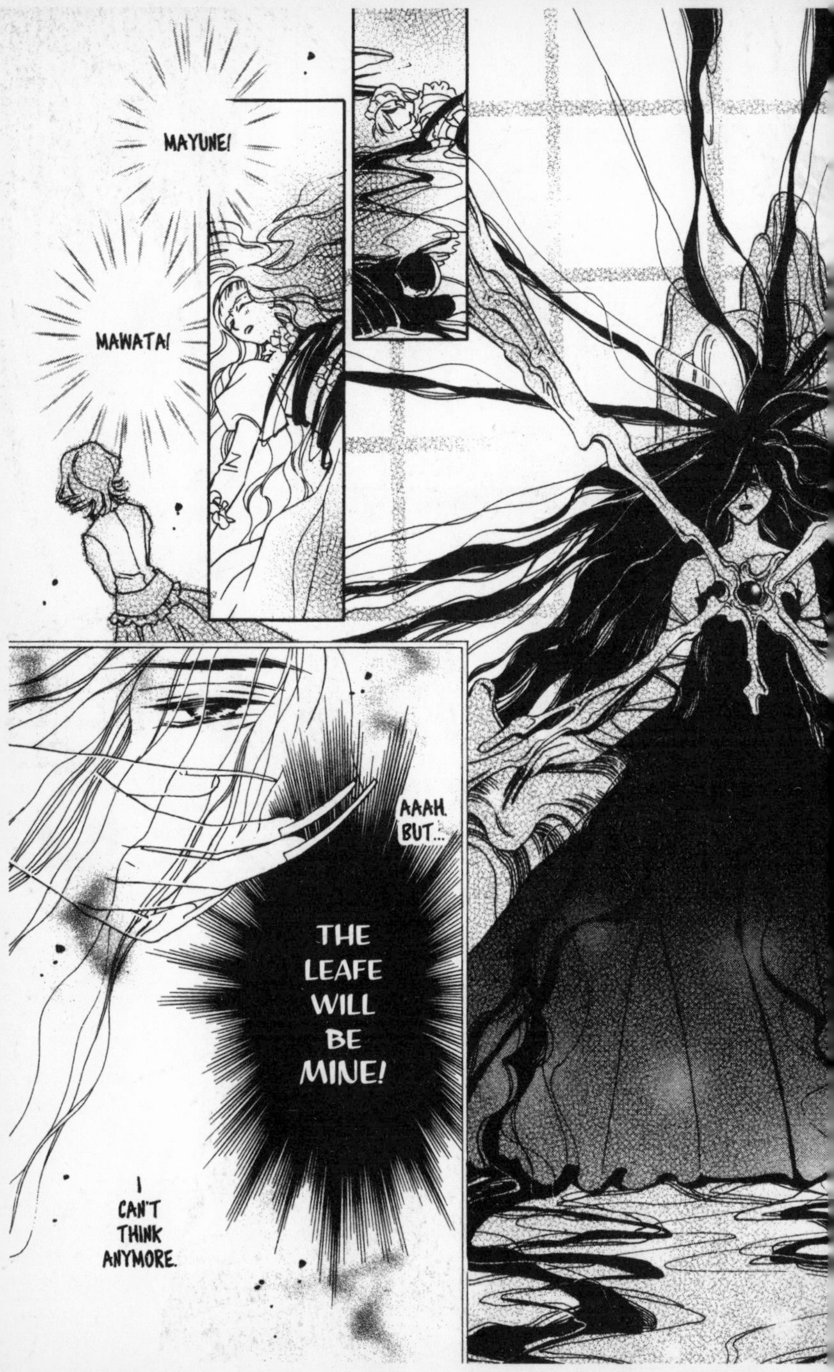
MAYUNE!
MAWATA!
AAAH, BUT...
THE LEAFE WILL BE MINE!
I CAN'T THINK ANYMORE.

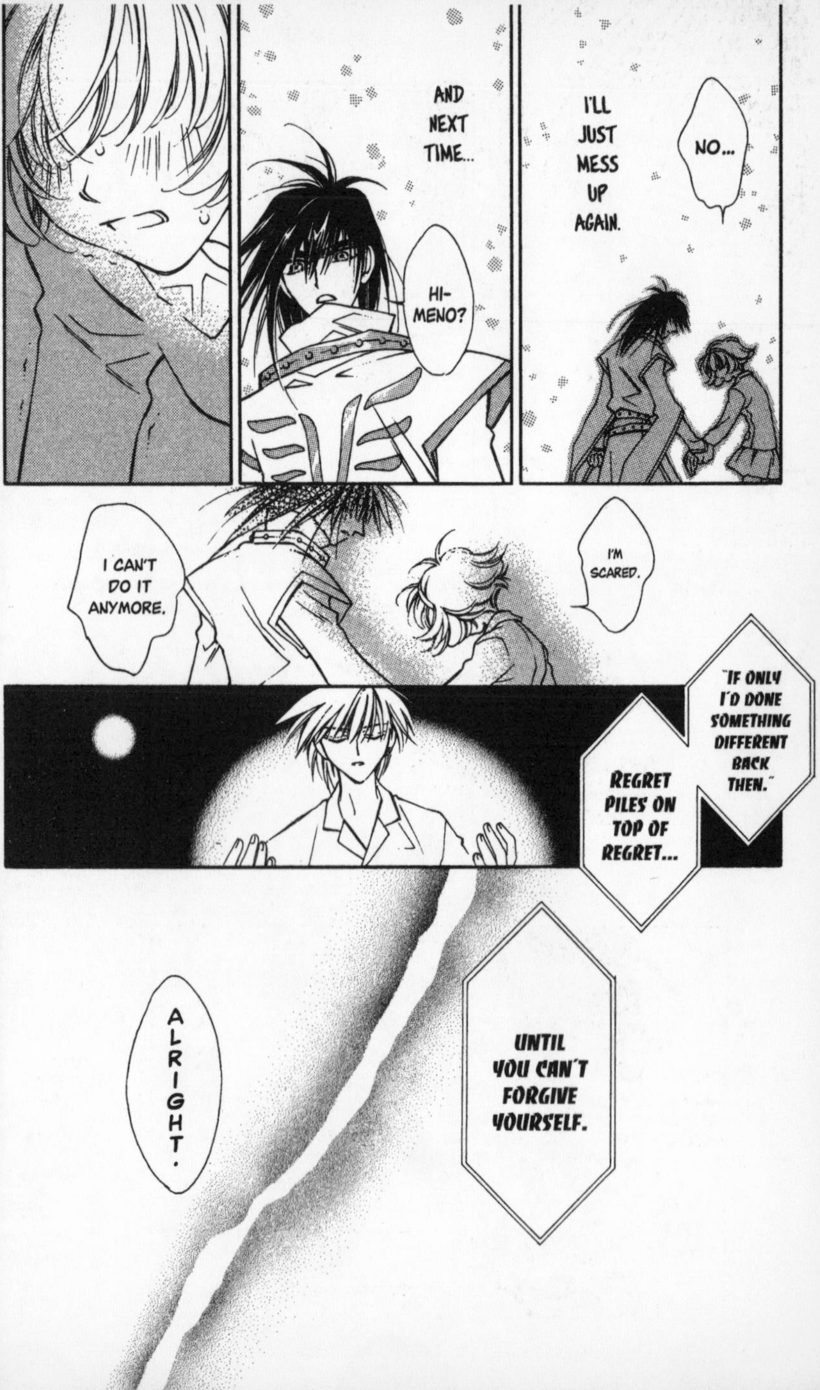
NO...
I'LL JUST MESS UP AGAIN.
AND NEXT TIME...
HI-MENO?
I'M SCARED.
I CAN'T DO IT ANYMORE.
"IF ONLY I'D DONE SOMETHING DIFFERENT BACK THEN."
REGRET PILES ON TOP OF REGRET...
UNTIL YOU CAN'T FORGIVE YOURSELF.
ALRIGHT.

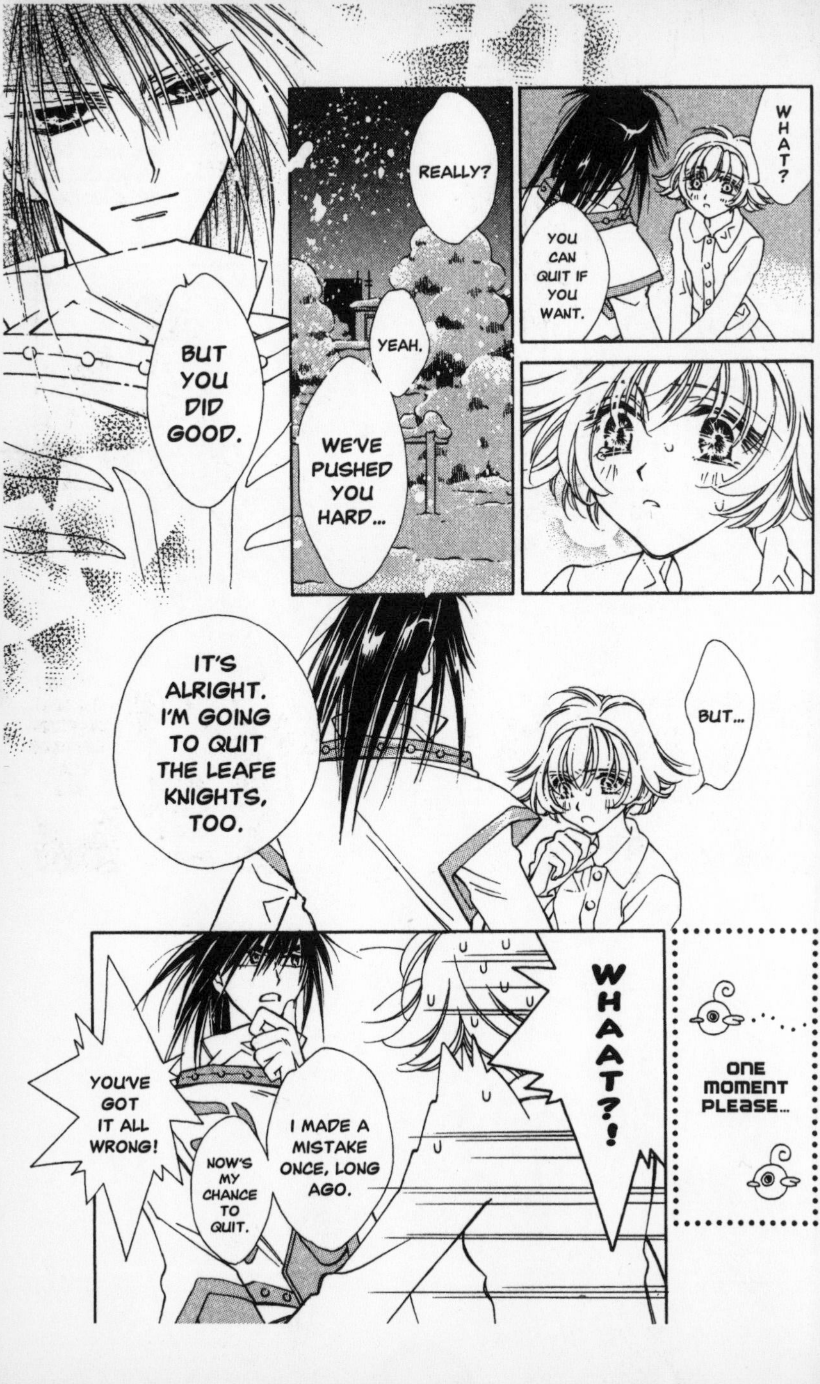
WHAT?
YOU CAN QUIT IF YOU WANT.
REALLY?
YEAH.
WE'VE PUSHED YOU HARD...
BUT YOU DID GOOD.
BUT...
IT'S ALRIGHT. I'M GOING TO QUIT THE LEAFE KNIGHTS, TOO.
ONE MOMENT PLEASE...
WHAAT?!
I MADE A MISTAKE ONCE, LONG AGO.
NOW'S MY CHANCE TO QUIT.
YOU'VE GOT IT ALL WRONG!

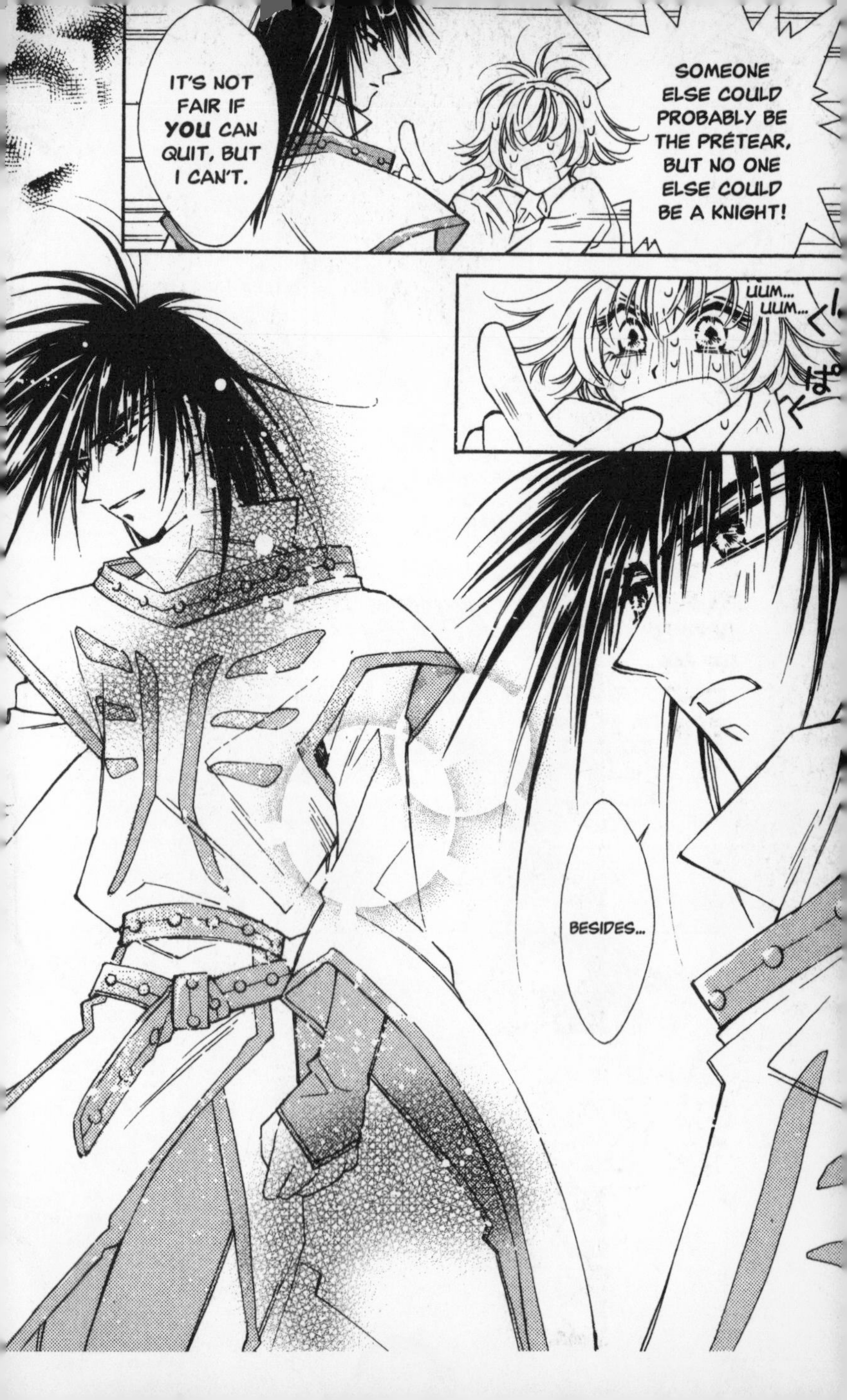

SOMEONE ELSE COULD PROBABLY BE THE PRÉTEAR, BUT NO ONE ELSE COULD BE A KNIGHT!
IT'S NOT FAIR IF **YOU** CAN QUIT, BUT I CAN'T.
UUM... UUM...
ぱ
BESIDES...

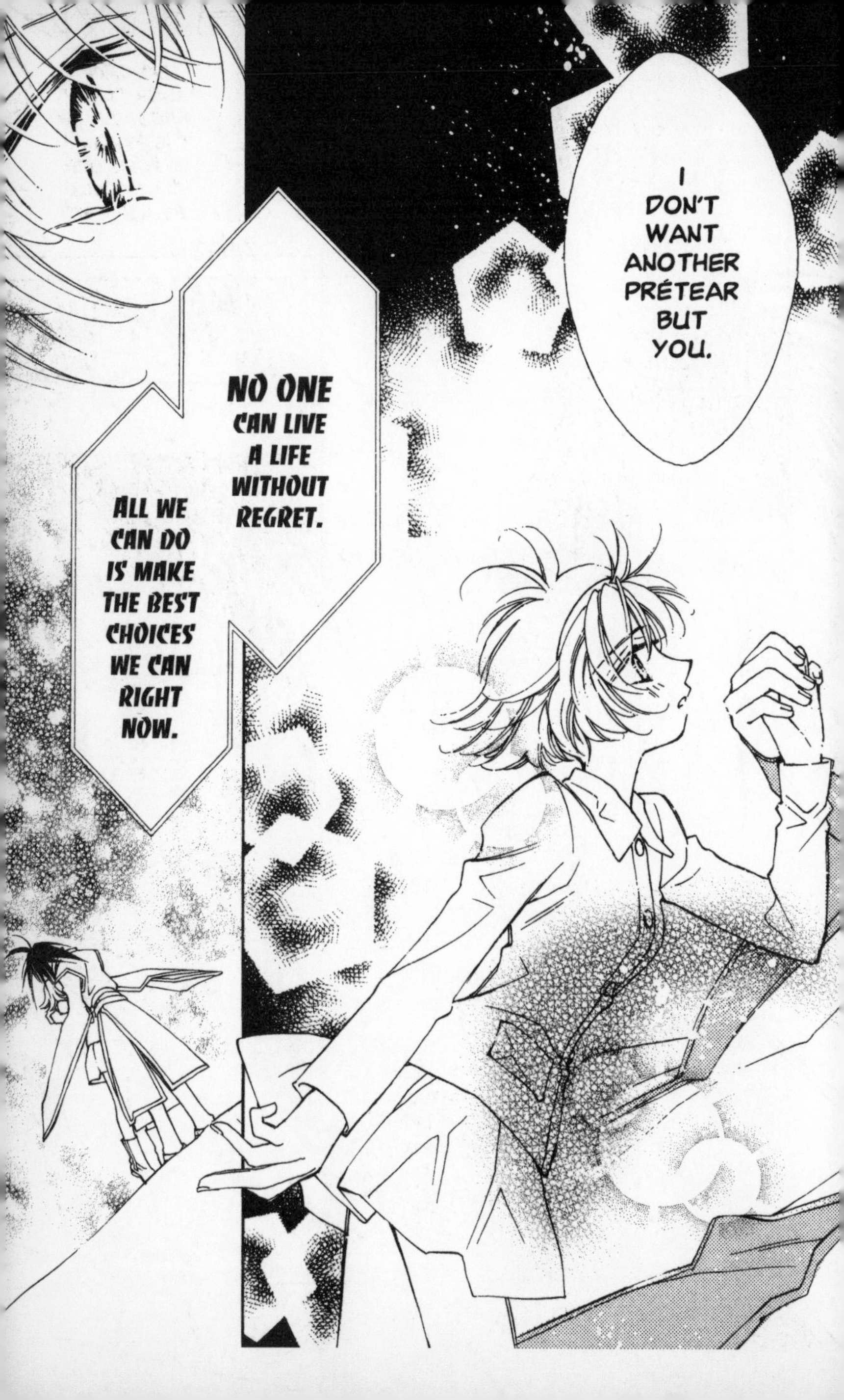
I DON'T WANT ANOTHER PRÉTEAR BUT YOU.
NO ONE CAN LIVE A LIFE WITHOUT REGRET.
ALL WE CAN DO IS MAKE THE BEST CHOICES WE CAN RIGHT NOW.

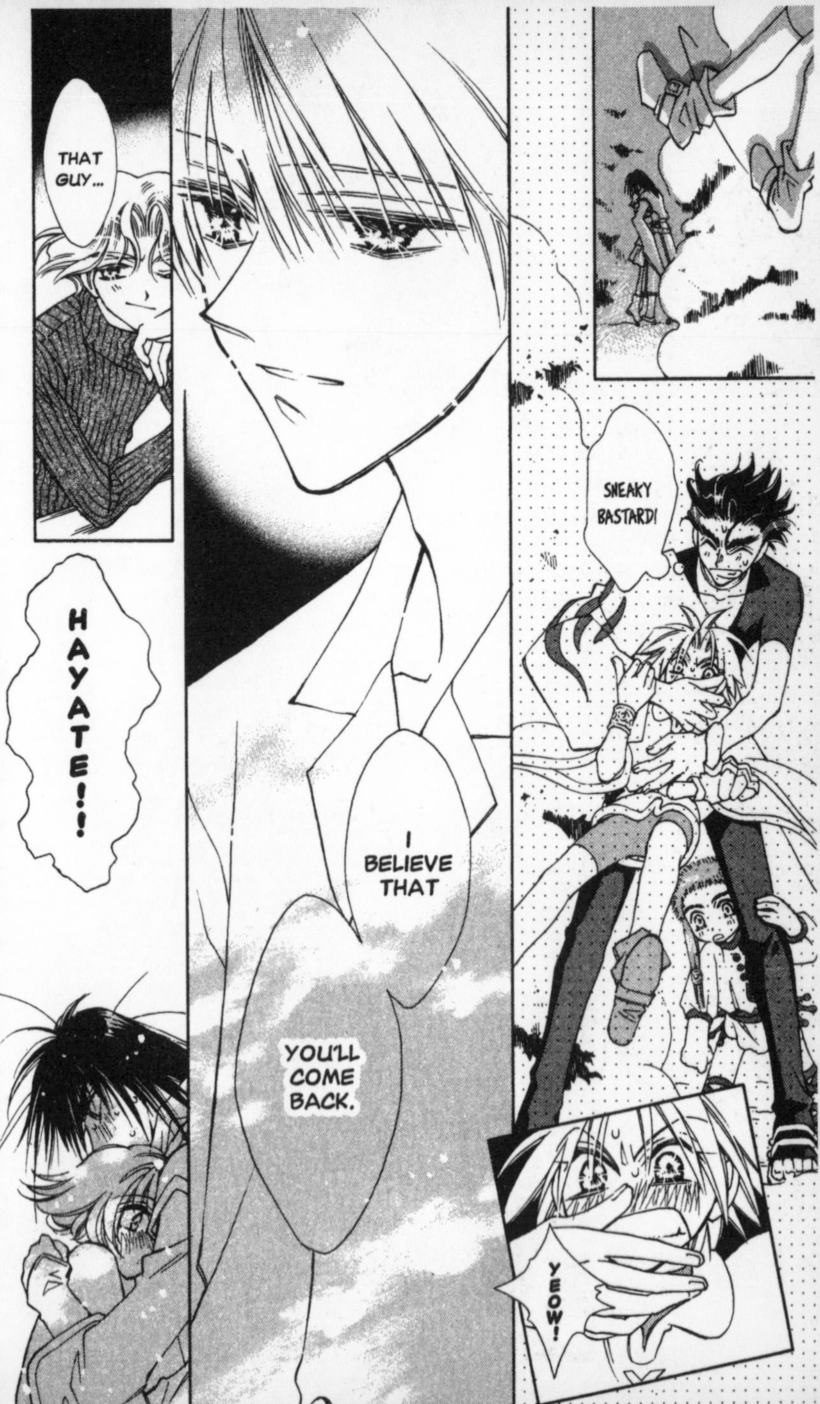
SNEAKY BASTARD!
YEOW!
I BELIEVE THAT
YOU'LL COME BACK.
THAT GUY...
HAYATE!!!

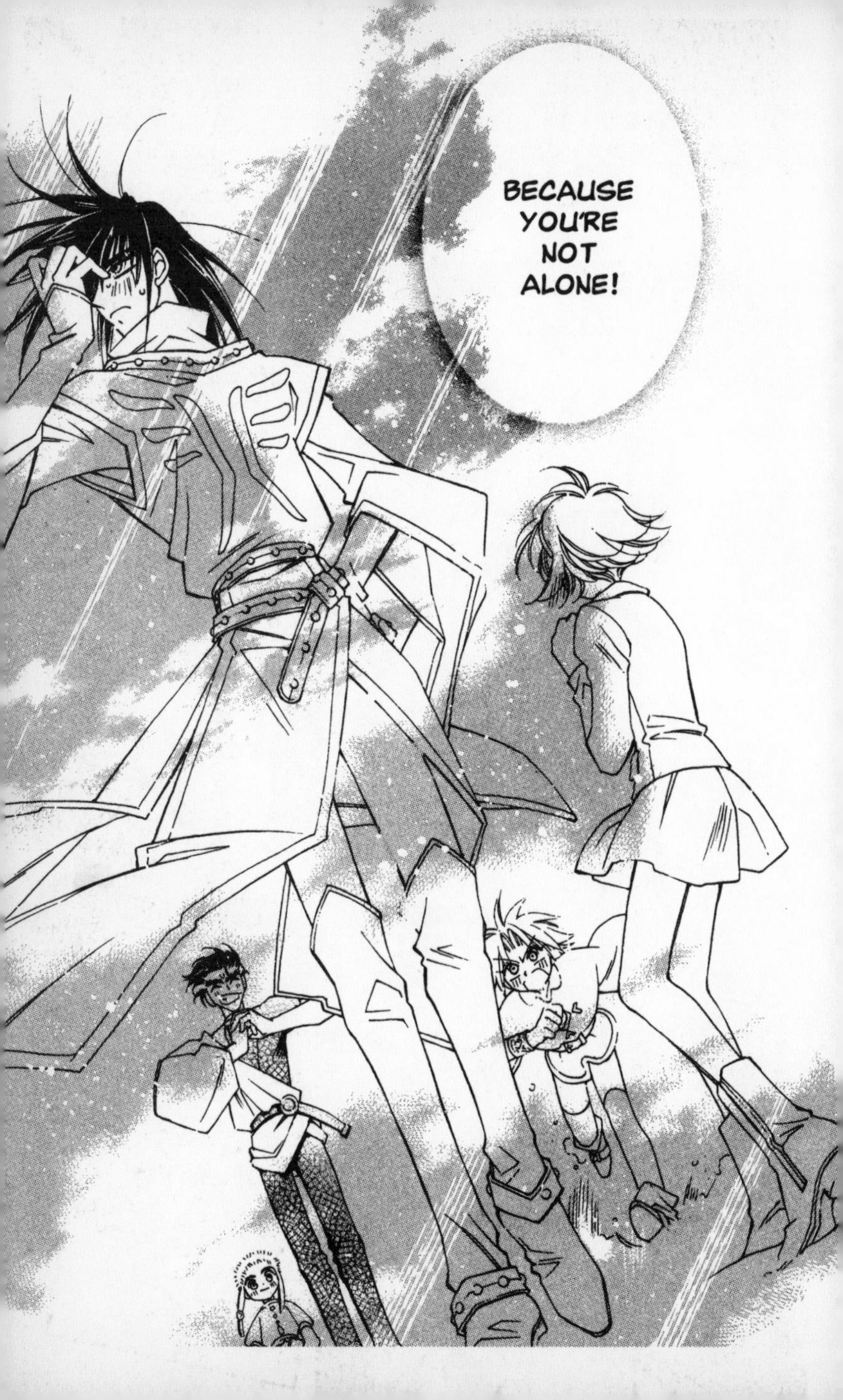
BECAUSE YOU'RE NOT ALONE!

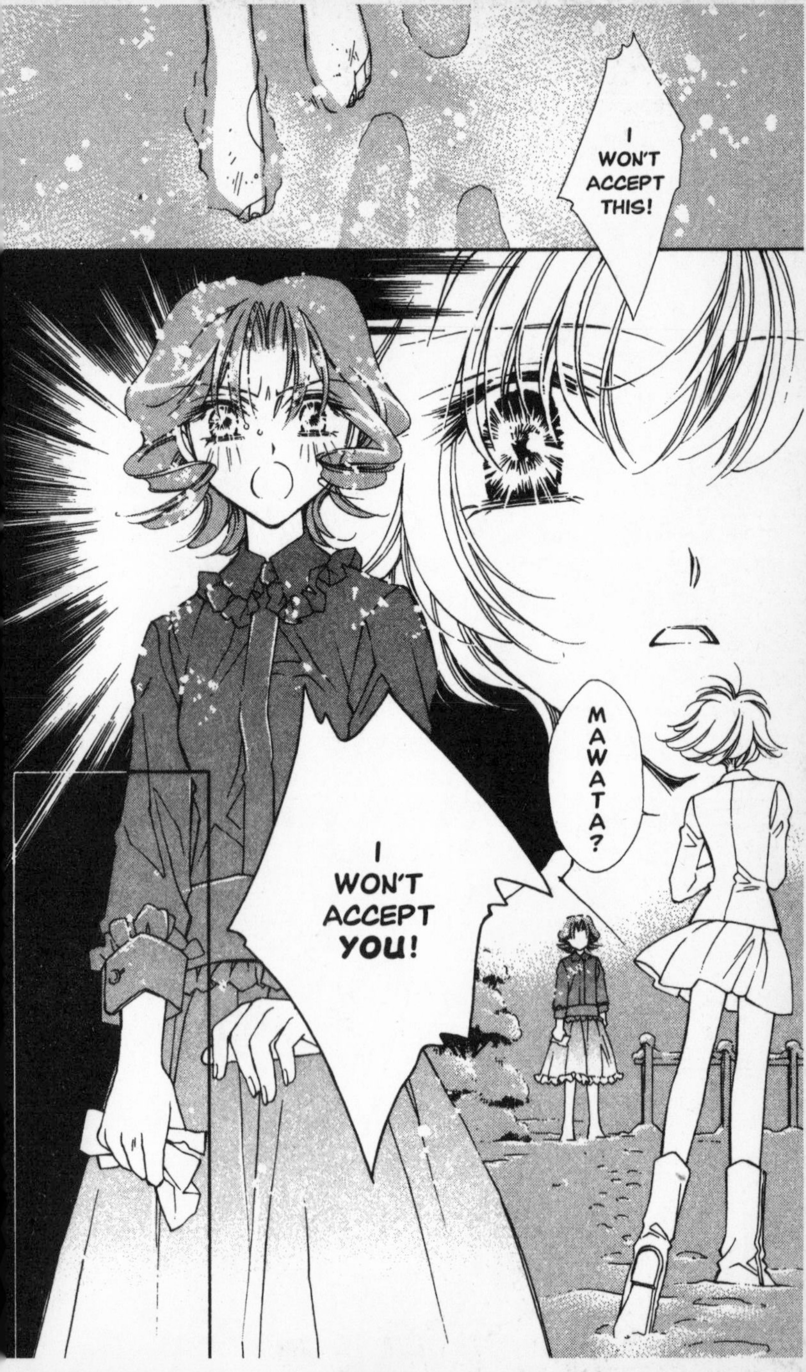
I WON'T ACCEPT THIS!
MAWATA?
I WON'T ACCEPT YOU!

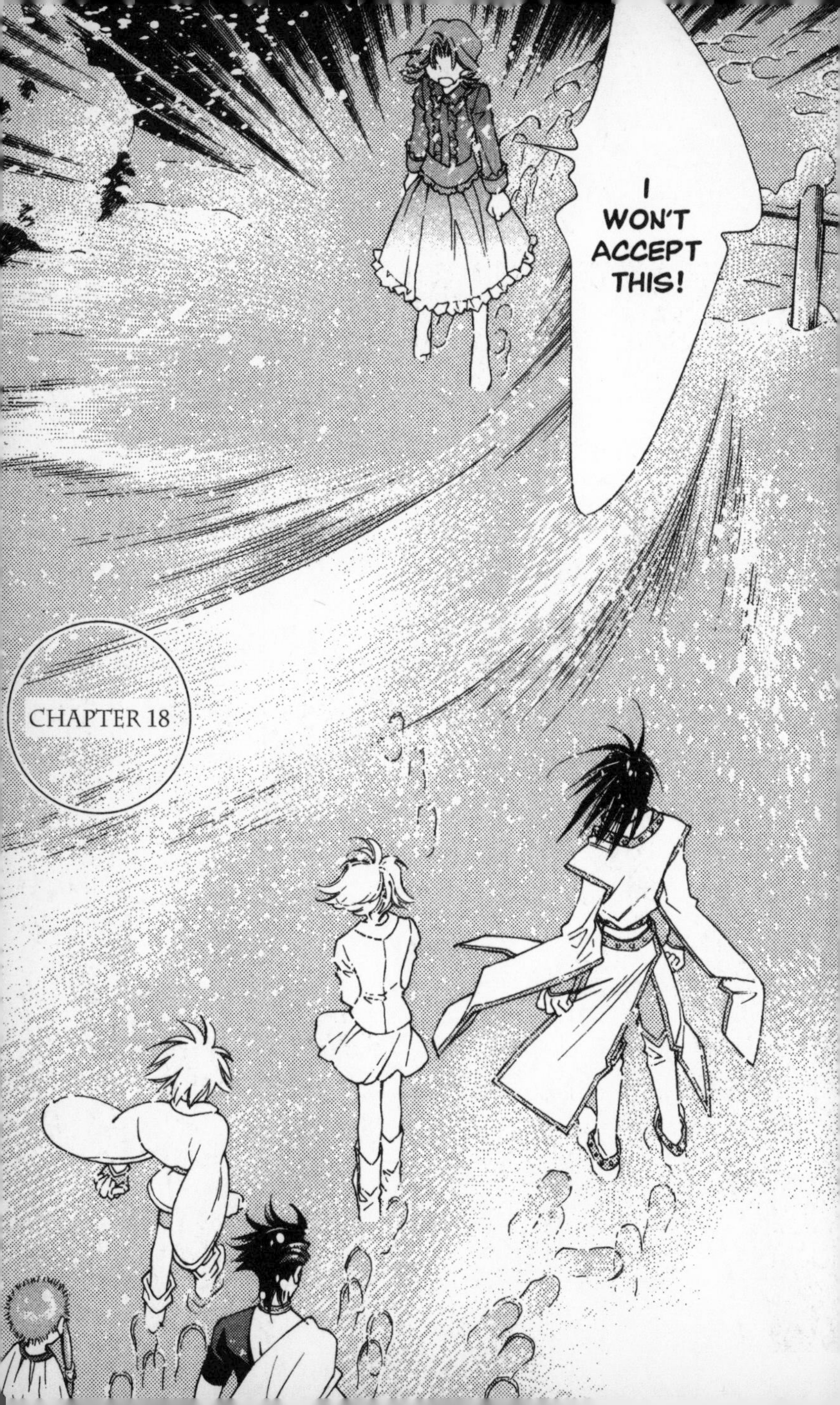
I WON'T ACCEPT THIS!
CHAPTER 18

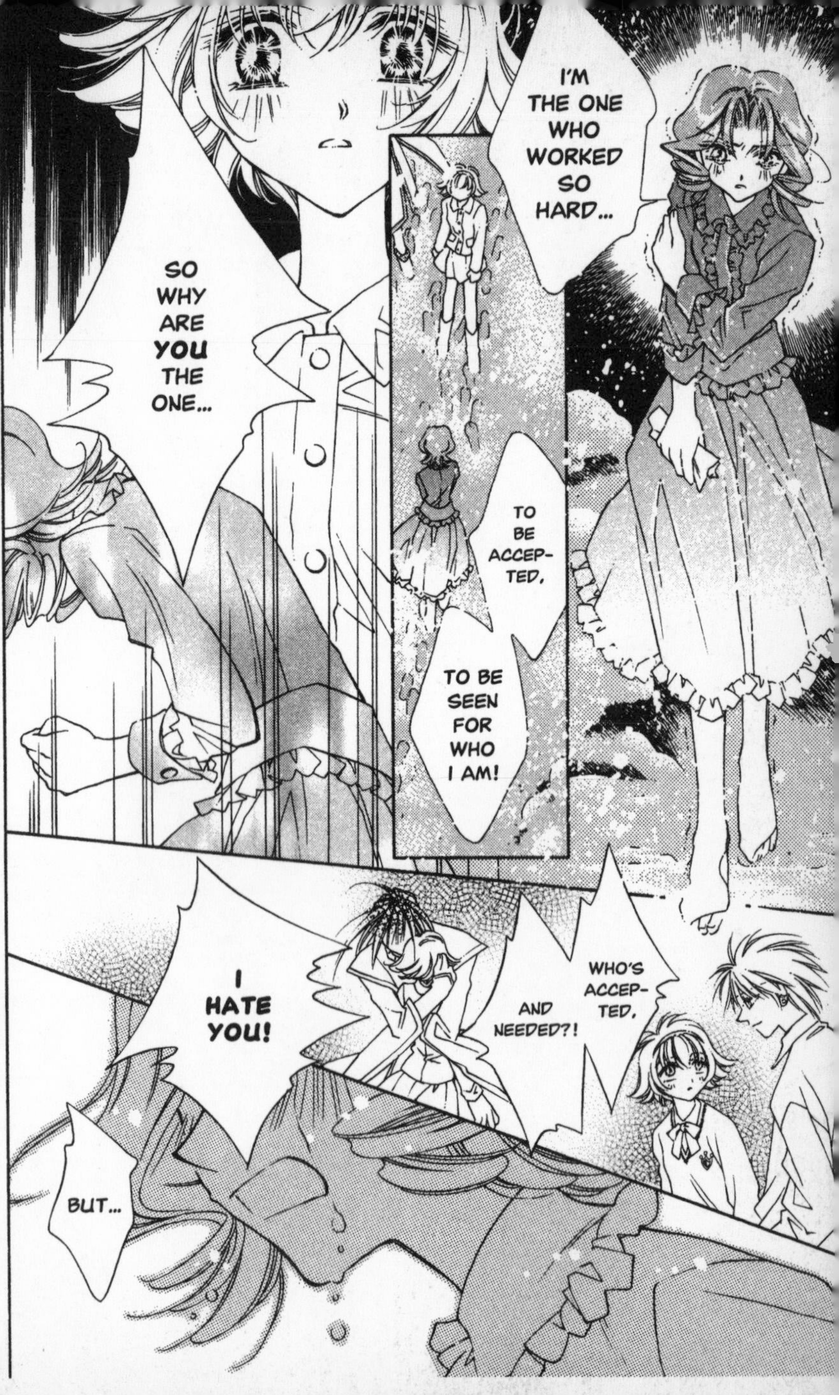
I'M THE ONE WHO WORKED SO HARD...
TO BE ACCEPTED,
TO BE SEEN FOR WHO I AM!
SO WHY ARE **YOU** THE ONE...
WHO'S ACCEPTED,
AND NEEDED?!
I HATE YOU!
BUT...

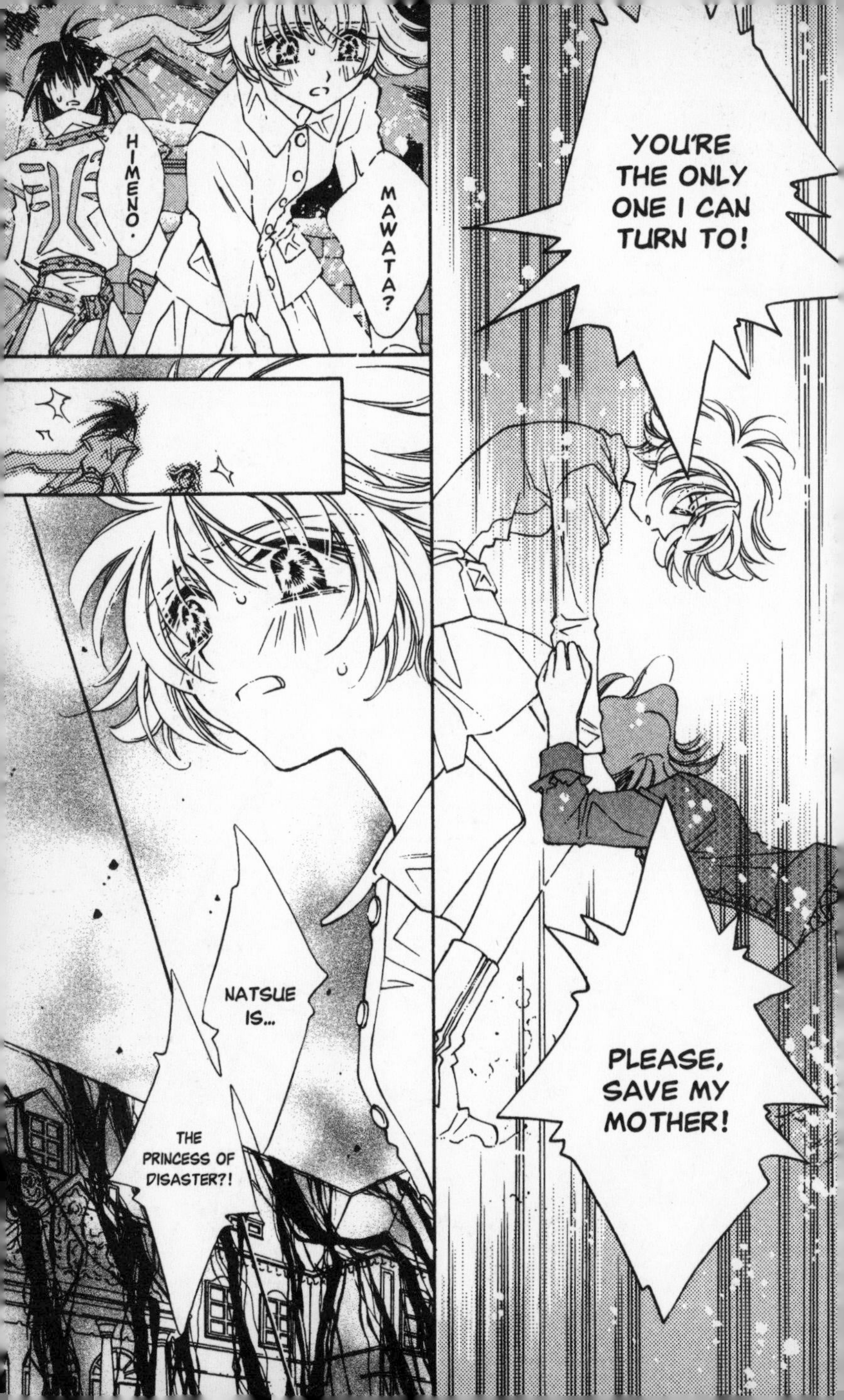
YOU'RE THE ONLY ONE I CAN TURN TO!
PLEASE, SAVE MY MOTHER!
MAWATA?
HIMENO.
NATSUE IS...
THE PRINCESS OF DISASTER?!

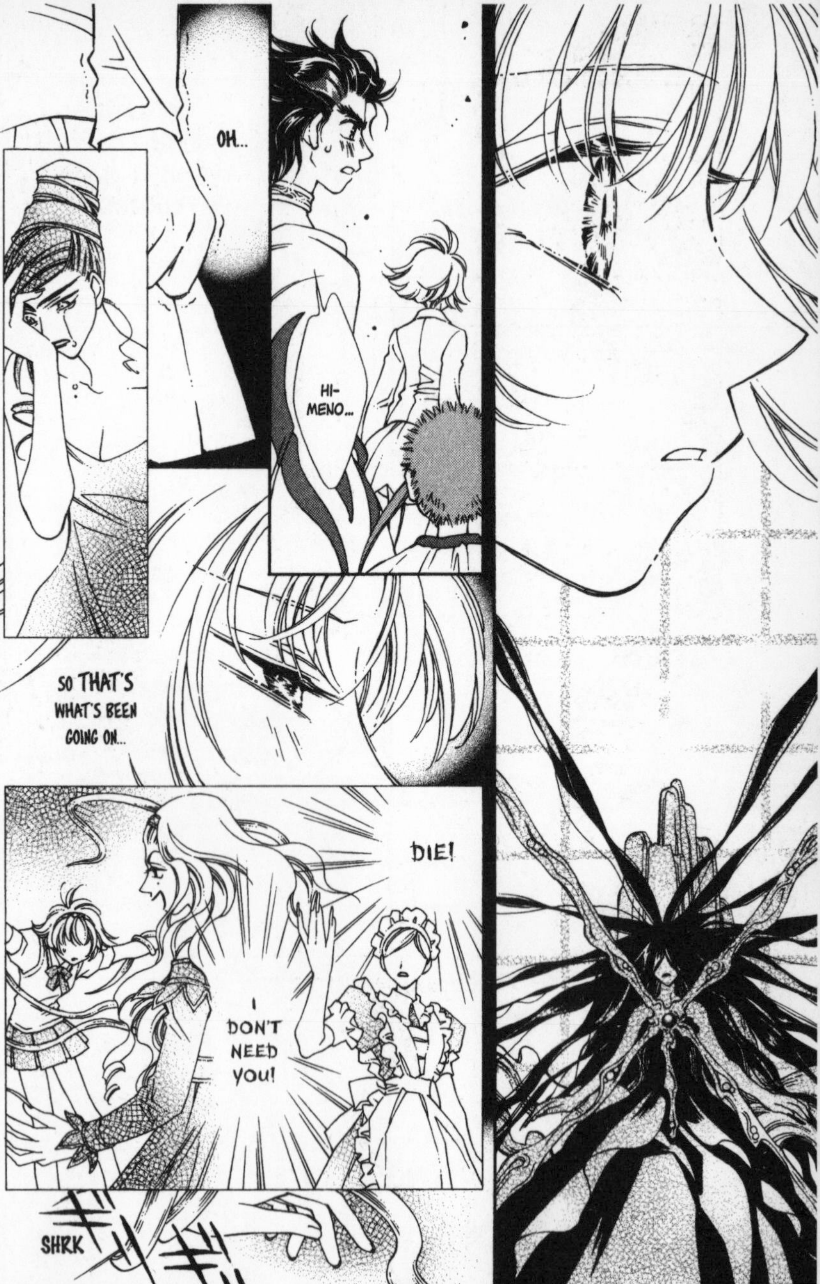
HI-
MENO...
OH...
SO THAT'S
WHAT'S BEEN
GOING ON...
DIE!
I
DON'T
NEED
YOU!
SHRK
SHRK

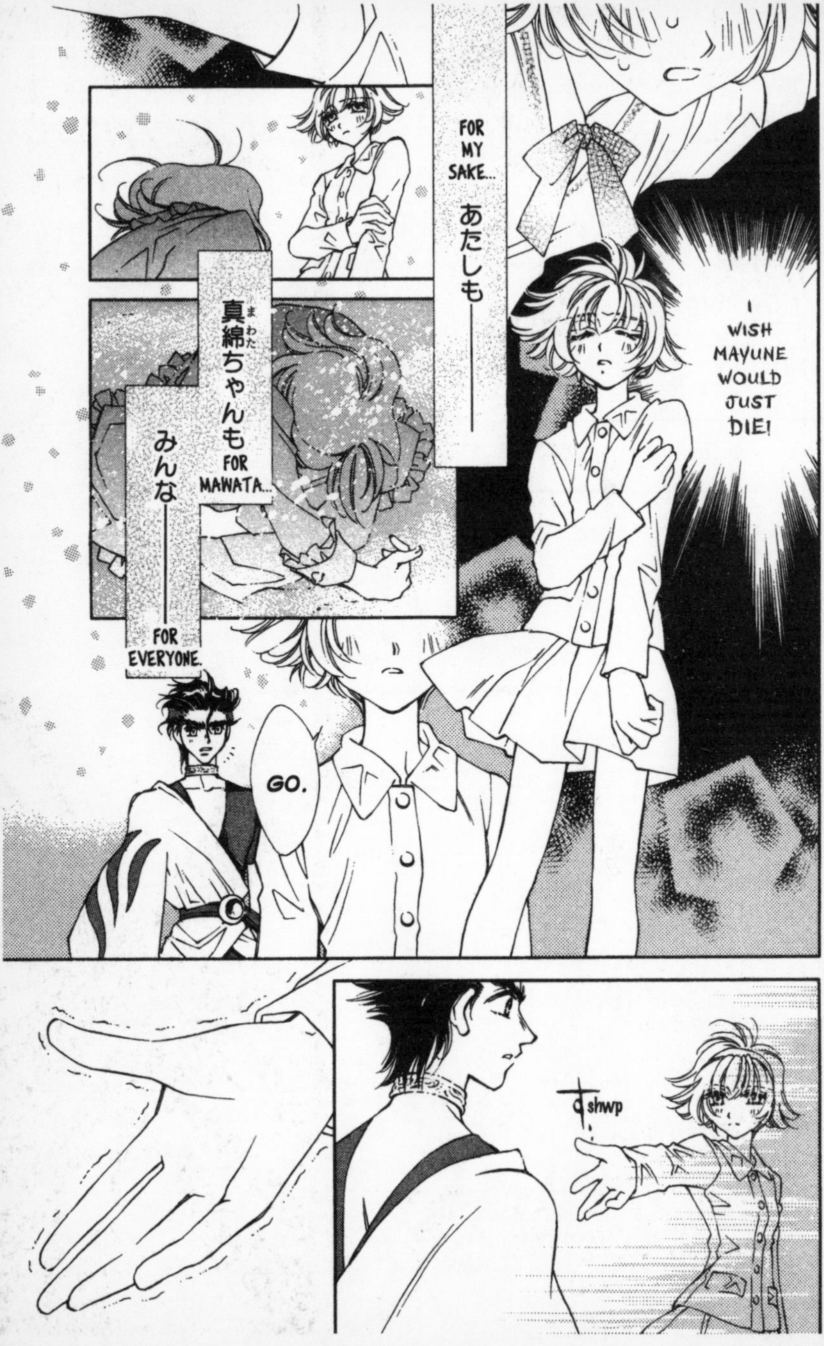
I WISH MAYUNE WOULD JUST DIE!
あたしも——
FOR MY SAKE...
真綿ちゃんも
FOR MAWATA...
みんな——
FOR EVERYONE.
GO.
shwp

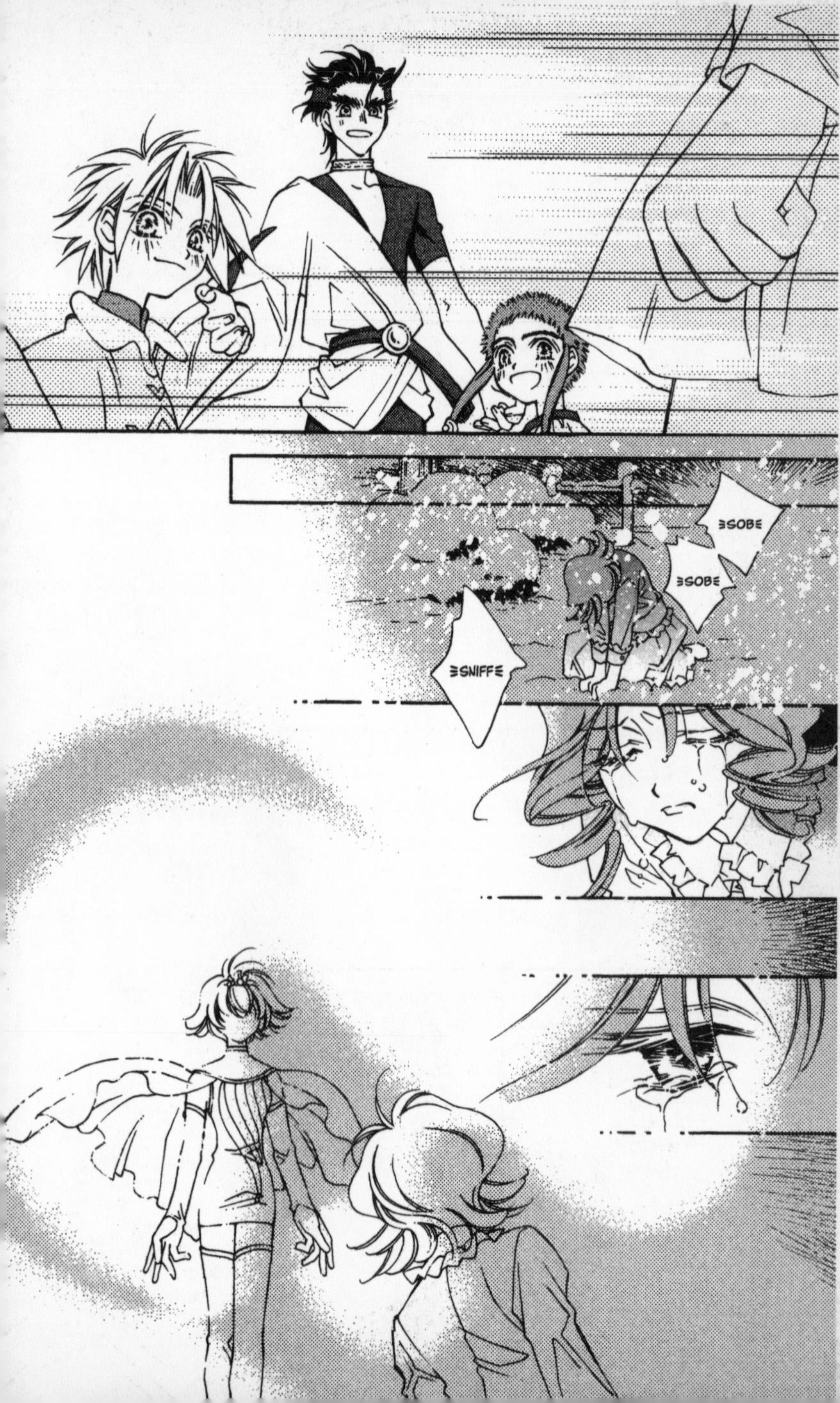

SOB
SOB
SNIFF

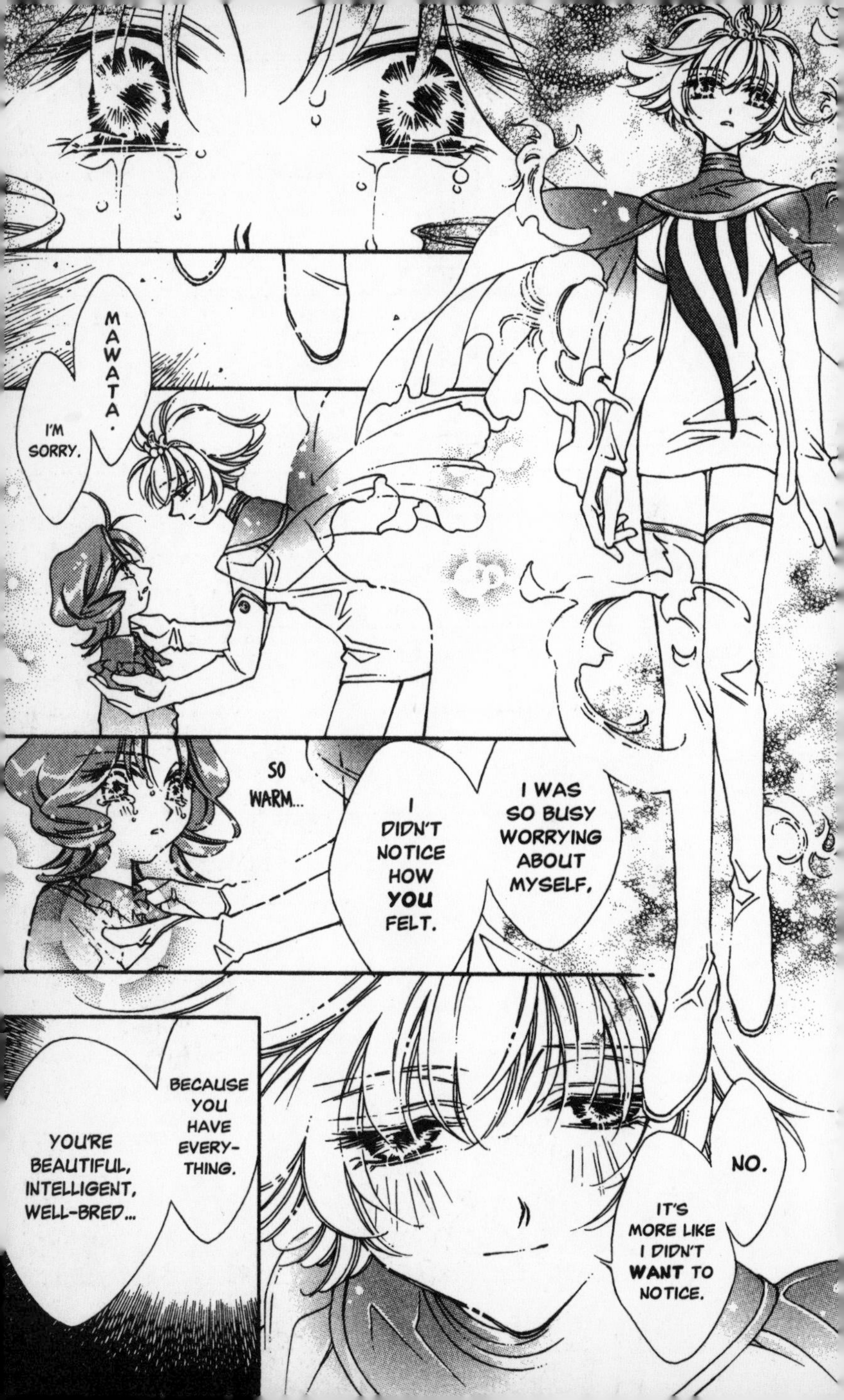
MAWATA.
I'M SORRY.
I WAS SO BUSY WORRYING ABOUT MYSELF,
I DIDN'T NOTICE HOW **YOU** FELT.
SO WARM...
NO.
IT'S MORE LIKE I DIDN'T **WANT** TO NOTICE.
BECAUSE YOU HAVE EVERY-THING.
YOU'RE BEAUTIFUL, INTELLIGENT, WELL-BRED...

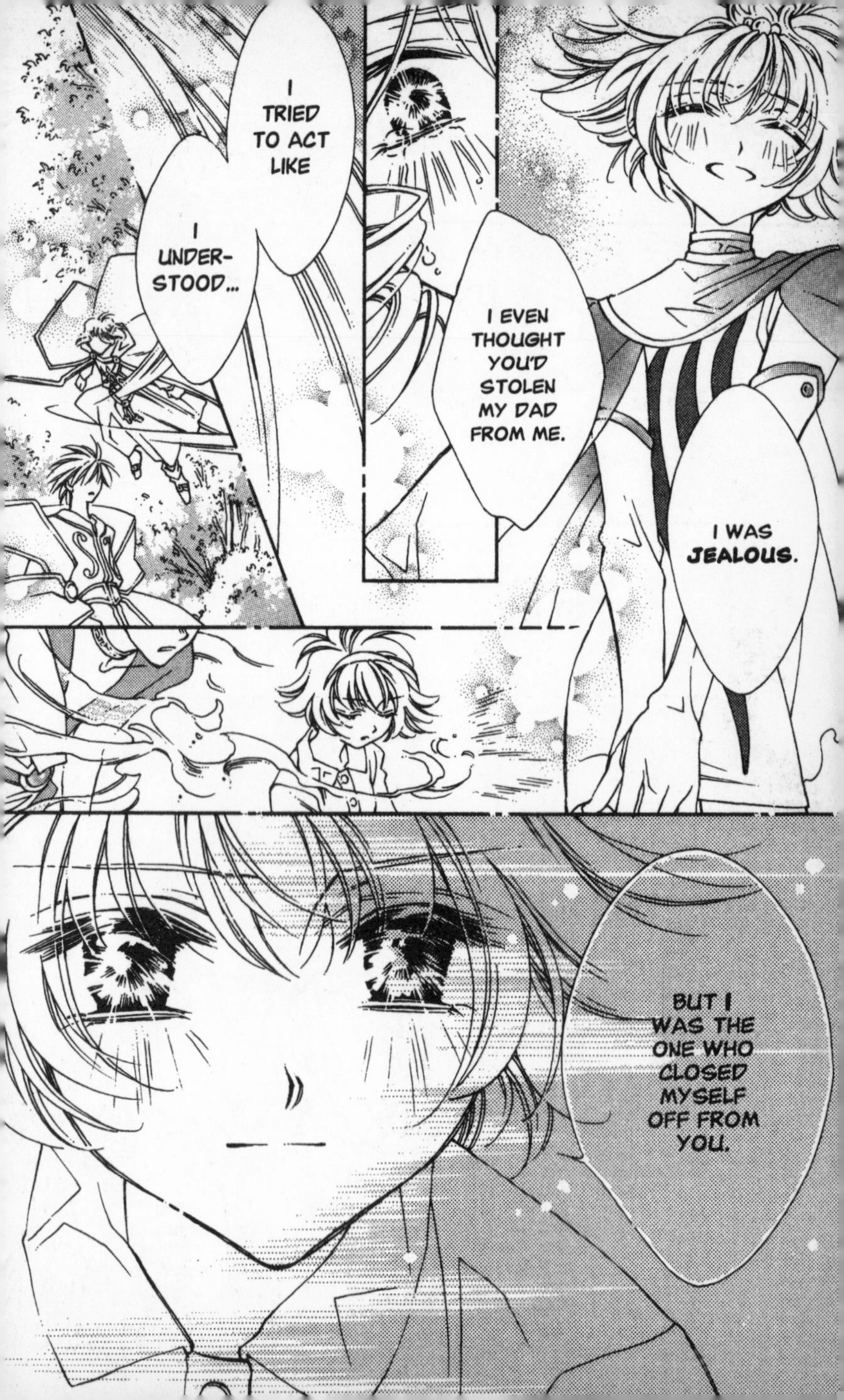
I WAS **JEALOUS.**
I EVEN THOUGHT YOU'D STOLEN MY DAD FROM ME.
I TRIED TO ACT LIKE
I UNDER-STOOD...
BUT I WAS THE ONE WHO CLOSED MYSELF OFF FROM YOU.

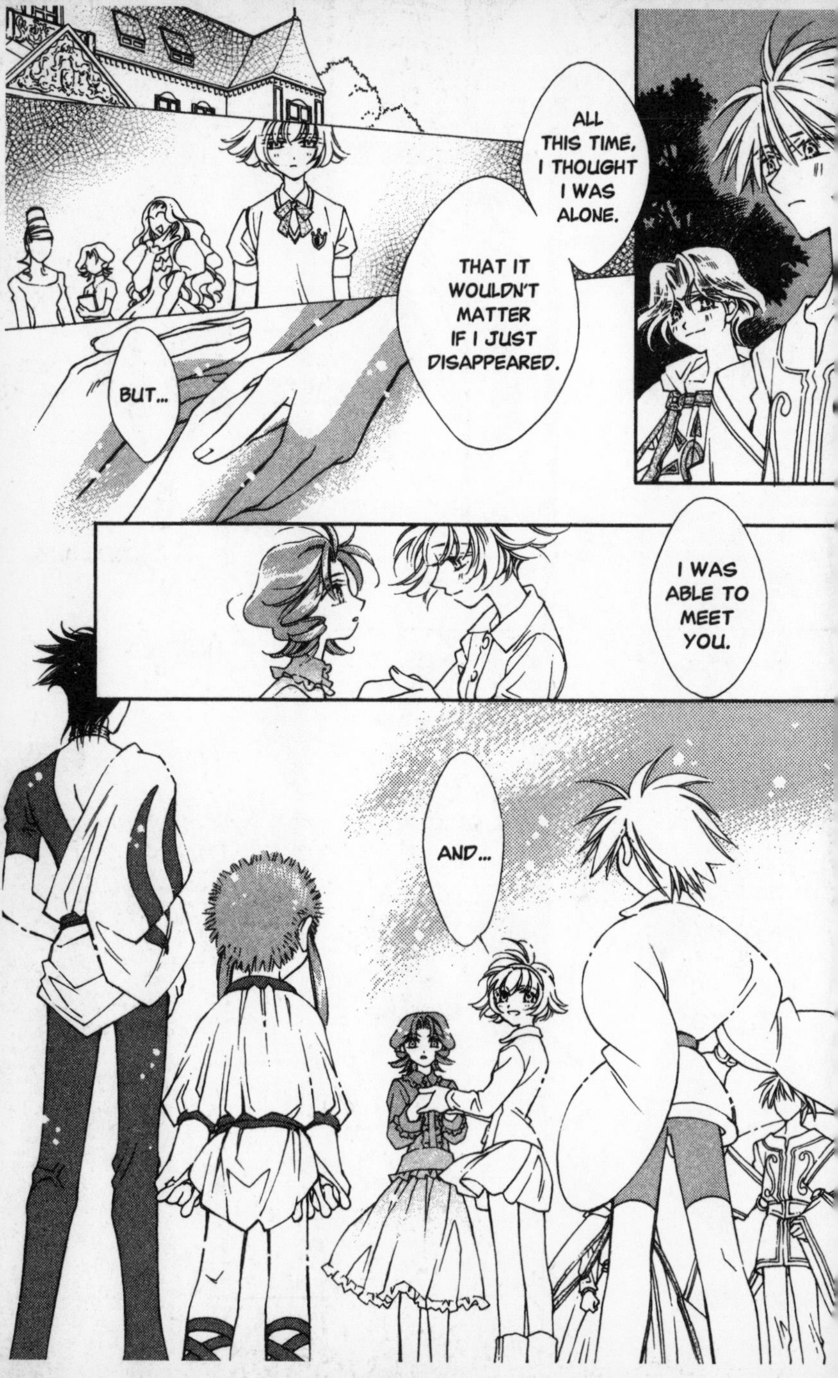
ALL THIS TIME, I THOUGHT I WAS ALONE.
THAT IT WOULDN'T MATTER IF I JUST DISAPPEARED.
BUT...
I WAS ABLE TO MEET YOU.
AND...

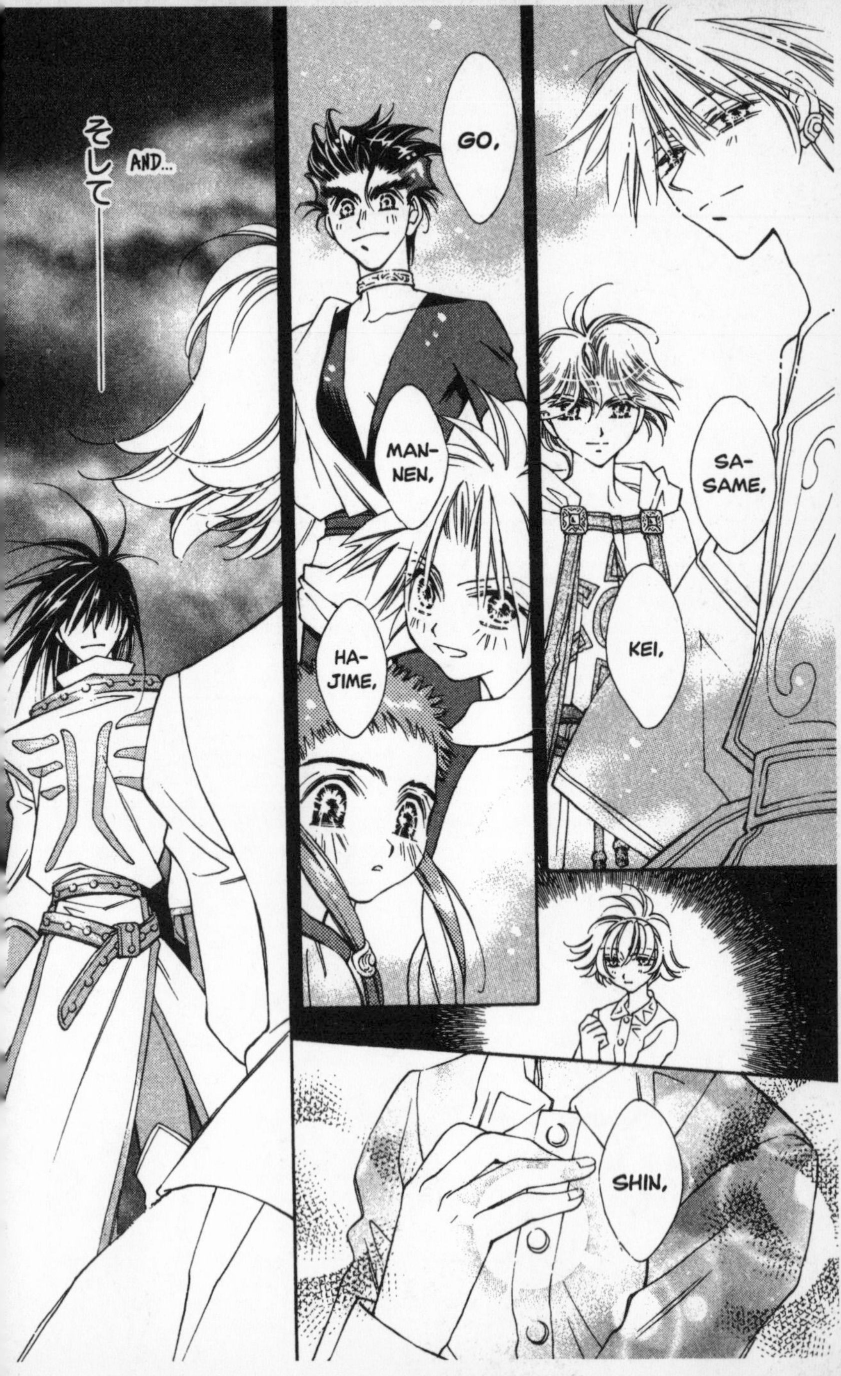
SA-SAME,
KEI,
SHIN,
GO,
MAN-NEN,
HA-JIME,
そして――
AND...

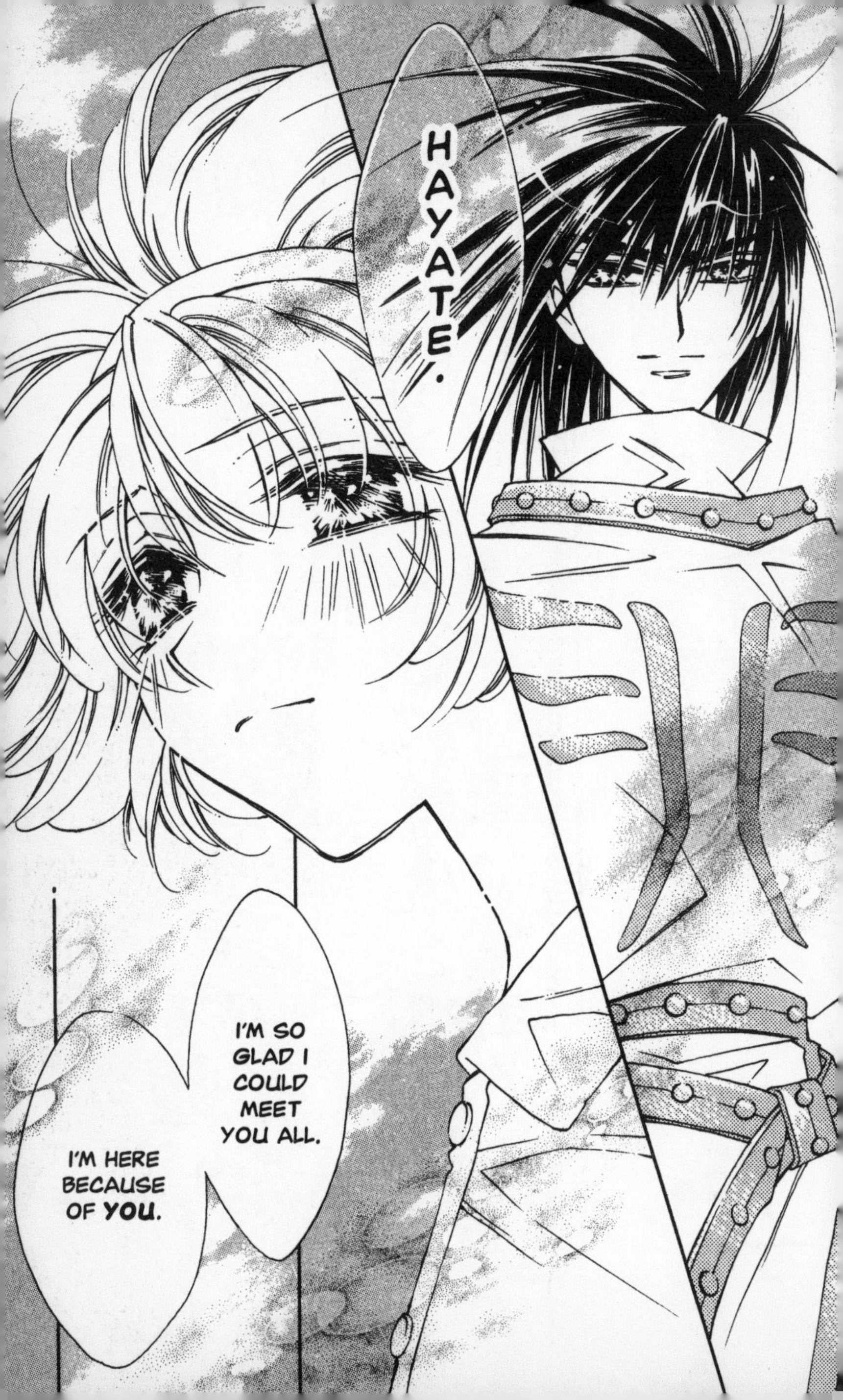
HAYATE.
I'M SO GLAD I COULD MEET YOU ALL.
I'M HERE BECAUSE OF **YOU**.

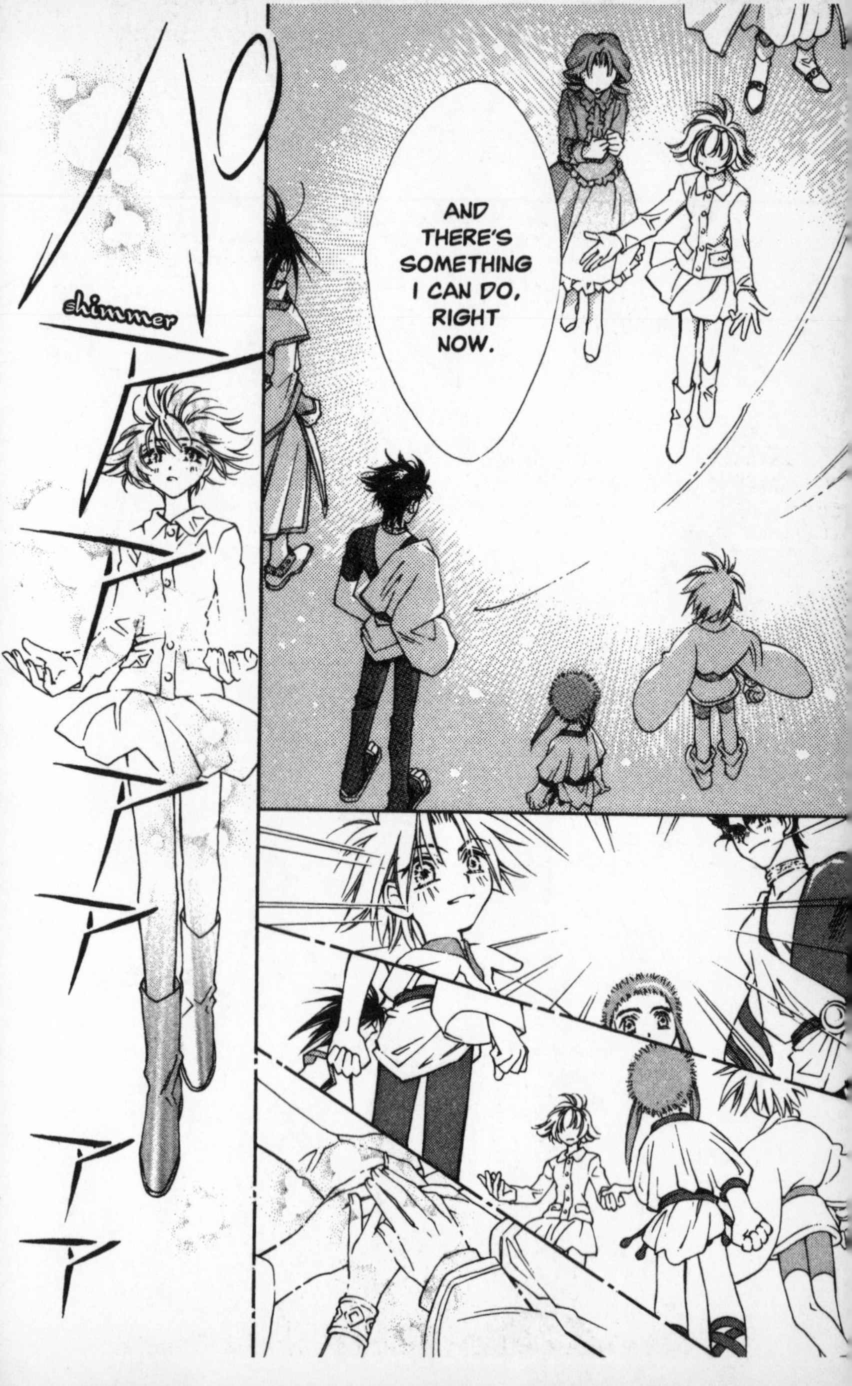
AND THERE'S SOMETHING I CAN DO, RIGHT NOW.
shimmer

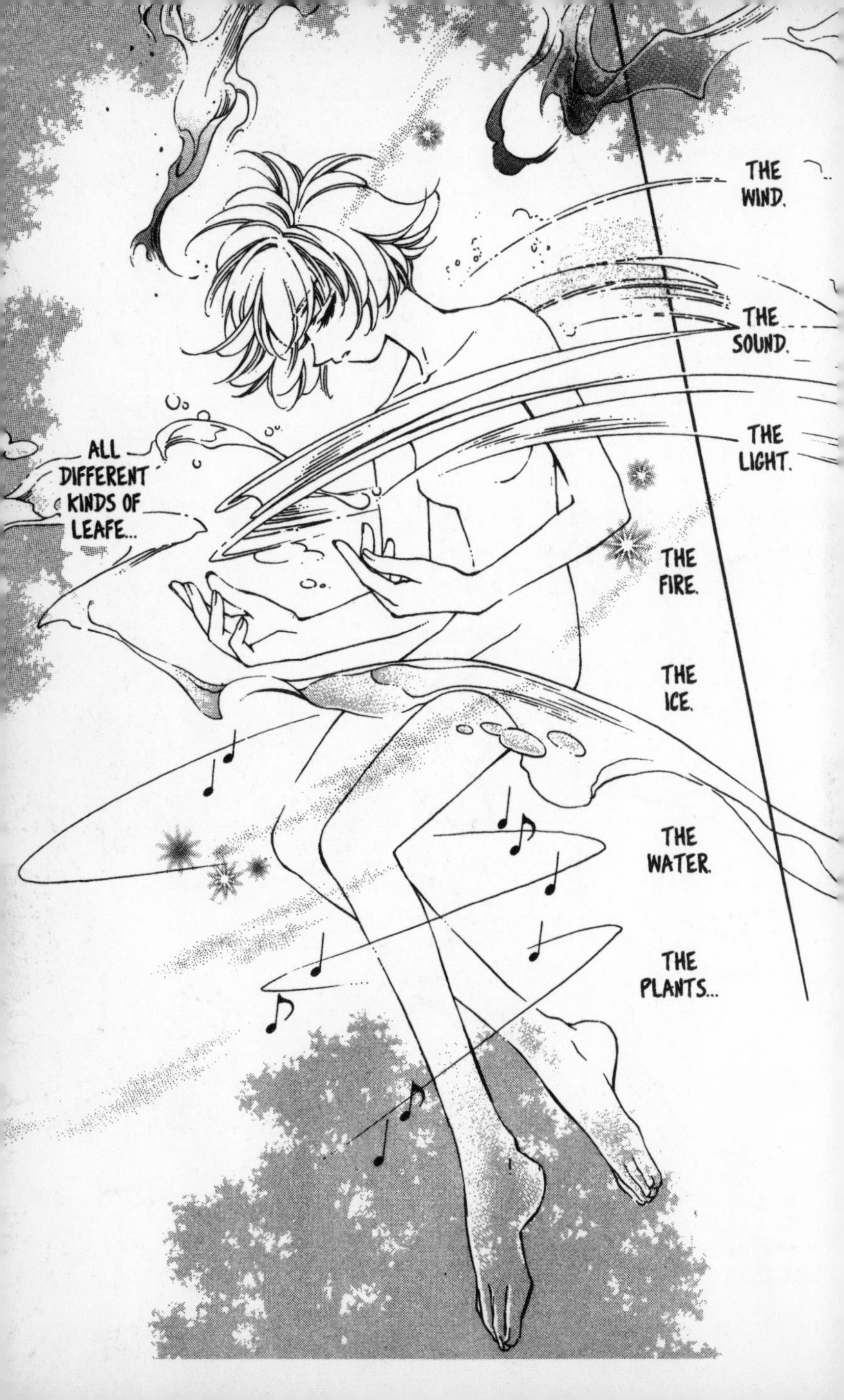
THE WIND.
THE SOUND.
THE LIGHT.
THE FIRE.
THE ICE.
THE WATER.
THE PLANTS...
ALL DIFFERENT KINDS OF LEAFE...

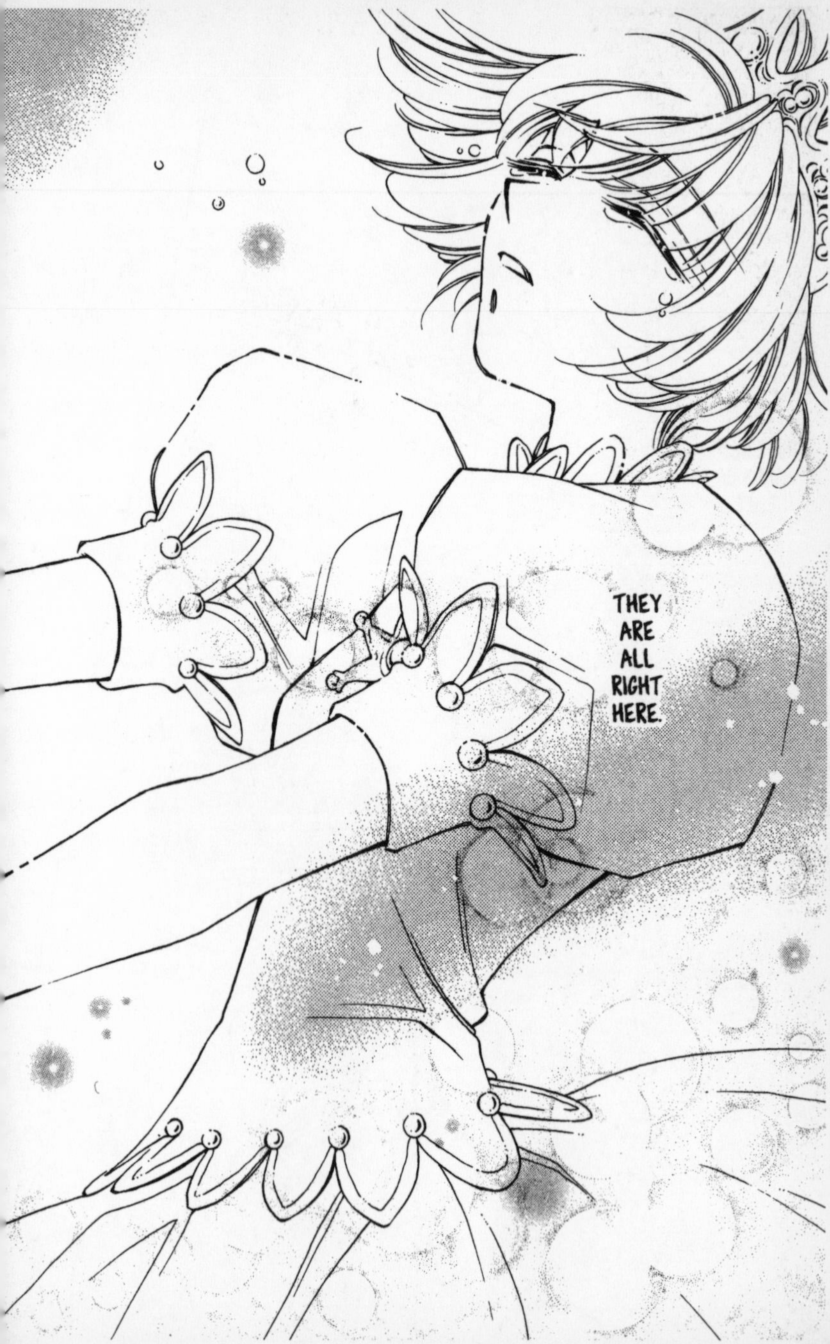
THEY ARE ALL RIGHT HERE.

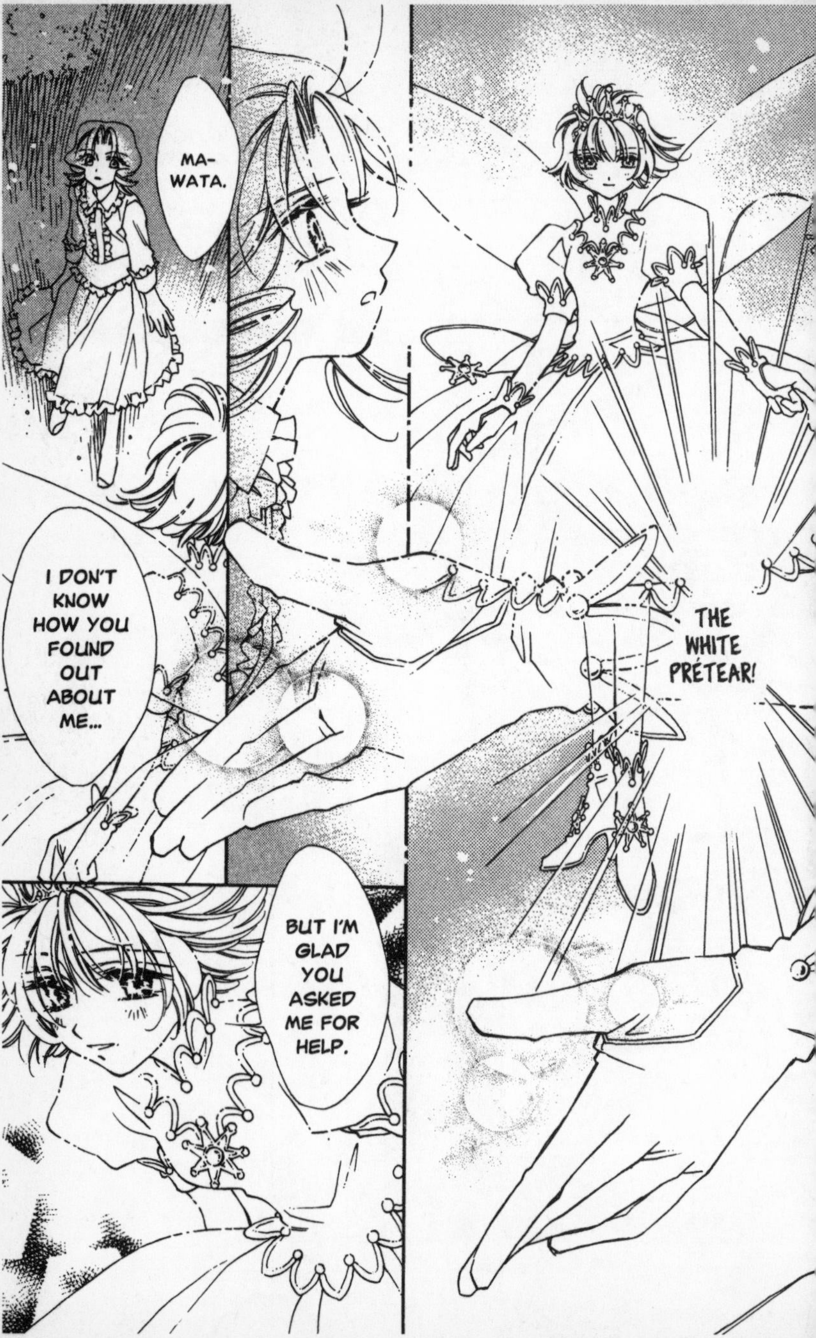
THE WHITE PRÉTEAR!
MA-WATA.
I DON'T KNOW HOW YOU FOUND OUT ABOUT ME...
BUT I'M GLAD YOU ASKED ME FOR HELP.

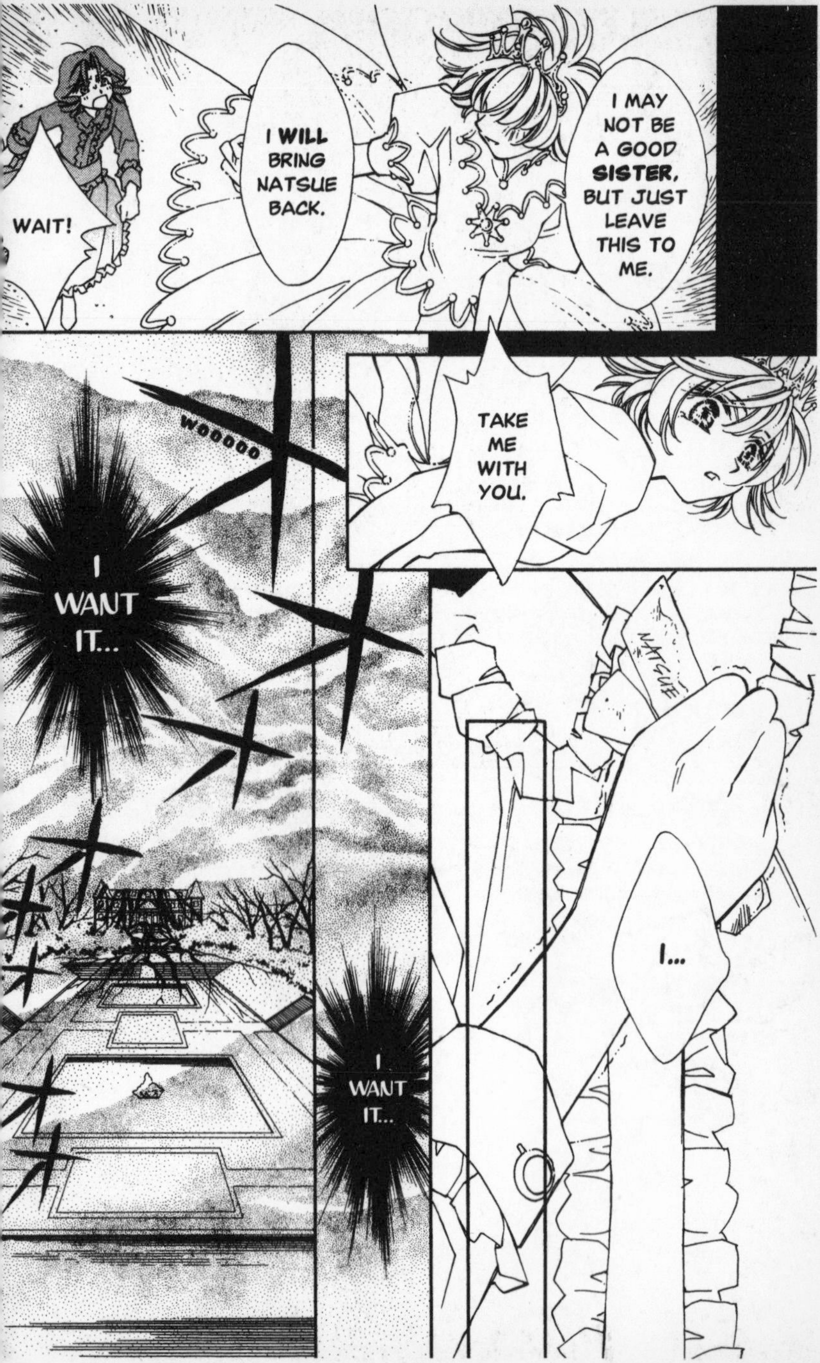
I MAY NOT BE A GOOD **SISTER,** BUT JUST LEAVE THIS TO ME.
I **WILL** BRING NATSUE BACK.
WAIT!
TAKE ME WITH YOU.
NATSUE
I...
I WANT IT...
WOOOOO
I WANT IT...

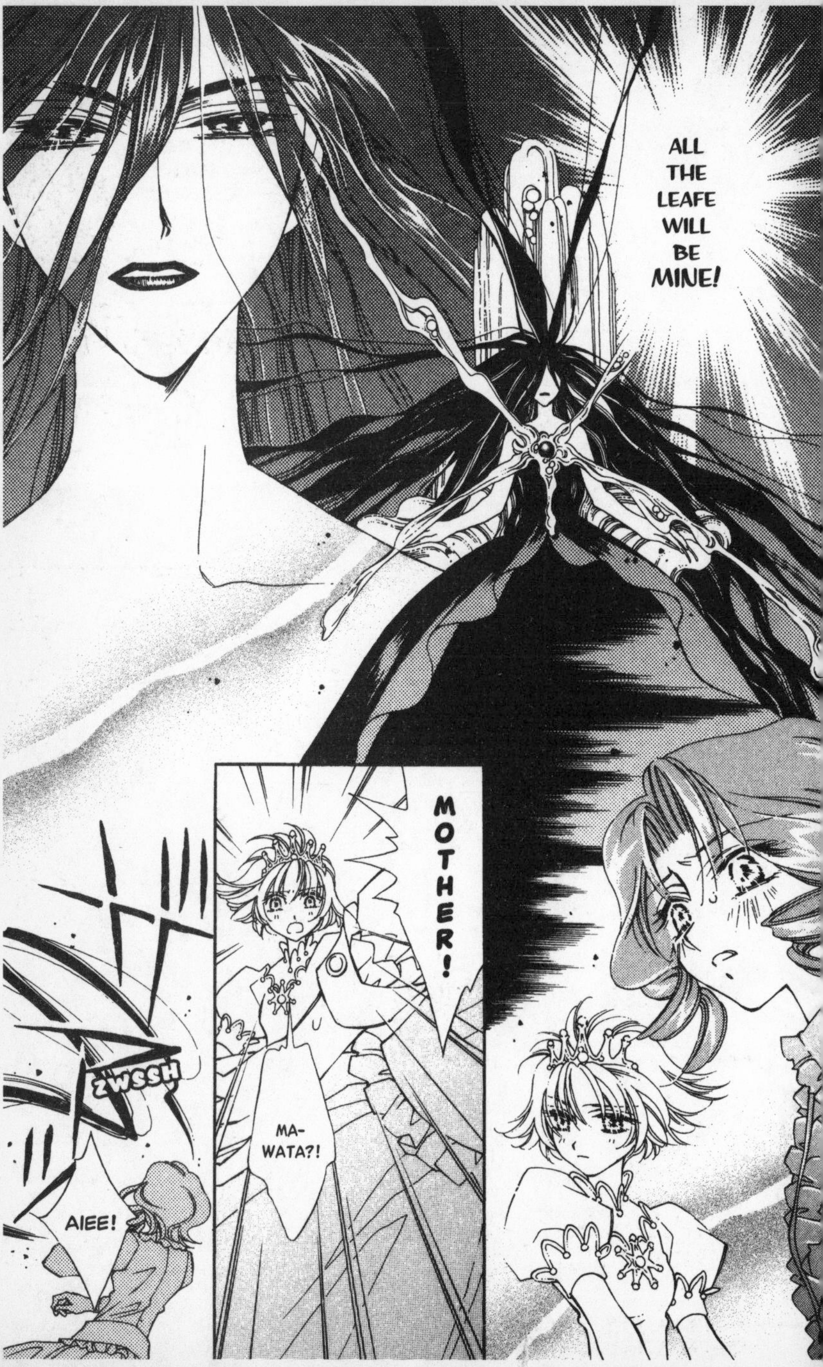
ALL THE LEAFE WILL BE MINE!
MOTHER!
MA-WATA?!
ZWSSH
AIEE!

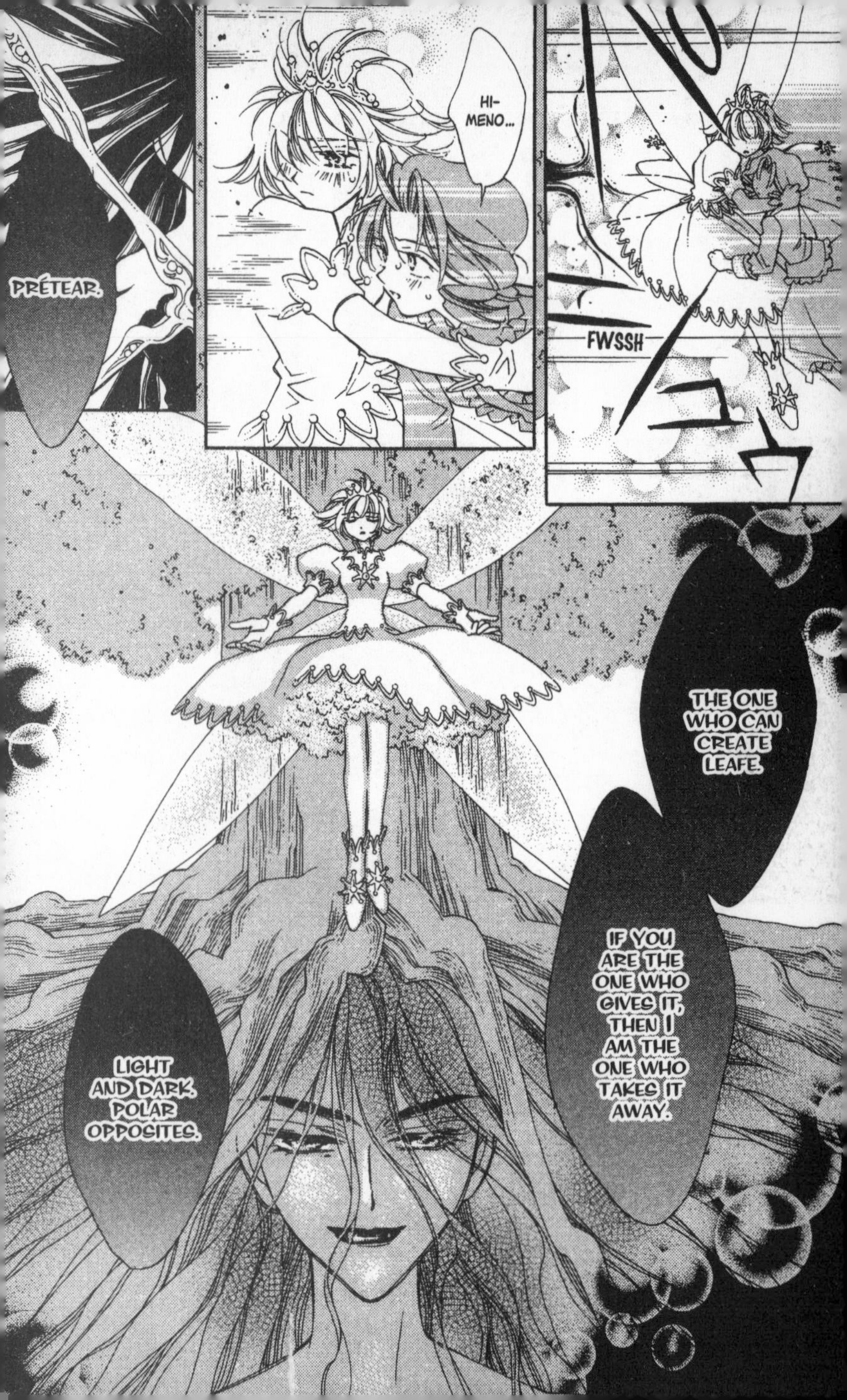
FWSSH
HI-MENO...
PRÉTEAR.
THE ONE WHO CAN CREATE LEAFE.
IF YOU ARE THE ONE WHO GIVES IT, THEN I AM THE ONE WHO TAKES IT AWAY.
LIGHT AND DARK. POLAR OPPOSITES.

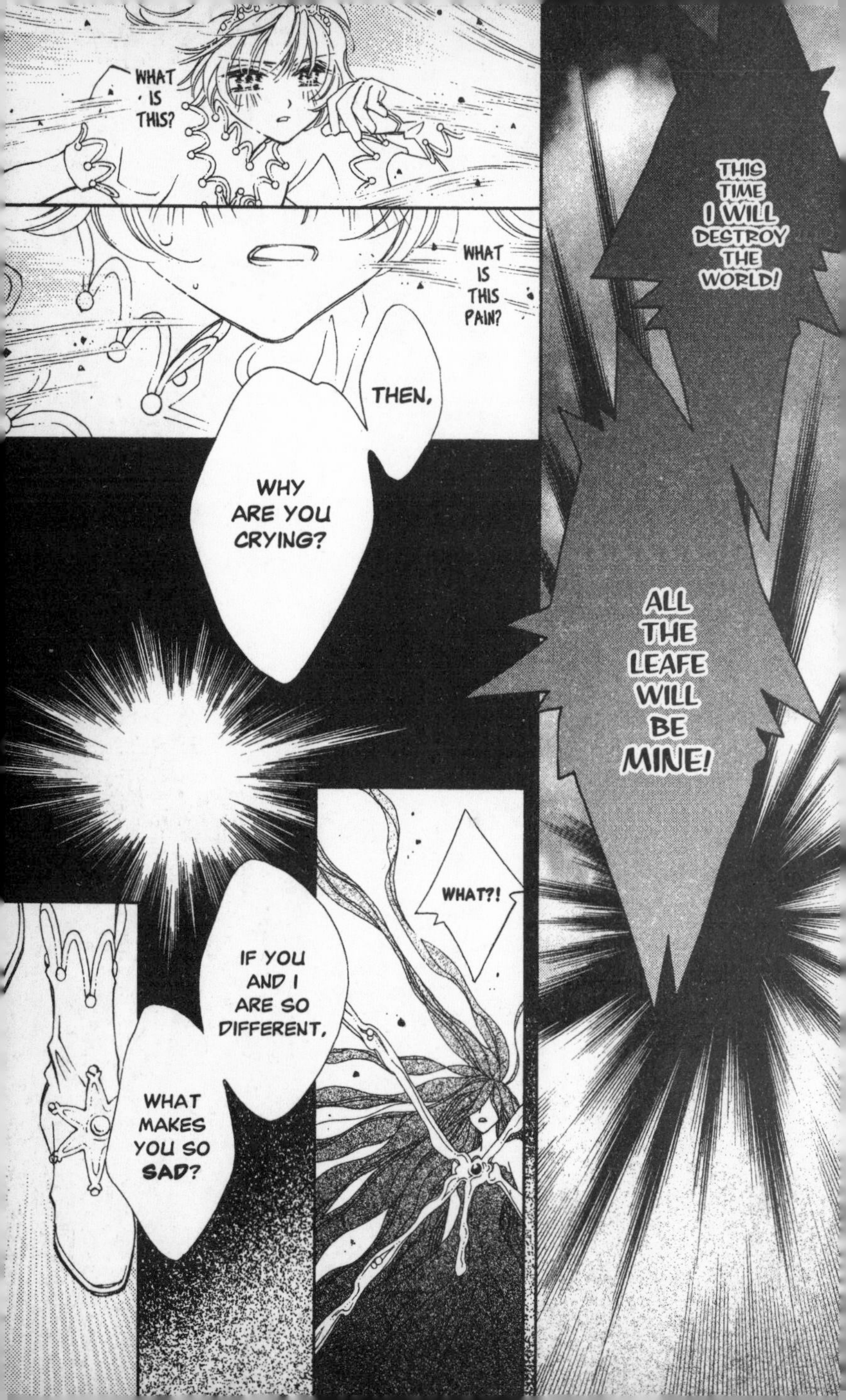
THIS TIME I WILL DESTROY THE WORLD!
ALL THE LEAFE WILL BE MINE!
WHAT IS THIS?
WHAT IS THIS PAIN?
THEN,
WHY ARE YOU CRYING?
WHAT?!
IF YOU AND I ARE SO DIFFERENT,
WHAT MAKES YOU SO SAD?

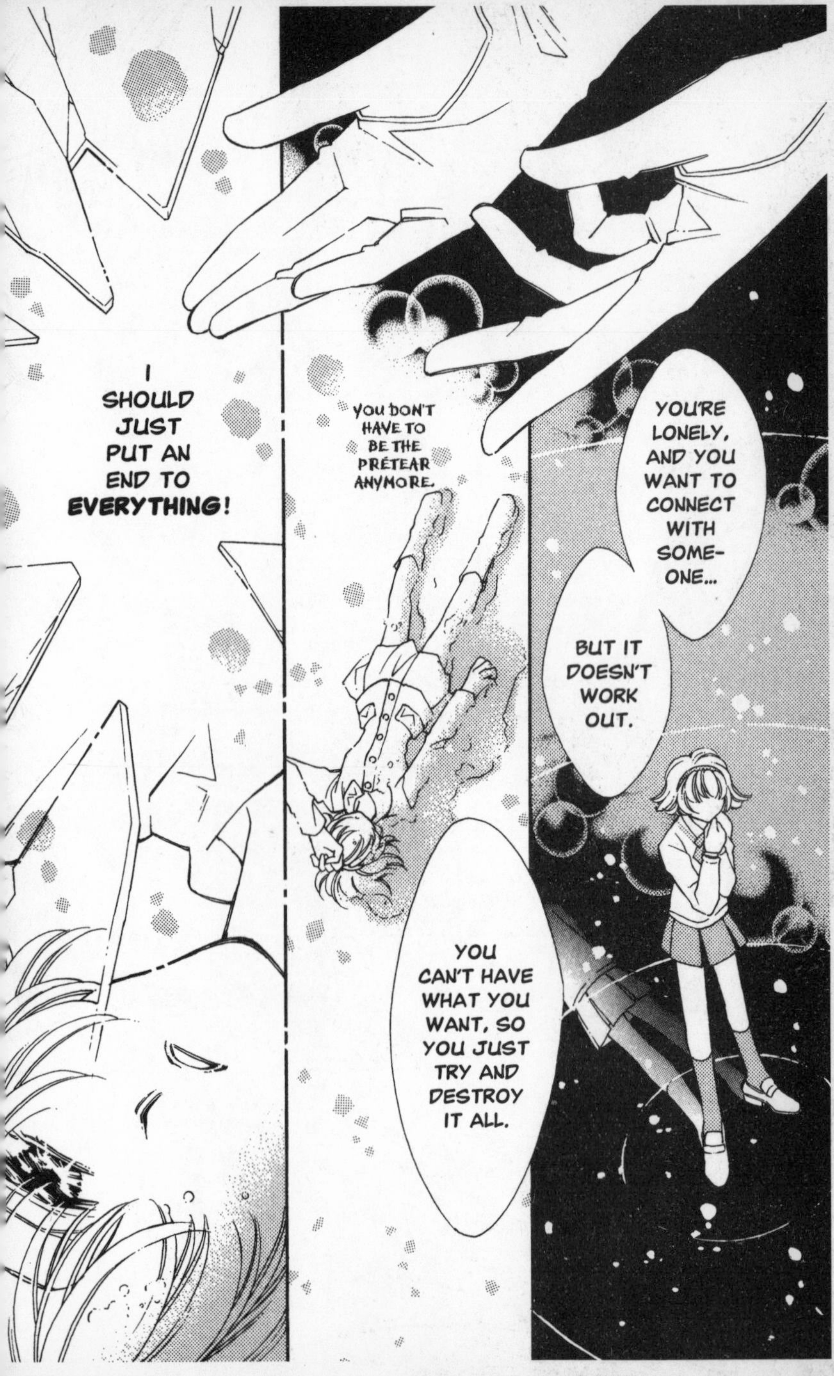
YOU'RE LONELY, AND YOU WANT TO CONNECT WITH SOME-ONE...
BUT IT DOESN'T WORK OUT.
YOU DON'T HAVE TO BE THE PRÉTEAR ANYMORE.
YOU CAN'T HAVE WHAT YOU WANT, SO YOU JUST TRY AND DESTROY IT ALL.
I SHOULD JUST PUT AN END TO **EVERYTHING!**

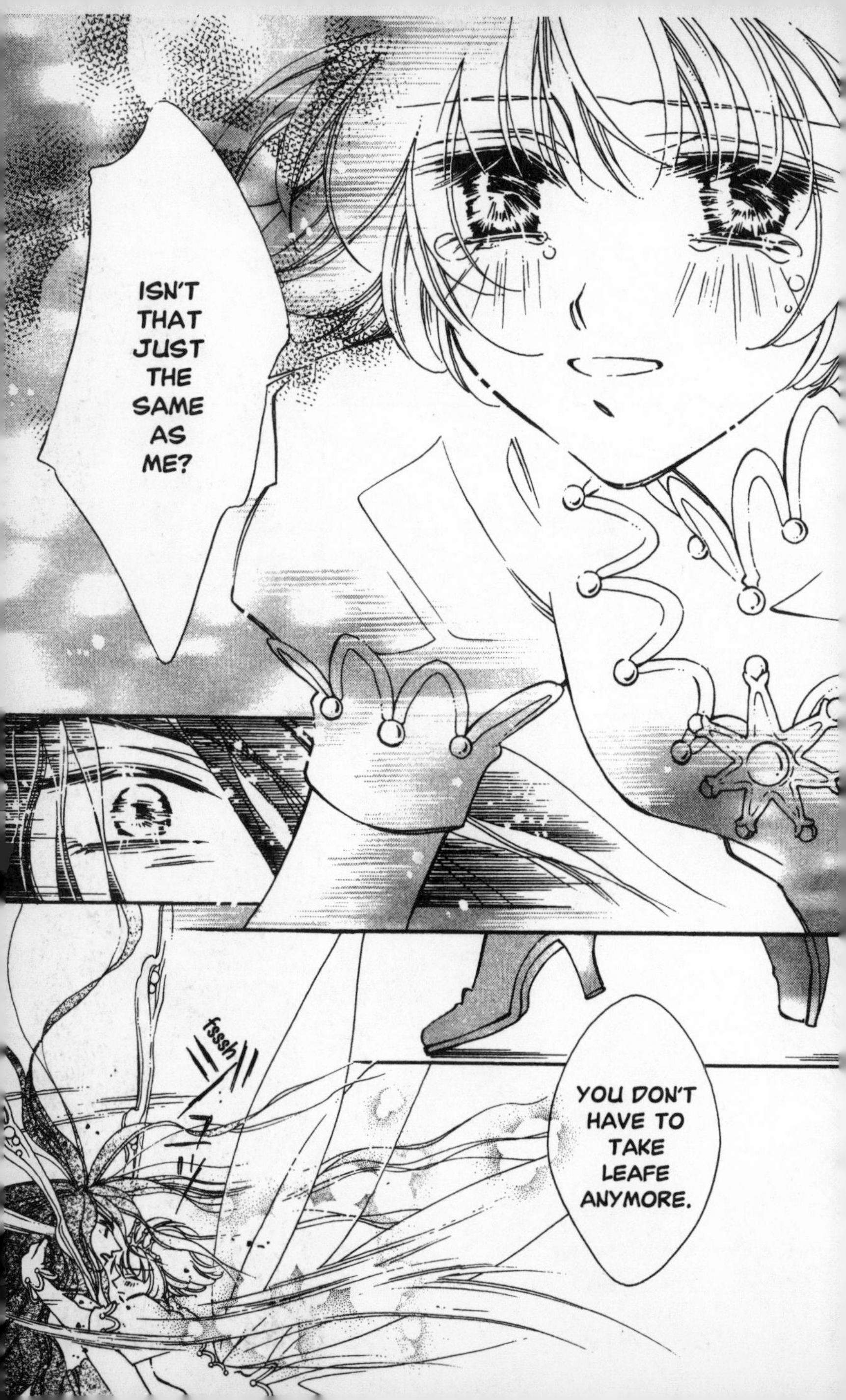
ISN'T THAT JUST THE SAME AS ME?
fsssh
YOU DON'T HAVE TO TAKE LEAFE ANYMORE.

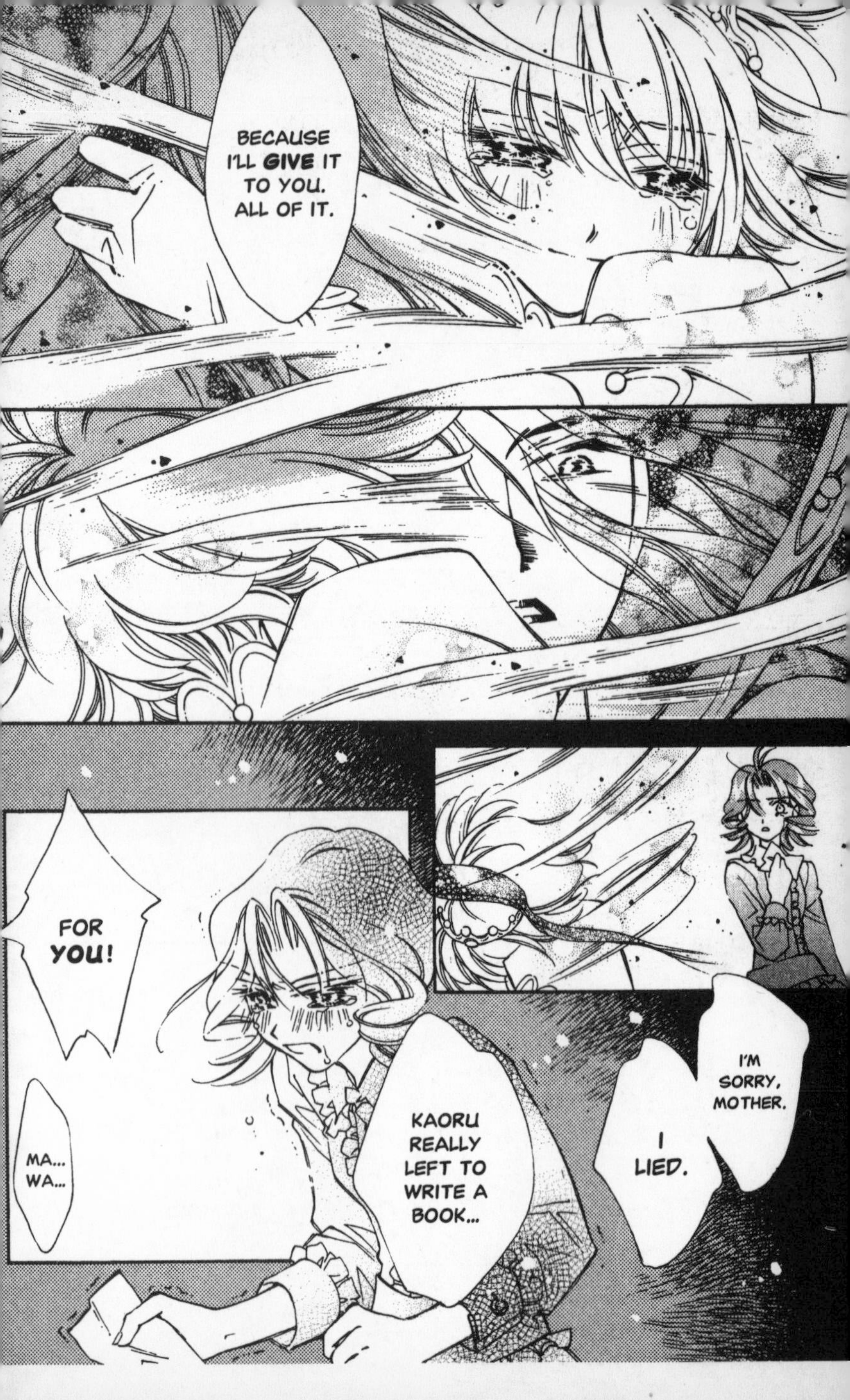
BECAUSE I'LL GIVE IT TO YOU. ALL OF IT.
I'M SORRY, MOTHER.
I LIED.
KAORU REALLY LEFT TO WRITE A BOOK...
FOR YOU!
MA... WA...

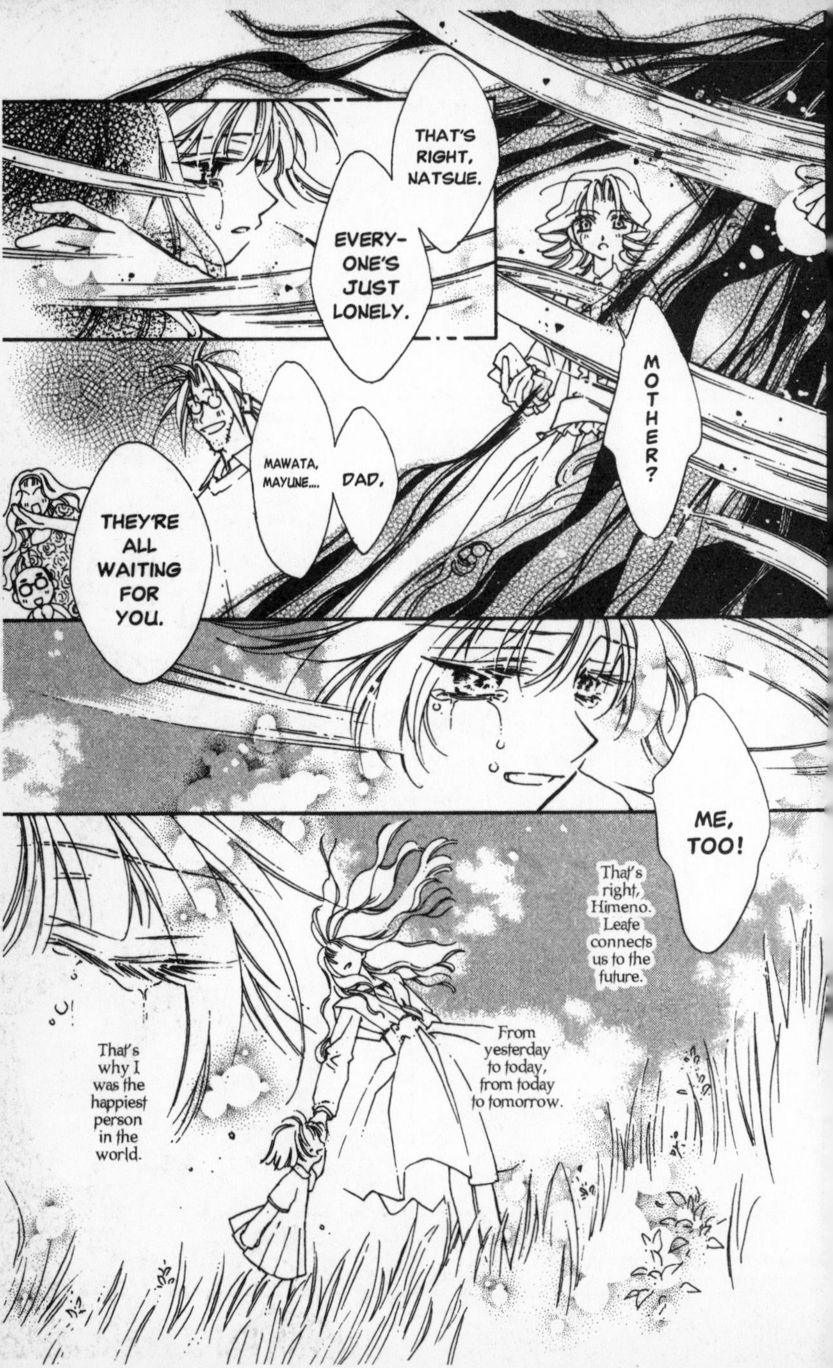
THAT'S RIGHT, NATSUE.
EVERY-ONE'S JUST LONELY.
MOTHER?
DAD,
MAWATA, MAYUNE....
THEY'RE ALL WAITING FOR YOU.
ME, TOO!
That's right, Himeno. Leafe connects us to the future.
From yesterday to today, from today to tomorrow.
That's why I was the happiest person in the world.

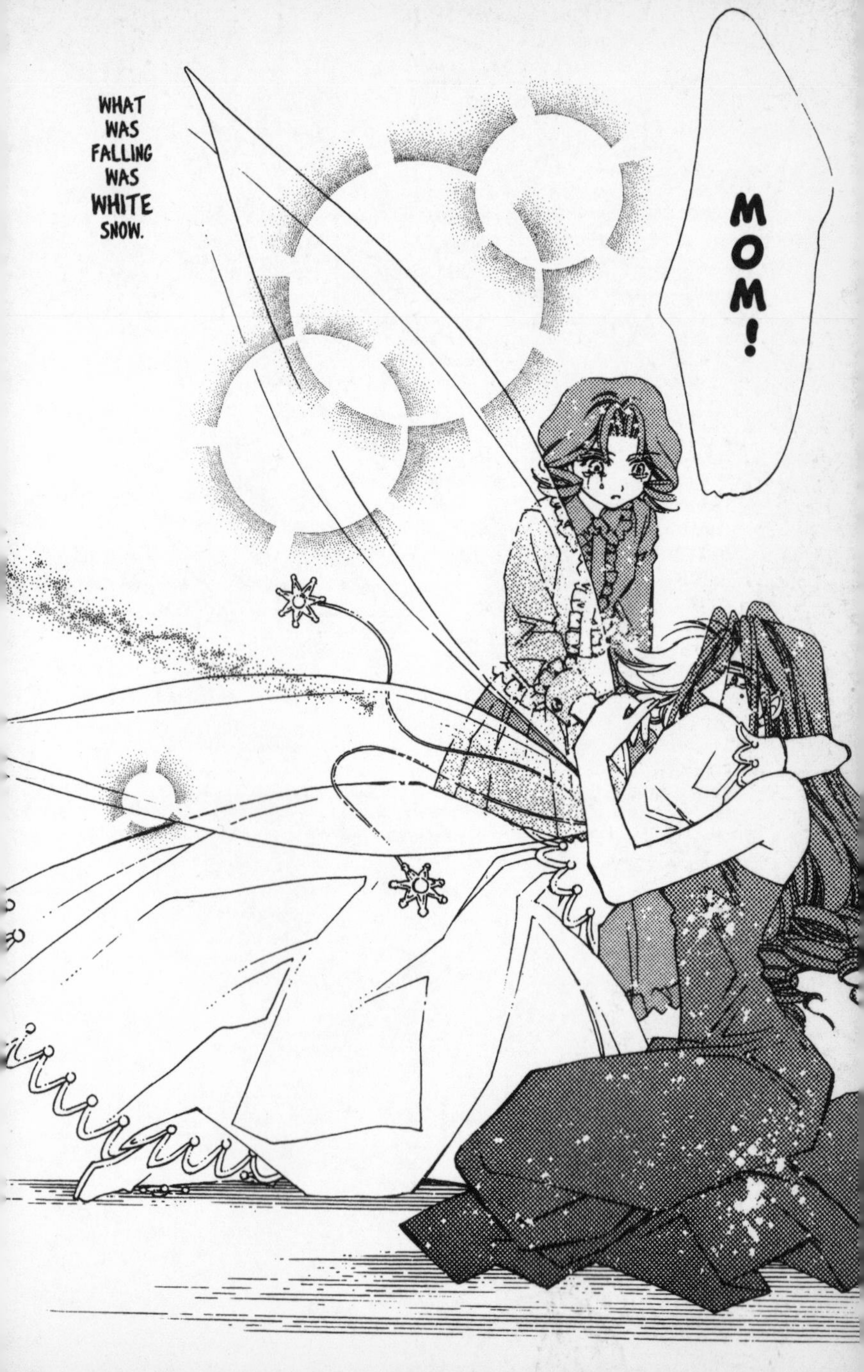
MOM!
WHAT WAS FALLING WAS WHITE SNOW.

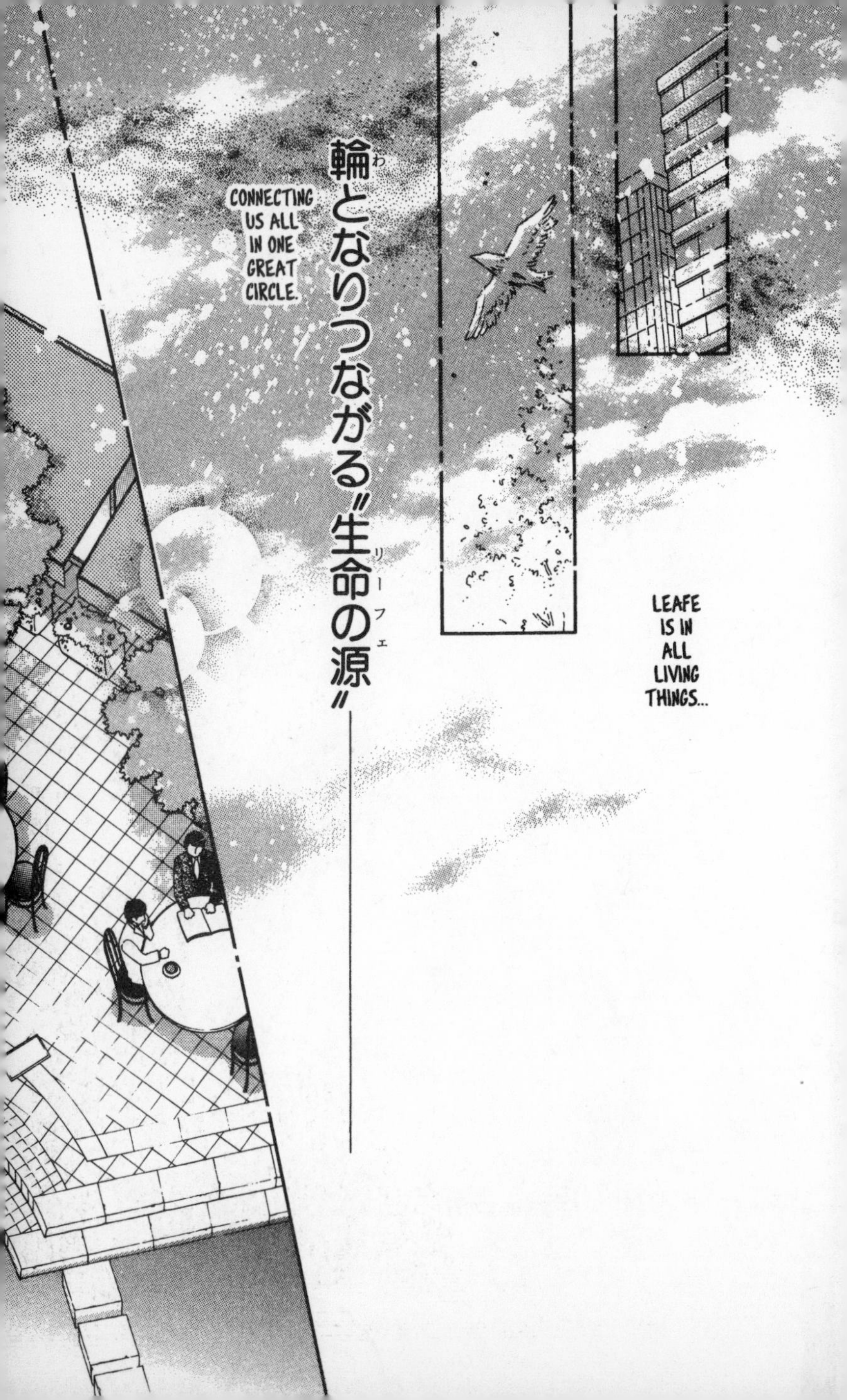
LEAFE IS IN ALL LIVING THINGS...
輪となりつながる〝生命の源〟
CONNECTING US ALL IN ONE GREAT CIRCLE.

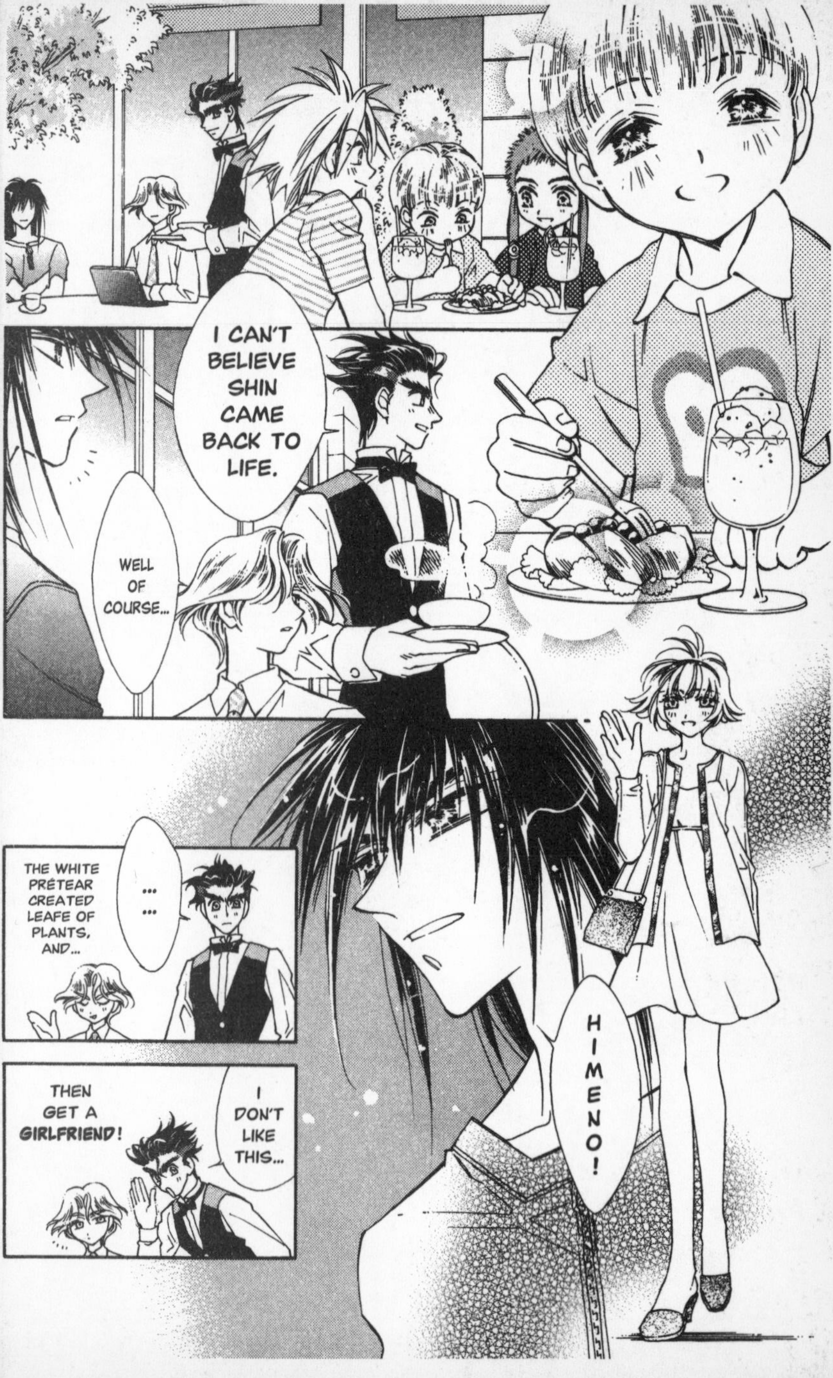
I CAN'T BELIEVE SHIN CAME BACK TO LIFE.
WELL OF COURSE...
HIMENO!
......
THE WHITE PRÉTEAR CREATED LEAFE OF PLANTS, AND...
I DON'T LIKE THIS...
THEN GET A **GIRLFRIEND**!

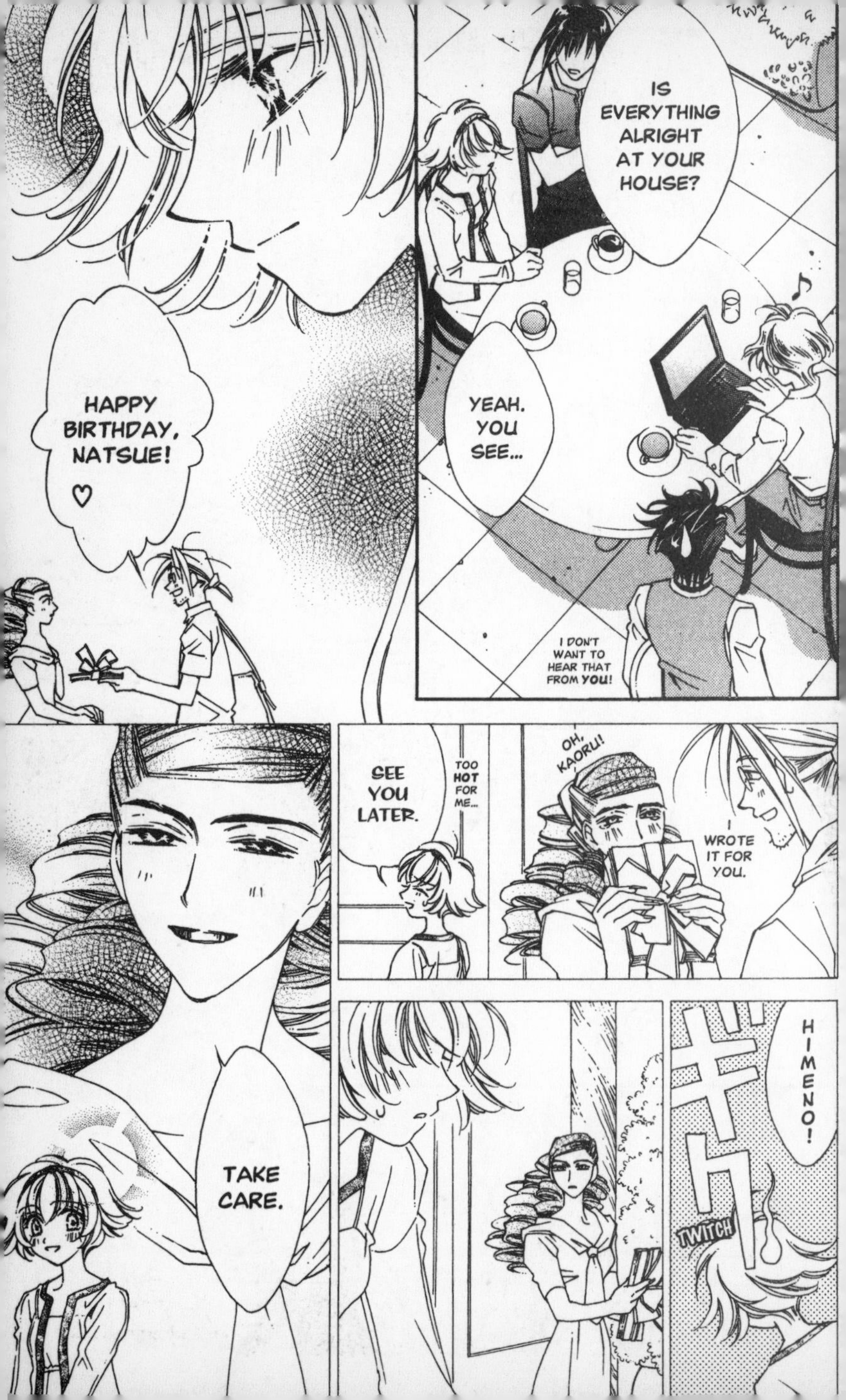
IS EVERYTHING ALRIGHT AT YOUR HOUSE?
YEAH. YOU SEE...
I DON'T WANT TO HEAR THAT FROM YOU!
HAPPY BIRTHDAY, NATSUE! ♡
OH, KAORU!
I WROTE IT FOR YOU.
SEE YOU LATER.
TOO HOT FOR ME...
HIMENO!
ギト
TWITCH
TAKE CARE.

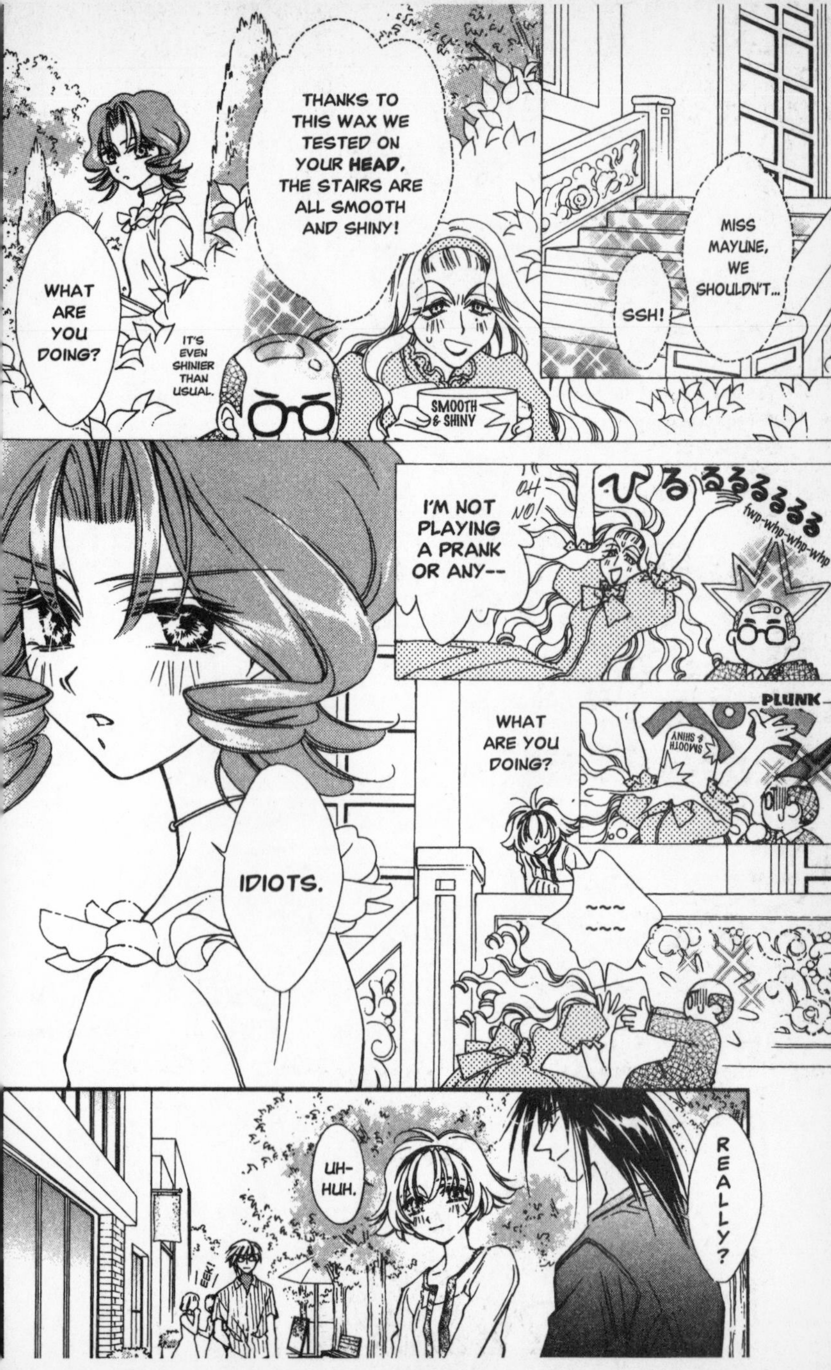

MISS MAYUNE, WE SHOULDN'T...
SSH!
THANKS TO THIS WAX WE TESTED ON YOUR **HEAD**, THE STAIRS ARE ALL SMOOTH AND SHINY!
IT'S EVEN SHINIER THAN USUAL.
SMOOTH & SHINY
WHAT ARE YOU DOING?
びるるるるるるる
fwp-whp-whp-whp
OH NO!
I'M NOT PLAYING A PRANK OR ANY--
PLUNK
SMOOTH & SHINY
WHAT ARE YOU DOING?
~~~ ~~~
IDIOTS.
REALLY?
UH-HUH.
EEK!
~~~

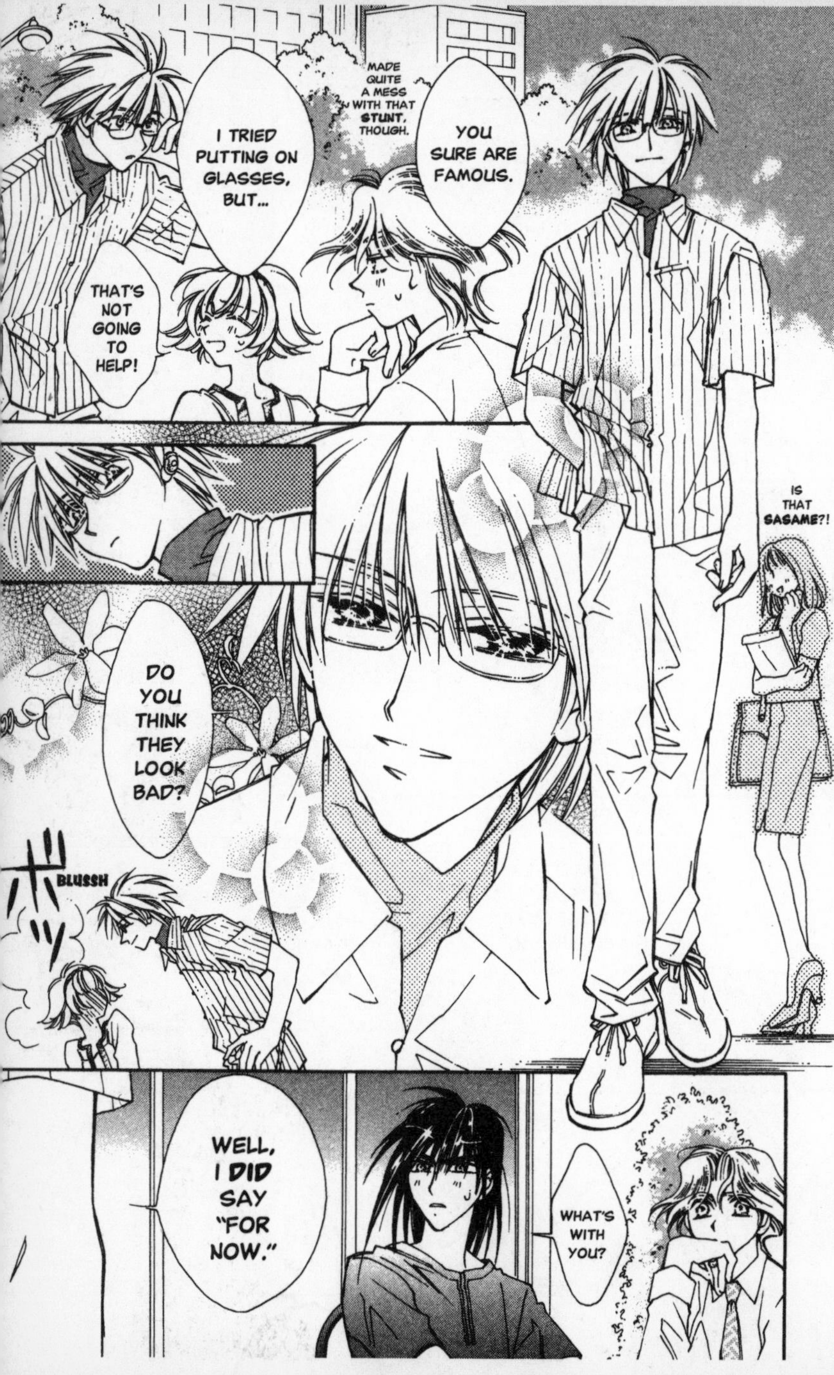
YOU SURE ARE FAMOUS.
MADE QUITE A MESS WITH THAT STUNT, THOUGH.
I TRIED PUTTING ON GLASSES, BUT...
THAT'S NOT GOING TO HELP!
IS THAT SASAME?!
DO YOU THINK THEY LOOK BAD?
BLUSSH
WHAT'S WITH YOU?
WELL, I DID SAY "FOR NOW."

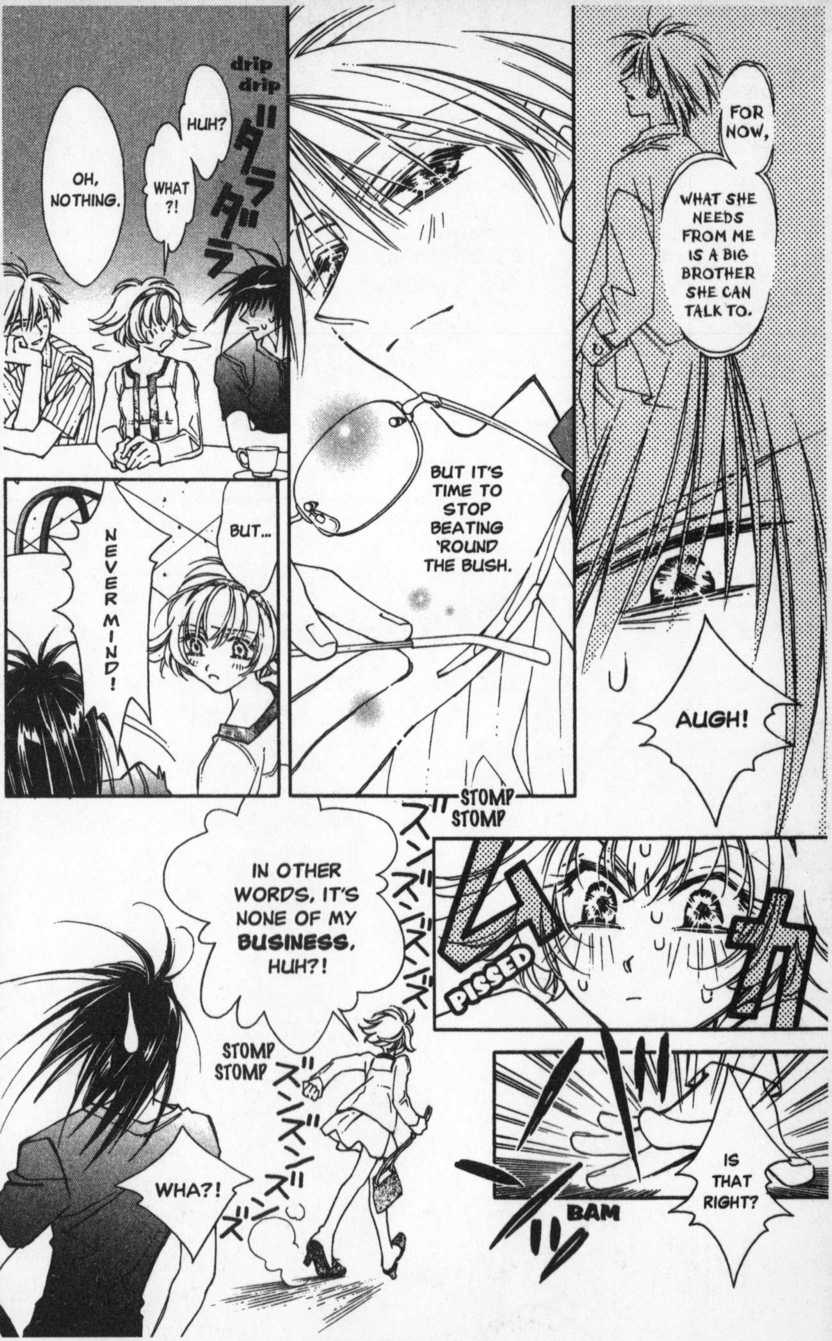

FOR NOW,
WHAT SHE NEEDS FROM ME IS A BIG BROTHER SHE CAN TALK TO.
AUGH!
BUT IT'S TIME TO STOP BEATING 'ROUND THE BUSH.
drip drip
ダラダラ
HUH?
WHAT?!
OH, NOTHING.
BUT...
NEVER MIND!
STOMP STOMP
ムカ
PISSED
IS THAT RIGHT?
BAM
IN OTHER WORDS, IT'S NONE OF MY BUSINESS, HUH?!
STOMP STOMP
WHA?!

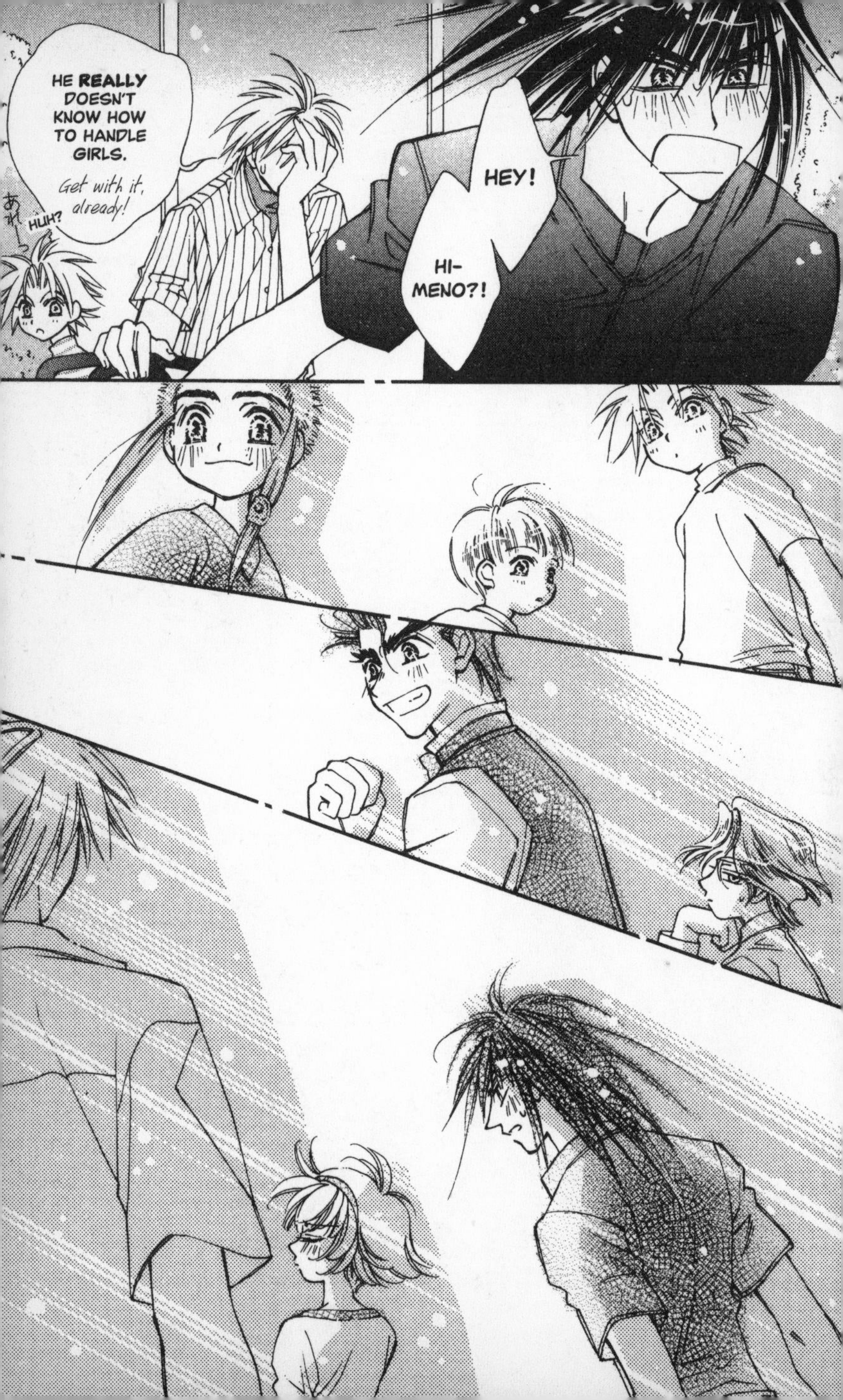
HEY!
HI-MENO?!
HE REALLY DOESN'T KNOW HOW TO HANDLE GIRLS.
Get with it, already!
HUH?

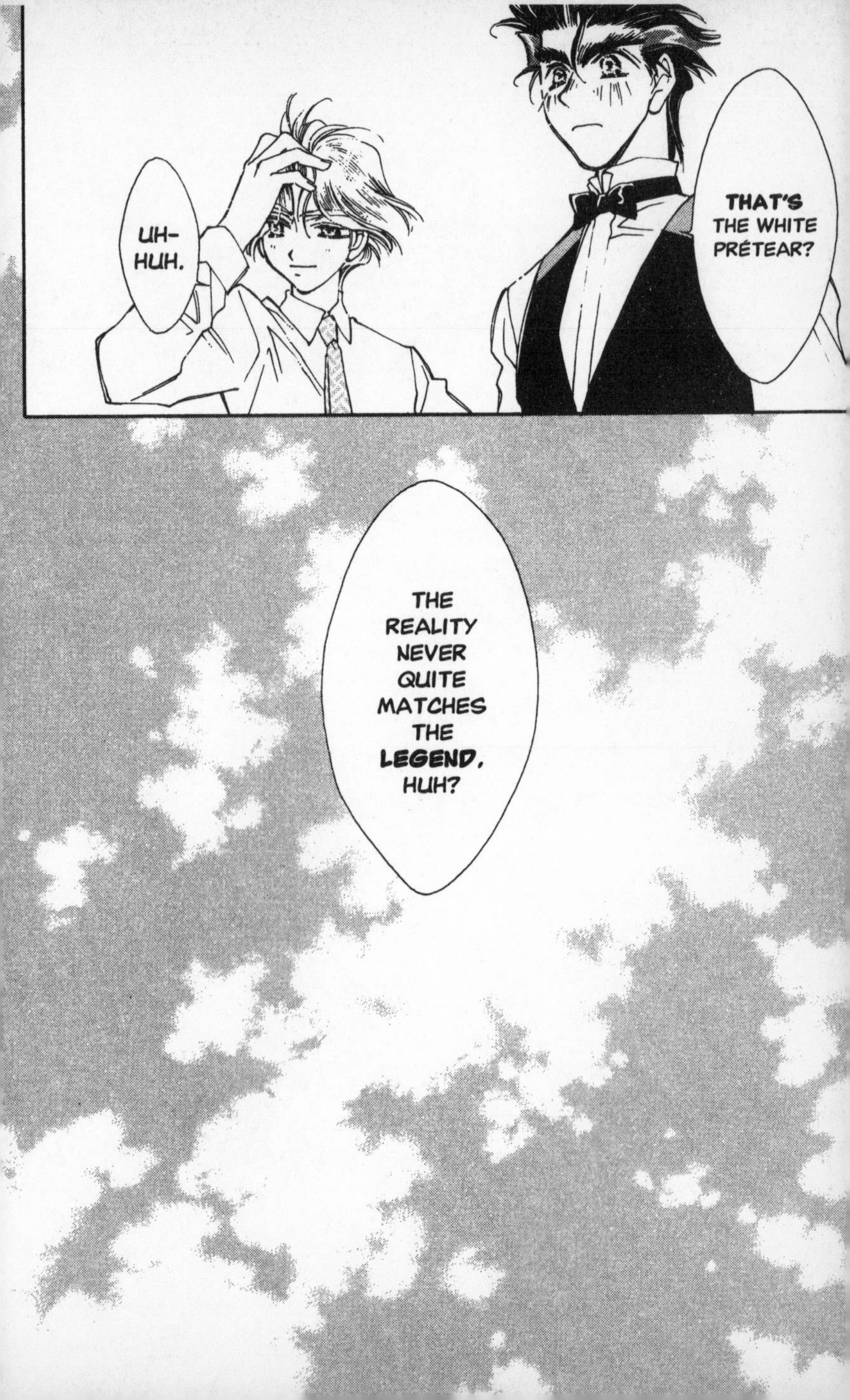
THAT'S THE WHITE PRÉTEAR?
UH-HUH.
THE REALITY NEVER QUITE MATCHES THE LEGEND, HUH?

Epilogue

THE WORLD TURNS

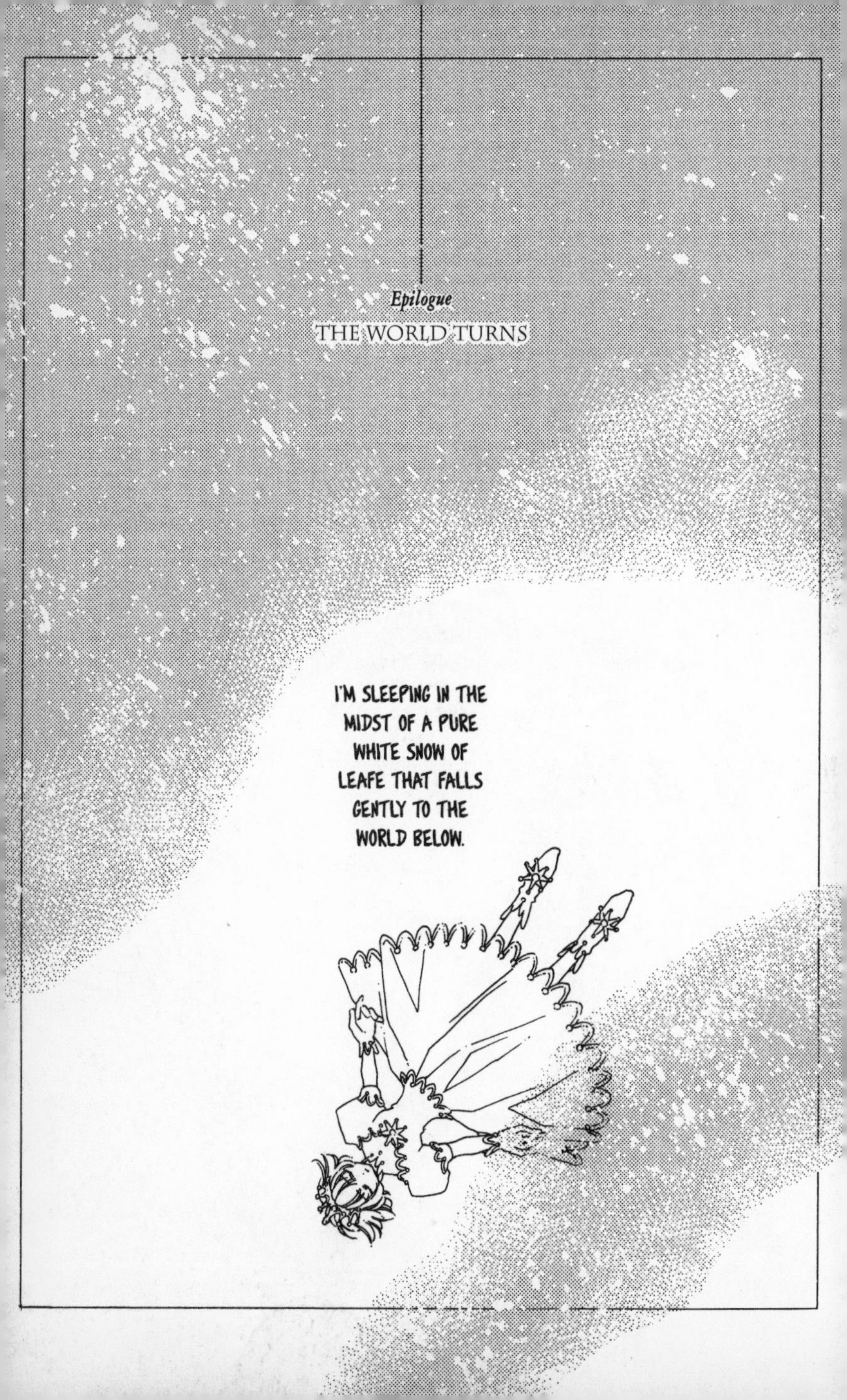
I'M SLEEPING IN THE MIDST OF A PURE WHITE SNOW OF LEAFE THAT FALLS GENTLY TO THE WORLD BELOW.

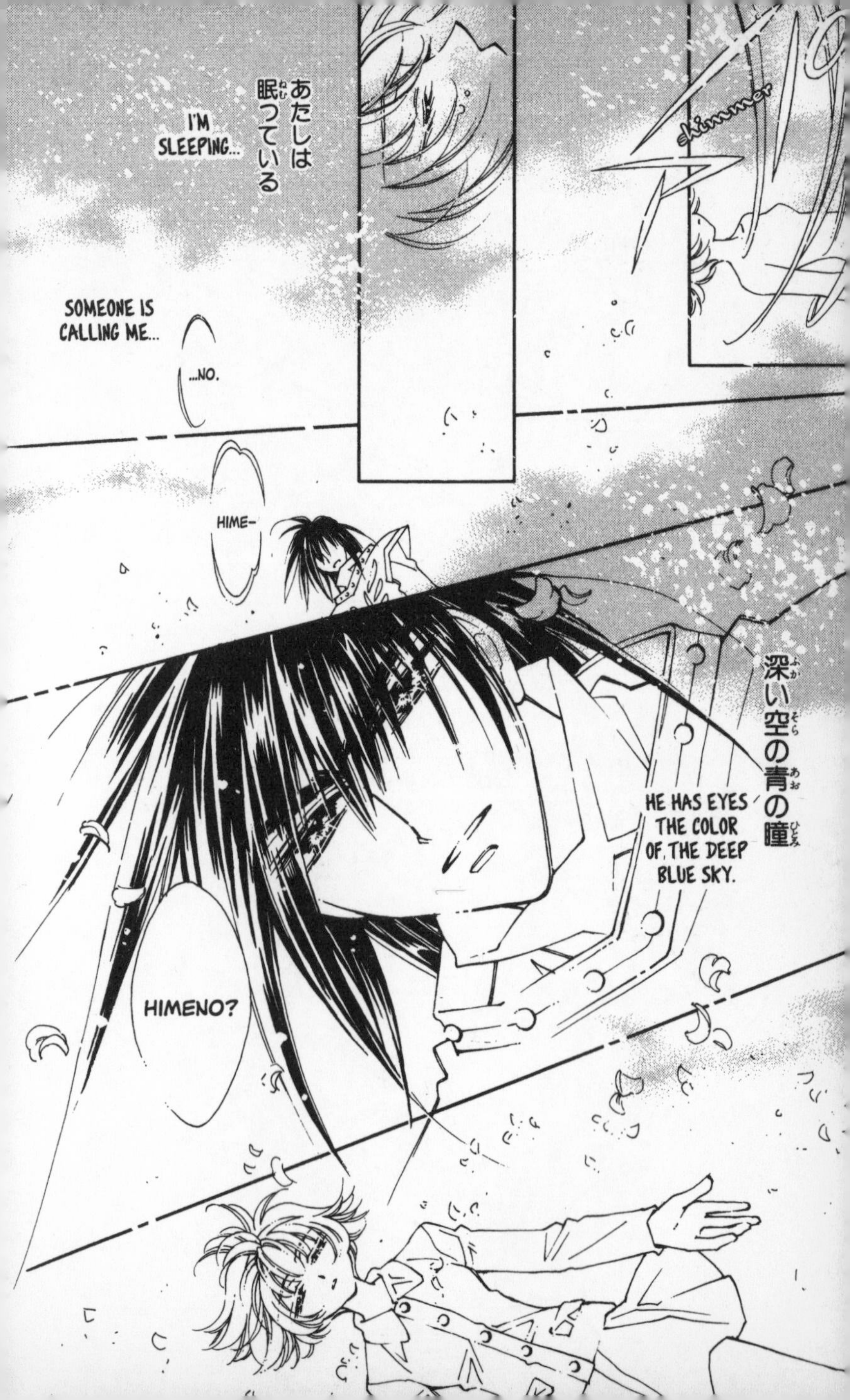
shimmer
あたしは眠っている
I'M SLEEPING...
SOMEONE IS CALLING ME...
...NO.
HIME-
深い空の青の瞳
HE HAS EYES THE COLOR OF THE DEEP BLUE SKY.
HIMENO?

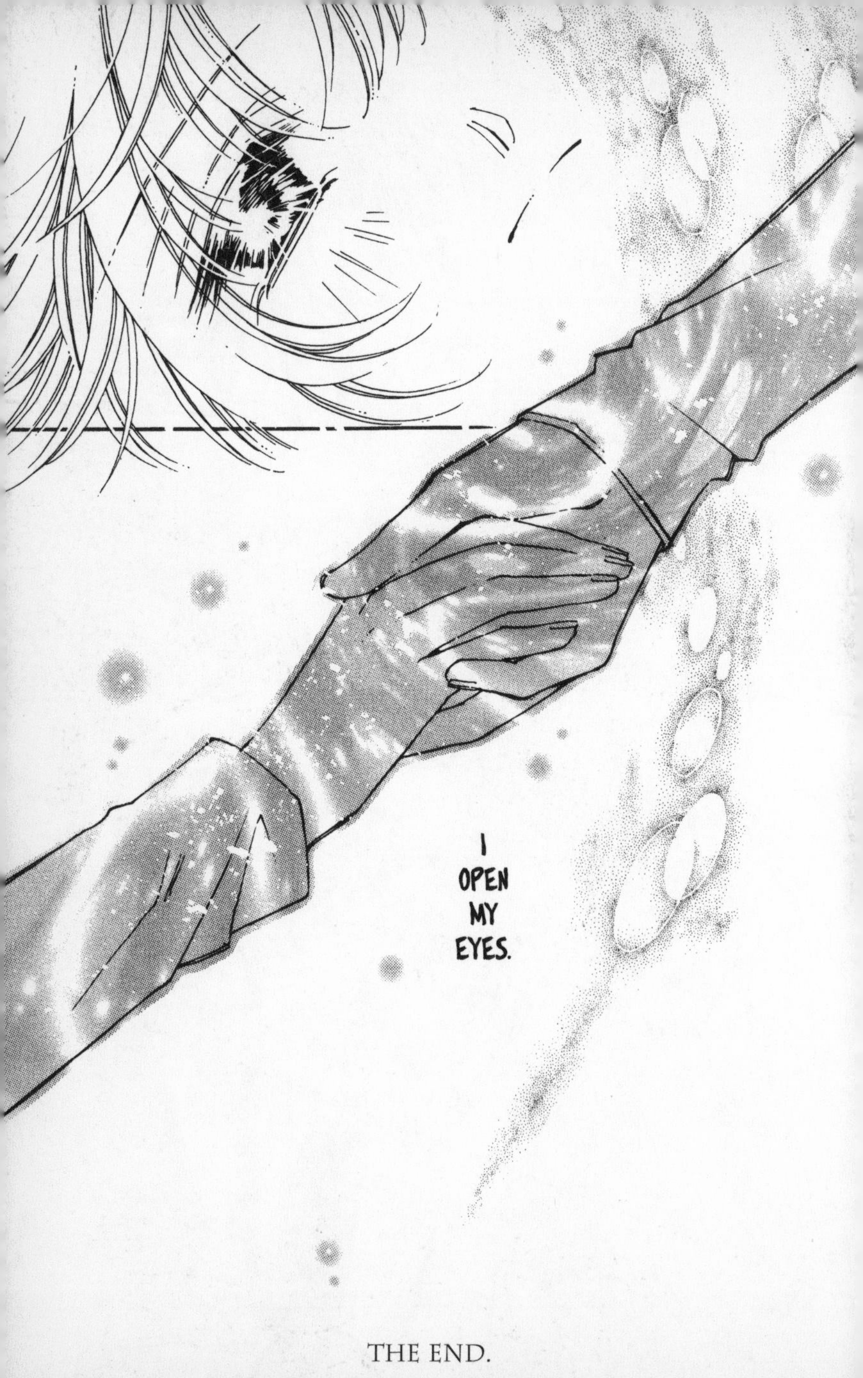
I OPEN MY EYES.

THE END.

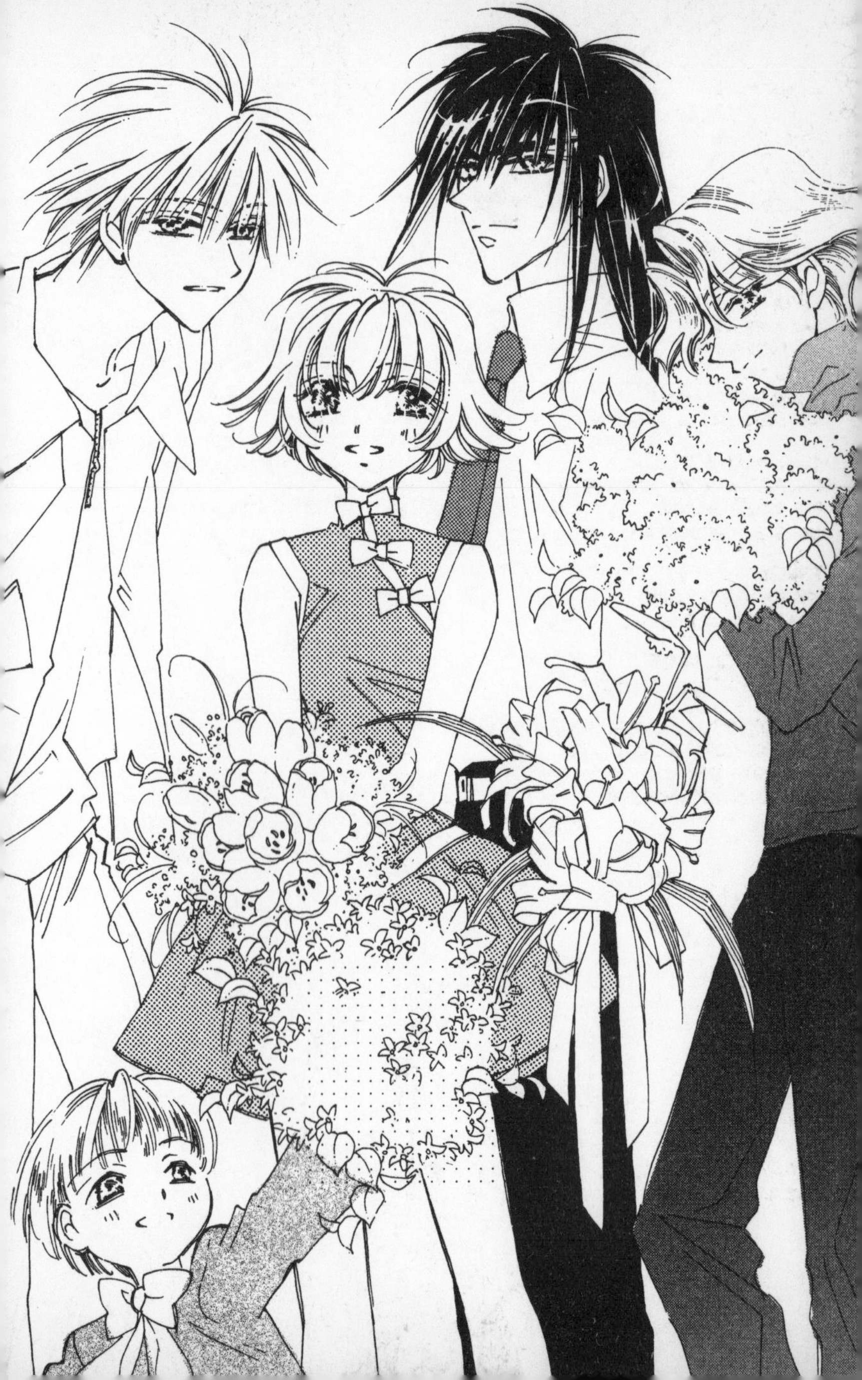

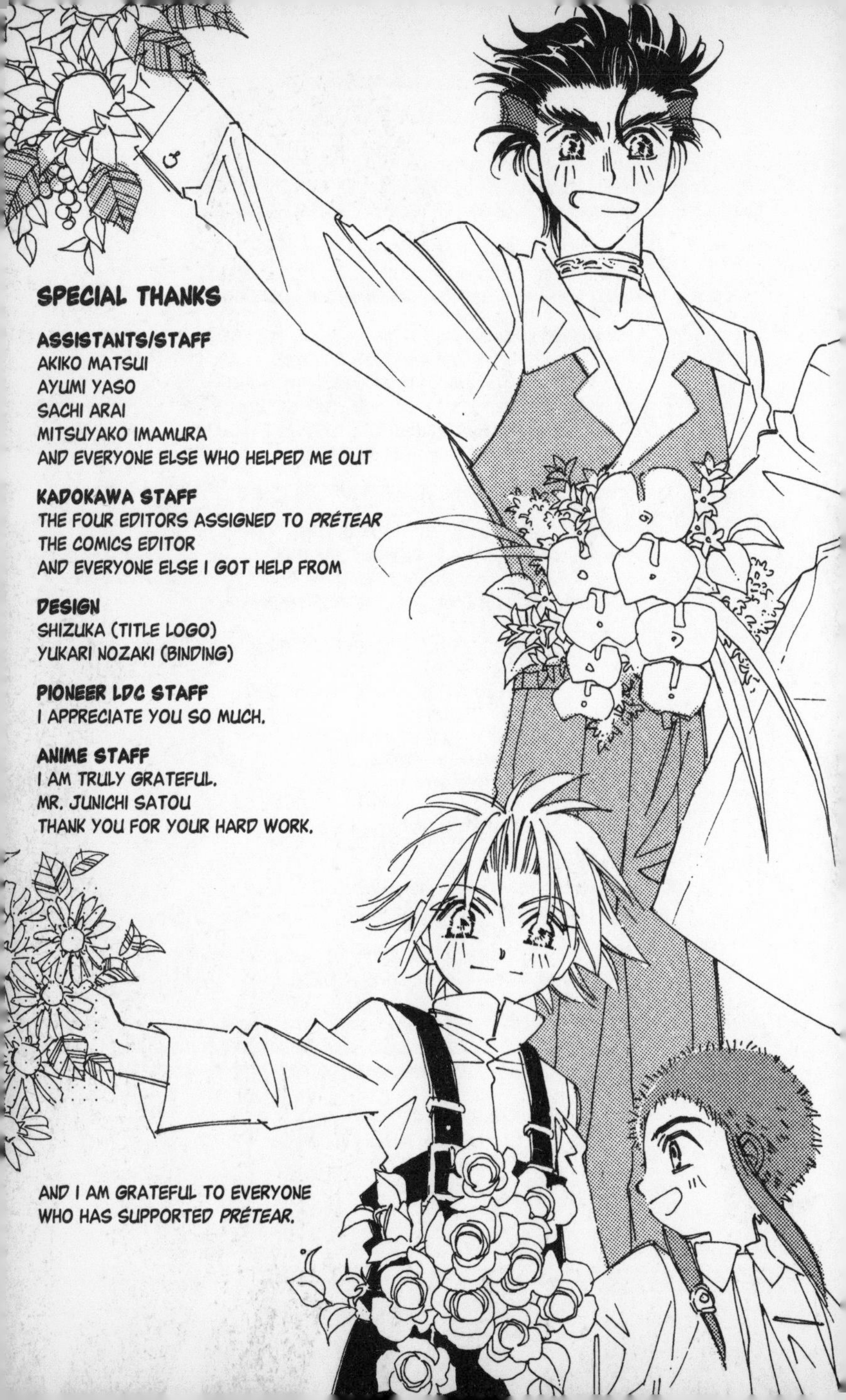

SPECIAL THANKS

ASSISTANTS/STAFF
AKIKO MATSUI
AYUMI YASO
SACHI ARAI
MITSUYAKO IMAMURA
AND EVERYONE ELSE WHO HELPED ME OUT

KADOKAWA STAFF
THE FOUR EDITORS ASSIGNED TO *PRÉTEAR*
THE COMICS EDITOR
AND EVERYONE ELSE I GOT HELP FROM

DESIGN
SHIZUKA (TITLE LOGO)
YUKARI NOZAKI (BINDING)

PIONEER LDC STAFF
I APPRECIATE YOU SO MUCH.

ANIME STAFF
I AM TRULY GRATEFUL.
MR. JUNICHI SATOU
THANK YOU FOR YOUR HARD WORK.

AND I AM GRATEFUL TO EVERYONE
WHO HAS SUPPORTED *PRÉTEAR*.

PRÉTEAR
VOLUME FOUR

© Kaori NARUSE 2001
© Junichi SATOU 2001

Originally published in Japan in 2001 by KADOKAWA SHOTEN PUBLISHING CO., LTD., Tokyo.
English translation rights arranged with KADOKAWA SHOTEN PUBLISHING CO., LTD., Tokyo.

Translator **AMY FORSYTH**
Lead Translator/Translation Supervisor **JAVIER LOPEZ**
ADV Manga Translation Staff **KAY BERTRAND & BRENDAN FRAYNE**

Print Production/Art Studio Manager **LISA PUCKETT**
Pre-press Manager **KLYS REEDYK**
Sr. Designer/Creative Manager **JORGE ALVARADO**
Graphic Designer/Group Leader **GEORGE REYNOLDS**
Graphic Designers **HEATHER GARY & NATALIA MORALES**
Graphic Intern **MARK MEZA**

International Coordinators **TORU IWAKAMI, ATSUSHI KANBAYASHI & KYOKO DRUMHELLER**

Publishing Editor **SUSAN ITIN**
Assistant Editor **MARGARET SCHAROLD**
Editorial Assistant **SHERIDAN JACOBS**
Research/Traffic Coordinator **MARSHA ARNOLD**

Executive VP, CFO, COO **KEVIN CORCORAN**

President, CEO & Publisher **JOHN LEDFORD**

Email: editor@adv-manga.com
www.adv-manga.com
www.advfilms.com

For sales and distribution inquiries please call 1.800.282.7202

ADV MANGA is a division of A.D. Vision, Inc.
10114 W. Sam Houston Parkway, Suite 200, Houston, Texas 77099

English text © 2005 published by A.D. Vision, Inc. under exclusive license.
ADV MANGA is a trademark of A.D. Vision, Inc.

ISBN: 1-4139-0147-6
First printing, January 2005
10 9 8 7 6 5 4 3 2 1
Printed in Canada

LETTER FROM THE ADV MANGA TRANSLATION STAFF

Dear Reader,

On behalf of the ADV Manga translation team, thank you for purchasing an ADV book. We are enthusiastic and committed to our work, and strive to carry our enthusiasm over into the book you hold in your hands.

Our goal is to retain the spirit of the original Japanese book. While great care has been taken to render a true and accurate translation, some cultural or readability issues may require a line to be adapted for greater accessibility to our readers. At times, manga titles that include culturally-specific concepts will feature a "Translator's Notes" section, which explains noteworthy references to the original text.

We hope our commitment to a faithful translation is evident in every ADV book you purchase.

Sincerely,

Javier Lopez
Lead Translator

Kay Bertrand

Brendan Frayne

Amy Forsyth

LETTTER
FROM THE
EDITOR

Dear Reader,

Thank you for purchasing an ADV Manga book. We hope you enjoyed the magical tale of *Prétear*.

It is our sincere commitment in reproducing Asian comics and graphic novels to retain as much of the character of the original book as possible. From the right-to-left format of the Japanese books to the meaning of the story in the original language, the ADV Manga team is working hard to publish a quality book for our fans and readers. Write to us with your questions or comments, and tell us how you liked this and other ADV books. Be sure to visit our website at www.adv-manga.com and view the list of upcoming titles, sign up for special announcements, and fill out our survey.

The ADV Manga team of translators, designers, graphic artists, production managers, traffic managers, and editors hope you will buy more ADV books—there's a lot more in store from ADV Manga!

www.adv-manga.com

Publishing Editor
Susan B. Itin

Assistant Editor
Margaret Scharold

EDITOR'S
PICKS

IF YOU LIKED *PRÉTEAR* VOLUME 4,
THEN YOU'LL LOVE THESE!

PICK 1

DESERT CORAL

©WATARU MURAYAMA 2002

WATARU MURAYAMA

Naoto Saki has an imagination so far-reaching that he has found an entire world within his dreams, filled with fascinating creatures and longstanding rivalries. After days and nights of escaping reality, he is summoned into this illusory land and into a battle between the Elphis and the Sand Dusts. Pain is real here, but the risk of certain injury and even death will not stave his eventual attachment to this world of fantasy. Ultimately, Naoto will be put to the test as he is forced to make a decision that will forever change him and the fate of *Desert Coral*.

PICK 2

BLUE INFERIOR

© 1999 Kyoko SHITOU

In a post-apocalyptic world, whatever life has survived subsists only in small pockets throughout the world. Existence is somewhat carefree, but certain fears obstruct complete happiness—fear of the outside world, the unknown, the stories about the subhumans. These creatures threaten entire populations, making the people quite unwelcoming to newcomers. A young girl with amnesia—Marine—who washes up on shore one day, is no exception to their apprehension. It is only through the kindness of a boy named Kazuya that Marine will be able to escape the hostile town and find out who she really is.

PICK 3

SWEET & SENSITIVE

© 1999 Park Eun-Ah / DAIWON C.I, Inc.

Life is tough for lovesick teenagers! Meet Ee-Ji, a high school freshman suffering from—or is, perhaps, the cause of—an adolescent love triangle. Torn between two men, she is racked with grief over her own indecision. The first man in the running is Han-Kyul, a classmate since elementary school and Ee-Ji's longtime lovable crush, or the safe bet. But, his competition is a far cry from his sweet and sensitive demeanor. Sae-Ryun is crude, offensive and constantly bullies Ee-Ji and her friends, but he has managed to catch her eye anyway. To make matters worse, these two contenders are best friends. This situation has the potential to explode into a sordid mess, but Ee-Ji will have to pick her favorite man first!

CHECK'EM OUT TODAY!

www.adv-manga.com

Dancing Queen

IN A MAGICAL WORLD, SHE FINDS THE GRACE TO LAND HER PRINCE

Art Mizuo Shinonome
Story Ikuko Itoh & Jun-ichi Satoh

© Ikuko Itoh • Jun-ichi Satoh/Mizuo Shinonome/Akita Shoten 2003

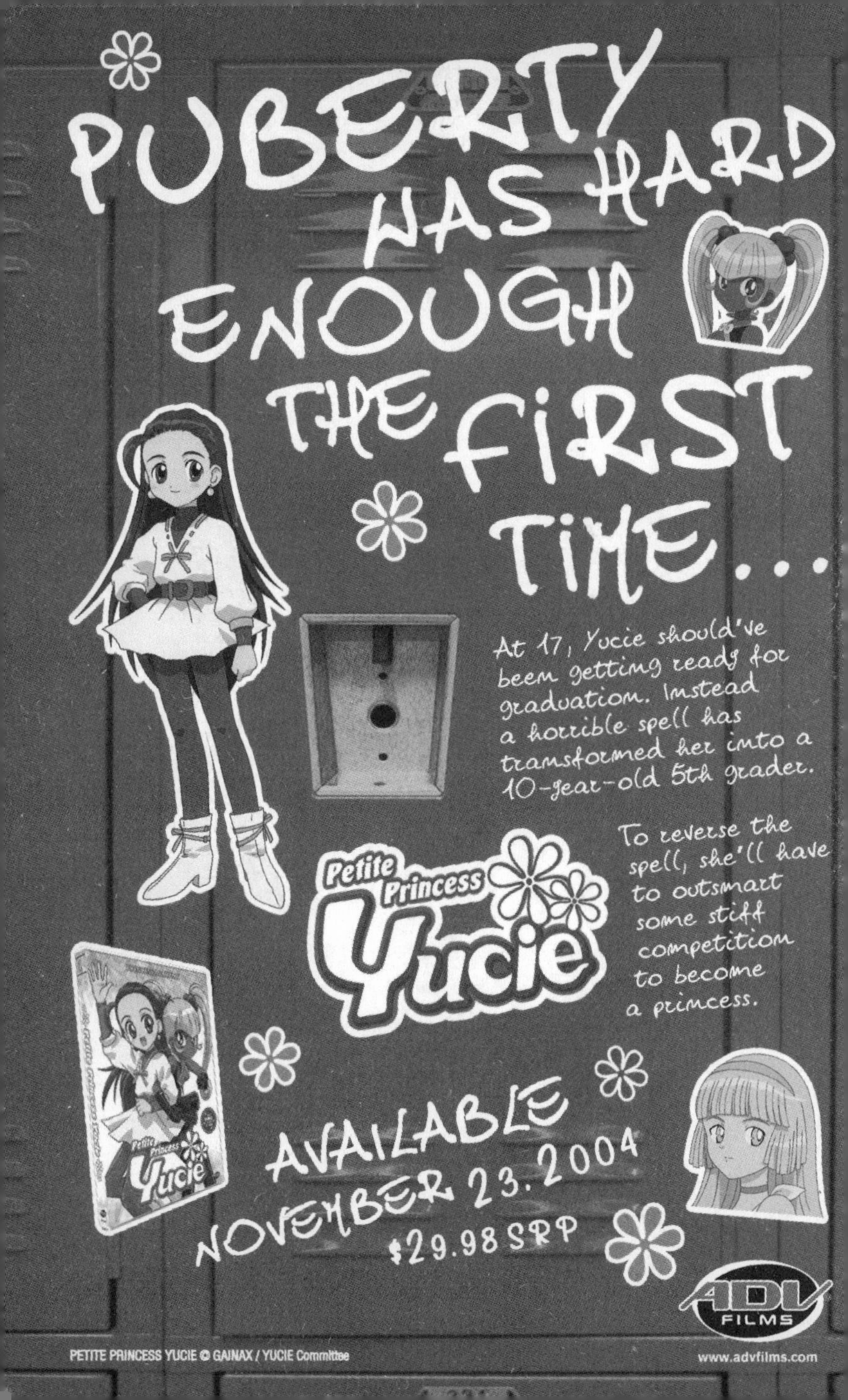
PUBERTY HAS HARD ENOUGH THE FIRST TIME...
At 17, Yucie should've been getting ready for graduation. Instead a horrible spell has transformed her into a 10-year-old 5th grader.
To reverse the spell, she'll have to outsmart some stiff competition to become a princess.
Petite Princess Yucie
AVAILABLE NOVEMBER 23. 2004
$29.98 SRP
ADV FILMS
PETITE PRINCESS YUCIE © GAINAX / YUCIE Committee
www.advfilms.com

LOOKING FOR
ANIME NETWORK?

THIS GUY WAS, THEN HE CALLED HIS LOCAL
CABLE PROVIDER AND DEMANDED HIS ANIME!

ANIME
NETWORK

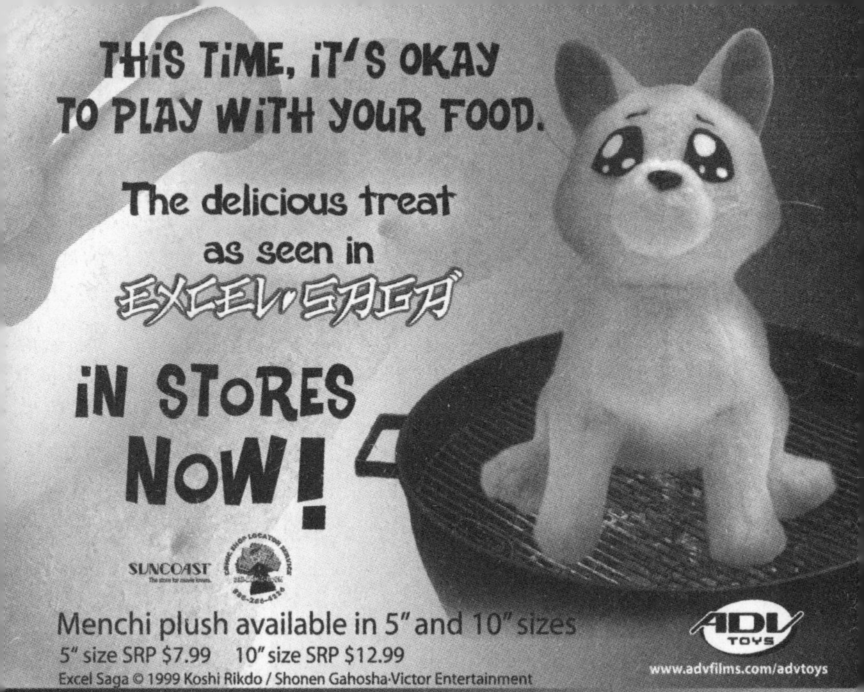
THIS TIME, IT'S OKAY
TO PLAY WITH YOUR FOOD.
The delicious treat
as seen in
EXCEL SAGA
IN STORES
NOW!
SUNCOAST
Menchi plush available in 5" and 10" sizes
5" size SRP $7.99 10" size SRP $12.99
Excel Saga © 1999 Koshi Rikdo / Shonen Gahosha·Victor Entertainment
ADV TOYS
www.advfilms.com/advtoys

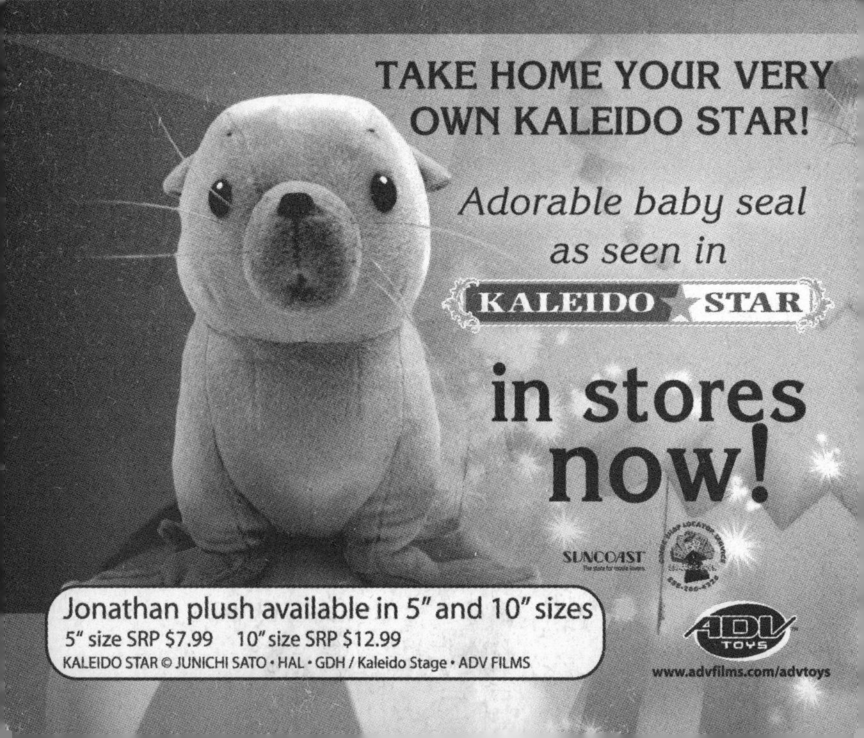
TAKE HOME YOUR VERY
OWN KALEIDO STAR!
Adorable baby seal
as seen in
KALEIDO STAR
in stores
now!
SUNCOAST
Jonathan plush available in 5" and 10" sizes
5" size SRP $7.99 10" size SRP $12.99
KALEIDO STAR © JUNICHI SATO • HAL • GDH / Kaleido Stage • ADV FILMS
ADV TOYS
www.advfilms.com/advtoys

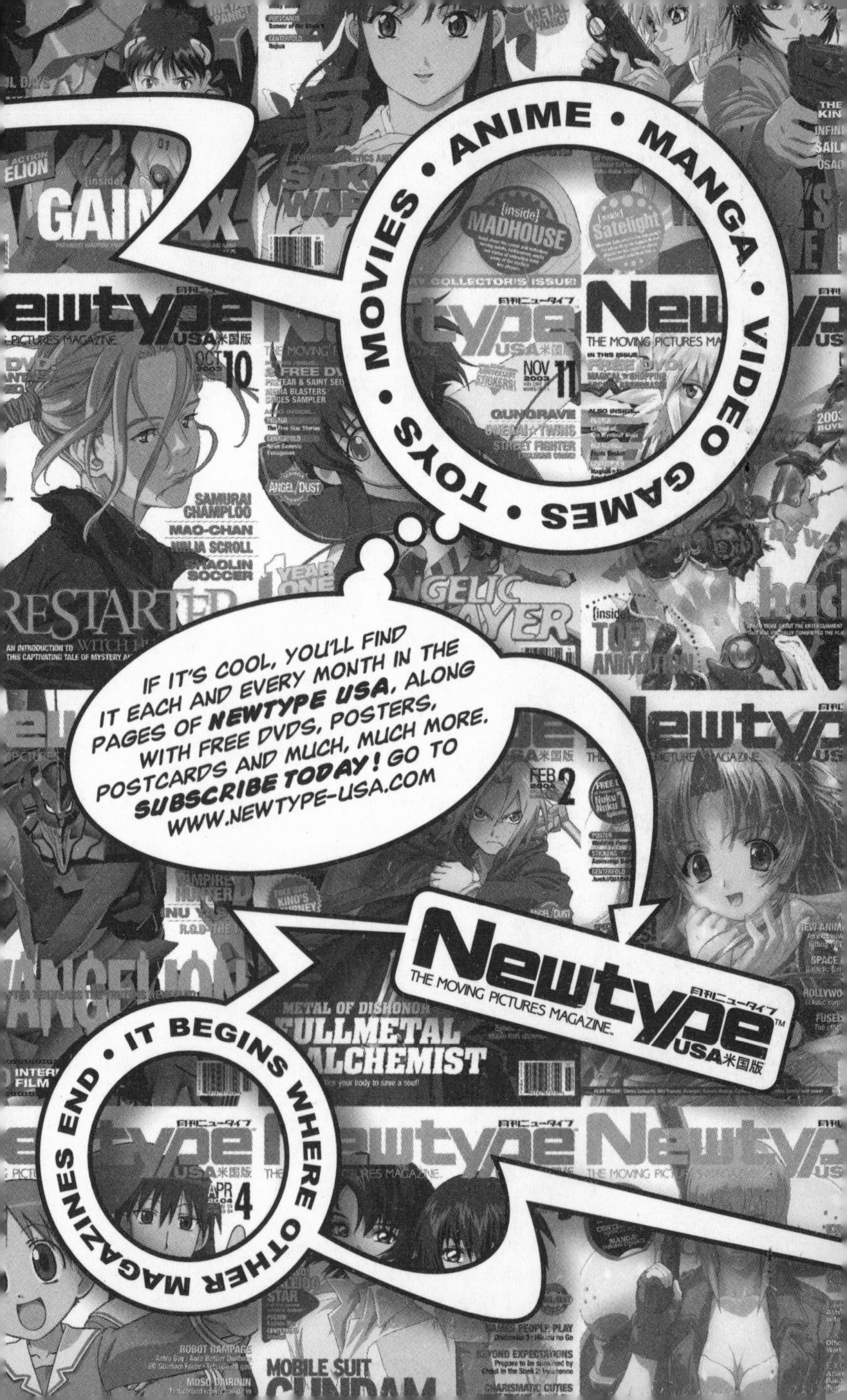
MOVIES • ANIME • MANGA • VIDEO GAMES • TOYS •
IF IT'S COOL, YOU'LL FIND IT EACH AND EVERY MONTH IN THE PAGES OF NEWTYPE USA, ALONG WITH FREE DVDS, POSTERS, POSTCARDS AND MUCH, MUCH MORE. SUBSCRIBE TODAY! GO TO WWW.NEWTYPE-USA.COM
Newtype USA 米国版
THE MOVING PICTURES MAGAZINE.
IT BEGINS WHERE OTHER MAGAZINES END •